SMALL PLANETS

SAUL BELLOW AND THE ART OF SHORT FICTION

SMALL PLANETS
SAUL BELLOW AND THE ART OF
SHORT FICTION

EDITED BY
GERHARD BACH AND GLORIA L. CRONIN

Michigan State University Press
East Lansing, Michigan

♾ The paper used in this publication meets the minimum requirements of
ANSI/NISO Z39.48-1992 (R 1997) (Permanence of Paper).

Michigan State University Press
East Lansing, Michigan 48823-5202

Printed and bound in the United States of America.

07 06 05 04 03 02 01 00   1 2 3 4 5 6 7 8 9 10

LIBRARY OF CONGRESS CATALOGING-IN-PUBLICATION DATA

Small planets : Saul Bellow and the art of short fiction / edited by Gerhard
    Bach and Gloria L. Cronin.
    p.   cm.
    Includes bibliographical references and index.
    ISBN 0-87013-529-5 (alk. paper)
1. Bach, Gerhard, 1943-. II. Cronin, Gloria L., 1947-.
813' .52-dc21   99-23854
                                                                         CIP

Cover design by Sharp Des!gns
Book design by Fara Sneddon

Cover artwork is "Saul Bellow" by Sarah M. Yuster. Used courtesy of The
National Portrait Gallery, Smithsonian Institute.

Visit Michigan State University Press on the World Wide Web at:
www.msu.edu/unit/msupress

CONTENTS

ACKNOWLEDGMENTS

The editors wish to give thanks and appreciation to the following: the contributors and the scholarly journals that granted us permission to reprint these essays; the contributors who wrote new material; editorial assistants Diana H. Tanner, Michael W. Hatch, Lynne Facer, Fara Sneddon and Ruth Liljenquist, who helped prepare the manuscript; and the Michigan State University Press for its expertise in publishing it. Special thanks to the guiding expertise of Linda Hunter Adams.

Introduction

Short views, for God's sake!
Artur Sammler

Short fiction is an apt form for a late twentieth-century audience because grand modernist "summations" are no longer expected of novelists, Saul Bellow stated in a lecture given in Haifa in 1987;[1] instead, smaller versions of life are perhaps more truthful. Two volumes of Bellow's fiction, Mosby's Memoirs and Other Stories (1968) and Him with His Foot in His Mouth (1984), are collections of short stories, and another four volumes are novellas: Seize the Day (1956), A Theft (1989), The Bellarosa Connection (1989), and The Actual (1997). Thus Bellow has been far more seriously involved in mastering the short fiction form than most of his literary critics have previously realized.

Both the short story and the novella have long and prestigious histories in nineteenth-and twentieth-century Anglo-American and European literature. Heir to this tradition, Bellow has become a master of this form, rejuvenating it for a late-twentieth-century audience in such commanding renditions as *Seize the Day* and *The Bellarosa Connection*. In "Novellas for the Nineties," Greg Johnson points out that this genre, often scorned by editors and writers alike, nevertheless has had a "long [if] uncertain tenancy in the house of fiction."[2] Too brief for a single-volume publication and too long for the format of most magazines and journals, it has enjoyed a sheltered existence in the niche of small presses. Bellow's unprecedented act of publishing *A Theft* and *The Bellarosa Connection* in 1989 in single volume paperbacks at a major publishing house with worldwide distribution has made recent publishing history, a feat topped only by the fact that his next novella, *The Actual*, appeared in 1997 in even more "exclusive" form—a slender hardback volume.

Several Bellow critics have devoted significant space in their books to Bellow's short fiction. Notably, Robert R. Dutton, in the Twayne Author Series, discusses mostly the stories from *Mosby's Memoirs* and the story "A Silver Dish."[3] Robert Kiernan's *Saul Bellow* contains a chapter each on *Mosby's Memoirs* and *Him with His Foot in His Mouth*, tracing a progression from early stories of social commentary to the more recent dense fictions of psychological sensibility.[4] Peter Hyland also includes a chapter on short fiction in his *Saul Bellow* and concludes that Bellow, "late in his career, seems to have turned away from the sprawling novels that are generally taken to be his *forte* to the cleaner lines of these shorter forms."[5] Ruth Miller, in *Saul Bellow: A Biography of the Imagination*, intersperses her account of Bellow's career as a writer with information on the biographical genesis of many of the characters in the short fiction.[6] Daniel Fuchs, in his *Saul Bellow: Vision and Revision*, reports finding evidence of considerable numbers of revised manuscripts of many of the stories.[7] A monograph devoted entirely to the subject of Bellow's short fiction has appeared recently: Marianne M. Friedrich's *Character and Narration in the Short Fiction of Saul Bellow*. In her introduction, Friedrich notes that "until the mid-1980s the opinion was widely accepted in Bellow research that, with few exceptions, the short form was not genuinely Bellow's strength." She points out that critics have looked to the short fiction only to illuminate the themes and characters of the long fiction. Thus it has been maintained that the central concern of each of his novels usually finds its first incarnation in the short fiction—that place where Bellow often developed and "tested" his fictional ideas and prototypical characters as well as his unique voice. As Friedrich shows, such critical short-circuiting generally fails to "recognize Bellow's short fictions independently as unique and complex works of art." Covering a representative collection of stories treated in separate chapters, Friedrich manages to reveal as a prevailing structural principle "the consistent dialectics of character and narration," thus revealing how Bellow's short fiction is uniquely distinct from his novels.[8]

It would seem that Bellow's lifelong preoccupation with short fiction has culminated with his last three novellas. While most critics support the notion that they were written a considerable time before publication, these later works confirm Bellow's ongoing commitment to short fiction as a discrete genre. Alongside the expansive forms of his novels, the short fiction appears to function somewhat like a corrective self-disciplining measure. In his foreword to the volume that contains his three late novellas, *Something to Remember Me By* (1991), Bellow himself says as much, implicitly criticizing some of his earlier work as unnecessarily verbose.[9]

The Early Years (1933–1958)

Saul Bellow's career as a writer of short fiction began in his mid-teens while he prowled 58th Street on the North Side of Chicago as a self-styled tough guy and first-generation Jewish American. The general atmosphere of the city was one of gangsterism, prohibition, violence, sex, bootlegging, and a corrupt city machine, and Bellow's self-confessed haunts were in lively pool rooms. According to critic David Anderson, graft was rampant, gangsters enjoyed a glamorous public existence, and the city swarmed with an upwardly mobile second-generation immigrant population who "found an open society, public schools and libraries, and the great university William Rainey Harper had built a generation earlier."[10] When the young Solly Bellow went to the public library, it was Chicago-based and midwestern writers such as Sherwood Anderson, Theodore Dreiser, Edgar Lee Masters, and Vachel Lindsay that he read, along with the works of the great European writers Chekhov, Dostoyevsky, and Tolstoy.[11] These combined traditions influenced his style in his earliest, distinctly Euro-American experiments in short fiction.

When Bellow graduated from Tuley High School in 1933, he had already formed the ambition to be a writer and begun his first literary experiments in the short story. While enrolled at Northwestern University, he published his first fiction, a short story entitled "The Hell It Can't," in the student newspaper, *The Daily Northwestern* (February 1936). Five years later "Two Morning Monologues" (1941) was published, followed by "The Mexican General" (1942). From about 1939 on he was also working on another project that loosely fit the short fiction genre—*Dangling Man*, published in 1944.[12] This book reveals how Bellow connects the European narrative traditions to an indigenous American modernism, as does his next book, *The Victim* (1947), in which Bellow tries to outdo his European models on whom this novel is grafted. *The Adventures of Augie March* (1953), also charged with experimental drive, is Bellow's breakthrough as a novelist who has found his own voice. During this formative phase, however, Bellow also continued his experiments with the short form, and a host of stories found their way into the major literary magazines: "Dora" (1949), "A Sermon by Dr. Pep" (1949), "The Trip to Galena" (1950), "Looking for Mr. Green" (1951), "By the Rock Wall" (1951), and "Address by Gooley MacDowell to the Hasbeens Club of Chicago" (1951). This auspicious apprenticeship culminated in 1956 with the publication of his most famous novella, *Seize the Day*, followed by two more short stories, "The Gonzaga Manuscripts," and "Leaving the Yellow House" (1958).

Mosby's Memoirs (1968)

The critical response to these early pieces has been surprisingly slight. Critics have mostly contented themselves with plot summaries and pointing out that these short fictions were probably only practice runs on the major novel themes.

Tony Tanner's 1969 review of *Mosby's Memoirs* was the first serious acknowledgment of Bellow's skills as a short story writer. He notes that Bellow has created characters who have to engage the great and ultimate questions of existence and that Bellow is attempting to depict the fact that excessive cerebration causes the characters to become "immobilized," "sealed off," or "glutted with thought." Tanner praises "Looking for Mr. Green" as the best thing Bellow has written to date and declares "Yellow House" to be outstanding. Tanner quickly identifies the fact that these "cool" narrators are related to those of the novels through their re-alization that life is very precious.[13] Denis Donoghue also sets about relating the style and content of the stories to each of the preceding novels through their relentless emphasis on feeling and finds the stories marked by intelligence, lucidity, irony, and felicity, as major American and existential themes are waged within them.[14] David D. Galloway expands this notion, recognizing the subtleties of "The Gonzaga Manuscripts" with its Talmudic sense of suffering and "quasi-Yiddish comic vision," as well as the author's "powerful allegiance to an optimistic and reverent" view of life. He suggests that the pattern of these short fictions follows that of the longer works: the movement of the hero "from estrangement to ritual acceptance."[15] Richard F. Dietrich's essay on "A Father-to-Be" describes the twin poles of scientific rationalism and human feeling along which the story is strung and notes that these are themes in every piece of Bellow fiction since 1944.[16] Irving Halperin's distinguished piece on this story additionally identifies Rogin as the typically Jewish schlemiel.[17] Noriko M. Lippit is the first to recognize that in "Leaving the Yellow House," with Lake Sego as the symbol of the lost new Eden, Bellow is adding to the theme of the failure of the American dream. Lippit argues that Hattie, like most Americans in this postwestward expansion period of history, can only answer to the question of who she is in self-referential terms: "I am I." Such solipsism reflects America's unique drama or archetypal theme, "man's (woman's) struggle for recovery from modern American alienation, which preoccupies all of the heroes of Bellow's long fictions."[18]

Constance Rooke, Bellow's first feminist critic, debates the critical issue of whether Bellow's first female protagonist can live up to the stature of her male counterparts. She concludes that while Hattie has much in common with her male counterparts Tommy Wilhelm and Moses Herzog, she generally lacks interest in ideas, fails to achieve peace and reconciliation, exists in conspicuous isolation, and does little with her gift of life—all symptoms of authorial sexism. Rooke concludes that living well in the Bellow novel is the province of men.[19]

David P. Demarest also suggests that "Looking for Mr. Green" and "A Father-to-Be" are important introductions to Bellow's general vision and style. He calls them "Popean middle-state" fictions, full of accounts of life's discontinuities and illogicalities, fallen appearances, and the general Bellovian injunction to accept things as they are.[20] Eusebio L. Rodrigues considers "Looking for Mr. Green" the most complete and compact of the stories and claims that it marks an important point in Bellow's transition as an artist since it issues from a creative mood poised precariously between the belief that humankind is somehow doomed and yet still able to transcend this condition. According to Rodrigues, Bellow transforms "a simple Dreiserian piece into a metaphysical parable," making it one of the great short stories of our time.[21]

Seize the Day (1956)

Significantly, *Seize the Day*, now considered Bellow's major breakthrough book, was also his first novella. Herbert Gold, immediately identifying it as a major expression of Bellow's "maelstrom fiction on inner-city life" and American alienation, suggests that it represents an important moment in Bellow's integration of the dense narrative and symbolic unity of *The Victim* and the wide-ranging playfulness and pathos of *The Adventures of Augie March*.[22] Some critics think the book "somewhat less than meaningful,"[23] "elliptical" and "obscure,"[24] or mere anthropology of social circumstance. Robert Baker, who recognized its importance as logically culminating the line of development begun with *Dangling Man* in 1944, *The Victim* in 1947, and *The Adventures of Augie March* in 1953, suggests that what interconnects these novels and the stories written up to this point is the very American theme of money and materialism.[25] Other critics complain that this is the third in Bellow's "mopery series," seeing *Seize the Day* as a mere "surface treatment" of that only too vogue American phenomenon—the middle-aged adolescent, that tour de force dear to the heart of the urban book reviewer. Still others agree that Tommy Wilhelm seems perversely unheroic and they note that, regardless of the pathos in the novel, this intellectually "small" book merely recasts the earlier themes.[26]

Leslie A. Fiedler, however, maintains that *Seize the Day* is a major achievement and praises its "slow, somber beauty" as well as its "modest," "authentic" demeanor producing that unmistakable shudder of truth found only in great writers.[27] Robert W. Flint likewise praises the novella for returning us to "that high, dazzling plateau of well-earned success where misery, joy, and love join hands and dance like crazy," labeling the book erudite and brilliantly original.[28] Ralph Ciancio, however, describes the book as a study in schizoid estrangement culminating in a salvific tale of a *tzadik*.[29] Richard Giannone identifies the book's romantic structures and mythological foundations, while several other critics explore the carpe diem and family themes.[30] Julius Raper in 1976 points out what so many critics have observed since—that the sheer economy and unity of this text mark an entirely new episode in Bellow's aesthetic command of form and style.[31]

Bellow's critics do not begin serious work on this novella until the 1980s. Allan Chavkin identifies the earliest draft of the work to be a manuscript entitled "One of these Days," a draft in which Bellow obviously began working out the character of Tommy Wilhelm.[32] Numerous other critics discuss the motif of the schlemiel, the enigmatic character of Dr. Tamkin, as well as the national, ethnic, and emotional roots of the three major characters. S. Lillian Kremer makes an important and complex analysis of several rich layers of anti-Hasidic satire in the text,[33] and in a further treatment of the text she discusses its rich intertextual echoes.[34] Gloria L. Cronin identifies the novella as a parody of the aesthetic and ideological formulas of the modernist novel which enacts farcical exploration of Bellow's ongoing philosophical quarrels with European modernism.[35] John J. Clayton sees it as another incarnation of the ongoing Bellovian dialectic between personal despair and romantic idealism, between Jewish humanism and Jewish guilt—a series of vacillations in which the American community has finally fallen to alienation, masochism, and despair.[36]

A significant body of psychological analysis finds Tommy alternately a victim of such personality disorders as passive aggression, alienation and depression, narcissism, masochism, and schizophrenia. In a more moderate mode, Clayton responds that Tommy is not a failed adult undergoing a midlife crisis, but an ordinary man with an oral regressive personality who is begging for love and mothering and whose moral masochism is nevertheless accompanied by seeds of moral greatness.[37] J. Brooks Bouson applies an Adlerian psychological model to Tommy Wilhelm, finding him to be a classic case of narcissistic personality disorder, a man who "inhabits not the glorious here-and-now fantasied by Tamkin but the bleak here-and-now of his own crippled self."[38]

Since its publication in 1956, *Seize the Day* has created a rich critical discourse, and as critics revisit it in the 1990s they invariably compare the more recently published novellas to this early masterpiece. In the wake of

The Bellarosa Connection, Gaye McCollum Simmons chides the majority of critics for avoiding the locus of Judaism and thereby failing to consider the book as an exploration of the Jewish religious theme of atonement. She also sees it as Bellow's attempt to awaken American Jews from the amnesia of assimilation.[39]

Critics continue to revisit this American classic in the light of current postmodern, gender, and other reading paradigms. Responding to the film version of *Seize the Day*, which appeared on American PBS in 1987 (the only film ever made of one of Bellow's novels or stories), Gerhard Bach ploughs some new territory by structurally relating the cinematic dynamics of film narrative to the novella structure[40] and Michael Shiels investigates the importance of space and place as structural devices in the novel and the film.[41] Significantly, throughout all of these recent critical approaches, the themes of narcissism and psychological disorder continue to dominate. In fact, Darryl Hattenhaur provides an even more pessimistic reading of Tommy Wilhelm. For him, Wilhelm is a classic passive-aggressive personality who swallows his feelings, is grandly circuitous, manifests self-destructive tendencies, engages in futility, and ultimately self-destructs.[42]

The Middle Years (1963–1988)

Firmly established as a preeminent twentieth-century author, Saul Bellow during these years of 1963 to 1988 received numerous awards and honorary degrees, culminating in 1976 in the Nobel Prize. During these great middle years in which Bellow produced his major novels—*Henderson the Rain King* (1959), *Herzog* (1964), *Mr. Sammler's Planet* (1970), *Humboldt's Gift* (1975), *The Dean's December* (1982), and *More Die of Heartbreak* (1987)—Bellow continued to demonstrate commitment to the short fiction form. He edited *Great Jewish Short Stories* (1963), published "The Old System" (1967) and "Zetland: By a Character Witness" (1974), and gathered up his stories into two collections—*Mosby's Memoirs* (1968), and *Him with His Foot in His Mouth* (1984). Coupled with the resounding critical success of his first novella, *Seize the Day*, in 1956, the considerable acclaim these two collections of short fiction received established Bellow's reputation as a master of the short story form.

"The Old System" (1967)

"The Old System" (1967) was largely ignored in the wake of the lively critical interest in *Herzog* (1964). Greg Johnson's essay establishes the connection between the novels and this story with its major themes of

American and Old World Jewish identity.[43] S. Lillian Kremer sees it as
Bellow's comment on Old and New World Judaism similar to the prismatic
vision found in Dante's account of Roman Catholic Florence, Tolstoy's
account of Tsarist Russia, and Joyce's vision of Roman Catholic Irish
ethnicity. This is the story, she argues, that establishes beyond doubt that
Judaism is vital to Bellow's belief in humanity, his veneration of life, and
his pervasive concern for morality. She points out that in commentary and
interviews Bellow has acknowledged the significance of Jewish thought
and experience during his formative years. Furthermore, he has identified
the Jewish view—that the world is sanctified and humankind is capable of
moral dignity and holiness—as the source of his own objection to
twentieth-century apocalyptic romanticism.[44]

Him with His Foot in His Mouth (1984)

Sanford Pinsker welcomes this new collection and notes that, mercifully,
these stories do not preach, as do some of the recent novels.[45] His
comments are echoed by most subsequent reviewers, who praise the
stories for their emphasis on style, voice, and memory. In "A New Look at
the Old System," Pinsker argues that this piece is much more than a dress
rehearsal for *Mr. Sammler's Planet*. Rather, it is "Braun's long, dark,
afternoon of the soul" as a scientist who has had to reckon with the "rigid
madness of the orthodox."[46] Cynthia Ozick offers the highest praise,
calling the collection a "concordance," a "reprise," and a summary of all
the old themes and obsessions "hauled up by a single tough rope." She too
sees it as cumulative art, concentrated, so to speak, "in a vial." She
concludes that Bellow, with his distinctly Chicagoan linguistic "bang and
blab," and brilliant "wiliness of predicament," is now an important
American and internationally distinguished master of the short fiction
form.[47] Peter Prescott is equally enthusiastic and laments that Bellow has
not written more of these "well-crafted and thickly textured" short
stories because they form a natural curb to his didacticism.[48] Robert Alter
notes that these stories provided a newer, younger Bellow audience with "a
vivid introduction to the distinctive allure of his fictional world," but Alter
is less impressed than either Ozick or Prescott. He sees the individual
stories as "vignettes" or "more like brilliant fragments than well-made
wholes," and he describes Bellow as a novelist more suited to the panoramic
form of the novel.[49] Molly McQuade strikes a new note when she praises the
collection for its skill and tenderness, "rhythmically personal talk," and
"unquenchable self-communion."[50] Only Oliver Conant feels the collection to
be less powerful than *Mosby's Memoirs*, but he concedes that it was done with

boldness, ease, a fine satiric insight, a carnival of ideas, as well as a rich and "yeasty brew of language."[51] D. Keith Mano, who also praises the stylistic innovation and bright linguistic elegance of the pieces, is the first critic to suggest the idea that in Bellow's fiction "remembering is a profound custodial event."[52]

All the stories in *Him with His Foot in His Mouth* had appeared previously in magazine publications. Hence, in 1979, Philip Stevick published the first comprehensive treatment of Bellow as a short fiction writer. Following the general trend of the initial reviews, he concurs that Bellow's short fiction carries all the linguistic sparkle, power, and integrity of his best novels as he works his usual territory: the "ludic," the "fabulous," and the "linguistic." Stevick's essential thesis—that the collection is unified by a certain "grammar of resistance and a complex analysis of the relationship between the community and the individual"—connects the stories in *Him with His Foot in His Mouth* to all of Bellow's previous novels.[53]

Critical response to the individual stories, however, has been almost as sparse as the critical response to the individual *Mosby's Memoirs* stories. Robert Alter relates "Cousins" to Kafka's and Agnon's depictions of family and notes that unlike both of these writers, Bellow is primarily interested in the extended family rather than in the contemporary nuclear family, which at this point in time has imploded upon itself. Alter comments on the "bulging familial grab bag" and the "familial sprawl" of this story of the Jewish immigrant family and concludes that despite the language of zoology that permeates the story, it remains firmly about "human stuff."[54] Allan Chavkin and Nancy Feyl Chavkin argue that in the title story, "Him with His Foot in His Mouth," Shawmut "shrewdly presents himself as a victim, thus robbing Miss Rose, for whom the letter is intended, of a genuine apology." Like the lawyer-narrator of Herman Melville's *Bartleby The Scrivener*, he is engaged in an act of self-justification and rhetorical manipulation. This central fact, they conclude, demonstrates this narrator's undeniable hostility to women.[55]

The Recent Harvest (1989–)

In 1989 critics and reviewers were amazed to hear of the unprecedented publication of two Bellow novellas in paperback first editions. *A Theft* appeared first, immediately followed by *The Bellarosa Connection*. "Something to Remember Me By" (1990), first published in *Esquire*, shortly after appeared in a paperback collection entitled *Something to Remember Me By: Three Tales* (1991), which also includes the previous two novellas. Although

Bellow has reportedly been working on two major novels during these intervening years, which have been marked by serious illness, he has added to this harvest his most recent novella, *The Actual* (1997). Thus it is evident that in this current decade Bellow has returned to his first interest, short fiction.

A Theft (1989)

Both Ithiel Regler and Clara Velde, the protagonists of *A Theft*, have antecedents in all the previous fictions in that whatever higher intuitions they attain have relatively little to do with the success or failure of "the human pair." Smaller in scale, more muted in tone, and done in reversed gender, *A Theft* deals with some very old Bellow themes related to the failures of heterosexual love. Indeed, this novella is representative of the typical Bellovian thematic matrix. There is the Hawthornian theft of the human heart, the lure of the intellect, the classic evasions of the male lover, the overweening romantic aspirations of just one partner (this time a female), the social chaos of "Gogmagogsville," the seeming impossibility of higher synthesis, the human comedy of sexual desire, the failure of psychiatry, the decreasing significance of the personal factor, the quest for the essential unified self, power politics, the loss of human qualities, the increasing absence of civilized spaces, the proliferation of ethnic others as confusing and lower types of the human, the diminished status of the individual, the problematic relation of love to being, and the issues of boredom, stewardship, and the human contract.

Reviewers of *A Theft* seem at best mildly interested and, at worst singularly unmoved, by this puzzling new fiction. At a loss to place it in context with the author's previous work, many provide a muted critical response and excessive commentary on the unprecedented act of a paperback first printing. Most critics are largely unconvinced by the belated appearance of Bellow's first major female protagonist and, furthermore, many seem unable to distinguish a central thrust or any genuine large-scale significance in the text. Susan Shapiro immediately identifies *A Theft* and *The Bellarosa Connection* as belonging together by virtue of their common theme of the "haunting lure of memory." She strikes the critical note many subsequent reviewers and critics echo: "One wishes Mr. Bellow would forget his 'Introduction's' silly justifications for avoiding lengthy books and get back to the novels that are his forte. Like Clara, Mr. Bellow's big head, with all its intriguing thoughts and insights, demands more space."[56] Others praise the book for its language, neatness, and control, while complaining of the lack of any genuine large-scale significance. Some critics praise it for its defense of heterosexual love, and yet others chastise it for its failure to present a non-sexist portrait of a woman who would be as significant as the famous male protagonists. Nearly all critics have found it lacking in focus and energy.[57]

Scholars have also been largely negative in their responses to *A Theft*. Liela Goldman roundly chastises Bellow for his stereotypically sexist portrayal of Clara Velde as a flighty, fashion maven,[58] while Elaine Safer points out comic irony in Bellow's use of the obtuse first-person narrator who fails, she argues, to "penetrate any of the ironies . . . involving the main character, Clara Velde."[59] Gloria Cronin argues that this text enacts only the latest permutation in Bellow's comic opera on the dynamics of the heterosexual human pair. Its situations parallel those of earlier novels as Clara and Ithiel alternately embrace and flee, seek higher consciousness, and become mired in temporal mundanities.[60]

The most positive response by far is that of Marianne Friedrich, who performs a creative manipulation of Jungian individuation theory, bringing together the twin romance paradigms embodied in the Hera and the Tristan and Isolde myths in an attempt to valorize Clara Velde.[61] Even Bellow himself has added to the debate: "[This story] gives an independent view of human reality different from the prevailing contemporary view. . . . And I can tell from the early reception of a story like this by my contemporaries that I have given a new view."[62]

The Bellarosa Connection (1989)

Set in the 1940s through the 1980s in New Jersey, Philadelphia, and Jerusalem, this novella functions both as a tribute to the victims and survivors of the Holocaust and as a morality play about the various failures of American Jewry to respond emotionally to this European tragedy. Perhaps the most "Jewish" of Bellow's books to date, this memorial and mea culpa is a richly worked and densely patterned tragicomedy about a man with a phenomenal memory who has come too late to the moment of genuine human feeling.

Many initial reviewers were lukewarm or patronizing about this book. Mark Feeney strikes a note many echoed, that this is "lesser Bellow," that the talkiness is like "wind bellying in sails," and that it has "a muffled ending." He concludes that at least it does "suggest a renewal after the crabbiness and lackadaisical manner of *A Theft*."[63] William H. Pritchard by contrast sees the novella as vintage Bellow, even though the book lacks closure,[64] while Bruce Bawer accuses Bellow of being too preoccupied with intellectual matters. Bawer does appreciate the elegant shaping and the compelling narrative strength of the book but concludes that it is an artificial work, overly schematic, too little engaged with telling, and ultimately lacking in passion and compassion.[65] David Denby calls the book a "seriously funny *jeu d'esprit*" of Bellow's old age. He praises the sentences which never "turn into a form of appropriation," and which remain "hard, resistant, rooted in the world, sitting on zippered plastic." He sees it as the classic Bellow story built from "a rush of declarative sentences—thought-tormented yet exuberant."[66] Greg Johnson, who finds the book a powerful meditation on the Holocaust and the history of the Jews, as well as on the relationship of the individual to a culture, concludes that the vigor and resourcefulness of America's most honored writer are as formidable as ever. He considers this short fiction "long on quality" and reminiscent of Bellow's earliest work because of its economy of form and essayistic elegance. A model of form, "its tightly organized but seemingly digressive and offhand style" is deceptive. At times the story strains credibility, but overall it is equal to Bellow's finest achievement in fiction, *Seize the Day* (1956).[67] Stronger and more accomplished than *A Theft*, and not quite as important as *Seize the Day*, *The Bellarosa Connection* thus seems to be garnering increasingly positive critical attention.

"Something to Remember Me By" (1990)

The story "Something to Remember Me By" is a memoir relating the narrator's (a septuagenarian's) story of how he was initiated into a "modern" world marked by a sequence of personal humiliations that culminate in an eventual return to grace. Andrew Gordon positions this story in the Bellow tradition of "the comedy of shame," describing it as a "ritual degradation of the Bellow hero," as an adolescent rite of passage that shows shame functioning as a "hopeful humanizing emotion," "penitential," and "reparative," a shame eventually leading to love.[68]

In contrast, Peter Hyland takes an "external" approach, suggesting that this story is not vintage Bellow streetwise comic realism but instead comes straight from the vault of old pieces waiting to be published. He indicates that the lack of critical responses to this collection can be attributed to what looks like the commercial recycling of a non-noteworthy story that had appeared in magazine form the previous year. Hyland believes that in re-situating this story in this new publication format and by providing a foreword to the volume, Bellow is presenting himself a victim of the "bitch-beauty," the well-known Bellovian seductress who "sometimes strips the protagonist materially, who always strips him of his dignity, and . . . who makes him compromise his intellectual work." Hyland then points out that since this volume has been dedicated by Bellow to his children and grandchildren, it is probably a farewell legacy, a Prosperan apologetics from this long-lived writer.[69]

The Actual (1997)

Bellow's latest novella, a love story about two elderly people, involves three main characters: Sigmund Adletsky, a now fragile, but fabulously rich old Chicago businessman; Harry Trellman, a vigilant intellectual scout; and Amy Wustrin, Harry's long-lost, unrequited, adolescent love. A woman in whom he has invested half a century of love, longing, and imaginary interaction, she is Harry's "actual." Told with bright flashes of Bellow's old descriptive power, it is a story about that perennial Bellow theme of the nature of the soul and the poignancy of a longtime love anticipated and remembered.

The critical response to this novella is just beginning. David Gates calls Harry Trellman an antiquities dealer who is really a first-class noticer and ambassador of the arts, who ironically notices a whole lot less than Sigmund Adletsky, the man he is supposedly "noticing" for. After all, it is Adletsky who discerns Harry's great love for Amy and who brings them together. Gates complains that this book, despite its upbeat ending, proves to be "thin gruel, with featureless characters and tin-ear dialogue." He surmises that were it not for his stature, Bellow might not have gotten away with this piece.[70] Justin Cartwright likewise notes that there are only a few flashes of vintage Bellow here. Bellow "has lost his sure touch" and now seems repetitive and pointless, producing characters who seem to be only poor repetitions of earlier richer versions. Worse, many passages seem like "bad pastiches of abstracts from other books," *Humboldt's Gift* in particular, while only a brief description or two of Chicago has the old Bellow power. "Age does take its toll, even on a genius like Saul Bellow," he concludes.[71]

Alfred Kazin, a lifelong Bellow admirer, sees in this book evidence that Bellow appears to be as sharp as ever. Though the Chicago Jews are much better off in *The Actual* than those of the *Augie March* years, they display just as much soul and Chicago angst about being sharp observers. Kazin suggests that Bellow has now reached the prophet stage, typical of old American Jewish radicals who "sigh over the mediocrity of our national arrangements." He notes some brilliant visual effects but acknowledges the lack of story and the fact that Amy is merely "a wistful attempt to redress the usual [gender] imbalances."[72] Michiko Kakutani likewise notes the much finer aesthetic scale of this later work and locates Bellow with the great existential master writers. Yet Kakutani also sees *The Actual* as a "Bellovian variation on James, a variation that oddly stands as a mature distillation of Mr. Bellow's work to date: a twinkling of a semiprecious gem that recapitulates in miniature the issues and ideas that have animated his fiction of the last 50 years."[73]

James Wood comments that although lacking the uninterrupted energy of the major works, *The Actual* has its own "nervous perfection" as it hits the familiar old theme of wrestling for the essential "amid piles of our emotional slack." Despite its "rationed power" it has plenty of sentences on which "Bellow has breathed," including many of the passages of remarkable physical description, of aged people, women's bodies, and the Chicago weather and landscape. Wood also recalls the stern fathers in Bellow's earlier work and suggests a mellowing in this late work containing a father–son relationship between Harry and old Sigmund Adletsky in which "communication was not arrested." He concludes that all Bellow's novels have been occupied with that most nineteenth-century and Russian of questions about what in life is essential and that in this late work Bellow finally tells us that "we are here [on earth] to seek what we are here for. That is our actual."[74]

Conclusion

Bellow's short stories have been read both individually and as companion pieces to the master works. Hence, though Bellow's universe has come to be known by its large planets—*The Adventures of Augie March, Henderson the Rain King, Herzog, Humboldt's Gift, Mr. Sammler's Planet, The Dean's December,* and *More Die of Heartbreak*—a surprisingly sizeable number of smaller Bellovian Planets adorn our literary universe. Their appearance, though not always fully recognized, is significant. Bellow's stories also reflect that his recurring themes have, like a fine vintage, aged with time to provide us now with a significant body of short fiction characterized by both its elegant brevity and its measured intensity. Their sharp wit, precise description, unforgettable portraits, and finely crafted dialogue remind us of the fiction of sensibility, character portraiture, and fine insights into the human heart characteristic of the best of Hawthorne and James. Like so many of the great modernists who preceded him Bellow too has become a master of the short story and the novella. His is a legacy of elegance, intensity, and clarity that spans Bellow's career all the way down to these, his silver years.

Gloria L. Cronin
Gerhard Bach

Notes

1. Saul Bellow, "The Silent Assumptions of the Novelist," Lecture Delivered at the Saul Bellow Conference in Haifa, 28 April 1987. Revised version published as "Summations" in *Saul Bellow: A Mosaic*, vol. 3 of Twentieth Century American Jewish Writers Series, ed. Liela Goldman, Gloria L. Cronin, and Ada Aharoni (New York: Peter Lang, 1992).

2. Greg Johnson, "Novellas for the Nineties," *Georgia Review* 45, no. 2 (1991): 363.

3. Robert R. Dutton, *Saul Bellow*, rev. ed., vol. 181 of Twayne's United States Author Series, (New York: Twayne, 1982).

4. Robert Kiernan, *Saul Bellow* (New York: Continuum, 1989).

5. Peter Hyland, *Saul Bellow*, Modern Novelists (New York: St. Martin's Press, 1992), 127.

6. Ruth Miller, *Saul Bellow: A Biography of the Imagination* (New York: St. Martin's Press, 1991).

7. Daniel Fuchs, *Saul Bellow: Vision and Revision* (Durham, N.C.: Duke University Press, 1984).

8. Marianne M. Friedrich, *Character and Narration in the Short Fiction of Saul Bellow*, vol. 5 of Twentieth Century American Jewish Writers, ed. Daniel Walden (New York: Peter Lang, 1995), pp. 3, 194.

9. Saul Bellow, foreword to *Something to Remember Me By* (New York: Viking Press, 1991), v–ix.

10. David Anderson, "Saul Bellow and the Midwestern Tradition: Beginnings," *Midwestern Miscellany* 16 (1988): 59–68.

11. "Starting Out in Chicago," *American Scholar* 44 (Winter 1974–75): 71–77.

12. Most critics have viewed *Dangling Man* as a novel. Viewed in retrospect it clearly belongs to the group of novellas that include *Seize the Day, A Thief, Bellarosa Connection*, and *The Actual*.

13. Tony Tanner, "Tony Tanner Writes about the American Novelist Saul Bellow" review of *Mosby's Memoirs and Other Stories*, by Saul Bellow, *Listener*, 23 January 1969, 113–14.

14. Denis Donoghue, "Bellow in Short," review of *Mosby's Memoirs and Other Stories*, by Saul Bellow, *Art International* 13 (1969):pp. 59–60, 64.

15. David D. Galloway, "Saul Bellow: 'The Gonzaga Manuscripts'" in *Die Amerikanische Short Story der Gegenwart: Interpretationen*, ed. Peter Freese (Berlin: Schmidt, 1976), 175–83.

16. Richard F. Dietrich, "The Biological Draft Dodger in Bellow's 'A Father–to–Be,'" *Studies in the Humanities* 9, no. 1 (1981): 45–51.

17. Irving Halperin, "Therefore Choose Life," review of "Mosby's Memoirs," by Saul Bellow, *Jewish Affairs*, March 1976, pp. 65, 67, 69.

18. Noriko M. Lippit, "A Perennial Survivor: Saul Bellow's Heroine in the Desert," *Studies in Short Fiction* 12, no. 3 (1975): 281.

19. Constance Rooke, "Saul Bellow's 'Leaving the Yellow House': The Trouble with Women," *Studies in Short Fiction* 14 (1977): 184–87.

20. David P. Demarest, Jr.,"The Theme of Discontinuity in Saul Bellow's Fiction: 'Looking for Mr. Green' and 'A Father-to-Be,'" *Studies in Short Fiction* 6, no. 2 (1969): 175.

21. Eusebio L. Rodrigues, "Koheleth in Chicago: Quest for the Real in 'Looking for Mr. Green,'" *Studies in Short Fiction* 11, no. 4 (1974): 387.

22. Herbert Gold, "The Discovered Self," *Nation*, 17 November 1956, 435.

23. John A. Lynch, "Prelude to Accomplishment," *Commonweal*, 30 November 1956, 238.

24. Charles J. Rolo, "Reader's Choice," *Atlantic*, January 1957, 86.

25. Robert Baker, "Bellow Comes of Age," *Chicago Review* 11, no. 1 (Spring 1957): 108.

26. Robert O. Bowen, "Bagels, Sour Cream and the Heart of the Current Novel," *Northwest Review* 1, no. 2 (1957): 52–56; Ray B. West, Jr., "Six Authors in Search of a Hero," *Sewanee Review* 65, no. 3 (1957): 498–508.

27. Leslie A. Fiedler, "Some Footnotes on the Fiction of '56," *Reporter*, 13 December 1956, 44.

28. Robert W. Flint, "The Undying Apocalypse," *Partisan Review* 24, no. 1 (1957): 139–45.

29. Ralph Ciancio, "The Achievement of Saul Bellow's *Seize the Day*," in *Literature and Theology*, vol. 7 in The University of Tulsa Department of English Monograph Series, ed. Thomas F. Staley and Lester F. Zimmerman (Tulsa, OK: University of Tulsa, 1969), 49–80.

30. Richard Giannone, "Saul Bellow's Idea of Self: A Reading of *Seize the Day*," *Renascence* 27, no. 4 (1975): 193–205.

31. Julius Raper, "Running Contrary Ways: Saul Bellow's *Seize the Day*," *Southern Humanities Review* 10, no. 2 (1976): 157–68.

32. Allan Chavkin, "'The Hollywood Thread' and the First Draft of Saul Bellow's *Seize the Day*," *Studies in the Novel* 14, no. 1 (1982): 82–94.

33. S. Lillian Kremer, "*Seize the Day*: Intimations of Anti–Hasidic Satire," *Yiddish* 4, no. 4 (1982): 32–40.

34. S. Lillian Kremer, "An Intertextual Reading of *Seize the Day*," *Saul Bellow Journal* 10, no. 1 (Fall 1991): 46–56.

35. Gloria L. Cronin, "The Seduction of Tommy Wilhelm: A Post-Modernist Appraisal of *Seize the Day*," *Saul Bellow Journal* 3, no. 1 (1983): 18–27.

36. John J. Clayton, "Alienation and Masochism," in *Saul Bellow: In Defense of Man*, 2ᵈ ed. (Bloomington: Indiana University Press, 1979), 49–76. Reprinted in *Saul Bellow*, Modern Critical Views, ed. Harold Bloom (New York: Chelsea, 1986), 65–85.

37. John J. Clayton, "Saul Bellow's *Seize the Day*: A Study in Midlife Transition," in *American Literature in Belgium*, ed. Gilbert Debusscher and Marc Maufort (Amsterdam: Rodopi, 1988), 135–47.

38. J. Brooks Bouson, "Empathy and Self-Validation in Bellow's *Seize the Day*," in *The Emphatic Reader: A Study of the Narcissistic Character and the Drama of the Self* (Amherst: University of Massachusetts Press, 1989), 64–81. Reprinted in *The Critical Response to Saul Bellow*, ed. Gerhard Bach (Westport, CT: Greenwood Press, 1995), 98.

39. Gaye McCollum Simmons, "Atonements in Saul Bellow's *Seize the Day*," *Saul Bellow Journal* 11, no. 2 & 12, no. 1 (Winter 1993): 30–53.

40. Gerhard Bach, "'Howling Like a Wolf from the City Window': The Cinematic Realization of *Seize the Day*," *Saul Bellow Journal* 7, no. 2 (Summer 1988): 71–83.

41. Michael Shiels, "Space, Place, and Pace: A Cinematic Reading of *Seize the Day*" in *Saul Bellow at Seventy-five: A Collection of Critical Essays*, ed. Gerhard Bach (Tubingen, Germany: Gunter Narr Verlag, 1991), 55–62.

42. Darryl Hattenhaur, "Tommy Wilhelm as Passive-Aggressive in *Seize the Day*," *Midwest Quarterly* 36, no. 3 (1995): 265–74.

43. Greg Johnson, "Spatial Dialogue in Bellow's Fiction," *Mosaic* 16, no. 3 (1983): 117–25.

44. S. Lillian Kremer, "Memoir and History: Saul Bellow's Old Men Remembering in 'Mosby's Memoirs,' 'The Old System,' and *The Bellarosa Connection*," *Saul Bellow Journal* 10, no. 1 (Fall 1991): 46–56.

45. Sanford Pinsker, review of *Him with His Foot in His Mouth and Other Stories*, by Saul Bellow, *Studies in Short Fiction* 21, no. 4 (1984): 404–5.

46. Sanford Pinsker, "A New Look at the Old System," *Saul Bellow Journal* 11, no. 2 & 12, no. 1 (Winter 1993): 54–65.

47. Cynthia Ozick, "Farcical Combat in a Busy World," review of *Him with His Foot in His Mouth and Other Stories*, by Saul Bellow, *New York Times Book Review*, 20 May 1984, 1.

48. Peter Prescott, "Him at His Most Impressive," review of *Him with His Foot in His Mouth and Other Stories*, by Saul Bellow, *Newsweek*, 14 May 1984, 76.

49. Robert Alter, "Mr. Bellow's Planet," review of *Him with His Foot in His Mouth and Other Stories*, by Saul Bellow, *New Republic*, 11 June 1984, 33–37.

50. Molly McQuade, review of *Him with His Foot in His Mouth and Other Stories*, by Saul Bellow, *Chicago* 33, no. 2 (1984): 108.

51. Oliver Conant, "Burlesquing Intellectuals," review of *Him with His Foot in His Mouth and Other Stories*, by Saul Bellow, *New Leader*, 11 June 1984, 16.

52. D. Keith Mano, "In Suspense," review of *Him with His Foot in His Mouth and Other Stories*, by Saul Bellow, *National Review*, 10 August 1984, 48.

53. Philip Stevick, "The Rhetoric of Bellow's Short Fiction," in *Critical Essays on Saul Bellow*, Critical Essays on American Literature, ed. Stanley Trachtenberg (Boston: Hall, 1979), 73–82. Reprinted in *The Critical Response to Saul Bellow*, ed. Gerhard Bach (Westport, CT: Greenwood Press, 1995), 272.

54. Robert Alter, "Kafka's Father, Agnon's Mother, Bellow's Cousins," *Commentary*, February 1986, 52.

55. Allan Chavkin and Nancy Feyl Chavkin, "Shamut's Hostile Joking and Stereotyping in 'Him with His Foot with His Mouth,'" *Saul Bellow Journal* 11, no. 2 & 12, no. 1 (Winter 1993): 23.

56. Susan Shapiro, "My Love Affair with Miami Beach," *New York Times Book Review*, 17 November 1991, 20.

57. See David Denby, "Memory in America," review of *The Bellarosa Connection* and *A Theft*, by Saul Bellow, *New Republic*, 1 January 1990, 37–38; John Seelye, "The Ring and the Book," review of *A Theft*, by Saul Bellow, *Chicago* 38 (April 1989): 101; Robert Boyers, "Losing Grip on Specifics," review of *A Theft*, by Saul Bellow, *Times Literary Supplement*, 24–30 March 1989, 299–300; Robert Towers, "Mystery Women," review of *A Theft*, by Saul Bellow, *New York Review*, 27 April 1989, 51; Anita Brookner, "Ring of Falsehood," review of *A Theft*, by Saul Bellow, *The Spectator*, 15 April 1989, 29; Joyce Carol Oates, "Clara's Gift," review of *A*

Theft, by Saul Bellow, *New York Times Book Review*, 5 March 1989, 3; John Updike, "Books: Nice Tries," review of *A Theft*, by Saul Bellow, *New Yorker*, 1 May 1989, 114.

58. Liela Goldman, "Revisioning Knowledge and the Curriculum: Feminist Perspectives," Conference at Michigan State University, East Lansing, May 1990.

59. Elaine Safer, "Degrees of Comic Irony in *A Theft* and *The Bellarosa Connection*," *Saul Bellow Journal* 9, no. 2 (1990): 8.

60. Gloria Cronin, "Bellow's *A Theft*: The Human Pair in Gogmagogsville," in *The Critical Response to Saul Bellow*, ed. Gerhard Bach (Westport, CT: Greenwood Press, 1995), 319.

61. Marianne Friedrich, "*A Theft*: Bellow's Clara between Anarchy and Utopia," in *Saul Bellow at Seventy-five: A Collection of Critical Essays*, ed. Gerhard Bach (Tubingen, Germany: Gunter Narr Verlag, 1991), 177–88.

62. Quoted in Sybil Steinberg, "Story behind the Book: A Conversation with Saul Bellow," review of *A Theft*, by Saul Bellow, *Publisher's Weekly*, 3 March 1989, 59.

63. Mark Feeney, "What Made Frederic Seize the Ring?" review of *A Theft*, by Saul Bellow, *Boston Globe*, 5 February 1989, 88.

64. William H. Pritchard, "Blackmailing Billy Rose," review of *The Bellarosa Connection*, by Saul Bellow, *New York Times Book Review*, 1 October 1989, 11.

65. Bruce Bawer, "Change of Pace for a Pair of Heavyweights," review of *The Bellarosa Connection*, by Saul Bellow, *Wall Street Journal*, 29 September 1989, sec. A, p. 12.

66. David Denby, "Memory in America," review of *The Bellarosa Connection* and *A Theft*, by Saul Bellow, *New Republic*, 1 January 1990, 37–40. Reprinted in *The Critical Response to Saul Bellow*, ed. Gerhard Bach (Westport, CT: Greenwood Press, 1995), 323.

67. Greg Johnson, "Saul Bellow's Short 'Bellarosa' Long on Quality," review of *The Bellarosa Connection*, by Saul Bellow, *Atlantic Journal/Constitution*, 8 October 1989, sec. L, p. 11.

68. Andrew Gordon, "Shame and Saul Bellow's 'Something to Remember Me By,'" *Saul Bellow Journal* 13, no. 1 (Winter 1995): 52, 53, 62.

69. Peter Hyland, "Something to Remember Me By," in *The Critical Response to Saul Bellow*, ed. Gerhard Bach (Westport, CT: Greenwood Press, 1995), 347.

70. David Gates, "The Heavy Hitters Are Up," *Newsweek*, 28 April 1997, 75.

71. Justin Cartwright, "Humboldt's Poor Relations," review of *The Actual*, by Saul Bellow, *London Financial Times*, 16 August 1997, 5.

72. Alfred Kazin, "Struggles of a Prophet," review of *The Actual*, by Saul Bellow, *New York Review of Books*, 26 June 1997, 17.

73. Michiko Kakutani, "Books of the Times: Eluding Entanglements, and So Eluded by Love," review of *The Actual*, by Saul Bellow, *New York Times*, 25 April 1997, sec. C, pp. 28, 30.

74. James Wood, "Essences Rising," review of *The Actual*, by Saul Bellow, *New Republic*, 16 June 1997, 41–45.

Works Cited

Alter, Robert. "Kafka's Father, Agnon's Mother, Bellow's Cousins." *Commentary*, February 1986, 46–52.

––––––. "Mr. Bellow's Planet." Review *of Him with His Foot in His Mouth and Other Stories*, by Saul Bellow. *New Republic*, 11 June 1984, 33-37.

Anderson, David. "Saul Bellow and the Midwestern Tradition: Beginnings." *Midwestern Miscellany* 16 (1988): 59–68.

Bach, Gerhard. "'Howling Like a Wolf From the City Window': The Cinematic Realization of *Seize the Day*." *Saul Bellow Journal* 7, no. 2 (Summer 1988): 71–83.

Baker, Robert. "Bellow Comes of Age." *Chicago Review* 11, no. 1 (Spring 1957): 107–10.

Bawer, Bruce. "Change of Pace for a Pair of Heavyweights." Review of *The Bellarosa Connection*, by Saul Bellow. *Wall Street Journal*, 29 September 1989, sec. A, p. 12.

Bellow, Saul. Foreword to *Something to Remember Me By*. New York: Viking Press, 1991.

––––––. "Summations." In *Saul Bellow: A Mosaic*. Vol. 3 of Twentieth Century American Jewish Writers Series, edited by Liela Goldman, Gloria L. Cronin, and Ada Aharoni, 185–199. New York: Peter Lang, 1992.

Bouson, J. Brooks. "Empathy and Self-Validation in Bellow's *Seize the Day*." In *The Critical Response to Saul Bellow*, edited by Gerhard Bach, 83–99. Westport, CT: Greenwood Press, 1995.

Bowen, Robert O. "Bagels, Sour Cream and the Heart of the Current Novel." *Northwest Review* 1, no. 2 (1957): 52–56.

Boyers, Robert. "Losing Grip on Specifics." Review of *A Theft*, by Saul Bellow. *Times Literary Supplement*, 24–30 March 1989, 299–300.

Brookner, Anita. "Ring of Falsehood." Review of *A Theft*, by Saul Bellow. *Spectator*, 15 April 1989, 29.

Cartwright, Justin. "Humboldt's Poor Relations." Review of *The Actual*, by Saul Bellow. *London Financial Times*, 16 August 1997, 5.

Chavkin, Allan. "'The Hollywood Thread' and the First Draft of Saul Bellow's Seize the Day." *Studies in the Novel* 14, no. 1 (1982): 82–94.

Chavkin, Allan, and Nancy Feyl Chavkin. "Shamut's Hostile Joking and Stereotyping in 'Him with His Foot with His Mouth.'" *Saul Bellow Journal* 11, no. 2 & 12, no. 1 (Winter 1993): 22–29.

Ciancio, Ralph. "The Achievement of Saul Bellow's Seize the Day." In *Literature and Theology*. Vol. 7 of The University of Tulsa Department of English Monograph Series, edited by Thomas F. Staley and Lester F. Zimmerman, 49–80. Tulsa, OK: University of Tulsa, 1969.

Clayton, John J. "Alienation and Masochism." In *Saul Bellow*, Modern Critical Views, edited by Harold Bloom, 65–85. New York: Chelsea, 1986.

––––––. "Saul Bellow's *Seize the Day*: A Study in Midlife Transition." In *American Literature in Belgium*, edited by Gilbert Debusscher and Marc Maufort, 135–47. Amsterdam: Rodopi, 1988.

Conant, Oliver. "Burlesquing Intellectuals." Review of *Him with His Foot in His Mouth and Other Stories*, by Saul Bellow. *New Leader*, 11 June 1984, 16–17.

Cronin, Gloria L. "Bellow's *A Theft*: The Human Pair in Gogmagogsville." In *The Critical Response to Saul Bellow*, edited by Gerhard Bach, 318–26. Westport, CT: Greenwood Press, 1995.

———. "The Seduction of Tommy Wilhelm: A Post-Modernist Appraisal of *Seize the Day*." *Saul Bellow Journal* 3, no. 1 (1983): 18–27.

Demarest, David P., Jr. "The Theme of Discontinuity in Saul Bellow's Fiction: 'Looking for Mr. Green' and 'A Father-to-Be.'" *Studies in Short Fiction* 6, no. 2 (1969): 175–86.

Denby, David. "Memory in America." Review of *The Bellarosa Connection* and *A Theft*, by Saul Bellow. In *The Critical Response to Saul Bellow*, edited by Gerhard Bach , 327–33. Westport, CT: Greenwood Press, 1995.

Dietrich, Richard F."The Biological Draft Dodger in Bellow's 'A Father–to–Be.'" *Studies in the Humanities* 9, no. 1 (1981): 45–51.

Donoghue, Denis. "Bellow in Short." Review of *Mosby's Memoirs and Other Stories*, by Saul Bellow. *Art International* 13 (1969): 59–60, 64.

Dutton, Robert R. *Saul Bellow*. Rev. ed. Vol. 181 of Twayne's United States Author Series. New York: Twayne, 1982.

Feeney, Mark. "What Made Frederic Seize the Ring?" Review of *A Theft*, by Saul Bellow. *Boston Globe*, 5 February 1989, 88.

Fiedler, Leslie A. "Some Footnotes on the Fiction of '56." *Reporter*, 13 December 1956, 44–46.

Flint, Robert W. "The Undying Apocalypse." *Partisan Review* 24, no. 1 (1957): 139–45.

Friedrich, Marianne M. *Character and Narration in the Short Fiction of Saul Bellow*. Vol. 5 of Twentieth Century American Jewish Writers, edited by Daniel Walden. New York: Peter Lang, 1995.

———. "*A Theft*: Bellow's Clara between Anarchy and Utopia." In *Saul Bellow at Seventy-five: A Collection of Critical Essays*, edited by Gerhard Bach, 177–88. Tubingen, Germany: Gunter Narr Verlag, 1991.

Fuchs, Daniel. *Saul Bellow: Vision and Revision*. Durham, N.C.: Duke University Press, 1984.

Galloway, David D. "Saul Bellow: 'The Gonzaga Manuscripts.'" In *Die Amerikanische Short Story der Gegenwart: Interpretationen*, edited by Peter Freese , 175–83. Berlin: Schmidt, 1976.

Gates, David. "The Heavy Hitters Are Up." *Newsweek*, 28 April 1997, 74–76.

Giannone, Richard. "Saul Bellow's Idea of Self: A Reading of *Seize the Day*." *Renascence* 27, no. 4 (1975): 193–205.

Gold, Herbert. "The Discovered Self." *Nation*, 17 November 1956, 435–36.

Goldman, Liela. "Revisioning Knowledge and the Curriculum: Feminist Perspectives." Conference at Michigan State University, East Lansing, May 1990.

Gordon, Andrew. "Shame and Saul Bellow's 'Something to Remember Me By.'" *Saul Bellow Journal* 13, no. 1 (Winter 1995): 52–63.

Halperin, Irving. "Therefore Choose Life." Review of "Mosby's Memoirs," by Saul Bellow. *Jewish Affairs*, March 1976, 65, 67, 69.

Hattenhaur, Darryl. "Tommy Wilhelm as Passive-Aggressive in *Seize the Day*." *Midwest Quarterly* 36, no. 3 (1995): 265–74.

Hyland, Peter. "Something to Remember Me By." In *The Critical Response to Saul Bellow*, edited by Gerhard Bach, 345–47. Westport, CT: Greenwood Press, 1995.

Johnson, Greg. "Novellas for the Nineties." *Georgia Review* 45, no. 2 (1991): 363–71.

———. "Saul Bellow's Short 'Bellarosa' Long on Quality." Review of *The Bellarosa Connection*, by Saul Bellow. *Atlantic Journal/ Constitution*, 8 October 1989, sec. L, p. 11.

———. "Spatial Dialogue in Bellow's Fiction." *Mosaic* 16, no. 3 (1983): 117–25.

Kakutani, Michiko. "Books of the Times: Eluding Entanglements, and So Eluded by Love." Review of *The Actual*, by Saul Bellow. *New York Times*, 25 April 1997, sec. C, pp. 28, 30.

Kazin, Alfred. "Struggles of a Prophet." Review of *The Actual*, by Saul Bellow. *New York Review of Books*, 26 June 1997, 17.

Kiernan, Robert. *Saul Bellow*. New York: Continuum, 1989.

Kremer, S. Lillian. "An Intertextual Reading of *Seize the Day*." *Saul Bellow Journal* 10, no. 1 (Fall 1991): 46–56.

———. "Memoir and History: Saul Bellow's Old Men Remembering in 'Mosby's Memoirs,' 'The Old System,' and *The Bellarosa Connection*." *Saul Bellow Journal* 10, no. 1 (Fall 1991): 46–56.

———. "*Seize the Day*: Intimations of Anti–Hasidic Satire." *Yiddish* 4, no. 4 (1982): 32–40.

Lippit, Noriko M. "A Perennial Survivor: Saul Bellow's Heroine in the Desert." *Studies in Short Fiction* 12, no. 3 (1975): 281–83.

Lynch, John A. "Prelude to Accomplishment." *Commonweal*, 30 November 1956, 238–39.

McQuade, Molly. Review of *Him with His Foot in His Mouth and Other Stories*, by Saul Bellow. *Chicago* 33, no. 2 (1984): 108.

Mano, D. Keith. "In Suspense." Review of *Him with His Foot in His Mouth and Other Stories*, by Saul Bellow. *National Review*, 10 August 1984, 48.

Miller, Ruth. *Saul Bellow: A Biography of the Imagination*. New York: St. Martin's Press, 1991.

Oates, Joyce Carol. "Clara's Gift." Review of *A Theft*, by Saul Bellow. *New York Times Book Review*, 5 March 1989, 3.

Ozick, Cynthia. "Farcical Combat in a Busy World." Review of *Him with His Foot in His Mouth and Other Stories*, by Saul Bellow. *New York Times Book Review*, 20 May 1984, 1, 34.

Pinsker, Sanford. "A New Look at the Old System." *Saul Bellow Journal* 11, no. 2 & 12, no. 1 (Winter 1993): 54–65.

———. Review of *Him with His Foot in His Mouth and Other Stories*, by Saul Bellow. *Studies in Short Fiction* 21, no. 4 (1984): 404–5.

Prescott, Peter. "Him at His Most Impressive." Review of *Him with His Foot in His Mouth and Other Stories*, by Saul Bellow. *Newsweek*, 14 May 1984, 76.

Pritchard, William H. "Blackmailing Billy Rose." Review of *The Bellarosa Connection*, by Saul Bellow. *New York Times Book Review*, 1 October 1989, 11.

Raper, Julius. "Running Contrary Ways: Saul Bellow's *Seize the Day*." *Southern Humanities Review* 10, no. 2 (1976): 157–68.

Rodrigues, Eusebio L. "Koheleth in Chicago: Quest for the Real in 'Looking for Mr. Green.'" *Studies in Short Fiction* 11, no. 4 (1974): 387-93.

Rolo, Charles J. "Reader's Choice." *Atlantic*, January 1957, 86–87.

Rooke, Constance. "Saul Bellow's 'Leaving the Yellow House': The Trouble with Women." *Studies in Short Fiction* 14 (1977): 184–87.

Safer, Elaine. "Degrees of Comic Irony in *A Theft* and *The Bellarosa Connection*." *Saul Bellow Journal* 9, no. 2 (1990): 8.

Seelye, John. "The Ring and the Book." Review of *A Theft*, by Saul Bellow. *Chicago* 38 (April 1989): 101.

Shapiro, Susan. "My Love Affair with Miami Beach." *New York Times Book Review*, 17 November 1991, 20.

Shiels, Michael. "Space, Place, and Pace: A Cinematic Reading of *Seize the Day*." In *Saul Bellow at Seventy-five: A Collection of Critical Essays*, edited by Gerhard Bach, 55–62. Tubingen, Germany: Gunter Narr Verlag, 1991.

Simmons, Gaye McCollum. "Atonements in Saul Bellow's *Seize the Day*." *Saul Bellow Journal* 11, no. 2 & 12, no. 1 (Winter 1993): 30–53.

"Starting Out in Chicago." *American Scholar* 44 (Winter 1974–75): 71–77.

Steinberg, Sybil. "Story behind the Book: A Conversation with Saul Bellow." Review of *A Theft*, by Saul Bellow. *Publisher's Weekly*, 3 March 1989, 59–60.

Stevick, Philip. "The Rhetoric of Bellow's Short Fiction." In *The Critical Response to Saul Bellow*, edited by Gerhard Bach, 271–81. Westport, CT: Greenwood Press, 1995.

Tanner, Tony. "Tony Tanner Writes about the American Novelist Saul Bellow." Review of *Mosby's Memoirs and Other Stories*, by Saul Bellow. *Listener*, 23 January 1969, 113–14.

Towers, Robert. "Mystery Women." Review of *A Theft*, by Saul Bellow. *New York Review*, 27 April 1989, 51.

Updike, John. "Books: Nice Tries." Review of *A Theft*, by Saul Bellow. *New Yorker*, 1 May 1989, 114.

West, Ray B., Jr. "Six Authors in Search of a Hero." *Sewanee Review* 65, no. 3 (1957): 498–508.

Wood, James. "Essences Rising." Review of *The Actual*, by Saul Bellow. *The New Republic*, 16 June 1997, 41–45.

THE EARLY STORIES

◆

Back to the Beginning:
A Late Look at Bellow's Early Stories

SANFORD MAROVITZ

SAUL BELLOW: THE EARLY STORIES, 1941–1951

By early 1951, when Saul Bellow published "Looking for Mr. Green," the first of many stories that exemplify his mastery of the genre, he had already established himself as an author of more than usual promise. In addition to five earlier stories, he had seen his first two novels through the press and had also brought out a few segments of them while in progress during those years. Only two of those stories preceded *Dangling Man* (1944). Of the eight that appeared through 1951, which closed his first decade as a publishing author, all but those two were written after *The Victim* (1947). Even though Bellow brought out no fiction during the interim between the two novels, the few years at mid-century constituted an especially prolific period for him. Six stories along with several reviews, miscellaneous essays, and excerpts from *The Adventures of Augie March* were forthcoming in 1953.

In an interview in 1991, Bellow referred to his earliest stories as "sketches,"[1] and the few critics who have commented on them also loosely categorized them as "character sketch[es]."[2] Because of this, critics anticipated the more fully developed character studies that constitute the bulk of his later fiction, from those collected in *Mosby's Memoirs and Other Stories* (1968) to such extended portraits as those of Henderson, Herzog, and Humboldt in the novels. Although his views on American culture and the possibility of an individual affecting it would change to a degree as he aged, Bellow's fiction shows a remarkable thematic and methodological consistency over the years after he frees himself from the self-conscious restraints that had inhibited him prior to the writing of *Augie March*.

Only a couple of months after "Looking for Mr. Green" appeared in the March 1951 *Commentary*, Bellow reviewed F. O. Matthiessen's posthumous biography of Theodore Dreiser and praised Dreiser for surmounting his initial limitations: "I think it is fair to judge a writer in part by the way he breaks through his first defects, the stiffness of his beginner's manner. . . . In writing, as in personal history, what a man overcomes is a measure of his quality."[3] By the time Matthiessen's book was published early in 1951, Bellow had spent more than two years living in Paris and traveling on the continent, acquiring experiences that would result in a new sense of openness and liberation as an author, readily apparent in the first few lines of *Augie March*: "I am an American, Chicago born . . . and go at things as I have taught myself, free-style, and will make the record in my own way."[4] It was in Paris, evidently, that Bellow himself developed the "free-style" that would mark the end of his early period as a writer of fiction.

Bellow's early period began in mid–1941 with the publication of "Two Morning Monologues," the first of three consecutive stories that would appear in *Partisan Review*, though the last of the three would be separated from the second by a span of seven years. "Two Morning Monologues" is a diptych comprising a pair of brief meditations, each by a different narrator with his own complaints; the nexus that links them is thematic and tonal. In the first, subtitled "9 A.M. without Work," Mandelbaum remains jobless after an extended period of job hunting during the latter part of the Great Depression of the 1930s, before the factories commenced their massive hiring in support of the war effort. He has lived his entire life in the same house on Chicago's South Side, owned for years by his father even before the young Mandelbaum was born; it had to be sold during the Depression presumably to allow the youth to complete his college education, an effort that required five years. Meanwhile his father wears overalls and goes to work every day carrying a trowel. Mandelbaum traces his educational career by recalling representative books that he read over the years on the same kitchen table: *Dapple Gray*, Scott's novels, and Gide's *The Counterfeiters*. The last of these was still roughly contemporary with Bellow's diptych; dealing broadly—and appropriately for this monologue—with intergenerational conflict, hypocrisy, and disillusionment, *The Counterfeiters* was published in 1925.

As with most of Bellow's characters to follow, Mandelbaum's fundamental problem is himself. Of his readings from the past, the one this college graduate seems to miss more than any other is "Dick Tracy," a daily comic strip in the *Chicago Tribune*. He resents that his guilt drives him from the house every morning to seek a job, a ritual enhanced by his daily allowance from his mother to cover the cost of carfare and his "essential" tobacco; he carries a sandwich for lunch along with him in his pocket. Mandelbaum blames his father for his distress; he is bored with killing time but lacks the initiative to do anything except go through the motions of job hunting until he finally stops that, too. Undoubtedly, jobs were scarce at the time, but Mandelbaum—with his father's urging—seeks one for which his education has prepared him rather than a position as a laborer that may bring in supplementary dollars but would undermine the value of his college training.

The second monologue—"11:30 A.M. The Gambler"—has an anonymous narrator who rises late in the morning and marginally supports himself by gambling on horses and cards while the "suckers" work for a living. Like Ishmael in the opening chapter of *Moby Dick*, the narrator feels subject to manipulations by Fate: "Who picks us out? Who decides or what decides my place and their place?"[5] Whereas Ishmael simply accepts his fate with an illusion of freedom, Bellow's narrator tries to find some way around it: "There's a way through the cracks. This city, this country is full of them and it's up to people like me to find a way through them" ("TMM," 235). But he loses more than he wins, he is in debt, and his clothes need mending; nevertheless, though knowing that his rationalizing is futile at bottom, he makes no effort to improve his life and literally sweats it out from day to day as "the stains grow under the arm" ("TMM," 236). In contrast to Mandelbaum's childish sense of inferiority and dependence, the narrator of the second monologue regards himself as superior to the laboring "suckers," but both are alienated marginal figures trapped by their own limitations on an urban treadmill. Mandelbaum's wish for an earlier draft number has a threefold significance, for it emphasizes the futility of his life without order, parallels the empty existence of narrator number two, and anticipates a central motif of *Dangling Man* three years later.

On the surface, Bellow's next story, "The Mexican General," has little in common with "Two Morning Monologues" because it incorporates several characters in a historical situation revealed largely through dialogue. In both style and content, a heavy Hemingway influence is immediately evident; according to Daniel Fuchs, it is "the only instance in Bellow where Hemingway's positive influence is apparent" (Fuchs, 283). The historical base of the story is the assassination of Leon Trotsky in Mexico in August 1940, an incident the general exploited two weeks earlier to make himself prominent in national affairs. The general had assumed authority over the proceedings from the time that Trotsky was struck down and hospitalized until shortly after his death; during this period he acted as a spokesman for the government. After the ordeal, he goes to a village for rest with three attractive, young concubines—"nieces" he calls them—and two lieutenants. The general is a vain, self-indulgent, self-promoting bureaucrat whose sexual play with his "nieces" contrasts sharply with the consequential past of the fallen Trotsky.

But the effect of the story is dependent less on the activities of the general himself than on the viewpoint of Citrón, whose prominent share of the dialogue informs his associate, Paco, of the general's past in the context of recent events. Both men are police lieutenants—Paco in uniform and Citrón in mufti. Detached and amused, Citrón provides the insight from which the story gains its ironic tone. Unlike the reporters and the mob around the hospital as Trotsky bled and died, and unlike the general himself, the reader can penetrate with Citrón's aid to the truth of the pompous officer's self-inflation. Although the difference between the general and the narrators of "Two Morning Monologues" is vast, thematically the stories are of a kind because both emphasize superficial values, hypocrisy, and a preoccupation with self. Indeed, these themes have remained central in Bellow's work throughout his career to date.

Seven years after "The Mexican General," Bellow brought out his next story, "A Sermon by Doctor Pep," another monologue that is oral rather than meditative like the earlier ones. Fuchs calls it Bellow's first "brilliant short fiction" in that it anticipates several of the "dazzling, . . . energetic" speakers in *Augie March* (Fuchs, 283). The language of Doctor Pep's Bughouse Square oration is energetic, to be sure, but many readers, including this one, are likely to find the story less than brilliant regardless, preferring to save that designation for such later short fiction as "Looking for Mr. Green," "The Old System," and "Leaving the Yellow House." Doctor Pep, on crutches after losing a leg in a train accident a quarter century earlier, addresses hygienic matters—"disease and health, and true and false nourishment"—for listeners in front of the Newberry Library on the Near-North Side of Chicago, an area called Bughouse Square, noted for its crackpot lecturers.[6] Earthly existence is hierarchical, he says, with the few at the top totally dependent upon everyone and everything below, hardly an earth-shattering observation. Spring and Easter make him contemplate such things, he says, and this leads him to consider the lamb: first, chocolate lambs made for children to eat with "hungry tongue and amorous teeth"; then, having learned "biting love," the children take in "the little pure divinity lamb" ("Sermon," 457). With this shift from the ludicrous profane to the absurd sacred, Doctor Pep legitimates meat-eating by suggesting that it has a religious foundation and is a necessary means of sustaining life. His harangue travels across a vast range of time and space;

he weaves in allusions to Osiris, Abraham's readiness to sacrifice Isaac, Robespierre, Auschwitz, even the Walrus and the Carpenter. He leaves us amused and a little breathless, echoing speakers that Bellow himself had probably heard at Bughouse Square and looking ahead to a multitude of others in such later works as *The Adventures of Augie March* and *Mr. Sammler's Planet.*

"Dora," Bellow's fourth story and the first one published outside of the *Partisan Review*, appeared in the November 1949 *Harper's Bazaar*. Still in the pattern of the monologue, "Dora" differs considerably from its two monologic predecessors by incorporating a developing situation that leads to a dramatic change in the regimented behavior of its narrator, Dora herself. She is a forty-five-year-old seamstress, a costume maker for the Metropolitan Opera who occasionally creates dresses for special clients. Dora prides herself on being consistent in her habits and highly dependable. Reared in an orphanage and now living alone, she feels neither lonely nor alienated because she finds other people "interesting"; she likes "to study" them and their "resemblances," which gives her a sense of control and makes her a detached observer of human behavior on the order of Citrón but lacking his ironic perspective. She feels most alone in her bedroom at night when through the window she hears people yelling and arguing, but she also knows that they, like nearly everyone else, can touch someone dear simply by reaching out to them, and she cannot. Until recently she has applied no makeup nor made other efforts to improve her appearance because she says, "It's too late for me to get a fellow" ("Dora," 188), which suggests a rarely acknowledged admission that something may be missing from her life.

Her decision to begin using lipstick seems to have occurred almost unconsciously as a result of her neighbor suffering a stroke. After hearing what sounded like a fall in a room next door, Dora investigated and discovered her neighbor, Mr. Regler, whom she recognized but did not know, lying naked, silent, and immobile on the floor of his apartment. Failing to gain information by which to identify him beyond his name and social security number, Dora perceives his nearly total alienation and wonders how anyone can be "so unattached"; she seeks personal information about him because, she says, "what isn't personal isn't really true" ("Dora," 198, 199). When this leads her to consider her own state, she understands that she is equally "unattached"; though not equally unknown, she sees that her associations are not personal, either, for to other people she is simply a reliable worker—a seamstress and house-sitter—upon whom they can depend.

This recognition comes as an epiphany to Dora and causes her to change her life, though nothing exists in the story to suggest that she grasps the reason for her change. Dora begins to use lipstick and fix her hair, and every day—that is, regularly—she rides the bus to Bellevue, where Mr. Regler has been hospitalized. In a sense she finds her fellow, after all, and becomes a de facto Mrs. Regler, though the stricken man cannot communicate with her, and she has no way to determine if he is conscious of her presence when she visits him. Dora learns the fundamental value of personal identity and distinction to someone not only as an individual but also as a social being. When she assumes her novel humane commitment, she feels a new "something" in herself as a consequence ("Dora," 199). What is that "something"? It is the human bond that many writers in addition to Bellow have described and that ultimately saves Dora from the total alienation and self-veneration toward which she was drifting.[8]

In her recent study of Bellow's short fiction, Marianne M. Friedrich discusses the relationship of "Dora" to Freud's well-known account of a woman with the same name: *"Dora: An Analysis of a Case of Hysteria."*[9] She points out that the differences between Bellow's character and Freud's victim of hysteria are far greater than the nominal identity would imply. But she also notes that Bellow's Dora, like Freud's, does undergo an "emotional upheaval" when a shocking reality overcomes "long-standing repressions" that had manifested themselves in her hostility to men and marriage, and in her absolute devotion to work. Despite the differences, Friedrich makes a persuasive case for Bellow's "absorbing the essence of the Freudian Dora concept to a conspicuously high degree" (Friedrich, 44).

Following "Dora" by exactly a year, "The Trip to Galena" appeared in the last issue of the *Partisan Review* for 1950. A footnote indicates that the story constitutes "a chapter from a novel in progress called *The Crab and the Butterfly*,"[10] but that novel was not completed. Like "The Mexican General," Bellow's fifth story is developed chiefly through a dialogue dominated by one speaker, in this case by an account related by Weyl to Mr. Scampi of his recent visit to the family of his sister's fiancé in Galena, a small city in northwestern Illinois. Scampi's role is simply to draw out the speaker, and his perspective is also that of the reader. Scampi has come to a hospital where Weyl is apparently recuperating from a mental breakdown; they stand talking on the fire escape, where Weyl tells him about his sister, Fanny, and relates what a fiasco he made of the visit to the Neff family in Galena. Although this story has more substance than "Two Morning Monologues," Weyl's basic dilemma resembles that of the earlier narrators—all are frustrated over their existence. He is bored, he says, as anyone would be "crawling around on the surface of life by himself" ("Trip," 781).

Yet he makes no real effort to end his isolation. Having recently broken off a dangerous liaison with a small-time gangster, Fanny successfully passes herself off to her fiancé and his family as a well-bred young woman from an exceptional background. To complement her story, she wanted Weyl to visit Galena; Weyl, bored with Chicago, was not eager. He felt that he could do nothing to support Fanny's claim to a good family, nor did he particularly wish to meet the fiancé's two sisters for a possible match. But he went, after all, became a little ill, made a fool of himself, and fled back to Chicago before the visit was scheduled to end.

Weyl attempts to explain his actions to Scampi without necessarily justifying them. He is oppressed by the Neffs' allegedly hypocritical expectations of proper conduct in Galena. While in Europe before this incident, he had lived by his wits with little concern for conventional morals. He admits that he acted in Galena as he generally does, that is, according to whim or emotional pressure rather than principle. This is characteristic of people these days, he says; they are less disciplined by convention and tradition than in the past and more inclined to act according to their original nature, which is dangerous:

> If we're murdered it will be because the original nature is murderous; if not, because there's something redeeming in the original thing and a reason for all the old talk about nobility. But before we can have [decent] conduct, everything will have to be proved all over again. The old props, manners. . . [T]he next conduct will have to come from the heart, from attachment to life despite the worst it has shown us, and it has shown us just about everything. Cruelty? Crime? Vanity? You name it. Is it millions shot, blasted, buried, burned? We have it. ("Trip," 788–89)

Yet Weyl does not advocate idealism, for he knows it is impossible to achieve. People should not be condemned for succumbing to creature comforts under the stress of terrible need, he tells Scampi. Possibly echoic of Plotinus Plinlimmon's pamphlet on Horologicals and Chronometricals in Melville's *Pierre* or of *The Ambiguities*, Weyl says: "You can't expect the meter-reader to take the burden of the world and imitate Jesus or walk his way into the communion of saints," but only to act politely under normal circumstances for the sake of community ("Trip," 789). Scampi does not understand Weyl's references or his point, though he has seen shocking examples of inhumanity in a Japanese prison camp during the war.

Weyl's desperado philosophy is ultimately less a plausible explanation for his inappropriate conduct than an unconsciously imposed facade for his confusion and self-disgust. In Rome he had hit a stranger standing in front of a hotel, fracturing the man's skull with a bottle. When Scampi asks why he had done it, Weyl responds that he could never figure it out and that recollection of the incident no longer bothers him. But Scampi perceives that "despite Weyl's denial, it was apparent that he was gruesomely suffering" ("Trip," 793–94), for in hitting the man physically, Weyl had subliminally struck out at himself, and he feels the wound anew each time he thinks of it.

His malaise-turned-violent resembles that of Joseph spanking his irksome niece in *Dangling Man*, but it goes a step further; at the edge of losing control, Joseph is saved by the draft, whereas Weyl sees no way out of his despair. In writing "The Trip to Galena," Bellow did not yet feel the release that would set him free as he portrayed Augie on his way to multitudinous new discoveries. Nor again would this quality be evident a few months later when *Commentary* brought out his next story in the March issue.

Indeed, from the perspective of setting and theme, "Looking for Mr. Green" is as restrained as any fiction that Bellow had published to that point, but it is also one of his career-long best. Several years later, he revised it slightly and included it in *Mosby's Memoirs* (1968), his only story through 1951 selected for this distinction.[11] "Looking for Mr. Green" is a quest story set in "the Negro district" of Chicago's South Side, now euphemistically called "the inner city." Grebe, a youngish thirty-five, has found a job delivering relief checks during the Depression, a difficult undertaking for a white college graduate because the slum-dwelling blacks do not trust Caucasians, especially those working for the government. Although he has few problems locating most check recipients, he cannot find one Tulliver Green, partly because he has no way of identifying the man but also because he can draw no information about Green from anyone living in the neighborhood. After distributing the other checks, Grebe returns to his search among the tenements late in the afternoon shortly before Thanksgiving; this implies early dark and biting cold in Chicago. He commits himself to fulfill his quest, as if guided in his determination by the story's epigraph from Ecclesiastes 9:10, "Whatsoever thy hand findeth to do, do it with thy might."[12]

Grebe is an innocent idealist—eager, good-natured, open to experience—and eventually he accomplishes his goal more or less to his satisfaction by bending the rules a little and handing the check to a woman who claims to be Mrs. Green rather than to Green himself. After an exhaustive search, the woman—heavy, drunk, talking to herself, and stark naked—bumps into him at the bottom of a dimly lit stairwell and holds out her hand for the check. He hesitates until "a moment came, illuminated from the greatest height, where you [*sic*] could not refuse to yield a check," and he turns it over to her, satisfied that he has done his best ("Looking," 261). Grebe's illumination corresponds with that ineffable "something" which Dora feels upon committing herself to Mr. Regler; the tone differs in the two stories, but the source in both seems to be divine revelation.

The impact of the later story is less attributable to the quest motif than to Bellow's manner of describing the setting and manipulating the tone. Echoes from earlier authors whose work Bellow knew are apparent throughout, but it would probably be an exaggeration to suggest that in writing this story he was actually influenced by, say, Hawthorne ("My Kinsman, Major Molineux"), Melville (Pierre entering New York City at night), Kafka (*The Trial* or *The Castle*), or Conrad (*Heart of Darkness*), among several other possibilities. An additional correspondence appears as the language of Eudora Welty's southern blacks seems to reverberate among the guarded remarks of Bellow's slum dwellers.

The manner of representation shifts between realism and surrealism with comic interludes as if conforming with Grebe's own changes of immediate circumstances and mood. Bellow believes that "the development of realism in the nineteenth century is still [in 1966] the major event of modern literature," and Keith M. Opdahl notes that Bellow and his high school friends were "at one time crazy about surrealism."[13] Descriptions in "Looking for Mr. Green" combine eons with the present moment when Grebe compares graffiti on the tenement walls with decorations on "the sealed rooms of pyramids and the caves of human dawn" ("Looking," 253). Grebe sees Chicago itself as an organism, rising and falling in rapid cycles that he tries to understand in covenantal terms. He speculates that things naturally collapse with time and thus lead to the rapid creation of other things to replace them only to fall under themselves a few decades later. With the cyclical changes, "you saw the common agreement or covenant, and you were forced to think about appearances and realities" ("Looking," 259), a problem that confronts Grebe later when he must decide whether or not to turn the check over to the drunken, naked woman who claims to be Mrs. Green.

Mr. Raynor, Grebe's supervisor, who has studied the Classics and holds a law degree, tells him that no matter how well educated and philosophical one becomes in distinguishing the ideal reality from the merely real, a vast difference exists between his weekly salary of thirty-seven dollars and Grebe's twenty-five, and that is a real difference, he says, that Grebe would easily recognize. The old Greeks were thoughtful, he adds, but they kept their slaves ("Looking," 255–56). As Daniel Fuchs put it, Grebe's search for Tulliver Green is like "trying to corner the reality by pursuing the shadow. If the story suggests an updated Plato, it suggests, similarly, a Kafkaesque metaphysical futility" (Fuchs, 287).

A different level of reality is exposed when the notorious Mrs. Staika totes her ironing board and children with her to complain at the Relief Office over inadequate support. Called by the employees the "Blood Mother of Federal Street," she is a "professional donor at the hospitals." An immense blond woman with "her great breasts, not much restrained by a man's undershirt," she appears as a grotesque earth mother with small eyes and a large voice, who dominates the station whenever she shows up there. "She'll get what she wants," Raynor tells Grebe as they stand watching her; "she'll submerge everybody in time, and that includes nations and governments" ("Looking," 256, 257). From his vantage point as author, Bellow remained essentially detached from the characters and situation in "Looking for Mr. Green," which enabled him to employ the tactics of a satirist without committing himself beyond touching everything in the story with irony; in the end he leaves his readers uncertain where entertainment stops and social criticism begins.

In April 1951, only a month after the publication of "Looking for Mr. Green," Bellow brought out his second story in *Harper's Bazaar*. "By the Rock Wall" is his least-known fiction, overlooked or disregarded as far as I can determine by all critics and by most early bibliographers. It is uncharacteristic of his work as a whole partly because it lacks his usual humor and sparkle. The story centers on two episodes in an unstable marriage between a presumably trustworthy woman and her philandering husband; perhaps the irony is particularly heavy because Willard, the cuckolded husband, is worse than a schlemiel like the comical Henderson, Herzog, and others. He is a vain solipsist who cannot see beyond his own nose and, even worse, cannot imagine anything of consequence happening there.

Because it is unfamiliar to most readers of this chapter, the story will be summarized briefly. Narrated in the third person from Willard's perspective, it is set in the couple's country home more than fifteen years after their marriage. The previous evening, they had decided to reveal their secrets, come clean, and start afresh. After disclosing the extent of his infidelity, Willard is astounded to learn that Genevieve had had an affair a few months after their wedding. Having received a small inheritance at the time, they had traveled to Rome, and although their marriage was still recent, Willard wanted a week of freedom, which would mean leaving Genevieve alone and vulnerable in an altogether unfamiliar country. He overruled her pleas and put her on the bus to Amalfi while he visited Siena. Quickly bored, he sent for her to meet him, but she responded that she would come later because she was having too good a time to leave just yet.

Some fifteen years later he is outraged when he discovers that she had lied to him about her intimate relationship with a young man in Amalfi. Both Willard and she are now ill at ease over the confessions and revelations, but neither wishes to cause a breach. The awkward situation is brought to a climax and at least tentatively resolved by a shocking incident more typical of D. H. Lawrence than Bellow. While working behind the house, Willard runs a large splinter into his hand and, in his attempt to remove it, draws a rapid flow of blood. He becomes a little faint when a sudden, sharp scream from behind or beneath a rock wall startles both him and Genevieve, who is standing nearby. As the penetrating screams continue, the couple trace them to a hole beneath the wall, where they see a rabbit being attacked by a mink. When Willard strikes the wall with a heavy rock, the mink releases its victim momentarily, but the rabbit flounders helplessly until the mink grabs it again and draws it, silently this time, back under the wall.[14] The bloody action leads Willard to identify with the stricken rabbit through his feeling victimized by Genevieve, and his hostility toward her reasserts itself when he refuses again to allow her to help remove the splinter. Instead, he insists on driving to the local pharmacy for first aid.

But he also understands that he and Genevieve will continue to hold secrets, the knowledge of which will remain in his flesh to disturb him as the splinter does, and that such things are not worth the destruction of their marriage. Convinced that he loves his wife, he prepares for a reconciliation. Despite the likelihood of that eventuality, the end of the story is less than uplifting. Although the immediate problem of the couple has been tenuously resolved, the final tone of "By the Rock Wall" is resignation, as if the marriage has long been without genuine warmth and compatibility, and its continuation promises only more of the same.

The final story to be discussed in this chapter, "Address by Gooley MacDowell to the Hasbeens Club of Chicago," was published in the *Hudson Review* during the summer of 1951. A monologue stylistically reminiscent of "A Sermon by Doctor Pep," it may be considered complementary to that earlier piece. In his "address," Gooley confirms that people recently have perceived what they believe to be his intellectual decline, and he explains his ambivalence over trying to maintain his intelligence. Praising the correspondence schools in his past, he claims to have written pamphlets on T. H. Huxley and a book on evolution with a foreword by Clarence Darrow, but he has lost his desire to intellectualize in favor of turning inward. In doing so, he compares his organs with pets and thinks of his heart caged in bone.[15] Fuchs suggests that Gooley's "creeping senility" reflects that of "a civilization," but this idea is not developed.

Gooley celebrates thought as a promising means for progress, regrets that its effectiveness is limited by natural inclinations, yet still retains his faith in it as, of course, does Bellow himself (Fuchs, 285).

For Gooley, "One thought leads to another as breath leads to breath" ("Address," 225), and he develops his address accordingly. In sharp contrast to earlier characters such as the narrators of "Two Morning Monologues," the Mexican general, Weyl and, most recently, Willard, Gooley recognizes the limitations of a preoccupation with the self and sees the merit of going beyond it. But this departure from egocentricity leads to another problem, Gooley says. We are burdened by a supera bundance of thought: "A person can no longer keep up, and plenty are dying of good ideas. . . . So we ask, will some good creature pull out the plug and ease our disgusted hearts a little?" ("Address," 225–26). Finally, however, he remains optimistic, and his conclusion borders on the transcendent: "There are feelings of being that go beyond and beyond all I ever knew of thought. . . . And [I] have the sense, as well, that there is always a furthest creature that wears various lives or forms as a garment, and the life of thought as one of the greatest of these" ("Address," 227). Although Fuchs assesses Gooley's "address" as a less successful "companion piece" to "A Sermon by Doctor Pep" (Fuchs, 285), each of these monologues is admirable in its own way, and if Doctor Pep is stylistically more dazzling, Gooley is no less amusing or provocative than he in his critical analysis of the human animal in the context of what Bellow has come to see as a modern world of seductive, interesting distractions. Because they are seductive, it is difficult to say "no," and because they seem worthwhile, we can easily rationalize and justify succumbing to them. The result is a lack of focus and a diffusion of purpose in our lives; as Gooley MacDowell says, "A person can no longer keep up, and plenty are dying of good ideas" ("Address," 225). From there it is only a step to Mr. Sammler's frenzied planet.

All told, between 1941 and 1951, Saul Bellow published eight short stories, all but two of which came out during the last three years of that decade. As Bellow himself recognized, most of these early pieces, especially those published in *Partisan Review*, are monological character sketches rather than fully developed stories; yet with his two novels of the 1940s, they establish the style that would become characteristically Bellovian in the decades to follow. Despite their similarities, most of the stories vary significantly from one to the other. Whereas "Two Morning Monologues" is a pair of meditations by different narrators, both under the influence of a solipsistic malaise, "Dora" is a personal revelation that exposes how a chance incident can lead to the resolution of heretofore unacknowledged repressed hostility and to a deeper, more compassionate association with others than alienation had previously allowed: through *tzedakah* (charity) comes *teshuvah* (repentance). "A Sermon by Doctor Pep" and "Address by Gooley MacDowell to the Hasbeens Club of Chicago" are also monologues, but in contrast to those mentioned immediately above, they are addressed to an implied listening audience, and their tone is zany—themes of high seriousness are treated with comic irony. "The Mexican General" and "The Trip to Galena" are more traditional in form, though both are mainly character portraits rendered through one speaker's predominant share of the extensive dialogue. A principal difference between them is that whereas "The Mexican General" characterizes the pompous title-figure from an observer's perspective, "The Trip to Galena" exposes Weyl's own psychological alienation attributable to self-directed hostility.

Of the two remaining titles, "By the Rock Wall" has gone virtually unknown, and "Looking for Mr. Green" has become an oft-anthologized literary classic. Both are developed stories rather than monologues or sketches, but "By the Rock Wall," which turns on an incident far more contrived and artificial than Mr. Regler's fall in "Dora," is neither satisfactorily resolved nor left open-ended with viable alternatives; it simply concludes on a note of resignation and doubt, highly uncharacteristic of Bellow's fiction. "Looking for Mr. Green," in contrast, combines realistic and surrealistic modes with a quest motif that sends an idealistic character seeking fulfilment of a mission in a labyrinth of moral uncertainty; a dark comic irony prevails, but the story ends on an upbeat.

After "Looking for Mr. Green," Bellow continued to write compelling short stories of distinction, but he never wrote a more engaging one. Its original publication early in 1951 testifies that he had clearly overcome "the stiffness of his [own] beginner's manner," an accomplishment that he attributed to Dreiser at about the same time, and his promise as an author of acclaimed short fiction had been realized.

Notes

1. *Bostonia*, "A Second Half Life . . . ," in, *Conversations with Saul Bellow*, ed. Gloria L. Cronin and Ben Siegel (Jackson: University Press of Mississippi, 1994), 280. Hereafter cited as *Conversations*.

2. Daniel Fuchs, *Saul Bellow: Vision and Revision* (Durham, N.C.: Duke University Press, 1984), 280; Marianne M. Friedrich retains the term *story* rather than *sketch*, but she sees all of his short fiction as based on the correlation of character and form; see her *Character and Narration in the Short Fiction of Saul Bellow* (New York: Peter Lang, 1995), 21.

3. Saul Bellow, "Dreiser and the Triumph of Art," review of *Theodore Dreiser*, by F. O. Matthiessen, *Commentary*, May 1951, 502.

4. Saul Bellow, *The Adventures of Augie March* (1953; New York: Viking, 1960), 3.

5. Saul Bellow, "Two Morning Monologues," *Partisan Review* 8 (May–June 1941): 235. Hereafter cited parenthetically as "TMM."

6. Saul Bellow, "A Sermon by Doctor Pep," *Partisan Review* 16 (May 1949): 456. Hereafter cited parenthetically as "Sermon."

7. Saul Bellow, "Dora," *Harper's Bazaar*, November 1949, 118.

8. For further insight into "Dora" in relation to selected writings by Bellow and others, see Sanford E. Marovitz, "That Certain 'Something': Dora, Dr. Braun, and Others," *Saul Bellow Journal* 12, no. 2 (Fall 1994): 3–12.

9. Friedrich, 42–45.

10. Saul Bellow, "The Trip to Galena," *Partisan Review* 17 (November–December 1950): 779. Hereafter cited parenthetically as "Trip."

11. See Friedrich for a brief but perceptive comparison of the texts, 50–52.

12. Saul Bellow, "Looking for Mr. Green," *Commentary*, March 1951, 251. Hereafter cited parenthetically as "Looking." Eusebio L. Rodrigues provides a useful commentary on the Ecclesiastes association in "Koheleth in Chicago: The Quest for the Real in 'Looking for Mr. Green,'" *Studies in Short Fiction* 11 (Fall 1974): 392–3.

13. Gordon Lloyd Harper, "The Art of Fiction: Saul Bellow," in *Conversations*, 60; Keith M. Opdahl, "Saul Bellow," in *Twentieth-Century American-Jewish Fiction Writers*, ed. Daniel Walden. *Dictionary of Literary Biography* (Detroit: Gale Research, 1984), vol. 28:10.

14. Although the differences are considerable, the violence and screams of the rabbit are reminiscent of chapter 18—"Rabbit"—in D. H. Lawrence's *Women in Love* (1921).

15. Saul Bellow, "Address by Gooley MacDowell to the Hasbeens Club of Chicago," *Hudson Review* 4 (Summer 1951): 224. Hereafter cited parenthetically as "Address."

Works Cited

Bellow, Saul. "Address by Gooley MacDowell to the Hasbeens Club of Chicago." *Hudson Review* 4 (Summer 1951): 222–27.

———. *The Adventures of Augie March.* 1953; New York: Viking, 1960.

———. "By the Rock Wall." *Harper's Bazaar*, April 1951, pp. 235, 205, 207–8, 214–16.

———. "Dreiser and the Triumph of Art." Review of *Theodore Dreiser*, by F. O. Matthiessen. *Commentary*, May 1951, 502–3.

———. "Looking for Mr. Green." *Commentary*, March 1951, 251–61.

———. "The Mexican General." *Partisan Review* 9 (May–June 1942): 178–94.

———. "A Second Half Life . . ." Reprinted in Cronin, 278–92.

———. "A Sermon by Doctor Pep." *Partisan Review* 16 (May 1949): 455–62.

———. "The Trip to Galena." *Partisan Review* 17 (November–December 1942): 779–84.

———. "Two Morning Monologues." *Partisan Review* 8 (May–June 1941): 230–36.

Cronin, Gloria L., and Ben Siegel, ed. *Conversations with Saul Bellow.* Jackson: University Press of Mississippi, 1994.

Friedrich, Marianne M. *Character and Narration in the Short Fiction of Saul Bellow.* New York: Peter Lang, 1995.

Fuchs, Daniel. *Saul Bellow: Vision and Revision.* Durham, N.C.: Duke University Press, 1984.

Harper, Gordon Lloyd. "The Art of Fiction." In Gloria L. Cronin and Ben Siegel, eds., *Conversations with Saul Bellow*, 58–76.

Marovitz, Sanford E. "That Certain 'Something': Dora, Dr. Braun, and Others." *Saul Bellow Journal* 12 (Fall 1994): 3–12.

Opdahl, Keith M. "Saul Bellow." In *Twentieth-Century American-Jewish Fiction Writers*, ed. Daniel Walden. *Dictionary of Literary Biography*, 28:8–25. Detroit: Gale Research, 1984.

Rodrigues, Eusebio L. "Koheleth in Chicago: The Quest for the Real in 'Looking for Mr. Green.'" *Studies in Short Fiction* 11 (Fall 1974): 387–93.

FROM *MOSBY'S MEMOIRS* TO *SEIZE THE DAY*

♦

Short Stories

PETER HYLAND

Although Bellow began his career with the small-scale works *Dangling Man* and *The Victim*, he is best known for substantial novels such as *The Adventures of Augie March* and *Herzog*, and it is generally accepted that his talents are best represented in these sprawling forms. He has, however, contributed excellent short stories to periodicals as diverse as *Partisan Review* and *Playboy*. He felt that at least some of these stories deserved a wider audience, and they have been reprinted in two collections, *Mosby's Memoirs and Other Stories* (1968) and *Him with His Foot in His Mouth and Other Stories* (1984).

Mosby's Memoirs brings together six stories written over a period of about seventeen years, including the three that were published with *Seize the Day*. Each of these latter three is in some way an attempt by an individual to establish for himself an identity in relation to the outside world which will allow inner and outer realities to give stable meaning to each other. The earliest, "Looking for Mr. Green" (1951), set in the bleak Chicago of the depression years, concerns the attempts of George Grebe, a displaced academic, to deliver a welfare check to a Mr. Green. During his journey through the black slum district he is met with suspicion and denials that make him ponder the insubstantiality of identity, and this leads him to question the possibility of establishing the existence of a stable reality. The misery and dismal ugliness of this world are one sort of reality, a product of human history and human consent, and he cannot bring himself to believe that there is not a higher reality beyond it. His quest to find Mr. Green becomes in his mind a quest for this higher reality, but when he finally finds Green's house he is confronted by a drunken, naked woman. Her refusal to either confirm or deny the presence of Mr. Green or that she is Mrs. Green

Reprinted with permission of St. Martin's Press, Incorporated, from *Saul Bellow*, 119-27. New York: St. Martin's, 1991. Copyright © Peter Hyland.

appears to discredit his idea of a higher reality, but he gives her the check, convincing himself that Mr. Green *is* there and can be found.

The protagonist of "The Gonzaga Manuscripts" (1954) also undertakes an unsuccessful quest, but unlike Grebe he is unable to allow himself the consolation of a conviction that what he seeks is, somehow, there. Clarence Feiler has gone to Spain to try to locate manuscripts of poems by a dead Spanish writer whom he admires for his positive acceptance of the world as it is and of his place as a "creature" in it. The existence of the Gonzaga manuscripts matters to him much as the existence of Mr. Green matters to Grebe. The people he meets in his search are not interested in Gonzaga, however, and show nothing of the Gonzagian spirit that Feiler so values, being more concerned with the weaknesses of Gonzaga's flesh and assuming that Feiler's own concerns with the poet must be materialistic. Benumbed by his experience, he has to abandon not only his quest but also the vision of human possibility that it has held out for him.

The material burden of the world weighs heavily on Rogin, the protagonist of "A Father-to-Be" (1955), in a different way. He is oppressed by his financial commitments to his brother and his mother and, most of all, by the lavish spending of Joan, his fiancée, who is beautiful, educated, and refined, but unable to find suitable employment. On his way to supper at her home one evening he sees on the subway a middle-aged man who is remarkably like Joan in appearance, and imagines that this is what their son will look like in forty years' time. But the man is all that Rogin despises: fourth rate, ordinary, dull, self-satisfied, and fundamentally bourgeois; Rogin becomes enraged at the injustice of this, the fact that his personal aims should count for nothing in the creation of the future, and also resentful at Joan for this further pressure he thinks she has imposed on him. When he arrives at her house, however, she persuades him to let her wash his hair, and overwhelmed by her female tenderness he abandons his determination to assert himself. Like the other two stories, "A Father-to-Be" is concerned in part with the crushing weight of the material on the human spirit. In all of them money is the source of the denial of this higher humanity: Grebe tries to hold on to a vision of something ulterior to the physical reality that money has created; Feiler's idealism is inextricably bound up with an idea of artistic value that is exploded by his discovery of the acquisitive and destructive interests of those he confronts; Rogin, worried about his own financial troubles, takes ironic comfort from the idea that all are oppressed and afflicted.

"Leaving the Yellow House" was first published in 1958, while Bellow was working on *Henderson the Rain King*. It is the story of Hattie Waggoner, an old woman living alone in an isolated house in the Utah Desert. Faced with her own declining powers and approaching death, Hattie decides to make her will. The only thing she has to bequeath is her house, which is, in a sense, her identity; she loves it, and yet it imprisons her, and its is olation is a metaphor for her own. As she considers the possible recipients of her bequest she goes back in memory over her life, finding there loss and defeat, and realizes that her only intimacy is with herself, and so in a gesture of defiance against a world that hasn't given her much she leaves her house to herself. Hattie is a large, cheerfully comic woman, both drunkenly self-destructive and resilient (she has much in common with Henderson). She combines snobbish pride in her Philadelphia family with a desire to show herself tough enough to flourish in the Western cowboy country, but the result is that she is an alien in the land she inhabits. Her gesture does nothing to save her, nothing to relieve the barrenness of her existence, but it is an act of persistence; like many Bellow heroes, she insists on survival against all odds. This is a good story, and it shows Bellow experimenting with a number of things. He tentatively employs the dual third-person/first-person narrative that he develops fully in Herzog, and he begins to explore the functions of memory (Hattie is made into a kind of spectator of her own life, watching it as if it were a film). Perhaps most notably, he creates his first female protagonist; and since she is not seen from a misogynist male perspective, like so many of Bellow's women, she is totally believable.

"The Old System" (1967) is more completely a story of memory. Dr. Samuel Braun is a biochemist whose work involves the chemistry of heredity, the science of biological connectedness and continuity. As a scientist he wants to look at life with a cold eye, to fit things into rational systems, but his story is concerned with the disordered vitality of human emotion. It begins with his love for his cousin Isaac, now dead. Isaac had offended his sister Tina over a matter of money; he was not at fault, but his sister's irrational resentment caused a rift between them that Isaac tried often to repair, but it was healed only on Tina's deathbed. Dr. Braun tries to understand this "crude circus of feelings," and to do so he excavates his memory, tracing his family's American history to its prehistory in Russia. The story he digs up ends with a reconciliation, which he sees as a reassertion of the "old laws and wisdom," the old Jewish system of blood ties, of obligation and acceptance, but his own scientific system remains inadequate as a means of understanding the demands of emotional life. "The Old System" appeared while Bellow was working on *Mr. Sammler's Planet*, and it shares some of the novel's concerns; the aging Dr. Braun, lying on his December bed, considering problems of memory, meaning, and mortality, foreshadows the more complex Mr. Sammler. It also takes up an issue that Bellow was later to pursue more fully in *The Dean's December* and *More Die of Heartbreak*: the ability of scientific thought to give order and meaning to human existence.

"Mosby's Memoirs" (1968) is the most complex of the six narratives. Willis Mosby is a retired academic and diplomat who is in Mexico writing his memoirs. He looks back with no small vanity on his successful career as confidant and advisor to distinguished men, a career founded on his intellectual arrogance and aggressiveness. In order to avoid what he calls "the common fate of intellectuals," the sin of pride (he is unaware of how deeply guilty he is of this sin), he decides to temper the serious stuff of his autobiography by introducing into it, as comic relief, the story of a Jewish radical named Lustgarten whom he had met in postwar Paris. Lustgarten was a born loser, a naive, well-meaning figure who failed in everything he did, a man doomed to be victimized by life. Mosby considers this man with detached irony and no compassion, seeing him purely as a comic figure. Only at the end of the story do we learn what Mosby has almost suppressed—that by making Lustgarten appear comic to his own wife as a means of seducing her, he had participated in Lustgarten's victimization. This memory triggers a wave of guilt in Mosby, expressed in a feeling of suffocation, as if he is being crushed by the realization that his stance of intellectual superiority has drained him of all humanity. Bellow provides us here with a further sophistication of the technique of moving in and out of the third-person narrative voice. Like the historian Henry Adams, with whom he compares himself favorably but inappropriately, Mosby thinks of himself in the third person. This is an attempt (like Dr. Braun's) to see life objectively, but also, as it turns out, to distance himself from what he does not wish to confront: his own coldness and isolation. For all his intellectual acumen (and, as presented in the story, that is very real), Mosby has been blind to the deeper truths of his existence and is doomed to live out his life being what he is.

The earliest of the five stories collected in *Him with His Foot in His Mouth* is "Zetland: By a Character Witness" (1974). This is hardly a story at all; it is a character sketch extracted from material developed for *Humboldt's Gift*, a memoir of the doomed poet Isaac Rosenfeld. It is an affectionate portrait of the son of a Russian immigrant family (not unlike Bellow's own). It follows him from his bookish boyhood in Chicago, where he becomes a student of philosophy, to his life in New York where, after reading *Moby Dick*, he decides he has to give up philosophy, moves to Greenwich Village, takes up a bohemian lifestyle, and becomes immersed in experimental literature and radical politics. Fragmentary though the story is, it builds the life of Zetland out of the piled-up detail of a rich world. If Bellow had developed the story, he would probably have clarified the character of the narrator, the character witness who retrieves Zetland from his own memory, perhaps as a kind of mirror to his own life.

In most of Bellow's novels the protagonist's relationship with his father, if it exists at all, is a marginal part of the story and is always uneasy and fractured, a source of pain in his memory, as it is for Henderson and Herzog; only in *Seize the Day* is it at the center of the story. Like *Seize the Day*, "A Silver Dish" (1978) is the story of a man whose life is blighted by his need to be loved by a father who is incapable of giving love. Woody Selbst is a successful businessman in his sixties who attempts to come to an understanding of his relationship with his recently deceased father. The cynically selfish Morris Selbst had abandoned his family while Woody was still a child but had always been able to cajole money out of his son. Woody's memory fixes on an incident that had taken place forty years earlier, when his father had persuaded him to ask for money from the wealthy widow who was paying for Woody's education at a seminary. Woody had reluctantly agreed, though he suspected (rightly) that his father wanted the money for gambling; Morris repaid the woman's generosity by stealing a silver tray from her.

Woody tries to understand his father's action in terms of a kind of noble manhood, a refusal to accept the hypocrisy and feminine religiosity of the respectable seminary world. He needs to believe that, in some way, his father loved him and that he himself shares some of that manhood (he likes to live slightly outside the law as proof of this), but in fact his father was incapable of loving anyone and indeed, frequently chided Woody for not being selfish enough. Woody is actually quite unlike his father, having visions of a world of love and being fully aware of his obligations to others (he supports his mother and sister, his wife, and his mistress all in different households). The story links two moments of physical struggle: Woody had grappled with his father in an attempt to make him return the silver dish but was unsuccessful; forty years later he had grappled with his father on his father's deathbed to prevent him from removing the tubes and needles that were keeping him alive, but Morris defeated him once again and died in his arms. Woody's real struggle, however, is with himself (the hint in the name—"Selbst," German for "self"—is perhaps a little too obvious) as he attempts to forge that impossible link: for his own emotional and spiritual equilibrium he needs to redeem a man who cannot be redeemed.

"Him with His Foot in His Mouth" (1982) also begins with an act of memory that instigates a self-examination. Shawmut, the narrator, is an aging intellectual, a musicologist and TV guru who is living in exile in British Columbia, waiting to be extradited because of his involvement in shady financial affairs. A letter from an old friend reminds him of an incident that took place thirty-five years before. Shawmut gratuitously insulted a librarian at the college where he was teaching and this, he is told, wounded her for life. The story is Shawmut's letter of apology to the woman, but it becomes a survey of his life and of the character traits that have led him to this exile. His insult was only one of a series of similar incidents, which he attributes to a kind of uncontrollable reflex of wit (what he calls a *fatum*). What he reveals about himself, however, is a general ineptitude at life, and especially a failure with American materialism, that has allowed him to be swindled by his loved brother and to care for his aged mother who doesn't recognize him even though she remembers all her other children. His sense of his own value and cleverness is thus weighed against a character that has brought him to spiritual barrenness and his isolation in an alien land, and the reader's response falls between sympathy for Shawmut's loneliness and an ironic awareness of his culpability.

In each of these stories the protagonist's recollection of the past leads to a reshaping of his life and a revelation to the reader of things that the protagonist himself does not clearly understand. "Cousins" (1984) presents another, more complex account of an attempt, through memory, to reconcile past and present. Ijah Brodsky, the narrator, is an expert in law, like Shawmut an ideas-man turned television celebrity. He is asked to intercede with a judge on behalf of his cousin Tanky and agrees to do so because of past ties (he calls his cousins "the elect of my memory"). This gets him involved in the affairs of a number of other cousins. Ijah wants to feel that he is loved and admired by his cousins, though it appears that most of them, materialists that they are, have a degree of contempt for him and are merely using him. One cousin, Scholem, is in genuine need of Ijah's help. Scholem is the other intellectual of the family; as a youth he was a philosopher with groundbreaking ideas and made Ijah feel inferior. He is now a taxi driver and seeks Ijah's help with publication of his papers and also with securing permission to be buried in East Germany.

For all his keen intelligence, Ijah has problems. He appears to have allowed his cousins to take the place of any closer family ties (he says nothing about his parents or siblings), and this may have been a stratagem for distancing people rather than connecting to them, for in spite of his professed love for his cousins he has seen them quite rarely; his cousin Mendy, for example, he contacts for the first time in decades, though he claims to have "friendly and even affectionate relations" with him. He seems to have problems with closer relationships; he divorced his wife years before, and she subsequently had other husbands, but Ijah still thinks vaguely that she wants him—another example of his need for the esteem of others. The one real love of his life, a concert harpist named Virgie Dunton whom he has met perhaps five times in thirty years, is unattainable and therefore safe. Perhaps his real state of being is represented in the darkness of his apartment with its strange, oriental corners, and in his interest in Arctic exploration. His eagerness to believe in cousinly ties as representing love in the world (he thinks of his school-days books with titles like *Our Little Russian Cousins*) coexists with the dark and cold of essential isolation. His final meeting with Scholem, when he suddenly realizes that he has been mistaken in his memories and his assessment of this cousin, comes as a kind of epiphany, a sudden reassessment of himself.

The remaining story, "What Kind of Day Did You Have?," is of interest first of all because in Katrina Goliger it has Bellow's second female protagonist. Katrina is a middle-aged woman who lives in a Chicago suburb; she is going through the messy fallout of a divorce that became necessary because of her affair with Victor Wulpy, "a world-class intellectual, big in the art world" (63), now in his seventies. The story covers a period of twenty-four hours, beginning as she is having dinner with her admirer, Sam Krieggstein, who claims to be a police lieutenant. Victor, who is giving a lecture in Buffalo, calls her to meet him there and then return with him to Chicago, and although this causes her much inconvenience with her psychiatrist, her children, and her housekeeper, she agrees to join him. It is a stormy day, and on the return journey they are marooned in the airport in Detroit. With growing anxiety she realizes that she will not be able to get back to Chicago before her daughters return home from school, and since she has had to lie about her trip, she fears that this will give ammunition to her vengeful ex-husband. Her fears seem to be justified when she finally gets back home and finds the house empty, and she rushes out in panic, only to discover that Krieggstein has taken care of the children. She ends her day on the verge of emotional collapse.

As this outline indicates, Katrina is something of a victim. She is an intelligent woman, but she has little self-esteem. She was mocked in childhood by a father who called her "Dumb Dora," and her marriage to a social climber who needed her only as a housewife gave her little opportunity to develop herself. Her envious sister Dorothea claims that Katrina has nothing to offer the intellectual high-flier but her body. Katrina half believes this, and in order to achieve some measure of independence and a sense of her own value she has been trying to write a story for children about an elephant trapped in a department store, but cannot find a way of ending it, which gives her a frustrating sense of failure. To be needed by Victor, therefore, allows her some sense of worth.

"How do you assess a woman who knows how to bind such a wizard to her?" (67–68) the narrative voice asks, and the problem of this story seems to be that Katrina is valued not for anything intrinsic in her, but as she is perceived by Victor. Victor is viewed by that same narrative voice with no little admiration: words like "wizard" and "giant" appear frequently. At parties, the only voice to be heard is Victor's, as he monopolizes all conversations; his opinions are sought at the highest levels of political and economic activity. To the reader, however, he may appear overbearingly arrogant. He gives a talk at a university, but perceives no signs of intelligence in his audience; pursued by an old acquaintance, a successful filmmaker who craves a good conversation about ideas, he is rude and hostile. Katrina herself remembers with pain how she was once the recipient of his long-lasting contempt when she persuaded him to go with her to see the film *M.A.S.H.*

Katrina craves distinction, and she believes she is getting it by having Victor confide his thoughts in her: "Abed, Victor and Katrina smoked, drank . . . they *thought*—my God, they thought" (77). But it is Victor's thinking that counts, because he doesn't listen to the thoughts of others. Indeed, he has little interest in Katrina's mind, let alone respect for it: "She could irritate him to the point of heartbreak" (105). He has erotic fantasies about her, she keeps him going, and this inexplicable sexual chemistry is the source of his tie to her. For all his genius, he is incapable of understanding a life different from his own, and her desire to have him say he loves her is meaningless to him; he can respond to it only with contempt. His need, perhaps, is summed up in the Picasso engravings described in the story, voyeuristic depictions of old men, satyr-artists gazing at submissive female bodies ("wide-open odalisques," 72).

Katrina wants to grow, to break out of the self defined by her father and her husband, and Victor's demanding intellectual company seems to be a way for her to do that. But the assumption of her inferiority by both Victor and herself means that she remains in the trap. She is like the elephant in her story and is no more capable of extricating herself than she is of freeing the elephant. "What Kind of Day Did You Have?" has much sympathy for Katrina, yet we can't help feeling, as we read, that Bellow's real interest is with Victor Wulpy.

"What Kind of Day Did You Have" is much more substantial than the other stories in this collection; it is really a novella. It is as long as *Seize the Day*, as long as the later work *A Theft*, with which it has much in common. Bellow, late in his career, seems to have turned away from the sprawling novels that are generally taken to be his forte to the cleaner lines of these shorter forms. The central issues of his larger novels are still here,

but the extended presentation of ideas in the novels from *Herzog* onward
is not possible, and there is less room for the didacticism, the lecturing that
for many readers mars his major work.

Works Cited

Bellow, Saul."Cousins." In *Him with His Foot in His Mouth and Other
  Stories.* New York: Harper: 1984, 225-94.
———. "A Father-to-Be." *New Yorker*, 5 February 1955, 56-30.
———. "The Gonzaga Manuscripts." *Discovery*, no. 4. New York: Pocket Books, 1954.
———. "Him with His Foot in His Mouth." *Atlantic*, November 1982, pp. 114-19,
  122, 125-26, 134-35, 144.
———. *Him with His Foot in His Mouth and Other Stories.* New York: Harper, 1984.
———. "Leaving the Yellow House." *Esquire*, January 1958, 112-26.
———. "Looking for Mr. Green." *Commentary*, March 1951, 251-61.
———. "Mosby's Memoirs." *New Yorker*, 20 July 1968: 36-42, 44-49.
———. *Mosby's Memoirs & Other Stories.* New York: Viking Press, 1968.
———. "The Old System." *Playboy*, January 1968.
———. "A Silver Dish." *New Yorker*, 25 September 1978, 40-50.
———. "What Kind of Day Did You Have?" *Vanity Fair.*
———. "Zetland: By a Character Witness." *Modern Occasions* 2, edited by Philip Rahv,
  9-30. Port Washington, NY: Kennikat, 1974.

The Theme of Discontinuity in Saul Bellow's Fiction: "Looking for Mr. Green" and "A Father-to-Be"

DAVID P. DEMAREST, JR.

Two of Saul Bellow's short stories, "Looking For Mr. Green" and "A Father-to-Be," serve as excellent introductions to his general vision. Both stories ask which of two responses to life is appropriate—a search, on the one hand, for intellectual order; a willingness, on the other, to take life as it is. The stories suggest Bellow's typical answer: both attitudes are inevitable and appropriate; and the man who does not recognize that humans alternate, often abruptly and illogically, between the two perspectives deludes himself with a half-vision of what life involves. Bellow, in short, places man in a rather Popean middle state and aims at an ironic knowledge similar to Pope's: man's final wisdom is to accept and affirm the contradictions of his position. Despite the differences among them, Joseph, Leventhal, Tommy Wilhelm, Henderson, and Herzog are all directed toward this wisdom as Bellow abruptly alters their perspectives at the end of their stories; none has solved the problems that caused his moral anguish throughout, but each has been made to respond less critically to an influx of life. "Looking for Mr. Green" lays down the terms of Bellow's dialectic: Grebe, the hero, struggles to connect logically the worlds of idea and experience ("being" and "seeming" are the specific terms of the story). Rogin of "A Father-to-Be" prefigures the protagonists of the novels in the inconsistencies of his own attitude: after a comically feeble revolt against the materialism of his life, he is wooed back to the way of the world, unresisting, by a warm shampoo. Both stories show Bellow's emphasis on life's discontinuity, the in consistency of human

Reprinted with permission from *Studies in Short Fiction* 6, no. 2 (1969): 175-86. Copyright © 1969 by Newberry College.

moods; both undercut narrow expectations that life can or should be ordered logically.

"Looking for Mr. Green" is by far the more complex of the two stories, creating a realistic picture of Chicago slums during the Depression and graphically showing the alienation of the urban Negro. These realistic social subjects become metaphors of the philosophic theme: the Negro environment suggests (much as it does toward the end of Ralph Ellison's *Invisible Man*) the inchoate world of experience; the urban relief agency is the pattern, the form that might impose organization on this flux. Grebe, the establishment's messenger, is allowed to test the relevance of a hopeful education and philosophy in this divided world of Chicago.

In the flashback that constitutes the middle of the story, Bellow makes consistent the philosophic terms of the argument. Raynor, the relief agency supervisor, twits Grebe for his ivory-tower college education in classical languages: " 'Were you brought up tenderly, with permission to go out and find out what were the last things that everything else stands for while everybody else labored in the fallen world of appearances' " (133). The question comes down to which world demands allegiance by being more real—the world of idea or the physical world. Should a man simply adjust to the raw facts of experience, or should he search for a pattern that might be discovered within or imposed upon that experience? Raynor announces his own allegiance to the physical facts of life:

> I'll tell you, as a man of culture, that even though nothing looks to be real, and everything stands for something else, and that thing for an-other thing, and that thing for a still further one—there ain't any comparison between twenty-five and thirty-seven dollars a week, regardless of the last reality. Don't you think that was clear to your Greeks? They were a thoughtful people, but they didn't part with their slaves. (132)

Raynor is a good-humored cynic who can smile at the characterization of the physical world that he imagines fits Grebe's view, "the fallen world of appearances"(147), who laughs at the irrelevance of his own language-learning at the Berlitz School, where he pictures himself one of the company of "office boys in China and braves in Tanganyika" seduced by the "attractive power of civilization" (145). Raynor has given up any belief that idea can be related significantly to experience; he has assumed the disparity of words and physical facts.

Grebe stands in contrast to Raynor, though he is not a simpleminded idealist. He is amused at the playful pedantry of Raynor's "fallen world of appearances"; it is not a phrase that Grebe would ever take seriously.

Grebe recognizes the force of raw, unorganized physical fact: his Depression experience has swept away collegiate naïveté, and he can look at Staika, Blood Mother of Federal Street, as she does her ironing in the relief office and see in her "the power that made people listen, . . . the war of flesh and blood . . . on this place and condition" (135). But granting the qualifications with which he hedges his idealism, Grebe has held to the faith that idea does and must organize experience. His central preoccupation in the story, matching the name on the check—Mr. Tulliver Green— to an actual person, dramatizes his faith: "'there must be a way to find a person'" (136); "'it almost doesn't do any good to have a name if you can't be found by it. It doesn't stand for anything'" (142). Grebe is painfully aware of the difficulty of his problem—applying labels in the anonymity of the ghetto: "When you saw them, how could you know them? They didn't carry bundles on their back or look picturesque. You only saw a man, a Negro, walking in the street or riding in the car, like everyone else, with his thumb closed on a transfer. And therefore how were you supposed to tell?" (130). But unlike Raynor, Grebe has not given up the assumption that one can fit idea to physical data, and we admire his stubborn faith. At the same time we feel that Grebe has yet to recognize, through experience, the true degree of discontinuity between the physical world and ideas that would govern it.

Just as he does in *The Victim, The Adventures of Augie March, Dangling Man,* and *Herzog,* in "Looking for Mr. Green" Bellow allows the weight of the urban environment to press home much of his theme. Chicago— blighted, desolated by the Depression, its neighborhoods always changing—graphically shows how fallen the world of appearances is: "trampled, frost-hardened lots on one side; on the other, an automobile junk yard and then the infinite work of the Elevated frames, weak-looking, gaping with rubbish fires; two sets of leaning brick porches three stories high and a flight of cement stairs to the cellar . . ." (126). The difficulty of dealing through intellection with this slum world is emphasized by its flux. In one shabby apartment jammed with transient Negroes, Grebe notes "a piano piled towering to the ceiling with papers, a dining-room table of the old style of prosperous Chicago" (128); in Raynor's relief office "a steel beam passed through the little make-shift room, from which machine belts once had hung. The building was an old factory" (131). Grebe's imagination suggests other pictures of how man's physical experience mocks efforts at civilized order. The Negroes in the apartment with the piano seem to be "sitting on benches like a parliament"; the halls of the buildings make their grotesque comment:

> he struck a match in the gloom and searched for names and numbers among the writings and scribbles on the walls. He saw WHOODY-DOODY GO TO JESUS, and zigzags, caricatures, sexual scrawls, and curses. So the sealed rooms of pyramids were also decorated, and the caves of human dawn. (127)

The darkness that pervades the apartment houses and that deepens through the streets as evening falls renders bizarre and feeble the lights of purposive, ordered life: "someone nursed a candle in a shed, where a man unloaded kindling wood from a sprawl-wheeled baby buggy" (139). Centrally, too, there is the inscrutability of the Negroes' identity—one Negro woman peers out at Grebe with "a dream-bound, dream-blind face, very soft and black, shut off" (128).

Such is the nature of the reality that Grebe still has cautious hopes he can deal with through the pattern of idea. He sets out like "a hunter inexperienced in the camouflage of his game" (123), armed with the weapons of tidy bureaucracy: "in his deep trenchcoat pocket he had the cardboard of checks, punctured for the spindles of the file" (123). At the start, Grebe, the ex-linguist, can believe seriously that one of his "great handicaps was that he hadn't looked at any of the case records" (125–26); if only he had spent "an hour in the files, taking a few notes, . . . he needn't have been at such a disadvantage" (130). The incongruity between the amorphous world Grebe faces and the tools of abstraction that form his mode of operation creates a comic undertone in the story. Grebe himself often feels the ridiculousness of his position and has to suppress despair and self-pity; the reader sympathizes with him but also smiles at the out-of-place figure he cuts: "he stood his ground and waited for a reply, his crimson wool scarf wound about his neck and drooping outside his trenchcoat, pockets weighted with the block of checks and official forms"(129). The expectation builds that Grebe will have to admit more openly to himself the disparity between the ordered symbols of society and the anonymity of the slum.

The climax of "Looking for Mr. Green" concentrates symbolically Grebe's philosophic problem—whether he can discover an intelligible relation between the world of idea and the brute force of the physical. Two Negroes—the old man, M. L. Field, and the naked woman with whom Grebe finally collides—are put forth very explicitly as symbols, yet Bellow manages to make each completely realistic. Mr. Field is the idealist, the supreme believer in order and civilization, in the creative reality of the word. Although Grebe hasn't doubted for a moment Field's identity, Field insists on piling up the kind of bureaucratic identifications with which Grebe has allied himself throughout the story:

> Field laid out his papers: Social Security card, relief certification, letters from the state hospital in Manteno, and a naval discharge dated San Diego, 1920. . . . "You got to know who I am," the old man said. "You're from the government. It's not your check, it's a government check and you got no business to hand it over till everything is proved. . . . There's everything I done and been. Just the death certificate and they can close the book on me." (137)

Grebe accepts all this bureaucratic "ceremony" with something of a comic sense that Field is a parody of his own reliance on numbers, names, and file cards. As the old man talks on, however, it becomes clear that Field is more than a card-carrying pedant. When he describes his "scheme," he sounds like a Platonist dreaming of a worldly utopia that will light the dark corners of the slums:

> The old man unfolded his scheme. This was to create one Negro millionaire a month by subscription. One clever, good-hearted young fellow elected every month would sign a contract to use the money to start a business employing Negroes. This would be advertised by chain letters and word of mouth, and every Negro wage-earner would contribute a dollar a month. Within five years there would be sixty millionaires.
>
> "That'll fetch respect," he said. . . . "You got to take and organize all the money that gets thrown away on the policy wheel and the horse race. . . . Money, that's d'sun of human kind! . . ." He sounded, speaking about a golden sun in this dark room, . . . like one of the underground kings of mythology, old judge Minos himself. (138)

Grebe may be too sophisticated for conversion to the details of the old man's dream, but his temperamental bias toward idealism is rekindled, after the day's discouragement, by Field; he begins a long review of the philosophic problem he's been facing.

As Grebe emerges through Field's yard, Bellow brings the details of the city into sharp focus for their climactic role in the working out of Grebe's final attitude. Grebe sees, above and beyond the debris in the foreground, the "needle-eye red of cable towers in the open icy height hundreds of feet above the river and the factories" (139). Those "keen points" of light, seen through the surrounding dark, perched, by suggestion, in the fragile framework of steel and wire, seem to sum up the precariousness of man's intermittent organizations. This impression leads Grebe to think of Chicago itself, its cyclical periods of construction and decay. What to his mind has been missing is a stable idea, a pattern (like Mr. Field's scheme) that could hold the city together and make it endure, make its appearance of physical solidity into something permanently real—"rebuilt after the Great Fire, this part of the city was, not fifty years later, in ruins again, factories boarded up, buildings deserted or fallen, gaps of prairie between. But it wasn't desolation that this made you feel, but rather a faltering of organization" (139). The dependence of the physical world on idea seems to Grebe clearer than ever. When these neighborhoods were new, they must have appeared to be objects "so concrete that it could never have occurred to anyone they stood for other things," but now it is obvious that their existence depended on a "common agreement or covenant" (140).

Grebe's imagination seizes on the El as ultimate symbol of the power of idea. He can understand how that skeletal structure might have inspired the schemes of Field:

> he had within sight of his kitchen window the chart, the very bones of a successful scheme—the El with its blue and green confetti of signals. People consented to pay dimes and ride the crash-box cars, and so it was a success. Yet how absurd it looked; how little reality there was to start with. (140–41)

Whimsically Grebe goes on to imagine the builder of the El, Mr. Yerkes, as a philosopher searching the fields of light for a realm where form and matter forever interpenetrate:

> Grebe remembered, too, that Mr. Yerkes had established the Yerkes Observatory and endowed it with millions. Now how did the notion come to him in his New York museum of a palace or his Aegean-bound yacht to give money to astronomers? Was he awed perhaps by his bizarre enterprise [the El] and therefore ready to spend money to find out where in the universe being and seeming were identical? (141)

The playfulness of this fantasy indicates that Grebe is alert to what may be absurd in the zeal of his own commitment to idea; for a moment Grebe turns bitterly on himself and asks whether it may be that what is most real, most permanent, is the fallen world of physical squalor he sees around him: Are he, and Mr. Field, and Yerkes the El building astronomer expecting too much of passing pipe-dreams? Grebe suppresses such disillusionment, and renewing the search for Mr. Green, clings to the check as at least one small instance in which he can assert the reality of idea: "he had a real check in his pocket for a Mr. Green who must be real beyond question" (141).

Grebe's collision with the nude Negro woman should smash his illusion that there can ever be a predictable relation between idea and physical experience. The woman is "heavy, . . . naked and drunk," and having stumbled down the stairs in response to Grebe's ring, "she blundered into him" (143). Grebe sees in her eyes, reminiscent of the Blood Mother of Federal Street, "a dot of blood in their enraged brilliance." As her huge body blocks the stairs that Grebe thinks might lead to Mr. Green, she tells him plainly what the scene has made uproariously clear—he's a damned fool; the check is undeliverable because Mr. Green can never be identified. At this point, faced with this final evidence that his faith in idea has been far too sanguine, Grebe cannot accept the truth. Breaking protocol, he gives the check to "Mrs. Green." As the comic fact rings in the reader's ear that Grebe has all along been trying to identify a Mr. Green among black people, Grebe consoles himself,

> It was important that there was a real Mr. Green whom they could not keep him from reaching because he seemed to come as an emissary from hostile appearances. And though the self-ridicule was slow to diminish, and his face still blazed with it, he had, nevertheless, a feeling of elation, too. 'For after all,' he said, 'he *could* be found!'. (144)

Our final attitude toward Grebe is complex. It is perfectly clear that after all Mr. Green *couldn't* be found; since it is also clear that Grebe really knows that he couldn't find him, Grebe has put himself in the position of deliberate self-deception. We cannot admire Grebe for refusing conscious knowledge of the discontinuity between idea and experience. On the other hand, however, we must sympathize with Grebe's predicament. Grebe's stubborn idealism is nothing less than the basic human need to construct the world according to intelligent, moral principles. His efforts have been admirable (he has fulfilled the epigraph of the story: "Whatsoever thy hand findeth to do, do it with thy might"), even if he has not been able to accept a balancing knowledge—admission of life's illogic and inconsistency.

Rogin of "A Father-to-Be" faces a philosophic choice similar to Grebe's—whether to view the world from a moral, ordering perspective or to bring himself to accept things uncritically as they are. Where Grebe took the first view, Rogin is interesting because he exhibits both attitudes himself and because he shows in these personal changes of perspective the illogic, the discontinuity of human mood. Man does not solve ideological problems, the story suggests; man merely changes his view of whether it is important to try to solve those problems.

As in "Looking for Mr. Green," the setting in "A Father-to-Be" carries a good deal of thematic weight. The sector of the city that we see now is that of the professional middle class. Joan, Rogin's fiancée, sums up the materialism of this world, the clutter of the affluent good life—"Joan bought him a velvet smoking jacket with frog fasteners, a beautiful pipe, and a pouch. She bought Phyllis a garnet brooch, an Italian silk umbrella, and a gold cigarette holder. For other friends, she bought Dutch pewter and Swedish glassware" (112). This sort of detail suggests one level on which the story operates—as satire of the materialistic frivolity of modern America. But again Bellow makes setting stand for a broader philosophic dilemma in the mind of the protagonist. From specific annoyance with Joan's spendthrift habits—"she had spent five hundred dollars of Rogin's money" for Christmas—Rogin generalizes his problem into a notion of material necessity:

> while the woman in the drugstore was wrapping the shampoo bottle, a clear idea suddenly arose in Rogin's thoughts. Money surrounds you in life as the earth does in death. Superimposition is the universal law. Who is free? No one is free. Who has no burdens? Everyone is under pressure. (112)

Rogin's problem is whether to surrender to the existential, the material, or to rebel and try to impose intellectual order upon it.

The structure of the story is the alternation of Rogin's moods between rebellion and submission. As the story opens, he is grousing about his lot—how his life is vexed by domineering women: "his mother was growing more and more difficult. On Friday night, she had neglected to cut up his meat for him, and he was hurt . . ." (115). "He recalled two dreams of the night before. In one, an undertaker had offered to cut his hair, and he had refused. In another, he had been carrying a woman on his head" (117). What emerges is not only Rogin's rebellious ill-humor but also the relative pettiness of his character compared to Grebe's. Bellow also establishes a stronger comic tone from the start in this story. We do not expect significant rebellion from a man who wants his mother to cut up his meat. Moreover, even in his complaints about Joan's materialism, Rogin implicates himself in her bourgeois values:

Joan had debts he was helping her to pay, for she wasn't working. She was looking for something suitable to do. Beautiful, well educated, aristocratic in her attitude, she couldn't clerk in a dime store; she couldn't model clothes (Rogin thought this made girls vain and stiff, and he didn't want her to) . . . (112)

Rogin's thin veneer of moral superiority is itself the target of satiric comedy. Nor is the reader inclined to take Rogin very seriously when his attitude abruptly alters, in the drugstore and delicatessen, to a happy submission to a material necessity:

The notion that all were under pressure and affliction, instead of sad-dening him, had the opposite influence. It put him in a wonderful mood. It was extraordinary how happy he became and, in addition, clear-sighted. His eyes all at once were opened to what was around him. He saw with delight how the druggist and the woman who wrapped the shampoo bottle were smiling and flirting, how the lines of worry in her face went over into the lines of cheer and the druggist's receding gums did not hinder his kidding and friendliness. (112–13)

Rogin's new mood, this affirmation of the world, seems comically superficial and strained—"his heart was torn with joy at those deeper thoughts of our ignorance" (115).

The rhythm of alternating moods of the story seems to deepen into a more serious tone when Rogin is again prompted to rebellion by the sight of a middle-aged man on the subway whom he can imagine as his son-to-be if he marries Joan. The material necessity that a few minutes before he had been able to rejoice in, he now sees as an indiscriminate life force that dooms him and his to mediocrity.

To suffer, to labor, to toil and force your way through the spikes of life, to crawl through its darkest caverns, to push through the worst, to struggle under the weight of economy, to make money—only to become the father of a fourth-rate man of the world like this, so flat-looking, with his ordinary, clean, rosy, uninteresting, self-satisfied, fundamentally bourgeois face. The Life force occupied each of us in turn in its progress toward its own fulfillment, trampling on our individual humanity, . . . making us . . . submit to the law of pressure, the universal law of layers, super-imposition! (118)

Rogin vows he will break loose from Joan: he won't be a "damned instru-ment," he "won't be used." But even this more sober depth of frustration does not cause the reader to see Rogin as an effective rebel: the terms of his argument are too hyperbolic, too fantastic, his outrage too much prompted by a snobbish objection to his son-to-be's appearance. Rogin remains comically futile.

What Bellow has thus established, up until the final pages of the story, seems to be a satire of American affluence and of a character who moves with shallow illogic between moods of rebellion against and submission to materialism. The reader expects that Rogin will give in to Joan at the end, but he might also expect that Bellow himself will stay satirically critical—that the point of the story will be that Americans need to look at themselves more truly than Rogin can from an intelligent, moral perspective. The final scene seems at first to go according to this script of expectations. Rogin's rebellion wavers as he looks around the apartment; "the carpeted, furnished, lamplit, curtained room seemed to stand against his vision" (120). And his rebellion vanishes completely as Joan plays Delilah with shampoo: "he sat with his breast against the cool enamel, his chin on the edge of the basin, the green, hot, radiant water reflecting the glass and the tile, and the sweet, cool, fragrant juice of the shampoo poured on his head" (121). The immediate irony here is at Rogin's expense: he has had his moments of rebellion, but now he gives in to material necessity; Bellow reveals as hollow his pretense of directing his life by some intellectual perspective. Like Grebe, Rogin has collided at the last moment with a potent physical experience; but where Grebe clung stubbornly to intellect, Rogin, wooed by pleasure, accepts unquestioningly the physical.

The final irony of the story, however, is at the reader's expense if he has been expecting nothing more than a satiric slant on Rogin's life. For the undeniable effect of the ending, surprising us, is that Rogin's submission is, in some measure, right. As Joan massages Rogin's scalp, we feel ourselves warmed by the rich sensuality of the scene:

> 'But there's absolutely nothing wrong with you,' she said, and pressed against him from behind, surrounding him, pouring the water gently over him until it seemed to him that the water came from within him, it was the warm fluid of his own secret loving spirit overflowing into the sink, green and foaming, and the words he had rehearsed he forgot, and his anger at his son-to-be disappeared altogether . . . (121)

The strength of this physical experience and the irrelevance for the moment of intellectual perspectives are clear. Bellow has managed to show both Rogin and the reader how pointless protest against physical experience can sometimes be. But as in the closing of "Looking for Mr. Green,"

Bellow also leaves an ambivalence here. He has shown us the discontinuity between idea and experience, first, in the alternations of Rogin's own mood and, finally, in the way the reader himself has been forced to drop suddenly his moralistic expectation. Bellow has made the point that men do not neatly shape their experience by idea; that what they can criticize, legitimately and severely at one moment, may at another time, in different circumstance and mood, be legitimately appealing to them. But though Rogin's final physical baptism may warm us, we are not impressed by Rogin's self-awareness; Rogin remains a shallow character. We must turn to the longer works to see Bellow's theme developed in empathic depth.

Deliberate discontinuity is a recurrent effect in the novels. As in the two short stories, Bellow seems typically to work against an expectation that fiction will reveal a logical learning process in its heroes, that the endings of works of fiction will exhibit a final resolution of moral problems posed. The starkest examples are *The Victim* and *Dangling Man*. *The Victim* ends with what amounts to an epilogue chapter in which action occurs several years after the climactic moment in the penultimate chapter in which Allbee has attempted suicide. There is no transition, no indicated resolution of the self-torturing hyper-awareness that bound Leventhal and Allbee together throughout. But both have prospered; both have avoided the collapse of their lives that had seemed imminent in the previous chapter. After their agonized attempts to understand the moral responsibilities of their lives, Allbee seems to pronounce the relaxed acceptance present in both of them in this epilogue chapter:

> 'I'm not the type that runs things. I never could be. I realized that long ago. I'm the type that comes to terms with whoever runs things. What do I care? The world wasn't made exactly for me. What am I going to do about it? . . . Approximately made for me will have to be good enough. All that stiffness of once upon a time, that's gone, that's gone'. (294, Compass Books)

Bellow is not invalidating the moral questions that the book has considered, but he asserts that life also consists of a prosy relaxation in which difficult questions don't seem very important. Men don't find answers; the mood, the perspective changes. Even more sharply abrupt is the ending of *Dangling Man*: the Army at last calls Joseph, and his final statement is a paean to the prospect of military life:

> I am no longer to be held accountable for myself; I am grateful for that.
> I am in other hands, relieved of self-determination, freedom canceled.

Hurray for regular hours!
And for the supervision of the spirit!
Long live regimentation! (191, Meridian Edition)

Again Bellow has maneuvered a protagonist into a position where he suspends critical judgment and gratefully accepts, without questioning, things as they are.

But it is in *Herzog* that the pattern laid down in "Looking for Mr. Green" and "A Father-to-Be" is fully developed. Herzog suffers like Grebe the anguish of the idealist, the romantic, who must make sense of his world by assigning moral responsibility to himself and others; and like Grebe, but more openly, Herzog feels the irrelevance of his efforts: many of his letters are not even addressed to living men. Late in the novel, Herzog's problem is put, as Grebe's was, in terms of the remoteness of legal protocols from actual life—first in court, when Herzog watches justice trying to comprehend the murder of a child, later when Herzog himself is booked by the police on an afternoon when he had meant to give his daughter a happy outing. As with Rogin, however, Herzog finally relaxes. There is the abrupt move to the country home in the last chapter, then the gradual unwinding, the warming toward affirmation, until Herzog can finally exclaim: *"But what do you want, Herzog?' 'But that's just it—not a solitary thing. I am pretty well satisfied to be, to be just as it is willed, and for as long as I may remain in occupancy'"* (340). Herzog has lived with an intellectual intensity like Grebe's and has experienced an alternation of perspectives like Rogin's. But Herzog has learned a full self-knowledge achieved by neither short-story hero: he has admitted the discontinuity of idea and experience and has understood that moral anguish and existential acceptance are alternations basic to human nature. In Herzog, Bellow has brought through to full self-awareness a hero prefigured in "Looking for Mr. Green" and "A Father to-Be."

Works Cited

Bellow, Saul. "Looking for Mr. Green." *Seize the Day.* New York: Viking Press, 1956.
———. "A Father-to-Be." *Seize the Day.* New York: Viking Press, 1956.
———. *Herzog.* New York: Viking Press, 1964.
———. *The Victim.* New York: Compass-Viking, 1956.
———. *Dangling Man.* New York: Meridian, 1960.

A la recherche du texte perdu:
"The Gonzaga Manuscripts"

BRIGITTE SCHEER-SCHAEZLER

It came to him business; it went from him poetry.
—Emerson, "The American Scholar"

Rereading Saul Bellow's early fiction and some of the contemporaneous commentaries on it is like taking a trip into the past. The sense of the mental sites of another era revisited is quite overpowering. The late forties and fifties, the time of the origin of "The Gonzaga Manuscripts," has, from our current vantage point, acquired an unmistakable sense of period, of historicity, with the Cold War looming in the background as ever-present threat and political matrix for the special and peculiar nature not only of Soviet–American but of European–American relations as well. These relations are one of the subjects of "The Gonzaga Manuscripts."

Bellow's material, dated as it may appear to us today, was by no means that in the fifties and sixties. On the contrary, European–American relations were a frequent theme of political, literary, and critical discourse. Remembering those days and rereading stories from these two decades one is led to conclude that Americans and Europeans could perceive one another only in clichés and stereotypes. In most European nations Americans were more welcome than Russians but sometimes only just. Europeans and Americans seemed endlessly strange to each other and commented on this with a vengeance, thus repeating what had become a settled pattern since the early nineteenth century. It makes one dizzy to recall what a role nationality played in these encounters and what a role it also played for self-definition on both sides. Topics such as the threat of nuclear extinction by an American atom bomb as well as the figure of the naive American tourist in postwar Europe abound in the short fiction of the time. Checking for instance the collections of short fiction of the year of the first publication of "The Gonzaga Manuscripts" (1954) and the year when it was reprinted in *Mosby's Memoirs & Other Stories* (1968), one comes across several unsuccessful encounters of Americans with Europeans in Europe.

One of the most perspicacious readers of short fiction, Martha Foley, the editor of *The Best American Short Stories 1954*, selects Irwin Shaw's "In the French Style" for her prestigious anthology (Shaw, 278–92); its Walter Beddoes is as ineffectual a protagonist and as unlucky in love as Bellow's Clarence Feiler, the insecurity being compounded by the foreign turf. When Foley in her introduction refers to "our culture" as "still fragmentary and not yet full-blown," one incredulously hears the echoes of Nathaniel Hawthorne and Henry James (Foley, ix). In her nutshell analysis of the state of American civilization she also names the atom bomb as the foremost object of dread in this "Age of Anxiety" (Foley, x).

Turning to 1968, both standard collections of short fiction—*The Best American Short Stories 1954* and *Mosby's Memoirs*—feature stories in which Americans suffer disappointment and defeat of their purposes in Europe. In Eldon Branda's "The Dark Days of Christmas," two elderly American ladies do not find social footing in Europe and leave a bleaker Ireland for a bleak United States (Branda, 246–58). Being snubbed and humiliated by an Italian contessa is the fate of two American ladies in Venice in Nancy Hale's rather bitter "The Most Elegant Drawing Room in Europe" (Hale, 97–115). A story almost parallel to Bellow's is James T. Farrell's "An American Student in Paris" (Farrell, 43–73). Alvin Dubrow is in several aspects a mirror image of Clarence Feiler, a student on a pilgrimage, hoping to give his life direction and purpose by exposing himself to the influence of European books, ideas, and culture. Dubrow is dazzled by Paris, its monuments, its history, the life of its streets; yet he ends up overwhelmed by complexities and by the weight of the very past that was his primary attraction: "Life was short and he was almost twenty-three and he had accomplished nothing" (Farrell, 73). His sojourn ends in frustration. Farrell indirectly makes a point of cultural comparison by drawing Dubrow as someone who reads Proust but "much less of American literature than he might have" (Farrell, 53). This, as will be shown, bears on Bellow's treatment of reading matter in "The Gonzaga Manuscripts."

Bellow's long short story that might almost be called a novella was first published in *Discovery* in 1954, republished in *Seize the Day* in 1956 together with "Looking for Mr. Green" and "A Father-to-Be," and published again in *Mosby's Memoirs* in 1968. Bellow must have valued it enough to retain it and juxtapose it with later stories such as "The Old System," first published in 1967, and "Mosby's Memoirs" of 1968. The critics were not exactly smitten with "The Gonzaga Manuscripts" and tended to focus on other stories when reviewing the two collections mentioned. The prevalent opinion seems to have been the one expressed in an unsigned review in *Choice* in 1969 in which it is stated bluntly that "The Gonzaga Manuscripts" is "a farcical 'Aspern Papers'" (*Choice*, 810). The flavor of bygoneness is acutely picked up by another reviewer of 1969, Maurice Capitanchik, who summarizes his impressions of Bellow's short stories to that date as contained in *Mosby's Memoirs* as follows: "Those who have a taste for a slightly outmoded type of literature will enjoy it" (Capitanchik, 212). Indeed, the note of something that is lost in the recesses of the past functions as atmospheric as well as substantive motif in "The Gonzaga Manuscripts."

Like "The Aspern Papers," Henry James's haunting 1887 nouvelle, "The Gonzaga Manuscripts" is a story about Europe revisited, revisited by Americans quite literally in quest of past culture and past culture's items. The protagonist Clarence Feiler employs the weighty term himself: "This time he came not as a tourist but on a quest" (112). Feiler is an early example of Bellow's many wanderers and travelers, such as Henderson in Africa, Herzog in Europe and the Near East, and Augie March in Mexico and Europe with a strong American sense of mission; all these characters seem to need to test their beliefs and personal substance abroad in what is now called intercultural encounters. Feiler's apparent reason for his European trip is, like James's narrator in search of the Aspern papers, to retrieve a lost text.

Feiler does not go to Italy like the protagonist of "The Aspern Papers" but to Spain—to Madrid, Alcalá de Henares, and Segovia. Bellow knew these places from his own tour of Spain in 1947 when he spent some time in Madrid and also at Alcalá, where he disgustedly watched Franco's system of justice at work in trials of his political opponents. He commented on his stay in a descriptive sketch entitled "Spanish Letter," first published in 1948. His observations and remarks, sharp and detailed as always, are strangely partisan, imbued, in spite of all their intelligence, with an unmistakable sense of American superiority elicited by a backward, corrupt, and destitute Europe. The continent was still struggling heavily with the aftereffects of World War II and, in the case of Spain, of the Civil War that brought Franco's fascists to power. If Bellow did not tell us— albeit very much later in "A Half Life" (cf. 311)—that he was charmed by Spain, we would not be able to guess it from the "Spanish Letter." In his early observations, Europeans on a train appear like ghostly hordes from another world:

> A crowd of *gente humilde*, sad, shabby, and world-worn, resting between the walls, leaning on the brass rods along the windows, with gloom-deepened eyes and black nostrils; in muffling shawls or berets that flattened their heads and made a disproportion in their long, brown faces; melancholy, but with a kind of resistance to dreariness, as if ready to succumb so far but no farther to it—the Spanish *dignidad*. (*SL*, 183)

His American separateness from them went directly into the making of Clarence Feiler. Feiler's constant suspicion that the police are after him, that people spy on him, that there is corruption on all levels of society, that the Spaniards are superficial and vain and crave mainly American consumer goods—"Buicks, nylons, Parker 52 pens, and cigarettes" (*SL*, 185)—and that they simultaneously envy, fear, and look down on Americans also have a basis in Bellow's own European impressions. As an American, Bellow remarks, he was regarded as "one of the new lords of the earth, a new Roman, full of the pride of machines and dollars" (*SL*, 195). "We are not strong enough to enjoy the Rights of Man,' a Spanish acquaintance told him; 'If Russia does not dominate us, your country will." (*SL*, 193). Thus the hysterical Cold War climate that caused the highly ambivalent reaction to any American presence in Europe accounts for the story's own pervasive, neurotic ambivalence affecting the political, social, and private assumptions made by its characters. The situation contributes to the mounting confusion, anxiety, and frustration of the visiting American who is himself lost in an unfathomable, backward, and bleak Europe.

Feiler's adventures are quickly summarized. The youngish man returns to Spain, a country that he knows from at least two former stays. He has studied Spanish Literature at the University of Minnesota, where he became entranced with the poetry of Manuel Gonzaga, "one of the greatest of modern Spanish geniuses" (112), whose work at the time is suppressed for political reasons. From a Spanish Republican refugee in California he has heard that more than a hundred unpublished poems are in someone's possession somewhere in Madrid. These poems are love poems by Gonzaga addressed to a certain Countess del Camino, who has died in the meantime. The refugee thinks that Gonzaga's literary executor, Guzman del Nido, might know where the poems could now be. Feiler visits Guzman, a wealthy member of the Cortes, in his Madrid home. Guzman seems quite indifferent to Feiler's quest, does not know where the poems are but sends him on to the nephews of the countess's former secretary, the Polvos, in Alcalá de Henares. The Polvos, it turns out, did not inherit any of their uncle's papers but think that one of their cousins, Pedro Alvarez-Polvo in Segovia, might have something. Feiler goes to see Pedro Alvarez-Polvo, who has inherited not the poems but shares in a uranium mine, which he mistakenly believes Feiler wants to buy. He also tells Feiler that the precious poems are long since lost as they were buried with the countess. Feiler is reduced to sitting "numb and motionless in his second-class seat" (142) on the train back to Madrid, taking in the full humiliating extent of the failure of his quest.

Any approach to the story with its overtones of a fool's errand is dependent, first, on an assessment of the character of Feiler and, second, on the intrinsic worth of his quest. By referring to James's story both these aspects can be elucidated to some extent. The intense desire for the possession of a text, which indeed becomes a "possession" for the craving person, is a trait that Feiler clearly shares with the narrator of James's "Aspern Papers." Already in 1958 Chester E. Eisinger stated that "The Gonzaga Manuscripts" is "in the Jamesian tradition that Bellow followed in the first two novels" (Eisinger, 200).

Bellow's indebtedness to James's nouvelle, one of James's many variations on his "international theme" of European–American relations, is obvious. When retracing the authorial steps involved in the making of "The Gonzaga Manuscripts," we come upon layers of story superimposed on one another, with the result that a palimpsest is an apt image. This stratification in the narrative process is already given in the etiology of James's text. James heard the original anecdote in 1887. An American art critic had discovered that two English ladies, namely Clara Godwin Clairmont and her niece, who were living in Florence, had letters by Shelley and Byron addressed to Clara; Clara was the mother of Byron's daughter Allegra. The American then took lodgings in their house with the purpose of somehow obtaining the letters. When the very old lady died, the niece offered him the letters in return for marriage. Since this price was higher than he was willing to pay, the precious letters never reached the public.

James already changed several features of the anecdote: The two ladies in his nouvelle, the Misses Bordereau, are not English but Americans and longtime residents in Europe; their city is not Florence but Venice; Byron and Shelley merge into the one figure of Henry Aspern, who is also an American. James then kept the central motif of the quest for the papers and the shady character of the critic-protagonist willing to go to great lengths to obtain the coveted documents. James also preserved the feature of his undignified flight once the price had been named, as a consequence of which the letters are burned by the owner (cf. Murdock, v–xi).

Bellow in turn changed several features of James's story. He relocates "The Gonzaga Manuscripts" to Madrid and to Alcalá de Henares, which is significant as Alcalá is the birthplace of Cervantes, whose work serves as a gauge for true poetic greatness. Bellow kept the quest motif, the search for the lost manuscript, as well as the love interest, although the missing documents are love poems and not love letters. He kept the intense urge of the protagonist to possess the poems as the driving force of his actions. Clara, also called Claire, Clairmont, and Clarence are also more than phonetically related; by taking up the etymological root in Clara's name Bellow may have wanted to stress the unfinished, late adolescent nature of his protagonist, who searches for clarity yet remains a "filer," a self-centered myopic clerk-type concerned with categorizing a world of which he has no encompassing vision. He added, however, a host of minor characters and changed the nature, if not the outcome, of the protagonist's experiences.

In summary, Bellow, to his own purposes, rewrote James's story who rewrote a story that he was told. In "The Gonzaga Manuscripts," what Feiler wants is relayed in words from one person to another and becomes distorted in the process—another text that is lost—thus adding to the sense of the palimpsestic "layeredness" of Feiler's experience. These complications in a protagonist's endeavors that he cannot disentangle constitute a plot element typical of Bellow at that period. Rogin of "A Father-to-Be" of 1955, for instance, complains about the life force that causes human beings to "engage in the social process, labor, struggle for money, and submit to the law of pressure, the universal law of layers, superimposition!" (*Mosby's Memoirs*, 147). In this context one is also strongly reminded of Bellow's great novel to come out of that period— *The Adventures of Augie March* (1953)—and especially of its last hundred pages with their plethora of events of which Augie is so painfully trying to make sense. Augie, of course, at that stage, is also a father-to-be. And George Grebe, yet another fictional contemporary, is desperately looking for Mr. Green in the story of that name, a quest whose ending remains wide open. These early protagonists seem to be somehow split off each other and thus intimately related. Possibly under the influence of James they are all ineffectual protagonists, a type that Bellow drew more elaborately in Tommy Wilhelm in *Seize the Day*.

Nevertheless, there are certainly differences between James's narrator and Feiler. Whereas the Jamesian character causes the catastrophe himself by rejecting the niece's offer to trade the Aspern papers for marriage, Feiler is mainly being acted upon. What matters for his endeavor—the fate of the papers—has been decided long before. The result of his search is that he ascertains the finality of their loss, with an additional good measure of demolition done to his self-image. He perceives himself as victim, and there is an element of self-pity in him that is not in the Jamesian figure nor in Augie March. An essential difference between Augie and Feiler is that Augie says no to the other characters (cf. *AM*, 515), whereas the other characters say no to Feiler, and in the very worst way, even belittle the object of his veneration: "Manuel? The soldier? The little fellow?" is how Alvarez-Polvo refers to Gonzaga with no recognition of the poet's rank (140).

No wonder Feiler suffers from a fading sense of his own worth. He is constantly concerned with his "dignity," which he feels is threatened by the European environment. Even the Spanish weather seems to play tricks on him, with a sudden cloudburst drenching him and making him feel smelly "like a wet dog" (125) right before his formal visit to Guzman del Nido. Bellow has always been concerned with human dignity but was especially aware of its significance for a character's sense of his standing in the world in the period under discussion. Schlossberg's "Have dignity, you understand me? Choose dignity" (*TV*, 46) was an early forceful expression of this. Dignity and its loss linked to the pressures of the Cold War reappear in the "Spanish Letter," in which Bellow mentions this as playing a great role for the Spaniards whom he meets. The Spanish, he writes, "feel the sway of American strength and American goods and the loss of their liberty and their strength" (*SL*, 194); yet:

> there is still something left—namely, an assertion of worth in a world in which worth is synonymous with power, and power has passed to featureless mass societies for which the past has little meaning, and machinery, wealth and organization topple the old dignity to replace it with contempt and discontent. (*SL*, 194).

Feiler encounters Spanish *dignidad* mainly in the form of pride. The Europeans are to him instruments for the destruction of his own dignity. There is really not one character in the story who, according to Feiler, treats him with respect. Miss Walsh at the pension ridicules Americans in general and even blames changes in the weather pattern on "their" atom bomb (117); Guzman del Nido "would make him look foolish if he could" (125); the Polvos are "a family of laughers" (131), and their repeated references to the atom bomb are "another assault on him" (133); the hotel manager even mistakes his nationality and attacks him as representative of ill-behaved English tourists: "'These Englishmen!' he said with fury, 'They don't know what hospitality is. They come here and enjoy themselves and criticize our country and complain about Spanish police!'" (141). The police supposedly search his valise in his absence. Even the pretty Miss Ungar drops him as soon as her fiancé returns—sad for him but not really amazing.

It is no wonder that, in reaction, Feiler is full of rage: "An ugly hatred for del Nido grew and knotted in his breast. He wanted to hit him, to strangle him, to trample him, to pick him up and hurl him at the wall" (127–28). When Miss Walsh involves him in a conversation at dinner in which she displays a simplistic bias against Americans, he becomes so enraged that he calls her "a nasty old bag" and leaves the table (118). It is evident why this has been called a *farcical* "Aspern Papers"; Feiler has developed a long way away from his gentlemanly Jamesian predecessor. In the history of the treatment of the "international theme," this story of Americans and Europeans is a story of mutual suspicion, misunderstandings, and misreadings. Feiler, through whose mind the story is told, is clearly an unreliable narrator as well as an unsteady character who confesses to his own immaturity: "I've never really been able to find the thing that I wanted to do" (123). He is one version of a dangling man, a "not-finder" and a loser. If a man's character is his fate (*AM*, 582), it is hard to imagine a satisfying future for him.

Critics have commented on Feiler's boorishness (e.g., Kiernan, 126), his lack of politeness and patience. He walks out on people who are talking to him (141), shouts at the hotel manager (141), curses (141) and clearly feels uncomfortable with his European counterparts from the very beginning. He arrives in Madrid "buttoned to the throat" (111), a feature which he shares again with Rogin in "A Father-to-Be," who is "buttoned to the chin" (*MM*, 143). He is bothered by the noise of the people in the Madrid train station but relaxes in the taxi where he listens "happily to the voice of the wonderful old motor" (111–12). One of his most burdensome and unattractive features is his constant suspicion of everyone and everything, even if Franco's Spain no doubt was an execrable police state with its concomitant scenarios of espionage and betrayal. He reacts "guardedly" (115) already in his first conversation with his landlady, not wanting to give her the true reason for his coming to Spain. As soon as he is seated for dinner at the pension next to a British lady, "he knows he must expect to have trouble with her" (115). The meetings with his Spanish hosts from whom, after all, he expects to get essential information, are a social disaster in all cases. The Europeans appear unappealing enough especially in their offensive, generalizing remarks on Americans, but it is difficult to establish with any degree of objectivity whether their behavior is not caused by the negative attitude that Feiler has toward them from the beginning: "Clarence at once sensed that del Nido would make him look foolish if he could, with his irony and his fine Spanish manners.

Del Nido was the sort of man who cut everyone down to size. Gonzaga himself would not have been spared by him" (125). This is the overreaction of a highly insecure man with low self-esteem. He is as naive as he is socially clumsy, and he may even be naive in his assessment of the quality of Gonzaga's verse. What he quotes from the extant works, even allowing for the fact of their English translation, is not only almost meaningless but simply dreadful poetry:

> These few bits of calcium my teeth are,
> And these few ohms my brain is,
> May make you think I am nothing but puny.
> Let me tell you, sir,
> I am like any creature—
> A creature. (113)

This is reminiscent of the poetic efforts of Griswold, a steward on the ship that takes Augie March to Europe and that is sunk by a torpedo:

> How much, you ask me, do I suffer.
> Now, baby, listen, I am not a good bluffer.
> My ambitions and aspirations don't leave me no rest;
> I am born with a high mind and aim for the best. (*AM*, 560)

The sentiment is indeed close to the one in the Gonzaga passage; the self-descriptions of the lyrical personas are remarkably similar yet Augie sees through Griswold and recognizes in him one of a number of "terrible strange personalities" (*AM*, 560) and can thus better protect himself from their influence than can naive, vulnerable Feiler. Feiler in Europe is lost in a maze that has social, moral, and aesthetic dimensions.

Still, to do justice to the character of Feiler, one must admit that he, too, has "a high mind" and aims "for the best." His one redeeming feature is his enthusiasm for a great man and for great literature as he sees it embodied in Gonzaga's works. If one regards him as nothing more than an "American buffoon just educated enough and just rich enough to loose himself upon postwar Spain in fancied service to mankind" (Kiernan, 128), one is not only judging him too harshly but one may also overlook the exploratory function he fulfills in Bellow's early work. It is more conducive to understanding the writer-in-the-making when one regards the story as an example of Bellow's attempt to capture the nature of a certain character-type or "a sort of mind," a phrase Bellow uses to describe his own working objective although in a later context (Roudané, 274). Seen from this vantage point it is improbable that Bellow meant to be "unrelievedly sardonic" (Kiernan, 128) in his treatment of Feiler. Although the irony in the story is undeniable and also touches upon the protagonist, there remains a seriousness of purpose about him that we know too well from other works of Bellow in the fifties as well as later periods to discard him too quickly. I believe that in the case of Feiler we have evidence of Bellow in the process of formulating some of the basic questions that were to occupy him throughout his career. He is still engaged in his discourse with the modernists, still in the clasp of James as one of their predecessors and one of his model writers as were Flaubert and Dostoyevsky. Thus in Feiler we get a protagonist who represents a literary and intellectual exercise, possibly of the trial-and-error mode. Feiler may be seen as a tentative case study, one of the several impersonations of a problem rather than a fully realized human being. If Bellow only made fun of him or treated him with contempt, he would be denigrating his own efforts.

Jack Richardson captures the quality of this probing process in a review of Bellow's *Mosby's Memoirs*: "So many times in his work one feels that he is encircling an incident, writing around it with an analytical caution that will never quite allow life an unannotated existence of its own" (Richardson, 12). The basic issue at hand was formulated by Bellow again and again and perceived by him as especially affecting the generation which, like him, grew up in the twenties and thirties: "We had to learn (if we could) how to reconcile high principle with low facts" ("The Writer as Moralist," 58). Always concerned with "the final assessment of human value" ("A Word from Writer Directly to Reader," 19), Bellow directs his searching glance at the past: "For the writer of the Fifties or for those of immediately preceding generations the questions have been these: Is man in this century what he was in times past?" ("A Word from Writer Directly to Reader," 19). In order to consider this question from as many angles as possible, Bellow held on to this story and did so in more than one sense.

In this connection there is yet another level of the palimpsest to be uncovered: as Daniel Fuchs has painstakingly reconstructed, "The Gonzaga Manuscripts" is taken from discarded drafts of *Augie March*. In these drafts, "Augie is an integral part of the Committee for a Reconstituted Europe, assuming a serious political character . . . the story and the novel both illustrate the contemporary climate of ideas, where people are taken as ideational objects rather than individual subjects" (Fuchs, 292). Although this observation does not apply to Augie in the published version in which he certainly is a fully realized character, the Feiler aspect of him that was not retained became a kind of lesser twin in the Feiler of the story. Augie's innocence, then, reflects on Feiler's, as do his craving for a worthwhile fate (*AM*, 491), his desire to live in accordance with some form of the "axial lines" (*AM*, 515), and his wish to continue being "a recruit of sublime ideas" (*AM*, 491), even if Feiler, like Augie, has yet to learn "how little people want you to succeed in an extraordinary project" (*AM*, 408). In addition, Feiler's rage can be detected in and deduced from the story's source in *Augie March*. Whereas it is decidedly not in Augie himself, it is abundant in his older brother Simon (cf. *AM*, 526, 527).

Even seemingly minor motifs, such as the rainfalls and downpours that mark the plot of "The Gonzaga Manuscripts" precisely at the beginning, the tempestuous middle, and the end, are revealed in their significance by relating them to their source. In a passage of great lyrical beauty, which proves how well Bellow distinguishes between fake versification and the real thing, he describes the state of mind of a young man, in this case Augie, who has to make decisions concerning his life just as Feiler is trying to do. It is interesting in the context of "The Gonzaga Manuscripts" that Bellow likens this state to European landscapes and cities in which darkness and rain prevail. It is:

> that darkness in which resolutions have to be made. . . . And what about the coldness of the rain? That doesn't deheat foolishness in its residence on the human face, nor take away deception nor change defects, but this rain is an emblem of the shared condition of all. It maybe means that what is needed to mitigate the foolishness or dissolve the deception is always superabundantly about and insistently offered to us. . . . With the dark, the solvent is in this way offered until the time when one thing is determined and the offers, mercies, and opportunities are finished. (*AM*, 201)

In this highly metaphorical discussion of the human condition Bellow emphasizes a democratic generality—"the shared condition of all"—as well as his belief in a "solvent" that is offered with the rain. When Feiler is so annoyed with the rain, he has forgotten—lost—a text most precious to him, a line of Gonzaga's that he himself quotes: "If it rained it was comforting" (113). Thus the persistently reappearing rain in "The Gonzaga Manuscripts" spells a more hopeful message for Feiler than he is able to make out at the moment, a message one would not have been able to gather without considering its emblematic meaning in *Augie March*.

Feiler, like Augie, has to make a decision concerning his life, what to do with it, what "shape" to give it (114). He believes that, if he accomplishes something that matters and that utilizes all his "good impulses" (114), he will be saved from not having "a good-enough fate"

(*AM*, 363). To "bring the testimony of a great man before the world" (114), to retrieve and publish Gonzaga's poems, would be such a saving act to him. He longs to possess, study, and share what is to him a sacred text. In it, he hopes to perceive:

> a sound
> Truly not my own;
> The voice of another,
> Truly other. (119)

Quite apart from anticipating Herzog's desire for "our employment by other human beings" (*H*, 283), Feiler's wish to resurrect Gonzaga's text is also a version of the desire of many of Bellow's major characters to communicate with the dead as, for example, Herzog does in many of his letters, thus once more turning to the past in search of meaning.

Feiler's search for meaning is rendered as a search for a text. The fact that the text has been lost accounts for much of the irony of the story but does not completely undercut the intentions nor the efforts of the protagonist. It is clear to any reader of Bellow that aesthetically shaped and condensed language has always mattered greatly to him. In *The Dean's December* Bellow equates poetry with "one's sense of existence" (*DD*, 265). Michael G. Yetman has written lucidly on Bellow's "logocentric understanding of language" (Yetman, 264). Poetic language, Yetman says, is both "the key which alone unlocks the human significance of things, events, perceptions," and it is also synonymous with "the older meaning of philosophy; implicit in each is an extraordinary power of intellectual discernment and ethical judgment" (Yetman, 264). Though such discernment is remarkably absent in Feiler, he at least shares with Bellow the high hopes and the high value placed on culture. Concerning possible psychological reasons for this, Peter Hyland establishes a connection between the rank assigned to culture and Bellow's life as the child of immigrants: "his early upbringing in the Montreal slums must have contributed much to . . . the intense desire for social and intellectual conquest that motivates so many of his protagonists" (Hyland, 3). Mario Maffi makes much the same point in his analysis of Jewish immigrant culture:

> The ethnic artist—outsider of necessity—thus directly plays the role Benjamin and Kracauer ascribed to the cultural outsider in the early years of the twentieth century, engaged in picking the rags and fragments, the secondhand goods and forgotten objects of the experience

of modernity, in order to reassemble its deep and current meaning.
(Maffi, 297)

Feiler is truly picking "the secondhand goods and forgotten objects"
of an earlier era.

Feiler, then, is a clumsy and uncharming version of Bellow's
clarity-and-meaning-seekers. Given his limited sense of judgment of
people, situations, and art, he is maybe better off not having retrieved the
poems, thus being saved from disappointment. The story ends on a note
of anticipating further unpleasant encounters with his fellow boarders, but
this ending in any case has the touch of a forward and not a backward
direction. The question finally arises whether Feiler, in his intense preoccupation with Gonzaga, has not been reading the wrong text all along.
Would it not have been better for him to be like Augie a "Columbus" of
what is "near-at-hand"? (*AM*, 607). It may be that the book of nature—a
text that is right there and is available all the time but remains unconsid-
ered—would have been "the voice of the truly other" that he craves. The
rain that falls on him at significant moments has not penetrated far enough
into his consciousness. Maybe, instead of reading Gonzaga, he should
have looked into Ralph Waldo Emerson, trusting the American rather than
the European word. In new-world antithesis to old-world antiquarianism
Emerson cut through Feiler's existential Gordian knot more innovatively
than Bellow did in this story of many losses when he stated in "The American Scholar" that "Books are for the scholar's idle times" (Emerson, 50).
Yet Bellow, the master of an irony that never excludes his own self, seems
to take up at precisely this point in the argument in a conversation with an
interviewer who is put in the unexpected position of having to
defend reading vis-à-vis Bellow. The interviewer is pressed into saying: "It's
not underprivileged to have a mind filled with books" ("A Half Life," 300).
To which a later Bellow, with the quests of his early years long since left
behind, replies now quite in the Emersonian sense:

> No, but it does create a terrible disorder, and you'd better make sense
> of it because the premise of the whole thing is your autonomy. You are
> going to govern yourself. And you don't realize what the cost of it will
> be. At first it fills you with pride and a sense of purpose and power, and
> then you begin to see that you are incapable of making the finer
> adjustment by yourself and life is going to be a mass of errors, that
> clarity is to be found only in spotting the mistakes. You are being
> educated by your mistakes. ("A Half Life," 300)

It may be overstating the case but Feiler's story might be read as an early bout in Bellow's lifelong struggle against historical pessimism. Feiler as protagonist is the exact reversal of Emerson's "scholar of the first age" for whom business turns into poetry (Emerson, 48). The modern era no longer permits such blessed conversions but rather turns matter around, offering the seeker of poetry a business opportunity. The bleakness of this venture is exacerbated by the nature of the merchandise: pitchblende contains uranium, which is used in the manufacture of atom bombs. Thus this business entails the threat of the annihilation of humankind. "From the dim past to the uncertain future" is Bellow's recent summary of the trajectory of historical development (*IAAU*, subtitle), along with "The classics themselves are shooting, not drifting, Letheward. We may lose everything at this rate" ("A Second Half Life," 327). Again, in this recent interview, Bellow uses the loss of texts as a metaphor for the direction civilization is currently taking. A sentence quoted in the *New Yorker* is painful to read for those of us who grew up with Augie, traveled with Henderson, suffered with Herzog, and survived with Sammler: "Everything worth living for has melted away," Bellow is reported to have uttered (*New Yorker*, 16 May 1994, 109). An early story such as "The Gonzaga Manuscripts" deals in "small ways and small souls" ("Bellow Exclusive," 40) trapped in the downhill slide of their particular historical moment, suffering defeat even if it is rendered as farcical defeat. Maybe Bellow's often-cited affirmative thrust must finally take second place to his having been such a sharply discriminating, minutely observant analyst and witness to our century, one of its keenest readers and, from the earliest phase of his career, a listener to its twice-told tales: "First, you heard the pure story. Then you heard the impure story. Both stories" ("Leaving the Yellow House," 44).

Works Cited

Bellow, Saul. *The Adventures of Augie March*. New York: Viking Press, 1953. Subsequent references to this edition are *AM*.

——. *The Dean's December*. New York: Harper, 1981. References to this work are *DD*.

——. "A Father-to-Be." *New Yorker*, 5 February 1955, 26–30. Reprinted in *Seize the Day* and *Mosby's Memoirs*. References are to the *Mosby's Memoirs* edition.

——. "The Gonzaga Manuscripts." *Discovery*, no. 4. New York: Pocket Books, 1954. Reprinted in *Seize the Day* and *Mosby's Memoirs*, 111–42.

——. "A Half Life." *It All Adds Up: From the Dim Past to the Uncertain Future*, 287–313. New York: Viking Penguin, 1994.

——. *Henderson the Rain King*. New York: Viking Press, 1959.

——. *Herzog*. New York: Viking Press, 1964. References to this work are *H*.

——. *It All Adds Up: From the Dim Past to the Uncertain Future*. New York: Viking Penguin, 1994. References to this work are *IAAU*.

——. "Leaving the Yellow House." *Esquire*, January 1958, 112–26. Reprinted in *Mosby's Memoirs*. References are to the *Mosby's Memoirs* edition.

——. "Looking for Mr. Green." *Commentary*, March 1951, 251–61. Reprinted in *Seize the Day* and *Mosby's Memoirs*.

——. *Mosby's Memoirs and Other Stories*. New York: Viking Press, 1968. References to this edition are *MM*.

——. "A Second Half Life." *It All Adds Up: From the Dim Past to the Uncertain Future*, 314–27. New York: Viking Penguin, 1994.

——. *Seize the Day*. New York: Viking Press, 1956.

——. "Spanish Letter." *Partisan Review* 15.2 (1948): 217–30. Reprinted in *It All Adds Up: From the Dim Past to the Uncertain Future*, 181–95. References to this edition are *SL*.

——. "A Word from Writer Directly to Reader." In *Fiction of the Fifties*, edited by Herbert Gold. New York: Doubleday, 1959.

——. "The Writer as Moralist." *Atlantic*, March 1963, 58–62.

——. *The Victim*. New York: Vanguard, 1947. References to this work are *TV*.

"Bellow Exclusive." Interview article, no author/interviewer given. *Observer Review*, 2 February 1969, 40.

Bourjaily, Vance. ed. *Discovery*. No. 4. New York: Pocket Books, 1954.

Branda, Eldon. "The Dark Days of Christmas." In *Prize Stories 1968: The O. Henry Awards*, edited by William Abrahams, 246–58. Garden City, N.Y.: Doubleday, 1968.

Capitanchik, Maurice. "Poet and Peasant." *Spectator* 222, 14 February 1969, 212.

Choice 6/7, September 1969, 810–11.

Eisinger, Chester. "Saul Bellow: Love and Identity." *Accent* 18, no. 3 (1958): 179–203.

Emerson, Ralph Waldo. "The American Scholar." In *The Complete Essays and Other Writings of Ralph Waldo Emerson*, The Modern Library, edited by Brooks Atkinson, 45–63. New York: Random House, 1940.

Farrell, James T. "An American Student in Paris." In *The Best American Short Stories 1968*, edited by Martha Foley and David Burnett, 43–73. Boston: Houghton Mifflin, 1968.

Foley, Martha. Foreword. In *The Best American Short Stories 1954*, edited by Martha Foley, ix–xii. Boston: Houghton Mifflin, 1954.

Fuchs, Daniel. *Saul Bellow: Vision and Revision*. Durham, N.C.: Duke University Press, 1984.

Hale, Nancy. "The Most Elegant Drawing Room in Europe." In *Prize Stories 1968: The O. Henry Awards*, edited by William Abrahams, 97–115. Garden City, N.Y.: Doubleday, 1968.

Hyland, Peter. *Saul Bellow*. Macmillan Modern Novelists. London: Macmillan, 1992.

James, Henry. "The Aspern Papers." In *The Turn of the Screw: The Aspern Papers*, Everyman's Library, 163–299. London: Dent, 1967.

Kiernan, Robert F. *Saul Bellow*. New York: Continuum, 1989.

Maffi, Mario. *Gateway to the Promised Land: Ethnic Cultures in New York's Lower East Side*. New York: New York University Press, 1995.

Murdock, Kenneth. Introduction. In Henry James, *The Turn of the Screw: The Aspern Papers*, Everyman's Library, v–xi. London: Dent, 1967.

Review of *It All Adds Up*, by Saul Bellow. *New Yorker*, 16 May 1994, 109.

Richardson, Jack. "Chasing Reality: *Mosby's Memoirs* by Saul Bellow." *New York Review of Books* 12, no. 5 (13 March 1969): 12–14.

Roudané, Matthew C. "An Interview with Saul Bellow." *Contemporary Literature* 25 (1984): 265–80.

Shaw, Irwin. "In the French Style." *The Best American Short Stories 1954*, edited by Martha Foley, 278–92. Boston: Houghton Mifflin, 1954.

Yetman, Michael G. "Toward a Language Irresistible: Saul Bellow and the Romance of Poetry." In *Saul Bellow in the 80s*, edited by Gloria L. Cronin and L. H. Goldman, 263–81. East Lansing: Michigan State University Press, 1989.

The Biological Draft Dodger in Bellow's "A Father-to-Be"

RICHARD F. DIETRICH

In *Ever Since Darwin*, Stephen Jay Gould writes about himself and his fellow scientists in a way that is occurring more often these days than used to be the case: "Science is not a heartless pursuit of objective information. It is a creative human activity, its geniuses acting more as artists than as information processors. . . . It is, after all (although we sometimes forget it), practiced by human beings."[1] The mere fact that Gould feels the need to point out that scientists are human beings implies that scientists are aware of being perceived as something more or less than human—Drs. Frankenstein and Strangelove being classic examples. The increasing number of people expressing opinions such as Gould's perhaps signals a desire on the part of scientists to once again rejoin humankind, admitting humbly that science suffers the same limitations as all other human endeavors and taking responsibility for the human consequence of science.[2] If so, this may be a welcome development, for Frankenstein's and Strangelove's respective monsters *have* gotten out of hand. Still, it's one thing to write, as Gould has, merely *asserting* a general truth, and it's another to write as Saul Bellow has in "A Father-to-Be," *showing* us very concretely how human a particular scientist can be. Bellow's story demonstrates how the humanity of a scientist, and the effect of that humanity on his work, is even more significant than a Gould would concede.[3]

Rogin is the scientist in question, a research chemist. We hear a great deal about his experiments, for they're never far from his thoughts, but the principal concern of Bellow's story is Rogin's relationship with a woman named Joan, his fiancée. Joan is a beautiful, expensive, and difficult woman; not the least of her difficulty is the sexual problem she poses to

Reprinted from *Studies in the Humanities* 9, no. 1 (1981) 45-51.

Rogin. On the brink of marriage, Rogin with his visionary mind sees the consequences of marriage to Joan. The principal thing he sees is that marriage means fatherhood. But fatherhood is a consequence so antithetical to who and what he is that Rogin feels he must rebel against that fate. What and who Rogin is and why therefore he must avoid the future *in the form of children* is the burden of this story.

Rogin is first seemingly characterized as the scientist is supposed to be—"his mind was generally serious and dependable" (143), befitting the ideal of the scientist as a calmly reflective, reasoning being. But gradually, in keeping with Gould's view of scientific creativity, we begin to see that Rogin's mind is essentially illogical and quixotic, "serious and dependable" only in pursuit of irrational goals. Rogin himself, humanly, does not perceive *himself* as fundamentally irrational. Rather he congratulates himself on his "clear-sightedness." In the delicatessen to which he has been sent by Joan's extravagant thoughtlessness, "he pitied the people who would buy the chicken salad and chopped herring; they could do it only because their sight was too dim to see what they were getting" (145). He pities most people, in fact, for it would seem that he alone, a philosopher among scientists, can see through to the essence of life. He sees clearly the universal "law of superimposition" and marvels at how ignorant people were of this, "how they slept through life, how small a light the light of consciousness was" (148). Rogin's Promethean mind makes him a unique figure in a society dedicated to self-delusion.

But note the comedy in this. Already comic is the leap in Rogin's mind from dimly perceived chopped herring to obtuse perceptions of cosmic law. We are dealing with a fast-moving mind, one very capable of jumping to conclusions and hasty generalizing—not in the cause of science, but in the purely personal cause of rationalizing his relationship to Joan and the world.

In male fiction, women often symbolize "the world," serving often as Earth Mother figures, and not infrequently they are seen as imposing crushing adult burdens, sometimes even threatening to swallow up the poor males. Adding to that burden in Rogin's case is a trying mother and a deadbeat brother. Even so, Rogin at first merely chafes at the burden and rationalizes it as cosmic law, to be cherished by the scientist. Seeing himself as in the service of "the life force" as he ferrets out its chemical mysteries, Rogin at first rejoices in the universal condition. When the law of superimposition first occurs to Rogin, "the notion that all were under pressure and affliction, instead of saddening him, had the opposite influence. It put him in a wonderful mood. It was extraordinary how happy he became and, in addition, clear-sighted" (145). And so, rejoicing at first in his participation in the human condition, Rogin seemingly does not resent the burden placed upon him by Joan.

But that is before Rogin's ride on the subway. Afterward his view of life changes radically and he transforms into something the very opposite of what we had supposed. On the subway he imagines that he has a prevision of what his future son will be, and the prospect is so revolting that he feels justified in fleeing from his biological duty:

> What a vision of existence it gave him. Man's personal aims were nothing, illusion. The life force occupies each of us in turn in its progress toward its own ends like mere dinosaurs or bees, exploiting love heartlessly, making us engage in the social process, labor, struggle for money, and submit to the law of pressure, the universal law of layers, superimposition! (152)

If he is to avoid becoming a helpless victim of the life force, Rogin sees that he must escape the clutches of Joan. He says to himself, "Rogin, you fool, don't be a damned instrument. Get out of the way!" (152). As he approaches the door of Joan's apartment, he declares to himself, "I won't be used . . . I have my own right to exist" (152). To no avail however. No sooner does Rogin enter the Earth Mother's lair than he is engulfed by her tender solicitude and apparently reduced to a mere instrument of her purpose, "his own secret loving spirit" (155) acquiescing in the reduction. For the bribe of "roast beef and shampoo" (food and love?), Rogin seemingly surrenders to his fate as breadwinner.

But is that the way it really is? Is Rogin really the helpless victim of female sexuality he appears to be, succumbing to his fate as mere procreator? Or is it that Rogin gets exactly what he wants, and in that satisfaction is there not a certain Thurberesque triumph of the male over the female? Let us turn to the beginning and follow Rogin step by step to his remarkable conclusion.

The clue to Rogin's real character is in the largely unconscious mental processes that he undergoes in the course of his journey to Joan's apartment. As a research chemist he is really less dependent on his rational deductions than on his intuitive powers. His inventions come to him out of the deepest recesses of his subconscious and bespeak his personal needs and weaknesses as much as they are rational solutions to universal problems. Indeed, his rational, conscious mind is shown to be subservient to the irrational impulses that press up from the depths.

As Rogin is on his way to have supper with Joan, Bellow writes that "he fell into a peculiar state" (143), a state that might best be described as a daydream. Figuratively, Rogin sleepwalks (note "his preposterous gait—feet turned outward" [143]) through something resembling a birth sequence; his daydreaming mind rationalizes his psychological preferences. That such a dreamer as Rogin prides himself on being so wide awake and clearsighted is obviously ironic.

Rogin's birth sequence seemingly begins with his initial vision (in the drugstore) of the law of superimposition, the idea that the life force puts pressure upon everything to bear the weight of life. His actual *mental* impregnation, however, occurs before that, as indicated by the story's first sentence—"The strangest ideas had a way of *forcing* themselves into Rogin's mind" (143, my italics). As the idea thrust upon him develops, he is delighted with his vision. "He saw with delight how the druggist and the woman who wrapped the shampoo bottle were smiling and flirting" (145). The sexual byplay seems natural to Rogin—"What happiness it gave him simply to be there" (145).

Rogin's lithe mind then notes the interaction between the storekeeper and the Puerto Rican boy in the delicatessen. As a gesture to his lost boyhood perhaps, Rogin helps the boy get chocolate cookies and empathizes, briefly, with the state in which the boy chews on the cookies—"the energetic dream of childhood" (146). This is the first of a series of regressions that will signal Rogin's deepest psychological need—to be a child again—and significantly it is interrupted by thoughts of Joan, returning him to the world of adult responsibilities. His problem is how to fit Joan into his psychological scheme. The answer comes only after a period of intellectual gestation upon the original conception of the law of superimposition. (By the way, does Rogin think of strawberries for Joan as a projection of his own pregnant cravings?)

That Rogin is steeped in self-deception is established by his encounter next with the two tall men in the subway (described as knightly symbols) who point up how easily one is self-deceived. The one man confesses that he has been an alcoholic for years, expecting that his friend will be surprised by the news. But the friend knew it all along, as the signs of alcoholism are evident in the man's face, and Rogin is amazed that anyone could be so self-deceived. The irony of Rogin's reactions is subtly exposed as the two men discuss further the possibility of a cure for alcoholism and in passing mention the fact that the Danes, unbeatable in science, "turned a man into a woman" (147). The Danes are "one-upped" by Rogin, however, who, having changed *himself* into a woman, so to speak, now incubates the egg of his original conception.

Rogin's "illuminated," agile mind then slips Freudian gears as it flits from level to level in pursuit of psychological fulfillment. His astonishment at the alcoholic's self-deception is followed immediately by thoughts about his own inventions, followed by thoughts about his need for money, followed by musings upon his mother, all linked together by the drive of Rogin's powerful mind toward emotional satisfaction. The comment on self-deception is followed by a subtle, free-association confession of his own secret "alcoholism"—namely, his need for regression.

What are Rogin's inventions? First, synthetic albumen. What need will there be for fathering upon the Earth Mother the children of the future if our scientist-philosophers can create life in the laboratory? Second, a cigarette that lit itself. Perhaps a comic reversal of the phallic need for a sexual spark (as in, "Baby, won't you light my fire?"). Or a mock heroic version of Prometheus's gift to humankind. Finally, a cheaper motor fuel. That is, a better way of making Detroit's favorite phallus ram on up the highway of life in blissful masturbatoriness ("Ford has a better idea"). In other words, all of Rogin's inventions are subversions (if not perversions) of ordinary adult sexuality. As for why, ask Rogin's mother: "On Friday night, she had neglected to cut up his meat, and he was hurt" (148). Mother senses a rival. Once a momma's boy, never a lover, and most certainly never a father.

Rogin's deluded mind (which he now thinks of as "clairvoyant") turns its attention to "a small girl with a new white muff" (148), with which she was very happy. "Her old man, stout and grim, with a huge scowling nose, kept picking her up and settling her in the seat, *as if he were trying to change her into something else*" (148, my italics). Rogin, who has unhappily suffered a similar forced transformation from child to adult, empathizes with the child again. As another little girl boards the train with an identical doll-muff, the parents of the two children express annoyance at this social put-down. "It seemed to Rogin that each child was in love with its own muff and didn't even see the other, but it was one of his foibles to think that he understood the hearts of little children" (149).

Without benefit of logical transition, but with obvious psychological connection, Rogin next turns his attention to a foreign family—composed of a mother, a son, and a dwarf of indeterminate sex who sat between them. Symbol of modern sexual ambiguity perhaps, the dwarf fascinates Rogin. Rogin "did not doubt . . . that this was a creature of remarkable understanding," and he was not free "from his consuming curiosity as to the dwarf's sex" until he resolved to read De la Mare's "Memoirs of a Midget," a book he had owned for years but had never read (149). The ambivalent sexuality which Rogin has repressed a knowledge of for years is now coming to the fore, and he will deal with it in his customary way, by regressing to the level of the sexually "midgeted," the sexually non-committed child.

Bellow now makes his point explicit as he opens the next section with the observation that "thoughts very often grow fertile in the subway . . ." (149). In the womb of the subway Rogin's gestating mind once again works on all levels, "following a train of reflection" (149). Again we have the connection between chemistry and money—he thought "first about the chemistry of sex determination, the X and Y chromosomes, hereditary linkages, the uterus, afterward about his brother as a tax exemption" (149–50)—connected by the fact that it is the biological accident of his maledom and of being the firstborn that places the burden of breadwinning upon him. Then he remembers "two dreams of the night before" (150), one of Samsonian castration, the other of the burden placed upon him by womankind. No sooner does he think of womanhood than he escapes into theorizing about synthetic albumen, which will indeed revolutionalize the entire egg industry—it eliminates the need for procreative sex.

Rogin has been sitting on his egg long enough, so to speak. It is now ready to hatch. Voila! The man next to him suddenly emerges into Rogin's consciousness as his son. Simultaneously Rogin gives birth to the idea that will help him escape his biological fate and that will fit Joan into his psychological scheme. This son-to-be repels Rogin because, inheritor of Joan's dominant genes, he would turn out to be like her father "a fourth-rate man of the world" (151). We should not be surprised that momma's boy would dislike father (where is Rogin's father incidentally?), but it is somewhat surprising to see this paragon of clarity so easily contradict his earlier reasoning about the life force. From a seemingly mature acceptance of his biological fate, Rogin passes to a baby's view of the life force as a vast merciless force that renders him helpless before the great Earth Mother's need to be sexually fulfilled. In short, Rogin's lofty philosophizing becomes a way of justifying and reconciling his infantilism and Oedipal urges.

And sure enough, the story closes with Rogin returning to the womb, not as impregnator but as embryo. His resolve not to be "used" as a mere instrument of the life force is fully realized in his regression. Joan, dressed in a motherly housecoat (ironically belonging to her divorcée roommate), greets him with appropriate diction—"Oh, my baby. You're covered with snow. Why didn't you wear your hat. It's all over its little head" (153). Rogin first complains about the overheated room (womb), but the comfort of it and Joan's mothering instinct gradually reconcile him to the domesticated fate he shares with her pet dog, Henri. (That Rogin and Henri are both French-named may be due to the French reputation for stifling bourgeois domesticity.)

But as Henri scratches in protest against his confinement, so too Rogin remains full of protest almost up to the end, although he never voices his thoughts about the injustice of being a man. Significantly, he conceives of his manhood as a matter of mere externals. Finally, his biology (that of an adult) in conflict with his psychology (that of a momma's boy), and his metaphysics serving as support for whichever is dominant at the moment, Rogin resolves his dilemma by denying his manhood and by regressing to an embryonic state. With scalp so baby pink ("It should be white. There must be something wrong with me" [154]), Rogin pronounces his own fate and floats in the amniotic fluid of Joan's shampoo, having pulled off one of the fastest Oedipal switches in the history of the West. Perhaps every man wishes to save his mother and his lover too, but not every man succeeds as well as Rogin.

These passages bring to mind certain turn-of-the-century works by such authors as Strindberg and Shaw. One thinks, for example, of Strindberg, the would-be scientist, on the one hand neurotically obsessed with the feminist conspiracy to exploit his disarmed manhood and, on the other hand, his astonishingly direct use of imagery that identifies the creative mind of the artist-man as essentially female—"My spirit has received in its uterus a tremendous outpouring of seed from Frederick Nietzsche, so that I feel as full as a pregnant bitch. He was my husband," or, "See now how my seed has fallen in Ibsen's brain-pan—and germinated. Now he carries my semen and is my uterus."[4] And one thinks of Shaw's notion of the archetypal "struggle to the death" between the artist-man and the mother-woman, in which the artist-man, recognizing his own female, creative nature, struggles to assert his own sort of intellectual creativity (his babies being the ideas, values, art, and civilization he creates) in the face of the mother-woman's overwhelming need to use him in fulfillment of her own biological creativity.

The hero of Shaw's play, *Man and Superman*, in characteristically exuberant Shavian fashion, at the end assents to both charges—to create babies of both kinds, intellectual and biological—because he is able to rationalize and romanticize both as part of the life force's creative, evolutionary drive. In contrast, Bellow's scientist-philosopher is not so heroic as Shaw's artist-philosopher, ultimately evading his biological duty as Shaw's hero does not, but both share a compulsion to place their own sort of intellectual creativity before that of biological procreation. Note how Shaw's hero puts the case in Act 1 before he changes his mind and accepts his biological destiny:

The true artist will let his wife starve, his children go barefoot, his mother drudge for his living at seventy, sooner than work at anything but his art. To women he is half vivisector, half vampire. He gets into intimate relations with them to study them, to strip the mask of conventions from them, to surprise their inmost secrets, knowing that they have the power to rouse his deepest creative energies, to rescue him from his cold reason, to make him see visions and dream dreams, to inspire him, as he calls it. He persuades women that they may do this for their own purpose whilst he really means them to do it for his. He steals the mother's milk and blackens it to make printer's ink to scoff at her and glorify ideal women with. *He pretends to spare her the pangs of child-bearing so that he may have for himself the tenderness and fostering that belong of right to her children.* Since marriage began, the great artist has been a bad husband. But he is worse: he is a child-robber, a blood-sucker, a hypocrite and a cheat [italics added].[5]

Very little of the above seems to apply to Rogin, at least not in any literal or obvious sense, perhaps because he is a respectable scientist rather than a bohemian artist; but significantly both scientist and artist, and the scientist *as* artist, imagine they can do without the Earth Mother as a creator of life. But as the italicized portion indicates, they cannot do without her as a mother-figure for themselves, and this, it seems to me, explains the capacity in which Joan serves Rogin. Rogin's clever and largely unconscious strategy is to provide the Earth Mother with a baby of *his* choosing rather than one of hers, in a sly subversion of the evolutionary effort.

And yet it's not as simple as that, either. There's more than one subversive in this story. The argument has assumed that Joan as Earth Mother *wants* actual babies. Rogin has made that assumption in projecting his son-to-be. But there is a strong suggestion that this particular Earth Mother is ironically sterile and is in complicity with her draft-dodging mate, however unbeknownst to him. The story's greatest irony may be that Rogin's fear about the consequences of procreation with Joan is totally unnecessary, for she appears to be satisfied with the baby she has, namely, Rogin. "Oh, my baby" is her first response to the sight of him. The shampooing, in which she lovingly engulfs him, may be a comic symbol for the "brain washing" that is necessary to keep her big baby unaware of his state, lest he become unruly. The Oedipus in Rogin may be chuckling at his marvelous success in finding a nice, "comfy" womb-room (as Dylan Thomas would put it) to relax in, but the Mother Woman in Joan must be equally pleased, for although he gets what he wants, a mother-lover, she also gets what she wants, a baby and a sugar-daddy all rolled into one. And they both get what they want without being subjected to the aggravation and responsibilities of procreation. That would be the perfect modern marriage—stalemate, so to speak.

What is Bellow implying here? His tone is more comic than anything else, so it would appear that there is more being celebrated than bemoaned. Human ingenuity is the fascination of this story, and thus perhaps the thing being celebrated. As modern man has gotten to know the life force a little better, scientifically speaking, he has found ever more ingenious ways of avoiding the biological draft and all the more reasons for doing so. The life force which Shaw so enthusiastically celebrated at the beginning of the century, a creative potential to be affirmed in ourselves and directed toward evolutionary ends has become, to some moderns, an appallingburden of biological imperatives, so weighted with economic implications that sensitive souls such as Rogin, geared for intellectual rather than biological creativity, are forced to take refuge in sexual ambivalence and infantile regression. But this is not to be understood as a purely negative thing, for this also suits who and what they are—these male artist-scientists possess minds that are childlike and feminine, playful and creative in intellectual terms, necessary to their being scientist-artist-philosophers.[6]

And that may suit the life force well, for there's no lack of other people to have babies. As long as there is no danger of universal sterility, and indeed as long as our biological evaders can invent such devices as synthetic albumen and test-tube babies, it's more amusing than sad or satirical that artist-philosophers and scientist-philosophers attempt to issue themselves biological draft deferments. Perhaps the best joke is that the women are in on it too.

Notes

1. Stephen Jay Gould, *Ever Since Darwin* (New York: W. W. Norton, 1977), 201 and 125.

2. See especially Freman Dyson's *Disturbing the Universe* (New York: Harper & Row, 1979).

3. Saul Bellow, "A Father-to-Be," in *Mosby's Memoirs and Other Stories* (New York: Viking, 1968). Further references are to this edition and will be noted parenthetically.

4. Cited in *Strindberg: Selected Plays and Prose*, edited by Robert Brustein (New York: Holt, Rinehart, and Winston, 1964), xxvii.

5. Bernard Shaw, *Man and Superman, Nine Plays with Prefaces and Notes* (New York: Dodd, Mead, 1946), 537–38. My italics.

6. I am reminded of the way in *Cesar and Cleopatra* Shaw's Cesar addresses the sphinx: "I am he of whose genius you are the symbol: part brute, part woman, and

part god—nothing of man in me at all. Have I read your riddle, sphinx?" And also Henrik Ibsen's sentence beginning "We women and poets." Bellow's contribution is to show how the same human equations pertain to the scientist.

Works Cited

Bellow, Saul. "A Father-to-Be." *Mosby's Memoirs and Other Stories*. New York: Viking, 1968.
Brustein, Robert, ed. *Strindberg: Selected Plays and Prose*. New York: Holt, Rinehart, and Winston, 1964.
Gould, Stephen Jay. *Ever Since Darwin*. New York: W. W. Norton, 1977.
Shaw, George Bernard. *Man and Superman, Nine Plays with Prefaces and Notes*. New York: Dodd, Mead, 1946.

Saul Bellow and the Absent Woman Syndrome: Traces of India in "Leaving the Yellow House"

MICHAEL AUSTIN

With increasing frequency, scholars are approaching Saul Bellow's texts with an eye on his female protagonists. While the vast majority of these critics focus on the inadequacy of Bellow's portrayal of women and the out-and-out misogyny evidenced in his male–female relationships, a few have tried to salvage something of the author's reputation by locating strong female characters in scattered Bellow texts and attempting to read these characters as rare examples of Bellow's ability to portray female characters with both sympathy and intelligence. With the publication of *A Theft* in 1989, Bellow critics were presented with a bonafide female Bellow heroine, someone who could serve as a focal point for debate over Bellow's (in)ability to create positive female protagonists. Though *A Theft* represents Bellow's first novel-length treatment of a female heroine, it is not his first attempt to tell a woman's story. Bellow's 1958 short story "Leaving the Yellow House," written three decades before the publication of *A Theft*, presents the story of Hattie Waggoner, an aging desert dweller whose only tangible possession, her Yellow House, becomes the focal point of what some have called a typically Bellovian quest for meaning and identity.

The scholarly debate over "Leaving the Yellow House" has tended to focus on whether or not Hattie Waggoner should be considered a female forerunner of such prominent male protagonists as Tommy Wilhelm and Moses Herzog. Noriko M. Lippit, in affirming the proposition, insists that Hattie constitutes a partial rebuttal to Charles Newman's charge that "there

Reprinted from *Saul Bellow Journal* 11, no. 2 & 12, no. 1 (Double Issue 1993): 146-55.

is not a single woman in all of Saul Bellow's work whose active search for identity is viewed compassionately" (qtd. in Lippit, 281). "While I agree, in the final analysis, with Mr. Newman's remark," Lippit writes, "I believe that Bellow's 'Leaving the Yellow House,' (1958) provides an exception; Hattie . . . is a female searcher" (281). In a later article, Constance Rooke insists that Hattie's quest for identity cannot be viewed as on par with that of other Bellow heroes because the author stops drastically short of granting Hattie

> the full status of "sympathetic intellectual" that he grants to male protagonists: Hattie Waggoner is not a typical Bellow protagonist. While Bellow can grant Hattie certain of the characteristics which he has parceled out from his own riches for the male protagonists, and can accord her the sympathy which is due to her participation in such qualities, he is obliged because she is a woman to withhold the Bellowesque *sine qua non* of a genuine intellectual life. He cannot in a single leap make of her a woman, a sympathetic character, and an intellectual. (185–86)

Both Lippit and Rooke ask the same important question: Does "Leaving the Yellow House" present a substantial portrait of a female character searching for meaning and identity—one that would allow us to acknowledge Hattie Waggoner as the one female star in Bellow's constellation of quest heroes? On an even more basic level, though, both scholars ask us to consider how we should read Bellow's fiction within a critical environment that values gender equality and rejects a long tradition of sexism in literature. Can Bellow's reputation as a misogynist be rehabilitated by examining a story like "Leaving the Yellow House," or does this story confirm, from yet another perspective, Bellow's reluctance or inability to portray women in a subject position?

While these are precisely the questions that concern me in this article, I propose to approach them from a slightly different perspective. Instead of looking only at Hattie Waggoner and her "active search for identity," I would like to consider Hattie in relation to the character I consider to be a second protagonist in the story—India (no last name given), the mysterious woman who brought Hattie into her house as a maidservant and subsequently left her the Yellow House in her will. Approaching "Leaving the Yellow House" from India's perspective presents certain challenges: she has been dead for years when the story begins, she is mentioned only a few times in the text, and what mention we do have of her comes almost entirely through Hattie's confused and unreliable memory. Nevertheless, given what we do know about India, I would argue that she exerts a tremendous influence over the way we should read the story, both because she successfully accomplished what Hattie seems unable to do—decide whom to leave the Yellow House to—and because she helps define, through opposition, the character traits that make Hattie unable to come to resolve this important matter. India's influence, and her importance to my analysis of gender relations in this story, stems directly from the way that she uses power in her relationship with Hattie. India is a very powerful woman, and while powerful women are not necessarily a rarity in Bellow's fiction, India seems to be able to access types of power that have generally been considered "masculine"—and this fact alone makes her worthy of substantial analysis by anyone concerned with the status of women on Mr. Bellow's planet.

As I have already suggested, India exists in this story, not as a full-fledged, present-tense character, but as a specter—the long-dead benefactor who managed simultaneously to both save and ruin Hattie's life by leaving her the Yellow House. In the deconstructionist's vernacular, India might be described as a "trace," or that part of a binary opposition that has been erased but that continues to define both the remaining term in the equation and the system as a whole. In typically dense prose, Jacques Derrida defines the trace as follows:

> The trace, where the relationship with the other is marked, articulates its possibility in the entire field of the entity, which metaphysics has defined as the being-present starting from the occulted movement of the trace. The trace must be thought before the entity. But the movement of the trace is necessarily occulted, it produces itself as self-occultation. When the other announces itself as such, it presents itself in the dissimulation of itself. . . . The presentation of the other as such, that is to say the dissimulation of itself "as such," has always already begun and no structure of the entity escapes it. (*OG*, 47)

As a trace, India functions in constant, unseen opposition to Hattie, the ostensible protagonist of the story, and represents a fixed nature against which the definition of "Hattie" can take place. The initial India–Hattie opposition serves as a focal point for all of the binary terms that go into the making of Hattie. India was rich, cultured, and well traveled; Hattie is poor, uneducated, and tied to one place. When they lived together, India was the property owner, the provider, and the master, while Hattie was the tenant, the beggar and, ultimately, the slave. Each of these binary oppositions stems from the one overarching dichotomy that feminist critics see as the organizing opposition of our culture: the masculine versus the feminine. These two terms, which should not be confused with the biological terms *male* and *female*, each represent a store of cultural constructions and stereotypes about power and gender-identity. India, who occupies the "male" space in each system, correspondingly exercises a masculine form of power on Hattie; Hattie, on the other hand, relegated to the "female" space, has access to a much more limited type of power—one that stems from passivity rather than action.

The gendered nature of the India–Hattie dichotomy becomes especially clear in view of what Bellow deigns to tell us about their past relationship. Though the text contains very little about the time Hattie spent with India—it is, after all, the story of Hattie's life years after India's death—what does come through suggests that it was an emotionally abusive relationship of the sort generally associated with a dominating male figure:

> Literature. Education. Breeding. But Hattie's interest in ideas was very small, whereas India had been all over the world. India was used to brilliant society. India wanted her to discuss Eastern religion, Bergson, and Proust, and Hattie had no head for this, and so India blamed her drinking on Hattie. "I can't talk to you," she would say. "You don't understand religion or culture." (21)

If India's criticisms of Hattie are stereotypically "male," Hattie's responses are equally "female." She submits patiently to India's tirades and never raises her voice to her benefactor. "I am a Christian person," Hattie would respond. "I never bear a grudge" (21). Of course, when Hattie was still living with India, she could not have afforded to bear a grudge even if she had wanted to. India owned the Yellow House and Hattie depended on the older woman completely for shelter and support.

Ultimately, India manipulated Hattie by creating an economic dependency. She seemed to compel both servitude and sycophancy by subtly promising the house to Hattie and tacitly threatening to take this gift away at any time. By manipulating Hattie in this way, India converted her one potential asset—the Yellow House—into a hard currency that enabled her to hire a servant, a nursemaid, and a court jester without ever having to spend any real money. The unstated threat of eviction kept Hattie's frontier spirit in check and ensured that India would have the physical and emotional needs of her final days met. We might realistically assume—though Bellow never says so directly—that India used Hattie's eventual inheritance of the Yellow House as a bargaining chip in whatever tacit negotiations for services occurred between the two. Hattie, who has never worked a day in her life and seems unable to perform even the smallest tasks in the world outside of the Yellow House, seemed to have no choice but to submit to India's regime.

What all of this amounts to is that India manipulated her wealth quite skillfully in her dying days. This might be, I admit, a somewhat cynical take on the relationship between the two women, but it points unquestionably to the point I wish to establish here: that India manifests an impressive ability to negotiate the traditionally male field of economic hegemony, an ability that makes her a singular character in the Bellow universe. While Bellow has created a number of extremely strong female characters, India is perhaps the only one who exercises power in such a typically male fashion. Other Bellow heroines—such as Valeria (the dying Rumanian matriarch in *The Dean's December*) and Sorella Fonstein (the indomitable wife in *The Bellarosa Connection*)—epitomize the perfection of traditionally female modes of power. They derive their ability to influence others precisely from the fact that they are good wives, good mothers, or powerful matriarchs. India, on the other hand, exhibits none of these qualities of a "good woman." Except for the unsubstantiated accusation of an affair with Wicks, India is never mentioned in connection with a man, be it a father, a husband, a son, or a lover. She does not depend on her relationship to a man for her power, but instead manipulates Hattie the same way that men have controlled women for centuries: by making herself the provider of a sustenance that can be taken away at any time.

Though reflections about India occupy only a few paragraphs in the story, she constantly peeks through the pages of the text as the buried half of the oppositions that define Hattie. When the story actually opens, Hattie finds herself in the same situation that India once faced: she is lonely, aging, and emotionally needy. Unlike India, however, Hattie cannot seem to find a solution. From the opening paragraph we are alerted to the fact that Hattie is in need of somebody to take care of her as she took care of India:

> The neighbors . . . told one another that old Hattie could no longer make it alone. The desert life, even with a forced-air furnace in the house and butane gas brought from the town in a truck, was still too difficult for her. . . . Hattie was not exactly a drunkard, but she hit the bottle pretty hard, and now she was in trouble and there was a limit to the help she could expect from even the best of neighbors. (7)

As the story progresses, we are increasingly made aware that Hattie has neither the financial nor the emotional resources necessary to live on her own and that she would have perished years ago had India not left her the Yellow House. When an automobile accident forces Hattie to acknowledge these needs, she sets out to find a way to do what India did: convert the Yellow House into some form of negotiable currency.

Like India, Hattie has clear title to the Yellow House, and even though she has little prospect of finding a buyer for it, she does have a number of options that would allow her to meet her temporal needs adequately. Throughout the story, Hattie receives and rejects two offers that would allow her to convert the potential asset of her house into tangible assets such as emotional and financial support. The first of these comes when Amy Walters offers, through Jerry Rolfe (who, knowing Hattie, refuses even to mention the matter to her), to make the same contract explicitly that Hattie made with India implicitly: to live with her and take care of her in exchange for the right to inherit the Yellow House. The second offer comes from her neighbor, Pace, who offers to give Hattie five hundred dollars up front and fifty dollars a month perpetually in exchange for the same privilege. While both Amy and Pace are clearly interested only in taking advantage of Hattie's needs, both of their offers represent the same type of bargain that Hattie once made with India: she would gain something that she needs now without having to part with anything until after she has died and doesn't need anything at all.

More than anything else about the house, however, Hattie seems to cherish the fact that the Yellow House is hers to bequeath or dispose of as she sees fit. Unlike India, she does not intend to exchange her birthright for economic sustenance. But even though she rejects economic gain as criterion for leaving the Yellow House to somebody, she seems unable to come up with an alternative, and so she chooses to do nothing at all. In her long interior monologue on the subject she brings up and rejects a number of possible bases for making a decision, including family loyalty, pride, love, and friendship:

> And first of all she wanted to do right by her family. None of them had ever dreamed that she, Hattie, would ever have something to bequeath. Until a few years ago it had certainly looked as if she would die a pauper. So now she could keep her head up with the proudest of them. And, as this actually occurred to her, she actually lifted up her face with its broad nose and victorious eyes. . . . She returned to the old point of her struggle. She had decided many times and many times changed her mind. She tried to think, *Who would get the most out of the yellow house?* It was a tearing thing to go through. (40)

The problem here is that, while Hattie revels in her ability to leave the house to somebody, she is unable to articulate a suitable criteria for deciding who to leave it to. Unlike India, who knew exactly what she wanted in exchange for the Yellow House, Hattie, playing with essentially the same cards, can come to only one decision: to get drunk and take up the decision later. India acted decisively and manipulated her economic assets, and she did so with some degree of skill. Hattie, on the other hand, even when presented with a fairly large set of options for disposing of the house and meeting her own needs, becomes impotent, crippled by her own indecision, and ultimately self-destructive.

To understand why Hattie cannot make these decisions, we must once again invoke the notion of India as part of the series of binary oppositions that define Hattie. As I have already argued, India and Hattie occupy spaces that our society has traditionally coded as "masculine" and "feminine." As a corollary to this statement, I would further propose that Hattie represents a feminine cultural space that can be considered "domestic," while India represents the masculine space that we would usually call "foreign." Even India's name—the name of an exotic foreign country—stresses her identification with the nondomestic sphere. The domestic–foreign dichotomy, when applied to a more localized gender economy, becomes the dichotomy between home and work, with the former generally considered the woman's sphere and the latter the domain of the man. This crucial opposition explains the differences in the way the two women treat "leaving the yellow house." India is able to see bequeathing the house as a business proposition—one that works particularly well for her in that it enables her to practically enslave Hattie. Hattie, on the other hand, operating from a culturally coded feminine/domestic viewpoint, sees the house as a home; it is part of the domesticity that defines her. Hattie's ultimate nondecision about the house reveals the extent to which her own identity is wrapped up in her home:

> Even though by my own fault I have put myself into this position. And I am not ready to give up on this. No, not yet. And so I'll tell you what, I leave this property, land, house, garden, and water rights, to Hattie Simmons Waggoner. Me! I realize this is bad and wrong. Not possible! Yet it is the only thing I really wish to do, so may God have mercy on my soul. (43)

I now return to my initial question: Does "Leaving the Yellow House" present an atypically sympathetic picture of a woman in Bellow's fiction? Yes and no. Certainly Hattie Waggoner resembles many of Bellow's men: she is confused, helpless, and desperately searching for both personal identity and metaphysical meaning. I would assert, however, that the portrait Bellow draws of Hattie does not, in any substantial sense, contradict Bellow's other characterizations of women; she, like most other Bellow females, is allowed to occupy only the various spaces that our culture has coded as feminine. India, on the other hand, represents something genuinely different: she represents the "male" half of the binary oppositions that Bellow often uses in his writing; she occupies, in other words, a masculine space. This statement has important implications. One of the most persistent problems for feminist Bellow critics is that the author forces most of his female characters into stereotypically female spaces—thus confirming the arbitrary social distinctions that serve as the basis for all gender inequality. Had "Leaving the Yellow House" actually been India's story, seeing her in this masculine space might force us to conclude that, at least once, Bellow indulged in a bit of feminist-postmodern gender bending. But such an optimistic reading of the story ignores the fact that India's character has been almost completely erased. India's character must be drawn from inferences, suppositions, and from seeing the space around Hattie that she must once have filled.

This brings us to the one vital Derridean opposition that I have consciously avoided so far: the presence–absence binary. India is a powerful character, true, but she is also an absent character; she has been erased from the text in a way that obscures her true importance. Next to Hattie, I would argue, India is the most important character in "Leaving the Yellow House"; however, the reasons for her importance must be re-created from a few fragments. But this reconstruction does not lie beyond our grasp. The ghost of India, though obscured by the text, cannot be completely excised as long as we can see her trace in and around Hattie. The vital terms we must use to define India exist, albeit inverted, in the terms that Bellow uses to describe his heroine, and the presence that India exerts throughout the story becomes increasingly visible as we survey the lack that surrounds Hattie. The deconstructive techniques that allow us to perceive India throughout the text also allow us to reconstruct the operative dichotomies—such as masculine–feminine, foreign–domestic, master–servant, and absent-present—that pervade the text, resulting in a picture of India as a powerful female character, occasionally obscured by the narrative, but unwilling to be completely suppressed by the text.

Works Cited

Bellow, Saul. *Mosby's Memoirs and Other Stories.* New York: Penguin, 1971.
Derrida, Jacques. *Of Grammatology.* Baltimore: Johns Hopkins University Press, 1974.
Lippit, Noriko M. "A Perennial Survivor: Saul Bellow's Heroine in the Desert." *Studies in Short Fiction* 12 (1975): 281–83.
Rooke, Constance. "Saul Bellow's 'Leaving the Yellow House': The Trouble with Women." *Studies in Short Fiction* 14 (1977): 184–87.

Two Women Protagonists from Bellow's Short Stories: Character Conception and Its Artistic Realization

MARIANNE M. FRIEDRICH

Two of Bellow's rather rare women protagonists are Dora, in the short story of the same name, and Hattie in "Leaving the Yellow House." Both stories were written in close proximity to a major novel, making it possible to trace genetic connections of the character in each story with its respective novelistic counterpart. Yet Bellow's short stories are not just "by-products" and "fictional fragments" as some critics have charged (i.e., Rodrigues). Rather they are independent works of art in their own right (Fuchs, "Bellow's Short Stories," 295). Each story has a unique structure that results from a highly original character conception.

This essay focuses on the close interrelation between the character conception and its narrative form, a significant achievement since Bellow uses each story to explore a major philosophical concept—Freud's theory of the individual in "Dora" and Proustian and Bergsonian concepts of time in "Leaving the Yellow House." A secondary benefit of analyzing character and narration is to see how clearly it reveals Bellow's progression from a traditional short-story form in "Dora" to a distinctive, personal concept of the short story in "Yellow House."

Bellow's fourth story, "Dora," appeared in *Harper's Bazaar* in 1949, the same year in which *The Adventures of Augie March* was copyrighted. Perhaps because it was never reprinted, it has been virtually neglected by critics to date. As an early story it is, thematically as well as structurally, much indebted to the literary tradition of the time. Yet its structure results from

Reprinted with permission from *Saul Bellow: A Mosaic*, edited by L. H. Goldman, Gloria L. Cronin, and Ada Aharoni, Twentieth-Century Jewish Literature, No. 3, series editor: Daniel Walden (New York: Peter Lang, 1992), 73-85.

a very specific character conception in which Bellow was clearly challenging a Freudian view of the individual.

Read against *Augie March*, it seems obvious that Dora is an amalgamation of Augie's Mama Rebecca and Grandma Lausch. Among other characteristics, Dora shares Grandma Lausch's autocratic behavior, her practical mind, her self-assurance, her assertiveness, and her pointed criticism of others. Like the seamstress Dora, Mamma March is a simple person, formerly a seamstress, who utterly neglects her appearance. Most striking is another similarity: all three women have missing teeth, and both Dora and Grandma Lausch refuse to be fitted with false teeth.

In one important aspect, however, Dora is distinctly different. Unlike Grandma Lausch, who represents "the main body of married womankind" (10), Dora represents the emancipated contemporary woman, "unmarried womankind"; in fact, this opposition—married versus unmarried—becomes an important leitmotif in the story. Repeatedly, Dora takes pride in not being married, feels sorry for married women, or mocks them. Dora's imaginative mind sees married women, with their constant concern about appearance, as caricatures "like . . . those African birds from the Bronx zoo with thick legs and red feathers" (188).

Like most of Bellow's short pieces that were published before *Mosby's Memoirs*, the whole story is a monologue with a circular structure. On a sunny afternoon, Dora sits before her dresser mirror, putting on lipstick. Her recollections during this short time period make up the whole story. Dora's interior monologue begins with a reflection on the recent disturbance of her mental state. She is puzzled by it and feels that she has lost her ordinary sense of direction: "You see the right way . . . , but it may be in reverse, like a thread that is winding one way instead of another . . . when out of the blue sky you see how the bobbin is running" (187). She reinforces this mechanical image with a natural one: "Each time there is lightning it divides the sky up in a new way" (187).

As the framing image of the story, reflections—Dora's physical reflection in the glass and her interior reflection—are a vital structural element. The combination of reflection and the circular structure of the narrative ultimately means that anything that enters Dora's horizon of subconsciousness reflects on her. Dora's thoughts constantly revolve around herself, her problems, and her life. She repeatedly circles back to certain themes and questions: married life as opposed to singleness with its accompanying loneliness, individuality as "a sign from God" (199), human detachment and alienation, moral responsibility and concern for others, and death.

But most frequently her thoughts return to her work. The first sentence of the story establishes this major theme: "I'm so far behind in my work, I couldn't be further if I was sick in bed" (187). Suffering from a puzzling inability to work, she keeps recalling how enthusiastically she normally pursues her dressmaking: "I'm a creative person in my own line" (188). In fact, Dora is absorbed by her work to the point of being a workaholic: "And when I really work, I'm devoted to it. It won't let me rest. I can't forget it ever" (189).

Dora's life story is the story of various jobs and customers. A surprising number of characters are introduced in this relatively short text, reflecting Dora's basic interest in people and her personal attachment to them. This narrative fact echoes Augie March's saying that by talking about his various jobs he is giving out the Rosetta Stone to his entire life (28). Similarly, Dora keeps talking about her customers and her jobs. But while the fascinating characters in Augie March almost lead a life of their own within its picaresque structure, the corresponding short-story characters function exclusively to reflect a limited number of Dora's characteristics.

In contrast to this narrative principle of abstraction and reduction, Dora's exuberant and sprawling interior monologue is striking. The reader can get lost in the random episodes of Dora's life, encumbered with accidental and sometimes grotesquely exaggerated detail. Flowery phrases, such as "if death does not collect me" (118), may be interpreted as characteristic language for a simple person who is occasionally inarticulate and uses faulty grammar. But at the same time, this phrase is almost baroque, unintentionally eloquent.

While the details serve the artistic intention of reproducing Dora's sprawling style, they simultaneously function to reduce and abbreviate. Dora's conspicuously long and involved review of her emphatic refusal to have a bridge made for her missing front teeth—almost two paragraphs— is a case in point. To her, this is not a matter of money but of principle. The dramatizing effect of dialogue adds to its intensity, disproportionately enlarging, grotesquely distorting, and isolating this detail within the context. And in its isolation, it stands for Dora's rigid opposition to married womanhood, an opposition to which she clings tenaciously and obsessively. At the same time, the detail sums up Dora's disregard of appearance, her extreme sense of independence and individuality, and her refusal to conform.

As Dora's monologue continues, the reader must register relevancies. Quite often, what seems accidental turns out to be revealing at a later point. The reader must also sort these apparently randomly presented events into chronological order, reconstructing the accident, anticipated in the introduction lightning imagery, that has caused Dora's crisis. Only at the very end does the reader fully realize what might have caused Dora's disturbance. As the bobbin thread reverses direction, the reader retraces the story step by step from its end to its beginning to fully realize its meaning.

Parallel to the linear development of the exterior plot culminating in Mr. Regler's fall next door is an interior plot. Dora's initial statement, "I myself haven't got anybody" (187), leads to a first climactic confession as Dora remembers listening to the lonely orgone scream at night: "I admit that's the time it counts with me that I'm alone. Most of the people lying there can just put out a hand and touch somebody" (189).

Ultimately, the climax of the story is not Mr. Regler's fall but the inner drama of Dora's reaction as she recalls putting her ear against his chest to see if he is still alive. This mental drama reads like a confession or an attempt at self-applied analysis in the theater of her consciousness. Dora's mind becomes the battlefield of opposing rational and irrational forces, she struggles for survival against the dehumanizing forces that surround her, and she triumphs by finally defining her inner state more precisely and accurately (199). The development of the interior plot has thus reached its climax; a self-applied analysis has reached its resolution.

How are we to understand the surprising end of the story? Is Dora, a strong and rational person who has always had her life under control, suddenly controlled and victimized by irrational life forces? Is Mr. Regler ("regulator" in German) the device that suddenly switches Dora's life into a drastically new direction, comparable to the mechanical process of a bobbin thread reversing direction? The circular structure of the story allows one reading to be Dora's total and hopeless victimization, but the open ending of the story leaves the reader confident that, no matter what, Dora is going to survive.

Bellow uses and challenges Freud's view in this short story. Despite the sudden epiphany at the story's end, the allusions and hints of repressed wishes in Dora are all relevant. Bellow deliberately echoes Freud by titling his story with a woman's first name, thus following the conventions of a case study. Freud's "Dora: An Analysis of a Case of Hysteria" describes a character who resembles Bellow's Dora in certain essential aspects, though the short story is far from being a fictional retelling of the Freudian source. (Interestingly, Freud comments on the "fine poetic conflicts" of his case study as suitable material for a short story ['Dora," 59–60]).

Freud's Dora is a member of a morbid aristocratic family. Bellow's is an orphan. Freud repeatedly emphasizes Dora's rejection of marriage and her complete absorption in her work. These characteristics intensify after

Dora witnesses a traffic accident in which Herr K. is run over by a cart ("Dora," 144). Although both Doras are phobic about men, Bellow's Dora speaks positively about the men she encounters in her work—Mr. Palmerin, Dr. Graffia, and Dr. Weisgard. That does not preclude the previous existence of a phobia but simply indicates the change in Dora caused by her recent crisis.

Bellow also uses such typical Freudian motifs as keys representing sexual desires, locking or not locking a room, and lightning, but he uses them as part of Dora's monologue rather than as dream elements. Bellow, as Daniel Fuchs points out, disagrees with Freud's dream interpretations ("Bellow and Freud"). The most striking correspondence between the two Doras is how clearly Dora's "shocking" experiences fulfill the Freudian prerequisites for producing a hysterical disorder (Freud, "Dora," 7:28).

From this basis, however, Bellow's character transcends the case history. His Dora lacks any signs of hysterical reactions. She is a strong and healthy person who reacts appropriately and efficiently to an alarming experience, enabling her to overcome her past repressions. As Freud had observed, "The barrier erected by repression can fall before the onslaught of a violent emotional excitement produced by a real cause; it is possible for a neurosis to be overcome by reality" ("Dora," 132). Her self-applied analysis before the mirror shows her, like Bummidge in *The Last Analysis* and many other Bellow characters, resolving her conflicts by herself. Bellow's Dora is ultimately not a pathologic victim like Freud's Dora but a woman who, though lonely, has the personal strength to survive.

Bellow's short story thus challenges the Freudian concept of human nature and his mechanistic view of victimization, which disregards the total personality (Fuchs, "Bellow and Freud," 59). By conceptualizing Dora as morally strong and religious, Bellow further implies that Freudianism does not exhaust the relevant aspects of being human. The human psyche remains an enigma, attracting ever new inquiries into human nature.

Much as Dora is linked to *Augie March*, *Henderson the Rain King* had a trial run in the character of Hattie in the short story "Leaving the Yellow House," which appeared in *Esquire* in 1958, one year before the publication of *Henderson*. Richard G. Stern comments: "The story is about a sort of female Henderson—but on her last legs—who drips out like hourglass sand in the Utah desert" (19).

Eugene Henderson, a picture of constant mobility, represents the *vita activa* ideal of Western civilization. In contrast, Hattie's more Eastern representation of the *vita passiva* or existence of a contemplative shows beneath the surface of her pathologic, ruinous, and slothful existence. Rendered almost immobile by her accident and old age but a "perennial survivor" (15), Hattie has become an expert at listening to her inner voice. She feels drawn to her dead friend, India, who had a special interest in Eastern religion. Hattie's body language suggests mystic inclinations, and an almost mystical awareness of God's presence frees her from the necessity of intellectual constructions. To develop Hattie's complex character, Bellow uses two strong intellectual concepts: Proust's idea of time and Henri Bergson's ideas of duration and motion.

"Yellow House" deals with Hattie's changing vision of her life as she approaches death. Her introspections focus on four major themes: death, identity, spiritual awakening, and love. Bellow casts Hattie as the opposite of Henderson, who affirms love as a means of self-transcendence. Incapable of true love, Hattie stays desperately and painfully imprisoned within herself (42). As an ultimate statement of her self-centeredness, she wills her house to herself. The ending in "Yellow House" brilliantly pulls together three of the major themes: love (its lack), death, and identity (Fuchs, "Bellow's Short Stories"; Rodrigues, "A Rough-Hewed Heroine"). The theme of Hattie's spiritual awakening, culminating in the last utterance of her inner voice, finds its conscious resolution in the concluding prayer of her will (42).

In "Leaving the Yellow House," Bellow creates and systematically utilizes an inner voice, a crucial development in his artistic maturing. He dates this development as occurring during the writing between *Augie March* and *Herzog*.

> I had to tame and restrain the style I developed in *Augie March* in order to write *Henderson* and *Herzog*. I don't care to trouble my mind to find an exact description for it, but it has something to do with a kind of readiness to record impressions arising from a source of which we know little. I suppose that all of us have a primitive prompter or commentator within. (Harper, "Saul Bellow: An Interview," 351)

In the same interview, Bellow refers to the momentous change in his writing as "an attempt to get nearer to that primitive commentator" (352). We see the same achievement in "Yellow House" and the same technique—a switch to mimetic fiction.

By establishing a double point of view in "Yellow House," Bellow deviates markedly from Henry James's artistic requirement that the point of view must reside in one central consciousness. We can read "Dora" as a trial run in inner monologue and "Leaving the Yellow House" as a decision for the greater artistic freedom and flexibility of a double point of view. The inner voice makes it possible for Bellow to experiment with the double point of view while retaining the immediacy of inner monologue, giving the reader direct insight into the conscious and unconscious levels of the character's mind. The inner voice is not totally emancipated from an objective narrator; in "Yellow House" it is consistently introduced like direct speech: "she thought," "she said to herself," "she swore," "she cried to herself," "she spoke to herself in silence."

In short, the inner voice in "Yellow House" represents the mimetic answer to the modern demand of inner monologue. By integrating the inner voice into the mimetic context, Bellow adds a new dimension of "speech" to the narrative tools for representing consciousness in a short story.

Bellow uses a free indirect style to make the transition from the authorial to the figural point of view. Both points of view often melt into one another until the reader can no longer recognize who is speaking, but the border between the two becomes clear each time Bellow switches to an inner voice. The tension between multiple dimensions of speech and the mimetic frame of the story adds to its density.

Bellow's deliberate choice of a mimetic artistic realization of this character is no small matter. The story rests on the silent mimetic assumption that a reality—visible and invisible—does exist outside of the character. Reality does not have to be achieved or constructed. Thanks to its mimetic foundation, the story can be read symbolically, with the inner voice becoming an acoustic echo of the visual symbol of the desert in a delicate balance between the exterior and interior points of view.

As a constant echo of and commentator on the fictional reality, the inner voice filters this reality, summarizes it, and gives it more structure. The occasional lyrical representation of the desert, in turn, is the music of the inner voice. The inner voice echoes and reflects itself, the individualizing attributes of the character, the major themes of the character conception, and the plot. Thus, the inner voice is not just added to the symbolism in the story but becomes an integral part of an interdependent dual structure. The grace and beauty of this story lie in such mutual echoes and reflections and in the delicate fusion of this duality into a whole. The inner voice, released at strategic points, makes possible the mutual echo and reflection, the occasional synchronization, the beautiful illumination and interpenetration of the inside and the outside world, and ultimately the protagonist's transcendence.

Since the multiple and gradual changes in Hattie's vision are the core of her character conception, Bellow uses the narrative principle of continuous progression, in contrast to "Dora," where the circularity of reflection opposes the linear development of a double-layered plot, halts the narrative at times, and underscores the basically static conceptualization of Dora to prepare the reader for the abrupt epiphany at the end. In

"Leaving the Yellow House," Hattie's introspective "movie" chronologically parallels the plot as the internal perspective intensifies and develops six chronological time periods in a straightforward way:

1. The last twenty years of Hattie's life at Sego Lake are summarized in the first three pages. Throughout the story, present time is skillfully intensified with flashbacks to past time that familiarize the reader with the major stations in Hattie's previous life: her education as an organist in Paris, her marriage to Waggoner, and her life with cowboy Wicks.

2. The progressive action of Hattie's accident is largely expanded, emphasizing its symbolic importance as a mirror of Hattie's spiritual situation and the trigger of her first serious crisis. At this point, the narrative begins to change to Hattie's perspective (Rodrigues, "A Rough Hewed Heroine," 12).

3. Hattie's subsequent hospitalization and recuperation take the relatively long space of about seven pages. The narrative aspect switches more noticeably to an internal perspective, the inner voice begins, and Hattie communes with India in a web of free indirect speech interwoven with the inner voice.

4. Hattie returns to the lake. The following ten pages record two mid-June crises: the Rolfes leave her and Pace makes her a cruel business offer. A temporary narrative slowdown permits Bellow to develop the story's symbolism through lyrical elements.

5. Hattie watches the "movie" of her life, extremely condensed, intercut with present time, and presented by an objective narrator (Rodrigues, "A Rough Hewed Heroine,"). Moreover, this movie represents a nearly chronological rerun of the major stages mentioned before. But the reader now gets the inside story in closeups of scenes most relevant for the interior perspective, with the inner voice serving as commentator. The inner voice becomes most frequent in this stage, then breaks off. This stage and the next, though taking only a short exterior time, are dramatically expanded and take up one-fourth of the short story.

6. Hattie writes her will.

This powerful and energetic principle of narrative progression manifests itself in the stylistic element of Bellow's sentence structure, short and clear-cut, streamlined for a fast-moving narration. For example: "But of course Hattie had no husband, no child, no skill, no savings" (19). This succinctness contrasts with Dora's discursive style.

Bellow captures Hattie's powerful feelings in the brevity of weighty nouns, but as nouns in dynamic processes rather than as permanent mental states: "A great fear took hold of her . . . not only for the future but spreading back into the past" (6). Feelings are captured in flux, as subject to constant change: "But her anger didn't last long. It was reabsorbed into the feeling of golden pleasure that enveloped her" (21). Bellow wrote to his friend Richard Stern: "The problem is to strike the richest kind of brevity" (qtd. in Kulshrestha, 38).

By using third-person narration, more fluid than the restrictive first-person style of "Dora," Bellow can more freely manipulate time, expanding or condensing its scale of narrative representation. The reader absorbs the significance of Hattie's changing vision against the background of her previous life and values—all seventy-two years of it.

The narrative expansion and representation of "interior time" is adjusted to the principles of brevity and progression. Bellow does not, for instance, like Proust, totally disregard the exterior temporal continuity (Auerbach, 542), though he comes very close to Bergson's notion of "pure memory" which retains the past as "pure time" and our conscious states "in the order in which they occur" (Goudge, 289). Bergson speaks of the mind's filtering "cinematographical method," comparing it to a movie camera which translates motion into a series of static frames (Goudge, 290). In the short story, these static frames dissolve into narrative progression; "pure time," *durée reélle*, is filtered, restrained, and presented by the omniscient narrator. So Bellow's concept deviates drastically from Proust's *memoire involontaire*.

Bellow's purposeful elaboration on the contrast between exterior and interior time in "Leaving the Yellow House" results in a symbolic simultaneity of past, present, and postmortal time. From Hattie's eternal perspective, the conventional concepts of a linear succession, with death as a decisive termination of time, seem to be eliminated.

The symbolism in "Leaving the Yellow House" derives from single objects, from objects which develop into plot, or from pure action which assumes symbolic meaning. In the latter case, the symbolism becomes completely assimilated by the dominating principle.

Hattie's story is firmly anchored in a coherent reality. The story takes place in 1947. The yellow house stands on the shore of Sego Lake in the Utah desert. Yet as the plot develops and the narrative perspective moves from outside Hattie to within her, the car, house, and desert gradually take on many meanings. Inside and outside reflect on one another; one can stand for the other, but the two never become identical. As a result, while the perspective shifts, so does the texture. The fictional reality in "Leaving the Yellow House" becomes increasingly transparent to the story's symbolism. For instance, the desert provides a literal physical setting but also functions symbolically to communicate the character of Hattie.

Gradually the reader also sees it as "a sarcastic symbol of America's Eden" (Lippit, 282). As it mirrors Hattie's mental process, the desert reflects the dynamism of change from "the most beautiful place in the world" to "Hell" (14, 31). It is only toward the end of the story that the ambiguous vision of the desert consolidates into hell: "ashes" that have "burned out" (31, 41). At this point, the desert symbol is finally anchored in a stable transcendental world: The narrative transformation of the Utah desert not only functions as a projection of Hattie's dynamic psychological character, but it also represents an ontologically stable entity that is different from the character. Once stabilized, the symbol of the desert vaults over the whole story, unifying and transcending the multiplicity of time and place.

At the end, Hattie's inner voice asks, "Have you eyes and see not?" (39), an echo of Jeremiah 5:21. Thus Bellow achieves an intricate fusion of the visual symbol of the desert and Hattie's inner voice.

Objects also bear symbolic weight in "Yellow House." The house more generally symbolizes Hattie, its dilapidated state reflecting her pathologic deterioration (Rooke). Bellow has positioned Hattie in a metaphysical world between good and evil. For example, on her night table is "the Bible her pious brother Angus—the other brother was a heller—had given her; but behind the little door of the commode was a bottle of bourbon" (61). The opposition of the bourbon and the Bible is reinforced later when Bellow juxtaposes the sofa and monastery table. Again a this-worldly and an other-worldly dimension are in tension. The three-hundred-year-old Spanish monastery table suggests the monasticism that flourished in Spain under the influence of such Christian mystics as John of the Cross. This relates to Bergson's view that Christian mysticism comes closest to his concept of an "open" or "dynamic" religion, the only reliable basis for assuming the existence of God and a continuation of life after death. Bellow's description of the sofa tufts "like the pads of dogs' paws" (22) is at first ambiguous, but the meaning crystallizes when we learn later that Hattie had killed her dog because suddenly she could "see . . . that he was evil" (36). The dog symbol may call to mind the Greek Psychopompos, the canine conductor of souls through the night of death to the afterworld.

Pure action becomes charged with symbolism as the plot deals with Hattie's spiritual awakening. Her indecision about whether to take care of the house may be read symbolically as her first realization that she cannot escape her responsibility to make moral decisions.

At one point, significant to her creation of self, she stands up, "and, rising, she had the sensation that she had gradually become a container for herself" (331). Thus, through a vehicle that is decaying and wasting away, she finds herself. This metaphor of her body as a container for her incorporeal existence is a further focusing and refinement of Hattie's self-view as "one single thing" whose existence stopped being "scattered" when she acquired the yellow house. It also echoes Proust's similar metaphor in *Remembrance of Things Past* (2:784).

Nor is this the only connection with Proust; he is specifically mentioned (18). Furthermore, in Proust's view, self "exists" only as long as this container is constantly filled and refilled with moments of "pure" time. This instability of self and its dependence on the constant artistic endeavor of re-creation ultimately results in dissolving the traditional concept of personality, leading Proust to a concept of fiction that is very different from Bellow's understanding of fiction as mimetic (Andreotti).

Bellow had, interestingly enough, used the container metaphor in connection with decay and death in "Dora" (198), though to focus on the suddenness and finality of death and decay. The metaphor in "Yellow House" is more differentiated; it focuses on the ongoing passage of time, of which Hattie's deteriorating body is the narratable visual manifestation. Physical mortality (the container) represents the passage of time, while the contents (the self) represent perpetuity. Thus Bellow alerts the reader to the possibility that the incorporeal self may never be subject to the finality of death. In Bergson's view, similarly, the real self is only duration and creation.

The subsequent strengthening and deepening of the theme of death in "Yellow House" extends the fictional technique of progressive continuation into a "hereafter," with death becoming a transition. This theme is realized in the dominant narrative principle of continuous progression. Hattie's concept of death is not a strictly Christian concept of resurrection. It comes closer to the Bergsonian concept of duration—*je suis une chose qui dure*—which, as a constant dynamic process of becoming, is accessible only by way of intuition. Its perception of time escapes the rational and is not measurable by traditional space-oriented categories of time.

As a result, Bellow concludes with Hattie's questioning and challenging our confined concepts of time:

> Then she thought that there was a beginning, and a middle. She shrank from the last term. She began once more—a beginning. After that there was the early middle, then middle middle, quite late middle. In fact the middle is all I know. The rest is just a rumor. (42)

The theme of death appears in many forms. After Hattie's accident she soliloquizes: "Pace would have sold her to the bone man. He'd give her to the knacker for a buck" (11). This vivid colloquial speech exemplifies Bellow's chosen narrative technique of brevity and directness, introduces the theme of death, describes Hattie's social environment, anticipates a later plot development, and connects with the theme of isolation. All of this is achieved within two lines of text.

Hattie's growing isolation (Fuchs, "Bellow's Short Stories," 297) is represented by the increasing breakdown of communication. For example, her conversation with Darly in the beginning starts out in direct speech but abruptly turns into free indirect speech. When Hattie learns that the Rolfes plan to leave her, the very brief introductory dialogue between Helen and her becomes disrupted and changes into an extensive description of what goes on in Hattie's mind immediately following this news. Bellow thus constructs an artful web of free indirect speech interwoven with inner voice to create the intensity of this "silent" inner drama of hatred ("bitch-eyes") and love (of a "sister").

Bellow's conceptualization of Hattie as exclusively intuitive results in an avoidance of noticeable ideation (Fuchs, "Bellow's Short Stories," 296). Nevertheless, the casual mention of Henri Bergson in the story, like the mention of Proust, works like a carefully hidden explosive.

I have already mentioned Bergsonian influence on the concept of death as part of "duration," the assumption of a life after death, mystic inclinations, the reliance on intuition, and the experience of self-becoming as creation and duration. More obvious, however, is Bellow's use of Bergson's two basic principles—motion and duration—as aesthetic values of narration.

Motion is an element of Hattie's characterization. She expresses defiance by the movement of her shoulders, while her face usually registers strong and violent changing moods (9). Progression and change permeate and transform narrative elements in the story. Hattie achieves a symbolic simultaneity of past time, present time, and postmortal time, an artistic representation of "duration."

"Leaving the Yellow House" was influenced by Henri Bergson and Marcel Proust. Bellow turns the two basic principles of Bergson's philosophy—motion and duration—into aesthetic categories of narration; and although he uses Proust in obvious points of contact, his concepts of the "self" and of the artistic representation of interior time deviate drastically from those of Proust's.

A comparison of Dora and Hattie in Bellow's short stories shows that the character conception of both was influenced by their respective novelistic counterparts. Freud's case study of "Dora" influenced the theme, structure, and narrative of Bellow's story; yet Bellow's "Dora" is not a case history but a challenge to Freud's concept of the individual.

Bellow's deliberate use of mimetic fiction facilitates a dramatic development in his short story form: the establishment of the inner voice as an integral part of a dual structure within the narrative progression. It accommodates the immediacy of inner monologue; yet, at the same time, its double point of view facilitates dealing with the difficult subject of death.

Works Cited

Andreotti, Mario. *Die Stuktur der modernen Literatur: Neue Wege in der Textanalyse.* Bern: Haupt, 1983.

Auerbach, Erich. "The Brown Stocking." In *Mimesis: The Representation of Reality in Western Literature,* translated by Willard R. Trask, 525–57. Princeton: Princeton University Press, 1968.

Bellow, Saul. *The Adventures of Augie March.* New York: Viking Press, 1953.

———. "Dora." *Harper's Bazaar,* November 1949, 118+.

———. "Leaving the Yellow House." In *Mosby's Memoirs and Other Stories.* New York: Viking Press, 1968.

Freud, Sigmund. *Dora: An Analysis of a Case of Hysteria,* edited by Philip Rieff. New York: Collier, 1971.

———. "Dora: An Analysis of a Case of Hysteria." In *The Standard Edition of the Complete Psychological Works of Sigmund Freud,* edited by James Strachey, et al.,vol. 7:3–122. London: Hogarth, 1974.

Fuchs, Daniel. "Bellow and Freud." *Philosophical Dimensions of Saul Bellow's Fiction.* Special issue of *Studies in the Literary Imagination* 17 (1984): 59–80.

———. "Bellow's Short Stories." In *Saul Bellow: Vision and Revision,* 280–304. Durham, N.C.: Duke University Press, 1984.

Goudge, T. A. "Bergson, Henri." In *The Encyclopedia of Philosophy,* edited by Paul Edwards, vol. 1:287–95. New York: Macmillan, 1972.

Harper, Gordon Lloyd. "Saul Bellow: An Interview." *Paris Review* (Winter 1996): 345–64.

Kulshrestha, Chirantan. "The Bellow Gyroscope: Letters to Richard G. Stern." *Saul Bellow Journal* 2, no. 1 (1982): 36–41.

Lippit, Noriko M. "A Perennial Survivor: Saul Bellow's Heroine in the Desert." *Studies in Short Fiction* 12 (Summer 1975): 281–83.

Proust, Marcel. *Remembrance of Things Past,* translated C. K. Scott Moncrieff and Terence Kilmartin. 3 vols. New York: Random, 1982.

Rodrigues, Eusebio. *The Quest for the Human: An Exploration of Saul Bellow's Fiction.* Lewisburg, P.A.: Bucknell University Press, 1981.

———. "A Rough-Hewed Heroine for Our Time: Saul Bellow's 'Leaving the Yellow House.'" *Saul Bellow Journal* 1, no. 1 (1981): 11–17.

Rooke, Constance. "Saul Bellow's 'Leaving the Yellow House': The Trouble with Women." *Studies in Short Fiction* 14 (Spring 1977): 184–87.

Stern, Richard G. "Henderson's Bellow." In *Critical Essays on Saul Bellow*, edited by Stanley Trachtenbert, 19–23. Boston: Hall, 1979.

The Logic of the Heart: Biblical Identity and American Culture in Saul Bellow's "The Old System"

ALAN BERGER

In one of his letters to Richard G. Stern, Saul Bellow describes himself as "a very imperfect and accidental sort of person, a poor over-interrogated witness" (Kulshrestha, "Bellow," 36). Like the prophets of antiquity, Bellow protests his unworthiness. Unlike his ancient counterparts, however, perhaps a portion of Bellow's lament stems from his being seen as a representative Jewish novelist, a designation that he vigorously resists. He told one interviewer that he has "never consciously written as a Jew" and that he "never thought of writing for Jews exclusively" (Kulshrestha, "Conversation," 8).[1] But Bellow's Jewishness permeates his writings and authorial stance. Moreover, this Jewishness serves as a judge of the surrounding culture. The Nobel prize winner in literature is, according to Nathan Scott, "a radically religious novelist concerned about the importance of covenants made with a God who has long since died." But another reason that the author may feel that he is an "over-interrogated witness" is the fact that his work profoundly touches a resonant societal chord among readers who are searching for a sense of meaning. Bellow's "Hebrew-Humanism" advocates moral responsibility while simultaneously viewing history through a covenantal lens. It is this fact which doubtless prompted Cynthia Ozick to term his works examples of "liturgical literature."

Bellow's literary covenantal characters speak and behave in terms of an a priori "contract." Leila Goldman argues, in my view correctly, that Bellow's later novels, *Herzog, Mr. Sammler's Planet* and *Humboldt's Gift* are

Reprinted from *Saul Bellow Journal* 11, no. 2 & 12, no. 1 (Double Issue 1993): 133-45.

"outspoken expressions of covenant Judaism as in each book man's life is viewed in terms of a contract with God, . . . which includes an attempt to reestablish the interrelatedness of the community of Man" (Goldman, 61). For example, eulogizing the dead Elya Gruner, Mr. Sammler implores God to remember the deceased's soul. Gruner was aware, continues Sammler, "that he must meet, and he did meet—through all the confusion and degraded clowning of this life through which we are speeding—he did meet the terms of his contract—the terms which, in his inmost heart, each man knows" (*MSP* 313).Bellow's contract is a secularized covenant which emphasizes concern for family, a distinctively prophetic moral code, memory, and a rejection of nihilism. The human complexity of Bellow's covenanted characters emerges in their struggle to merge both the Old (Hebraic/Yiddish) and the New (American) worlds.

Far less attention, however, has been paid either to the covenant or to other biblical and Jewish mystical strands in Bellow's short stories and novellas. "The Old System" (1967), included in the collection *Mosby's Memoirs and Other Stories* (published the following year), is the most unambiguously Jewish of Bellow's short stories—and one which he confides having "liked writing" (Boyers et al., 21). Curiously, however, the work has received very little sustained critical interrogation/analysis concerning its specifically Jewish content. Published more than twenty-five years ago, the story can be read on many levels. For example, it is a canny social history of Jewish assimilation: an insider's description of the "old system" of *Ostjuden* (East European Jews) with its emphasis on feeling and emotion, and an empathic portrayal of biblical and Hasidic components of Jewish identity. Further, this identity conflicts both with American mores and the Enlightenment's dispassionate scientific worldview. While portraying the role of traditional religion in a post–traditional world, Bellow astutely comments on both the form and content of Jewish survival. In short, the themes of "The Old System" remain vital ones in contemporary Jewish American culture.

I shall argue that "The Old System," which Gregory Johnson has intelligently analyzed as "the waning of the 'old system' of Jewish manners in early twentieth-century America" (Johnson, 49), should be read as a distinctive type of covenantal tale putting into sharp relief the millennial struggle between traditional and assimilationist modes of being. Moreover, Bellow's use of biblical themes, religious ritual—even in a secular context—and Jewish languages (Hebrew and Yiddish) underscores the continuing dilemma of Jews who attempt to "sing the Lord's song in a foreign land." The old system is, as Norma Rosen observes, one which displayed "the old-time religious passion. With that gone, only grotesqueries, passions without real goals, are left" (Rosen, 56). Practices of ancestral religion are juxtaposed against a morally flaccid American culture, an infantalized and sterile notion of religion, and an American restraint which has use for neither feeling nor emotion.

Isaac Braun, the protagonist, lives among immigrants and blacks in upstate New York in the 1920s. He models a particular form of biblical and mystical behavior. Like his biblical namesake, the twentieth-century Isaac is a "man in the direct Old Testament sense" (Bellow, 46). Although lacking a theonomic name, the second patriarch was named by God. The biblical Isaac is the true inheritor of the Abrahamic tradition and was the first to be circumcised in accordance with divine command. Isaac's silence as he and Abraham walked towards the place of binding (the *Akedah)* is interpreted as a sign of his acceptance of God's test of Abraham. Similarly, Bellow's Isaac is a survivor or, rather, embodies Jewish survival— he becomes wealthy, has deep feelings for his family, and is a believer. Merging biblical and Hasidic motifs, Isaac has a rebbe in Brooklyn, reads *Tehellim* (psalms) in his air-conditioned Cadillac, prays at his construction sites, and speaks both Hebrew and Yiddish. "His orthodoxy," the reader is told, "increased with his wealth" (54).

Isaac's orthodoxy, however, is not shared by his sister Tina. An obese and spiteful woman, she wrongly accuses him of excluding his siblings from an illicit real estate deal which netted enormous profit. In truth, the family had backed out at the last moment leaving Isaac to risk all that he has—and could borrow from the bank—in order to pay $100,000 to Ilkington, a Protestant whose own CASP (Capitalist, Anglo-Saxon, Protestant) culture is so alien to Judaism. The cash is a bribe meant to insure that Ilkington vote for the sale of the antisemitic Robbstown Country Club to Isaac. Sealing the transaction underscores the clash between the Hebraic Old System and America's CASP culture. Ilkington neither refers to their arrangement nor even counts the money. Isaac, for his part, feels "lost to his people, his family, lost to God, lost in the void of America" (59). Yet this cultural accommodation paves the way for Isaac's subsequent financial successes. Years later, Tina refuses to allow Isaac to visit her deathbed unless he pays her $20,000. A dramatic deathbed reconciliation scene reveals the depth of familial emotions which characterize the old system.

The Old System Remembered

Dr. Samuel Braun, Isaac's nephew, narrates the tale many years later. The *form* of his narrative is as crucial as its content. A specialist in the chemistry of heredity, Braun is committed to the dispassionate method of scientific inquiry. Yet, in the twilight of his own life, he laments the inadequacy of contemporary civilization's cultivation of unhealthy self-detachment. Braun, whose first name may be rendered as *Shmu-el,* God hears, thinks of his two cousins, Isaac and Tina, long dead, who had lived in upstate New York. His reflections occur on a Saturday in late December. Waking late, he lies in bed in the darkened room until noon. Amidst this numinous setting, he rises and bathes in a ritual fashion reminiscent of the *mikveh* to which both men and women go in order to purify themselves. Braun dries himself, "with the self-respecting expression human beings inherit from ancestors for whom bathing was a solemnity. A sadness" (44).

Dr. Braun in fact is engaging in *heshbon Ha-nefesh,* an interrogation of the soul. This interrogation will lead him on a twofold path. He admits the limitations of scientific detachments, and he acknowledges the powerful lure of tribal emotions. He engages his memories in an awe-ful silence, recalling both the people and the ways of the old system. Braun's reminiscence is a *yizkor* for a Jewish worldview which seems increasingly archaic while simultaneously serving as a spiritual yardstick against which one may measure the extent of loss of Jewish identity in the New World.

The novella is also psychologically rich in describing Dr. Braun's adult return to memories of long-suppressed emotions. Recalling a summer visit to his cousins' cottage in the Adirondacks when he was seven years old, the scientist remembers being sexually initiated by the hulking Tina who "promised nothing, told him nothing" (50). He also recalls attempting to club Isaac, fifteen years his senior, to death because the youngster was not allowed to join Isaac and his fianceé as they walked in the woods. The young boy was sent home to Albany because he lacked self-control. Subsequently, he repressed his emotions and became "a docile, bookish child (who) did very well at school" (51). Childhood repression paved the way for Braun's adult career of scientific detachment. Isaac and Tina, on the other hand, repressed nothing.

The Old System in America

Literary exploration of the tensions between the demands of ancestral faith—the old system—and American culture received early attention in the works of Abraham Cahan and Anzia Yezierska. Bellow's Isaac Braun differs, however, from his literary forebears in immigrant novels. Whereas his predecessors believed it was difficult to be both authentically Jewish and American, Isaac's orthodoxy keeps apace with his material success.

Isaac's wealth is in fact inextricably linked to his adherence to the old system of beliefs, values, and practices. Bellow writes:

> The world had done for him [Isaac] exactly what he had demanded. That meant he had made the right demand and in the right place. It meant *his reading of life was metaphysically true.* Or that the Old Testament, the Talmud, and Polish Ashkenazi Orthodoxy were irresistible. (Italics mine; 60–61)

But there was more to Isaac than piety. His sexual escapades were also of biblical proportion. Braun remembers his cousin contending that he "fought on many fronts, meaning women's bellies" (62).

The American-born Dr. Braun discovers that he himself is not entirely free of the demands of the logic of the heart. The old system, replete with its emotionalism, its openness, and its familiarity with Jewish religion, has a prior claim on Jewish allegiance. By contrast, the American experience appeals both to the superficial and to a type of "operatic excess" that derived from the "old system." Braun notes that "this native American boastfulness had aggravated a certain weakness in Jewish immigrants" (45). Jews were becoming antiseptic creatures in America—"the land of historical redress" where "abuses of the Old World were righted" (65). Yet material details were not the abiding concerns. In Dr. Braun's words, "the largest strokes were made by the spirit. Had to be!! People who said this were right" (65). Uninformed about or disinterested in the old ways, successive generations of American Jews appear concerned only with escaping their own history and embracing the ways of CASP culture. In fact, Braun's observation reveals that the tension between the old system and CASP modes of being displayed in Isaac's anguished reaction to bribing Ilkington had, for the majority of America's Jews, been resolved by abandoning the old system.

Belying his self-description as one unable to love, Braun nostalgically describes his Aunt Rose and Uncle Braun, the parents of Isaac and Tina. Uncle Braun personifies early-twentieth-century Jewish history. Conscripted into the czar's army—"How those old time Jews," thinks Dr. Braun, "despised the *[dummheit]* goy wars"—Uncle Braun escaped through Manchuria, came to Vancouver, and arrived finally in New York State's Mohawk Valley, where he became "monarch of used stoves and fumigated mattresses" (47). In addition to his business success, Uncle Braun was also respected for his religious learning, an example that will be followed by his son Isaac. Aunt Rose, for her part, "was the original dura mater" whose "straight sharp nose [could] cut mercy like a cotton thread" (48). If Uncle Braun personally experienced the travails of Jewish males in the "Pale of Settlement," Aunt Rose herself exuded the stereotypical aura of Jewish females. Braun recalls that she "had a large bust, wide hips, and old-fashioned thighs of those corrupted shapes that belong to history" (48). A determined woman who, recalls Braun, "was building a kingdom with the labor of Uncle Braun and the strength of her obedient sons"(48). Far removed from the Tradition's *eshet hayil* (woman of valor) and having little use for Jewish religious practices, Aunt Rose was adept in Yiddish sarcasm, vetoing each of Isaac's women friends with vicious epithets: "a false dog," "candied poison," "An open ditch. A sewer. A born whore" (52).

Isaac eventually marries the daughter of a Jewish farmer. Against his mother's inevitable verbal assault, Isaac defends his father-in-law, citing his honesty, hard work, and the fact that he "recites the Psalms" even when driving his wagon. This practice of *avodah begashmiyyut* (worship in corporeal things) is a well-attested one among the Hasidim, and it allows them to transform their work into a form of worship. The Berditchever, Levi-Yitzhak of Berditchev, observed a coachman praying while fixing his wagon. This prompted the zaddik to cry out to God: "Look at Your people, God of Israel, and be proud. What does this man do while working on his cart? He prays. Tell me, do You know of any other nation that has You so completely in its thoughts?" (Wiesel, 89). Unmollified, Aunt Rose intensifies her attack, terming the man a "son of Ham." This is a vile insult as those who remember the tale of Noah and his son recall. Ham uncovered his father's nakedness, was cursed by Noah, and destined to be a servant to his brothers. Aunt Rose then speaks to her daughter-in-law in Yiddish:

> "Be so good as to wash thy father before bringing him to the synagogue, Get a bucket and scalding water, and 20 Mule Team Borax and ammonia, and a horse brush. The filth is ingrained. Be sure to scrub his hands." (52)

At least part of Bellow's descriptive genius resides in portraying the various types of individuals who lived according to the old system. Even rabid secularists and atheists knew the Bible and many of them spoke Yiddish. Uncle Braun died angry with his wife who, in turn, broke the terms of his will. While lamenting the loss of this system, Bellow clearly refrains from sentimentalizing it.

Isaac and Tina's emotional relationship is the tale's centerpiece. Tina commits the sin of causeless hatred *(sinat hinom)*, one of the rabbinical explanations for the destruction of the Temple, in blaming Isaac for excluding his siblings from the deal with Ilkington. Isaac, for his part, continues to observe biblical ritual. He visits the graves of his parents before the High Holidays—according to the ways of the pious—to forgive and ask forgiveness. The practice of *kever avot,* visiting the graves of the dead, is enjoined at the time of Rosh Hashanah and Yom Kippur. Also at this time, one is commanded to pray for forgiveness of sins. But there are two types of sins: those transgressions committed by humans against God *(beyn Adam le Makom)* and those committed by humans against each other *(beyn Adam le Adam).* God can forgive only transgressions committed against the divine. Those committed against other humans must be forgiven by the one sinned against.

Isaac's appeals to Tina are, however, crudely rejected. He reminds Tina that they are sister and brother. Further, he begs her to remember Judaism's central ritual. His appeal is to remember their parents, the fact that they are Jews, and siblings. She, in turn, remembers or, rather, dismembers the past by clinging to the false accusation against her brother. She screams at him, "You son of a bitch, I *do* remember! Now get the hell out of here" (67). Denying Isaac a pardon for a sin he did not commit, Tina symbolically prevents her brother from achieving penance *(tshuva).* *Tshuva* means a turning away from sin and a turning toward Torah. For Tina, this was an act of spite. For Isaac, it was a metaphysical rebuke.

Isaac's European ways embarrass the new rabbi who, with his Madison Avenue airs, embraces the way of understatement and Anglo-Saxon restraint. "European Judaic, operatic fist-clenchings" had no place in America. Isaac, however, wrapped in his late father's *tallith,* continued to pray and weep near the ark. His is the logic of the heart which impels him to feel and play the role of an "old-fashioned Jewish paterfamilias." Despite his accommodation to CASP mores in financial matters, Isaac "had the look of ancient generations on the New World. Tents and kine and wives and maidservants and manservants" (46). The extent to which the old system has been lost is present even, or rather especially, in the synagogue, where it is apparent that among the congregants only Isaac's voice and gesture "belong to history." He has, writes Bellow, "no place or parallel in upstate New York." In the synagogue, Isaac prays the *Al Chait* (public confession of sin), "striking breast with fist in old-fashioned penitence" (67).

Dr. Braun recalls vividly Tina's behavior toward Isaac during her terminal illness. Refusing to see him because he wants a "Jewish deathbed scene," she proposes to allow her brother to visit only on condition that he pay $20,000. Ostensibly, this money is to be for her young daughter. In fact, Tina's demand was an act of extortion. "Tina," writes Bellow, "had discovered that one need not be bound by the old rules" (69). Dr. Braun believes that his cousin Tina had created a situation of parody and opera. Isaac's longing to see his sister would be denied unless he paid up. "Hyperbole," notes Dr. Braun, "was Tina's greatest weakness" (62). This parodic *Akeda* informs the remainder of the story.

Isaac has two encounters following receipt of Tina's terms. The first meeting occurs when, as a member of the governor's environmental commission, Isaac takes a boat tour of the Hudson River. One of his fellow delegates is Ilkington Junior. The man knows about the $100,000 bribe and, although somewhat reserved, does not snub Isaac. In fact, young Ilkington "behaved with courtesy." Although naturally inclined to show gratitude, Isaac understands that "what you showed among these people, you showed with silence." Commenting on the New World's flight from feeling, Isaac muses that "the more they had in their heads, the less people seemed to know how to tell it" (72–73).

The religious value of the old system is strongly underscored by Isaac's decision to seek guidance from his rebbe in Williamsburg. Realizing that the agonizing dilemma imposed on him by Tina can be faced in no other way, Isaac takes a train to New York City. Awaiting his *yehidut* (private audience) with the Lubavitcher Rebbe, Isaac is in the company of the master's bearded followers, many of whom were Holocaust survivors, as is the rebbe himself, who had survived the *Shoah* as a boy. As an aside, it is noteworthy that Menachem Mendel Schneerson—the Lubavitcher Rebbe—had studied mechanical engineering at the Sorbonne. Unlike Samuel Braun, he had abandoned science in order to wholeheartedly embrace the old system. Speaking in Yiddish, Isaac explains his situation to the rebbe, who—in contrast to the American rabbi—"had the old tones, the manner, the burly poise, the universal calm judgment of the Jewish moral genius" (77). Isaac, for his part, distinguishes his payment to Ilkington (a business risk) from the situation with Tina, who is family. The Rebbe remarks that "our Jews love deathbed jokes." Nevertheless, he counsels Isaac to pay.

Understanding of the Rebbe's counsel is an imperative and Isaac decides that he must fly home. Never having flown before, he is understandably apprehensive. On the airport bus he opens his father's copy of the Psalms. As the airplane leaves the runway, Isaac intones the words of *Shema Yisroel.* The *Shema* asserts the oneness of God. Further, it is the central credal statement of Judaism and, following the legends associated with the martyrdom of Rabbi Akiba, pious Jews say the *Shema* on their deathbeds. Arriving home, Isaac collects the money and rushes to the hospital. Opening the door to Tina's room, he hears his sister say, "I wondered." Isaac assures her that the money is all there. There ensues an overwrought and prearranged ceremony. Tina, consumed by her disease, not only refuses the money but returns a ring which had rightfully belonged to Isaac's wife, and which the jealous sister had, years earlier, taken from their mother's corpse. Tina's demand, like the *Akeda* of old, was a test. Brother and sister embrace and weep. The old system of concern for family and the old style of emotional expressiveness have, at least temporarily, overcome the CASP restraint and detachment of the New World.

Dr. Braun is "bitterly moved" when attempting to grasp what emotions are. He has tears in his eyes and thinks, "Oh these Jews—these Jews! Their feelings, their hearts!" (82). The scientist of heredity wonders, "why these particular forms—these Isaacs and these Tinas?" Tears from the heart make one feel that one understood something. But this something was only an "intimation of understanding. A promise," muses Braun, "that mankind might—*might*, mind you—eventually, through its gift which might—*might* again!—be a divine gift, comprehend why it lived. Why life, why death" (82–83).

Braun derides himself on the one hand for the "useless love" of his dead relatives. On the other hand, although the old system ostensibly dies with Tina and Isaac, there are hopeful signs. For example, as noted earlier, Tina has a daughter whose behavior may display certain dimensions of the old system. Dr. Braun himself is at least a partial participant in this system. He, too, remembers and has a deep attachment to his now-deceased family. Braun, like Jacob of antiquity, struggles for an unambiguous identity. Unlike that of his biblical forebear, Dr. Braun's struggle remains unresolved. A scientist who craves that which is neat and orderly, he is drawn by the emotional expressiveness of his long-dead relatives. As one commentator—correctly in my view—notes, the entire narration is a "cry of longing for the old system rather than the statement of bemusement that Braun tries to make it seem" (Kiernan, 121).

The promise of Enlightenment ended in the gas chambers of Europe. Describing Isaac's household, the narrator notes that it was "an ample plan of old-fashioned respectable life on an Eastern European model completely destroyed in 1939 by Hitler and Stalin. Those two saw to the eradication of the old conditions, made sure that certain modern concepts became social realities" (64–65). Consequently, on the one hand, tyrants had literally exterminated both the old system and its adherents. In a world which is increasingly murderous and religiously infantilized, there appears none of the certitude of either covenant or a meaningful sense of history. On the other hand, Isaac both seeks and embodies the consolations of the old system. For him, adjustment to American culture entails neither abandonment of Jewish identity nor family commitment. Dr. Braun, representing the next generation, can only reflect on, yet not fully embrace, this system. The emotional, moral, and religious yearning which comprise the old system remain as both a historical chapter and a future goal. Even Braun's story-ending look at the cold, impersonal stars, "things cast outward by a great begetting spasm billions of years ago," will—the reader knows—do little to assuage his longing for the personal and emotional ways of the old system.

Notes

1. Bellow clearly distinguishes between his public role as a novelist and his private role as a father in disseminating Judaism. I remember, nearly three decades ago, as a graduate student at the University of Chicago meeting Bellow's son, Gregory. He told me that his father would give him the family Bible only if Gregory learned to read its Hebrew text.

Works Cited

Bellow, Saul. *Mr. Sammler's Planet.* New York: Viking Press, 1964. Further references are to this edition and will be noted parenthetically as *MSP*.

——. "The Old System." In *Mosby's Memoirs and Other Stories.* New York: Penguin Books, 1968.

Boyers, Robert, et al. "Literature and Culture: An Interview with Saul Bellow." *Salmagundi* 30 (1975): 21.

Goldman, L. H. "Saul Bellow and the Philosophy of Judaism." In *Saul Bellow in the 1980s: A Collection of Critical Essays*, edited by Gloria L. Cronin and L. H. Goldman. East Lansing: Michigan University Press, 1989.

Johnson, Gregory. "Jewish Assimilation and Codes of Manners in Saul Bellow's 'The Old System.'" *Studies in American Jewish Literature* 9, no. 1 (Spring 1990): 49.

Kiernan, Robert F. *Saul Bellow.* New York: Continuum Publishing Company, 1989.

Kulshrestha, Chirantan. "The Bellow Gyroscope: Letters to Richard G. Stern." *Saul Bellow Journal* 2, no. 1 (1982): 36.

——. "A Conversation with Saul Bellow." *Chicago Review* 23, no. 4 & 24, no. 1 (1971–72): 7–15.

Rosen, Norma. "The Second Life of Holocaust Imagery." *Midstream* 33, no. 4 (1987): 56.

Wiesel, Elie. *Souls on Fire: Portraits and Legends of Hasidic Masters*, translated by Marion Wiesel. New York: Random House, 1972.

A New Look at "The Old System"

SANFORD PINSKER

B ecause his congenial turf is the large canvas of the novel, one tends to forget how impressive Saul Bellow can be within more restrictive forms. A novella such as *Seize the Day* (1956) springs immediately to mind and, indeed, it has long been cited as Exhibit A in the case for Bellow as a writer of great compression and extraordinary fictive power. No doubt part of the adulation springs from the undeniable fact that *Seize the Day* is what those of us in the lit. crit. business call an "eminently teachable text." After all, one can guide students to an understanding of how the water imagery functions or how the story's richly textured allusions work. There is, in short, God's plenty to talk about, even if many students are not quite sure what the literary fuss is about or why Tommy Wilhelm can't be written off in a single word: "loser."

What I'm suggesting, of course, may sound like yet another nail driven into the coffin of close, New Critical reading, and in the sense that I will be arguing that literature is finally about more than image clusters and symbolic meanings, perhaps it is. But let me hasten to add that I am even less persuaded by much that travels under the banner of the *au courant*. As I watch fashionable theoreticians busily dismantling what they insist upon calling texts or others just as busily converting works of the imagination into political tracts, I find myself vacillating between curiosity and skepticism, an amusement that figures this too will pass and what Marlow, in another country, as it were, called a "fascination with the abomination." Yiddish is better equipped to deal with such foolishness, not only because it has a richer word for the phenomenon—namely, *narishkeit*—but also because it has the saltiness and the good sense to know when to say "*Me redt, me redt un me shushkit zich*" (They talk and talk and say nothing).

Reprinted from *Saul Bellow Journal* 11, no. 2 & 12, no. 1 (Double Issue 1993): 54-65.

All of which brings me to "The Old System," a short story that has
been largely ignored by Bellow's critics and that I would argue is more,
much more, than its usual characterization as a dress rehearsal for
Mr. Sammler's Planet. Granted, Dr. Samuel Braun's meditations of a winter
afternoon bear more than a few resemblances to the extended social
critique Artur Sammler will dispense a few years later. Both characters
share much in terms of ambiance and essential attitude. Compare, for
example, this description of Samuel Braun preparing for the spiritual
exercises that await him with the description of Artur Sammler, who
paddles around his apartment in much the same regimen. First, Braun:

> Every civilized man today cultivated an unhealthy self-detachment. Had
> learned from art the art of amusing self-observation and objectivity.
> Which, since there had to be something assuming to watch, required art
> in one's conduct. Existence for the sake of such practices did not seem
> worthwhile. Mankind was in a confusing, uncomfortable, disagreeable
> stage in the evolution of its consciousness. Dr. Braun (Samuel) did not
> like it. It made him sad to feel that the thought, art, belief of great
> traditions should be so misemployed. Elevation? Beauty? Turn into
> shreds, into ribbons for girls' costumes, or trailed like the tail of a kite
> at Happenings. Plato and the Buddha raided by looters. The tombs of
> Pharaohs broken into by desert rabble. And so on, thought Dr. Braun
> as he passed into his neat kitchen. He was well pleased by the
> blue-and-white Dutch dishes, cups hanging, saucers standing in slots.
>
> He opened a fresh can of coffee, much enjoyed the fragrance from
> the punctured can. Only an instant, but not to be missed. Next he sliced
> bread for the toaster, got out the butter, chewed an orange; and he was
> admiring long icicles on the huge red, circular roof tank when he
> discovered that a sentiment was approaching. (*MM*, 44)

And now, Artur Sammler:

> New York was getting worse than Naples or Salonika. It was like an
> Asian, an African town, from this viewpoint. The opulent sections of
> the city were not immune. You opened a jeweled door into degradation,
> from hypercivilized Byzantine luxury straight into the state of nature,
> the barbarous world of color erupting from beneath. It might well be
> barbarous on either side of the jeweled door. Sexually, for example. The
> thing evidently, as Mr. Sammler was beginning to grasp, consisted in
> obtaining the privileges, and the free ways of barbarism, under the

protection of civilized order, property rights, refined technological organization, and so on. Yes, that must be it.

Mr. Sammler ground his coffee in a square box, cranking counterclockwise between long knees. To commonplace actions he brought a special pedantic awkwardness. In Poland, France, England, students, young gentlemen of his time, had been unacquainted with kitchens. Now he did things that cooks and maids had once done. He did them with a certain priestly stiffness. Acknowledgment of social descent. Historical ruin. Transformation of society. It was beyond personal humbling. (*MSP*, 6–7)

Granted, Sammler can never quite resist delivering jeremiads, however much he protests that the trouble with contemporary life is people who insist "on being right" and who end up as tiresome, explaining creatures— "Fathers to children, wives to husbands, lecturers to listeners, experts to laymen, colleagues to colleagues, doctors to patients, man to his own soul, explained" (3).

By contrast, Braun's extended meditation is as private as it is necessarily hesitant, for on the afternoon set aside to take stock of his family, what he confronts is nothing less than what Bellow likes to call the Death Question. Into a life given over almost entirely to orderliness and the scientific process, a certain messiness seems fated to intrude:

The sentiment, as he drank his coffee, was for two cousins in upstate New York, the Mohawk Valley. They were dead. Isaac Braun and his sister Tina. Tina was the first to go. Two years later, Isaac died. Braun now discovered that he and Cousin Isaac had loved each other. For whatever use or meaning this fact might have within the peculiar system of light, movement, contact, and perishing in which he tried to find stability. (45)

Bellow's title is carefully chosen to suggest a contrast between systems old and new, between the melodramatic excesses of the Jewish immigrant experience and the newer order represented by scientific inquiry. Not surprisingly, Dr. Braun would prefer a tidy, high-tech explanation that would account for an Isaac, a Tina, but none is forthcoming: "One could not help thinking what fertility of metaphor there was in all of these Brauns. Dr. Braun himself was no exception. And what the exception might be, despite twenty-five years of specialization in the chemistry of heredity, he couldn't say. How a protein molecule might carry such propensities of ingenuity and creative malice and negative power" (55). In short, Bellow's character may retain a certain faith in what his computer-generated studies of genetic chemistry might reveal, but its author knows better. To understand human personality at the extremes of love and hatred—and perhaps more important, to understand how these emotions are inextricably connected—requires more than is dreamt of in philosophy or logged into a computer.

As a number of critics have suggested, Bellow's narrative techniques keep the "old system" at an arm's length at the same time that they distance us from Braun himself. Robert F. Kiernan puts it this way: "Braun's story is as interesting for its suppressions as for its inclusions" (120). Put a slightly different way, "The Old System" *is* Braun's story much more than it is Isaac's or Tina's or even, as Gregory Johnson argues, a sociological account of "the waning of the 'old system' of Jewish manners in early twentieth-century America" (49). For it is Dr. Braun who worries that "it has been said of him, occasionally, that he did not love anyone" (44) and who insists that the accusation is not strictly true: "He did not love anyone steadily. But unsteadily he loved, he guessed, at an average rate" (44–45).

Granted, the social costs of acculturation, as outlined in studies such as John Murray Cuddihy's *The Ordeal of Civility* (1974), not only provide the necessary background against which the emblematic saga of Isaac and Tina is played out, but also help explain why he became a "docile, bookish child" and, later, an adult who prefers scientific precision to immigrant Jewish hyperbole. Nonetheless, "The Old System" is much more than sociology gussied up as fiction. Rather, I would argue that Bellow has yet another meaning for "the old system" tucked up his sleeve—namely, the very *American* preoccupation with interior meditation that generated countless Puritan diaries. In such a world, one's spiritual condition mattered greatly and while Bellow is hardly a Calvinist, he is surely one of the few contemporary American writers not embarrassed by the word *soul*.

"The Old System," then, is Dr. Braun's long, dark afternoon of the soul. Like Herzog, he means to "have it out, to justify, to put in perspective, to clarify, to make amends" (*H*, 2)—not by compulsively writing a series of mental letters (as Herzog does) but, rather, by narrowing the focus of his significant dead to Isaac and Tina. To be sure, other Bellow protagonists have an easier time reconnecting with their roots. One thinks, for example, of the Moses Herzog who nostalgically remembers his childhood on Napleoan Street ("Here was a wider range of human feelings than he had ever again been able to find" [*H*, 140]), or even of the cranky Artur Sammler who ends his novel-long tirade by insisting that Elya Gruner had fulfilled his contract—"the terms which, in his inmost heart, each man knows. As I know mine. As all know. For that is the truth of it—that we all know, God, that we know, that we know, we know, we know" (*MSP*, 316).

By contrast, Dr. Braun teeters uneasily between attraction and repulsion, affection and disgust, certainty and doubt. He can neither give himself over to the large, volatile emotions that characterized immigrant Jewish life nor can he entirely dismiss the tugs of memory. Images, in short, intrude—a sycamore tree beside the Mohawk River, a gray-and-blue fish hawk, an old coarse-tailed horse pulling a wagon—and with them, vivid memories of Aunt Rose, the "original dura mater—the primal hard mother" (54), and of his cousins Isaac and Tina. Dr. Braun has long had his doubts about their fierce family pride and the large claims they would make on its behalf. When, for example, Isaac once insisted that the Brauns were descended from the tribe of Naphtali, the young Samuel Braun, then a mere ten-year-old, wondered aloud, "How do we know?" (49). What he means, without quite knowing that he means it, is how could one *prove* such a thing? What would constitute evidence, data, hypothesis, and procedure—in short, the very stuff of the scientific method? Isaac, of course, marches to the drummer of an older system: "People—families—know."

And in their own way, the Brauns *did* know not only about their tribal origins, but also about how to unpack their hearts in the face of life's elemental moments. They know, in short, how to laugh and how to cry. But it is also true that they know how to scream and how to bicker. By contrast, a character like Ilkington stands for old money and the "new system" of manners and restraint, the stiff upper lip and the perfectly shaken martini. If Dr. Braun shares something of this reserve, his generates from the regimen that science requires and, of course, from what he has seen firsthand of "the rigid madness of the orthodox" (52).

Small wonder, then, that he is overwhelmed by the sheer excess his extended family represents—their boastfulness and hyperbole, their propensities for creative malice and negative power, their fierce loves and often fiercer hatreds. "And Dr. Braun, bitterly moved, tried to grasp what emotions were. What good were they! What were they for! . . . Oh, these Jews—these Jews! Their feelings, their hearts!" (82). Kiernan argues that the irony buried most deeply in the story is "that Isaac finds consolation in the old system as it becomes increasingly clear that his life is in every other way a failure, whereas Braun, facing the same sense of failure, spurns the consolations of the old system that might soothe him" (121). But, as Hemingway once wrote, "isn't it pretty to think so?" especially for those enough removed from immigrant Jewish life to wax nostalgic about its benefits.

Bellow, of course, is neither a social historian nor a professional apologist; what he seeks is a way of dramatizing how a character such as Dr. Samuel Braun might respond to the deaths of his cousins—indeed, to death itself—as he juggles past against present, what he observed as a child against what he remembers as a man. Moreover, I suspect that Kiernan is not the only critic made uncomfortable by Bellow's ending, with its careful balancing of pros and cons, affirmations and doubts. After all, Dr. Braun might share a good many of Bellow's pet gripes and characteristic flourishes, but he is, finally, a *scientist*; and scientists, as they say, just don't get it.

On the other hand, a character such as Philip Roth's Nathan Zuckerman *is* one of us. But does "Higher Education," the story about Jews squabbling over money that sets *The Ghost Writer* into motion, suggest that Nathan sees a "truth" that the conflicted Dr. Braun has missed? I think not. Indeed, Nathan's story strikes me as mean-spirited and smart-alecky, exactly the sort of fare that might have slipped easily inside the covers of *Goodbye, Columbus* and its other stories. Granted, that is precisely Roth's point, as his protagonist battles against his father's worries and Judge Wapter's criticisms. But that always seems to be Roth's point— namely, to filter everything through the prism of the self.

Indeed, intimations of the self—as rebel, as free-spirit, as no-goodnik—are what draw Nathan to the materials of "higher education" in the first place. For here, after all, is the stuff of Jewish-American conflict in vivid miniature: Meema Chaya's years of hard work against Sidney's life of inveterate laziness, Richard's and Robert's track record of studiousness against Sidney's shiftiness. Add the complications of deciding what does, or does not, constitute "higher education" (college? medical school? both?) and the result is precisely the sort of tale a younger Philip Roth might have included as one of *Goodbye, Columbus*'s "other stories."

My point, however, is that Nathan's sympathies flow easily, perhaps too easily, toward Sidney:

My admiration was longstanding, dating back to Sidney's Navy days, when he had won four thousand dollars on the homeward journey of the battleship *Kansas*, and was said to have thrown into the South Pacific, for the sharks to dispose of, a Mississippi sore loser who at the end of an all-night poker game had referred to the big winner as a dirty Jew. (*Ghost Writer*, 82)

In a family governed by a sha-sha approach to what the *goyim* might say, who fear the consequences of speaking up, much less hitting back, Sidney is the stuff of which heroism is made. But Sidney is also the embarrassment, the bum that Nathan's family insists he is: "for four years Sidney had been waiting for Richard and Robert to graduate from Rutgers—waiting mostly in pool rooms and saloons, to hear the family tell it—so he could buy a downtown parking lot with his legacy" (*Ghost Writer*, 81).

For those immigrant Jews who translated opportunity into their version of the American Dream (first college, then medical school, then a lucrative suburban practice), Sidney is the giddy freedom of America gone sour. He represents neither what was best in the old system (a reverence for learning, a feeling for family) nor what might be possible, through hard work, in the new. By contrast, Nathan sees him as both a source of inspiration and the subject of an ambitious 15,000-word story. As Amy Bellette puts it, the master—E. I. Lonoff—is "counter-suggestible"; one manipulates him via reverse psychology in much the same manner that, say, Poe's cerebral detectives match their wits against master criminals. Much the same thing might be said of the young Nathan Zuckerman, who finds that his latest manuscript can have surprising, even wounding, consequences. The "games" that result are both subtle and stylistically dazzling. To be sure, Nathan Zuckerman *dreams* many of the complications—for example, that Amy Bellette is *the* Anne Frank, an Anne Frank who survived, who "got away," and that her extraordinary book exacts a silence, an ostensible death, in short, the shadowy life as a "ghost writer," if it is to retain its raw emotional power. But this countertext, if you will, is also an extended exercise in defending, in justifying, and, I would add, in deconstructing the knotty question of an artist's responsibility.

For Doc Zuckerman, the consequences of art are as clear, as undeniable, as the Jewish nose on Nathan's face: "From a lifetime of experience I happen to know what ordinary people will think when they read something like this story ["Higher Education"]. And you don't. You can't. . . . But I will tell you. They don't think about how it's a great work of art. They don't know about art." (*Ghost Writer*, 92) The young Nathan Zuckerman, surprised by his father's surprise, hurt by his father's hurt, thinks about loftier matters: the shape and ring of individual sentences, the rise and resolution of dramatic tensions, in short, about aesthetic considerations far removed from those messy interferences that now travel under the banner of "reader response," but that, in suburban Newark, boil down to the existential business of what is, or is not, good for the Jews. Read *this* way, Nathan's story strikes his father as an accident waiting to happen; it confirms, from one of their own no less and in public print to boot, what anti-Semites have long suspected—namely, that Jews squabble over money, that they are, in a word, kikes.

Small wonder, then, that Nathan seeks the "sponsorship," the surrogate fatherhood, of E. I. Lonoff. As a consummate Jewish American fictionist, *he* will be able to extend the welcoming hand that Nathan's own father has refused. What Nathan discovers, however, is a man so committed to "fantasy" that the slightest hint of Life has been rigorously, systematically, crowded out. "I turn sentences around," Lonoff declares. "That's my life. I write a sentence and then I turn it around. Then I look at it and turn it around again. Then I have lunch" (*Ghost Writer*, 124). Although Lonoff tells his writing students that "there is no life without patience," he has little patience with the "deep thinkers" who are attracted to his work, and no doubt he would have even less patience with a deconstructive reading of his working habits.

Zuckerman, however, is an artistic horse of a very different color. His aesthetic feeds on turbulence, on mounting tensions, on a world where sentences are shouted across a kitchen table and end in exclamation points. "You are not somebody who writes this kind of story," Doc Zuckerman insists, "and then pretends it's the truth" (*Ghost Writer*, 95). But Nathan *did* write such a story; moreover he *is* precisely "the kind of person who writes this kind of story!" For Lonoff, such truths are as much a part of the artistic landscape as the regimen of daily reading and obsessive scribbling. Zuckerman may be a nice polite boy when invited into somebody's home, but he is not likely to be so politic when he writes up the report of his visit. With a pen in his hand, Nathan becomes a different person, and if Lonoff's "blessing" is anywhere in the text, it is in his understanding, accepting wish that Nathan continue to be this "different" person when he sets about composing the novel we know as *The Ghost Writer*.

For those who would brand him as self-hating, as an enemy of his people, nothing short of marrying Anne Frank will suffice. And indeed, Zuckerman imagines exactly this triumph as a logical consequence of his imaginative rescue. Not only would he who had been misunderstood now be forgiven, but his father would utter the very words Nathan most wants to hear: "Anne, says my father—the Anne? Oh, how I have misunderstood my son. How mistaken we have been!" (*Ghost Writer*, 159).

To be sure, the Anne Frank that Nathan resurrects—the impassioned little sister of Kafka who lived out in Amsterdam the indictments, the hidden attics, the camouflaged doors he had dreamed about in Prague—is a psychological ringer for Nathan himself. Both exact their rebellions against family, synagogue, and state in the pages of their respective works; both suffer the loss of fathers for their art; and interesting enough, *neither* could answer Judge Wapter's questions (number 3, for example, asks: "Do you practice Judaism? If so, how? If not, what credentials qualify you for writing about Jewish life for national magazines?"[*Ghost Writer*, 131]) in ways that Wapter would find satisfactory.

The Ghost Writer is, of course, a version of the modernist *Bildungsroman* as reflected through the lens of a Nathan Zuckerman some twenty years old and presumably light years sadder and wiser about the "madness of art" and the human costs that come with landscaping a fictional territory. For better or worse, Nathan's congenial turf turns out to be the Jews. Unfortunately, what he discovers—after publishing a scandalously successful expose entitled *Carnovsky*—is that no analogs to his modernist precursors will wash. Try as he might, the mantle of exile that slipped so easily, so convincingly, around James Joyce's shoulders will not quite fit. Granted, there are no end of attacks, no end of those who would add Zuckerman to the list of Hamen and Hitler—names that deserve being blotted out—but Zuckerman craves approval rather than martyrdom. Down deep, he really can't believe that his antagonists are as angry as they claim or that they would stay mad if he just had a chance to explain himself. In a similar way, Roth continues to be driven by the need to explain and to be loved. His insistence of late that *Operation Shylock* is true, that he worked as an agent for the Mossad, the Israeli Secret Service, is simply the latest chapter in a long trail of tears and misunderstandings. But if the truth be told, if "confession" is the operative word for Roth these days, he is a writer both blessed and cursed with an uncanny eye for controversial material and an ear for dialogue so brilliant that one nearly forgives his excesses. And if an even deeper truth be told, what delimits Roth is nothing more or less than Roth himself, for one could argue that psychic projections and internecine battles were *always* his most congenial subject; sadly enough, his art pays the price for his continuing inability to see life as somehow wider, deeper, more significant than book-after-book accounts of his own *kvetches*. "Higher Education" is a good example of Zuckerman/Roth at "their" most representative. Doc Zuckerman is not entirely right about the story but, then again, he is not entirely wrong either.

By contrast, Bellow is both more expansive and more humane. In "The Old System," arguably his best short story, he not only assesses the costs of assimilation, but also the larger matters of life's ultimate meaning: "It was only an intimation of understanding. A promise that mankind might—*might* mind you—eventually, through its gift which might—*might* again!—be a divine gift, comprehend why it lived. Why life, why death" (82–82). Granted, Dr. Braun's "might" is tentative (how could it *not* be?), but as Faulkner liked to put it, the words speak eloquently to a human heart in conflict with itself.

I readily admit that my "new look" at "The Old System" will not much interest those who define the *new* in terms of Lacan or Derrida, Kristeva or Foucault. But, then again, Bellow's story does not particularly lend itself to such discussion. Rather, it strikes me as a richer example of "what we talk about when we talk about love" than anything in Raymond Carver's canon or, indeed, in most contemporary American fiction.

Works Cited

Bellow, Saul. *Herzog*. New York: Viking Press, 1964.
———. *Mr. Sammler's Planet*. New York: Viking Press, 1970.
———. "The Old System." In *Mosby's Memoirs*, 43–83. New York: Viking Press, 1968.
Johnson, Gregory. "Jewish Assimilation and Codes of Manners in Saul Bellow's 'The Old System.'" *Studies in American-Jewish Literature* 9, no. 1 (Spring 1990): 48–60.
Kiernan, Robert F. *Saul Bellow*. New York: Frederick Ungar, 1989.
Roth, Philip. *The Ghost Writer*. New York: Farrar, Straus & Giroux, 1979.

Zapotec Man and the Torajan Granny: "Mosby's Memoirs" and the Sacrifice of the Heart

JUDIE NEWMAN

"Do you know what that is?" my host reached out and patted a large bundle in one corner of his living room. It looked like the bundle of old clothes you pick out for the charity shop. . . . "It's my grandmother." Before the advent of television, no Western house was complete without a granny to sit with the children and spout idiotic wisdoms at them. Many Torajan houses still have one, but she may be dead. The body is wrapped in vast amounts of absorbent cloth to soak up the juices of putrefaction. Quite quickly, the whole bundle becomes relatively inoffensive . . .

"Aren't you going to greet her?"

"Pleased to meet you granny." A gesture was difficult: a handshake was impossible, but it would have been overly familiar to pat the bundle.

"Wah, that's good."

"How long has she been dead?"

He looked at me appalled. "We don't say that. She's 'sleeping' or 'has a headache.' She won't die until she leaves the house. She's been sleeping for three years now." He reached over and took down a huge cassette player to offer musical entertainment. The tapes, I noticed, were stored in alphabetical order on the body which made a handy shelf.

"You'll miss her when she dies," I said (Barley, 54, 55).

Nigel Barley's account of his encounter with a Torajan grandmother offers a convenient point of entry to Saul Bellow's "Mosby's

Memoirs," a tale in which the imaginative remapping of the border between life and death is a key operation. As Barley demonstrates (in the longer anthropological study of death customs, from which the above is extracted), death may be seen in the West as a precise point in time, but in many cultures it is a continuing process, even, indeed, a process capable of going into reverse. Any reader who has contemplated the enormous variety of mortuary practices and concepts chronicled by anthropology will concur that "it is striking how little other people's views on the borders of death coincide with our own" (Barley, 55). The geography of death is not universal: the Styx has a pronounced tendency to wander in its course. Chinese who die abroad and are brought home for burial, for example, are treated as alive and welcomed as such; they will officially die only much later. In Hindu ritual the deceased dies only at the moment when the skull is split on the funeral pyre. Conversely, an ascetic who has renounced the world through symbolic death needs no further rites and is slid into the Ganges without further ado. His social death has preceded the arrival of the biological Grim Reaper. Among the African Dowayos a person who faints has "died," even if revival immediately follows. This is not (unlike say, Western orgasmic imagery) a metaphor. The Dowayos insist that such people did die, but then they simply stopped being dead (Barley, 47).

As several commentators have argued, the decline of the belief in purgatory in the West after the Reformation has encouraged the tendency to assume that we have no social relation with previous generations, that those on this side of the frontier can no longer affect those on the other—and vice versa. Each individual henceforth keeps his own balance sheet and the next world withers away (Barley, 79). In much of the world, however, as the Torajan granny demonstrates, the dead remain an important part of society. Even in the West, vestiges of the concept of residual death persist in such beliefs as the bleeding of the wounds of the murder victim in the presence of the killer or in our uncertainties concerning the status of the brain dead, the aborted foetus, or the "heart-beating cadaver" necessary for successful kidney transplants. Western culture feels the need to pin down the precise moment and cause of death. (How often does a death certificate ascribe death to "old age"?) Other cultures are less "rational" and meet different social needs in different ways. In the Solomons there are no precise equivalents for the English terms "dead" or "alive"; one term includes the dead, the very old and the very sick (Barley, 54–57). Memorial practices may deny death—or anticipate it. Amongst the Dogon of Mali, when funerary rites have been performed for a person who is "missing presumed dead," there is no possibility of accepting him as alive again, even if he returns in robust good health. In other cultures the anticipation of death finds its clearest application in the entombment of the living—the live burial of wives or servants with the deceased, or the walling up of saintly recluses. In the West the segregation of the living from the dead is rigidly observed. No photographs are taken of the dead, for example, whereas in Java (as in many other cultures) it is normal to photograph the corpse with the family who imitate the "tenseless" expression on the face of the dead (Barley, 72). As Barley comments, our photographs are forgeries of memory in which everyone is always smiling. "In the Western album, the last scene, the funeral, is always missing" (Barley, 72). Memoirs are, for obvious reasons, a similar case in point. Although ostensibly anticipating death which is implicitly acknowledged as imminent, they also deny it. When Willis Mosby sets out to memorialize himself, his intention is to defeat death rather than to acknowledge it, to keep his reputation alive and to prolong his social existence by assuring himself a place in the historical record. The ambiguity of the borders of life and death is powerfully asserted in the tale, in a fantasy which obsesses Mosby. As he tours the ruins of Mitla,

> Mosby was going once more through an odd and complex fantasy. It was that he was dead. He had died. He continued however to live. His doom was to live life to the end as Mosby. In the fantasy he considered this his purgatory. And when had death occurred? In a collision years ago. He had thought it a near thing then. The cars were demolished. The actual Mosby was killed. But another Mosby was pulled from the car. (171)

It is particularly appropriate that Mosby's fantasy of self-impersonation, doubling, and death as an open frontier should occur in Mitla, near Oaxaca in Mexico. The Oaxaca valley is an area which has attracted anthropologists in droves, including Bronislaw Malinowski, and Elsie Clews Parsons, whose magnum opus, *Mitla: Town of the Souls*, is referred to by Mosby (171).[1] Interest in the area and scholarly work shows a marked increase from 1965 onward (Whitecotton, vii). Susan Drucker-Brown notes that an anthropological bibliography of Oaxaca lists 1,002 items between 1974 and 1979 (Malinowski, 43). As Bellow would have known from his anthropological background (Newman, 1991) and from personal visits to Oaxaca, Mitla was the focus for the mortuary cults of the Zapotecs. According to local tradition Mitla was the center of the world of the dead (Leslie). In Mitla the Spanish term for hell was translated into Zapotec as "gabihl"—a realm of the dead coexistent with this world, where souls lived much as in their own lifetime. Heaven was not a dwelling place of souls, but a vague, faraway place where God and the saints lived. People who died lived on in the "gabihl," close to their living relatives. Tombs in the area have been exhaustively studied. (To vary an old joke, the typical Mitlan family appears to consist of parents, children, an anthropologist, and an archaeologist.) The monuments reveal powerful images of both denied and anticipated death. According to tradition the more fanatical Zapotecs practiced a form of self-sacrifice by being voluntarily cast into the subterranean charnel house, there to wander amidst festering corpses until they also died (Verrill, 71). One of the most recent commentators on the tombs, Arthur G. Miller, notes that in pre-Hispanic history Mitla (the name derives from Nahuatl "Miquitla"—land of the many dead) was primarily a place for the interaction of the dead with the living (Miller, 221). In the pre-Hispanic past the Zapotecs, like the Torajan, literally lived with their dead in houses which included tombs beneath the living quarters. These residential tombs were not sealed up for eternity but periodically reentered and rearranged, the walls repainted, as the death of a family member necessitated a social reorganization of the tomb. The walls were painted with red hematite pigment, as was the corpse, perhaps as an image of life-giving blood. In short, "the Zapotec response to mortality was to live with it and to make it part of everyday and ritual life" (Miller, xix). As a result whole generations of the dead were incorporated into the family unit. "For the Zapotec, death was a particularly powerful social bond that literally cemented the present with the past. They lived with death" (Miller, 31).

It is significant that, although Bellow's frame tale situates his memorialist in Mitla, Mosby's memories center upon Europe in the immediate aftermath of the Second World War and upon a Jewish character, Lustgarten, who is repeatedly characterized as "Zapotec" because of his squat, black-haired look and the shape of his nose (155). Lustgarten is introduced into the memoirs as comic relief and essentially takes over the tale. The conjunction of Mitla with post-Holocaust Europe suggests that the topic at the heart of the story concerns other images of mass death, of families dead together, and of combined anticipation and denial of death. Mexico provides a substitute place of death—an area which may be envisaged either as a place where there are many dead—or no dead at all; a place where nobody is dead because people remain in close contact across the boundary between life and death, a place where a fantasy of dying-but-not-dying can be fully staged. Staginess is a particularly appropriate term. Bellow stages the act of writing within the tale, as Mosby writes memoirs which we read over his shoulder, in order to distance himself protectively from the material and to accentuate the impression of a stagy, self-conscious dramatization, a ritual.

Let us return for a moment to the Torajan granny. While the tale makes serious points about liminality and death, it is also a funny story. Indeed the "blurb" for Barley's study describes the whole volume as "blackly comic." Barley himself notes that

> comedy and indulgence too have their place at death. Madness and pantomime, the slapstick flinging of excrement and insults, attempts to copulate with one's grandmother or the deceased, heavy sexual trading, gluttony and drunkenness are all well documented as part of regular, obligatory funeral arrangements. (Barley, 34)

In Britain few funeral games survived the liturgical controversies of the sixteenth century (though an Irish wake may offer some degree of counterexample.) The "joke slot" in the Western funeral has been largely reduced to the variety of ways in which cremated ashes can be disposed (Barley, 39). The Mexican Day of the Dead, however, involves a joking relationship to the dead, even today, with much jollity, dancing, excess, and the mass consumption of skulls made of chocolate or sugar paste. Essentially the dead are being welcomed back to the land of the living and royally entertained. Joking, however, need not simply represent an affirmation of life. It may function less as an image of irrepressible vitality than as a counterirritant. Ritual jokes may be quite aggressive in content, using dirt, insult, and ambiguity to express the nature of a dangerous and marginal event, with a very thin line between solace and aggression. (Shakespearean fools are a case in point.) Ritual joking, then, may not involve "real" amusement any more than ritual mourning involves real grief (Barley, 40). In some cultures smiles and laughter are not necessarily signs of joy. One of Barley's colleagues who worked in West Africa after the war could never explain why, when she showed local people the first pictures coming out of the concentration camps, they laughed. If she had witnessed a funeral among the Nyakusa (Barley, 34), who have formal joking partners whose function is to continually exasperate both dead and bereaved, or the Betsilea of Madagascar (who have fights between men and bulls, drink themselves into unconsciousness, and cover their faces with the shroud-cloths in order to engage in blind, orgiastic, and incestuous sex), she might have understood that there is more than one "right response" to death. Her experience has a particular relevance to "Mosby's Memoirs" in which Bellow performs his own comic mourning ritual, as a means to confront the deaths of millions in the

Holocaust, and as a reflexive investigation of his own writerly activity. Published in 1968, immediately before *Mr. Sammler's Planet* in which the Holocaust is finally treated directly (albeit in the memories of Sammler, an intellectual as sure of his own self-importance as Mosby and similarly scornful of those who fail to meet his high standards), "Mosby's Memoirs" approaches its buried topic circumspectly, through layers of indirection, surrogate characters, and substitute geograph-ies, until at its close the narrator is finally able to enter the tomb.

This is not the first time that Bellow has used an oblique strategy to approach material of this sort. Bellow's treatment of the Holocaust in his fiction has been characterized by indirection. In a 1990 interview Bellow was asked about the relative absence of the Holocaust in his writing. He agreed that

> there were lots of things I hadn't been able to incorporate. Things that got away from me. The Holocaust for one . . . . I may even have been partly sealed off from it. (*IAAU*, 312)

According to Bellow, it was only in 1959, when he visited Auschwitz, that the Holocaust "landed its whole weight on me" (313). He admitted to finding it odd that he had not been moved to write about it. "I can't interpret it creditably to myself. I'm still wondering at it. I lost close relatives" (313). Bellow's reluctance to confront the topic—understandable as it is—becomes potentially more comprehensible in the description offered, in the same interview, of his childhood. At the age of eight, Bellow spent six months in hospital with T.B. Already a good reader, he could read his chart at the end of the bed and knew, even at that age, that "it was very unpromising" (289). In the ward he was constantly exposed to the death of children. As a result, Bellow felt forever after that he had been in some fashion "excused from death" (289), "that it was a triumph, that I had gotten away with it" (289). Survival guilt therefore marks Bellow's fiction from an early age. As an American Jew, of course, Bellow escaped the fate of European Jewry. In an interview, Bellow was asked about the intellectual impact of the Second World War. He replied that he had completely misunderstood the war because he was under the influence of Marxism. Although Kristallnacht gave him pause, Bellow, as a Trotskyist, stood by the belief that a workers' state, however degenerate, could not wage an Imperialist war. Bellow was indeed such a committed Trotskyist that he arranged to meet the great man in Mexico. Unfortunately, death got there first. On the morning of their scheduled meeting Trotsky was assassinated; Bellow saw him only in the emergency room of the hospital, just after he had died.[2] Later he drew the moral, commenting that as a result he understood

> what a far-reaching power could do with us; how easy it was for a despot to order a death; how little it took to kill us; how slight a hold we, with our historical philosophies, our ideas, programs, purposes, wills, had on the matter we were made of. (*IAAU*, 101)

After France fell, Bellow came to his senses: "not only did I feel that my Jewish Marxist friends were wrong in theory, but I was horrified by the positions they—we—had taken" (*IAAU*, 310). Later Bellow looked back on his political views as comically naive:

> Our own movement. . . . was often foolish, even comically absurd. During the Spanish civil war, the issue of material aid for the Spanish republic was furiously debated by comrades who didn't have a dime to contribute. (*IAAU*, 100–101)

In *The Victim*, as I have argued elsewhere (Newman, 1996), Bellow constructs in Allbee an anti-Semitic double for his hero, Leventhal. In allowing Allbee to persecute him, Leventhal finally exorcizes his own guilt at surviving and confronts the degree of responsibility which he owes to the past. As an alter ego, Allbee is drawn very much in terms of Otto Rank's analysis of the figure of the double. Originally an insurance against death (as in the first double, the immortal soul), the double is also a figure which may reverse its aspect, becoming a harbinger of death and the enemy of the survivor. In Rank's analysis the double appears as a defense against the dissolution of the ego—whether in death or in sexual love (hence the frequency with which doubles interrupt sexual activity or thwart relationships). In "Mosby's Memoirs" death hangs over the action; Mosby is old and writing his memoirs. He describes himself as a ruin (154). It is therefore unsurprising that a double appears in the shape of Lustgarten. Importantly, Jewish Lustgarten suffers from the same political naivety as the younger Bellow. Mosby chronicles the recondite examination which he and his friends made of the same issues: "Whether the American working class should give material aid to the Loyalist government of Spain. . . . There was, of course, no material aid to give. But had there been any, should it have been given" (155). Lustgarten also displays an agonized ability to split hairs over the issue of Finland. "Here the painful point of doctrine to be resolved was whether a Workers' State like the Soviet Union . . . could wage an Imperialistic War" (156). Jewish Lustgarten remains in America throughout the war "just sitting around" (163), but arrives in Europe immediately after its end, intent on making a fortune. Mosby's comments foreground the Holocaust:

> Lustgarten may have felt, qua Jew, that he had a right to grow rich in the German boom. That all Jews had natural claims beyond the Rhine. On land enriched by Jewish ashes. And you never could be sure, seated on a sofa, that it was not stuffed or upholstered with Jewish hair. And he would not use German soap. (159)

If Lustgarten is a double to Mosby, he is also an emblematic figure of the Jew who has survived unscathed. The evocation of the ubiquity of Jewish remains recalls the description of Mitla as a place of death. Mosby, in poetic mode, registers the mountains

> Whose fat laps are rolling
> On the skulls of whole families. (170)

Mitla offers a seductive locale for Bellow's imaginative response to the Holocaust, a place marked by sacrifice and expiation, where death is emphasized as a negotiable frontier, where one's family dead can be maintained in close social proximity, where the relationship between the generations and the community of human beings is insisted upon. "Mosby's Memoirs" evolves in response to the questions posed by mass death: how can the dead be accepted as dead and properly mourned? Does a less "rational," non-Western belief system offer the right way to carry out the process of mourning?

"Mosby's Memoirs" shares many features with *The Victim*— doubles, Holocaust material, a near-death experience. The startling difference is that of tone. In *The Victim* the mode is largely tragic. In the denouement Allbee almost succeeds in gassing Leventhal. The later tale is comic— though it is a comedy which has a very black edge. More than one reader has, indeed, found that the unstable mixture of comedy, irony, farce, and horror creates a problem in reading the tale. Robert F. Kiernan describes it perceptively (132) as "a scenario which owes more to the Marx brothers than to Marx" whereas others have emphasized Mosby's guilt (Hyland), the purgatorial nature of the experience (Dutton), and the satire on Mosby's intellectualism (Fuchs). If, however, the tale is read within the context of ritual mourning comedy, it becomes more comprehensible.

The characteristic note is struck from the beginning, in the association of comedy and aggression:

> The birds chirped away. Fweet, Fweet, Bootchee-Fweet. Doing all the
> things naturalists say they do. Expressing abysmal depths of aggression,
> which only man—Stupid Man—heard as innocent. (149)

The nonsense language foregrounds the conventional association of fools
with birdsong as noted by Willeford in his study of fools in culture, and
exemplified in the fool's coxcomb. Fools are associated also with death
(death as jester, death who makes fools of us all) and are therefore
unkillable—because already liminal. (The obvious example is that of the
circus clown who jumps to his feet after being hit over the head with a
sledgehammer.) Forms of duality also run through the range of clowns
and fools, as in the ventriloquist and his dummy, the comedy "team" of
straight man and comic, mirrors in a fun house, and the device of the
foolpair (Lear and Fool, Don Quixote and Sancho Panza, Don Giovanni
and Leporello). "Often when we recognize someone as a fool we do so
partly because we sense that he is somehow double, even if he is alone"
(Willeford, 42). Although Mosby is emphatically alone in Oaxaca, his
activity as a memoir writer effectively doubles him. The narration oscillates
between Mosby as first-person narrator and Mosby as third-person
character: "Mosby speaking of himself in the third person as Henry
Adams had done in *The Education of Henry Adams*" (156). Doubling
himself in his memoirs as a defense against death effectively delivers him,
however, into the hands of another double, Lustgarten. Initially
Lustgarten also has a defensive role. Mosby is concerned that his memoirs
are not very funny. His own wit has more in common with death than with
life. His jokes are killing. One example is indicative: "Willis Mosby, who
was in Toledo with me when the Alcázar fell, made me die laughing" (150).
As in "Him with His Foot in His Mouth," Mosby's satirical sallies are
deadly: "He was like the Guerrilla Mosby of the Civil War. When he
galloped in, all were slaughtered" (166). In order to inject some comic
relief into his account (and thus keep the reader reading and Mosby's name
alive), Mosby re-creates Lustgarten as a foil, a comic figure to his own
straight man. If Lustgarten's political pretensions are absurd, his later
attempts to storm the bastions of capitalism are even more laughable.
Swindled by his business partner, betrayed by his wife, he is comprehen-
sively fooled by all and sundry. He, too, has connections with death,
however. When Mosby first meets him in Paris, he is recalled in the blood
red interior of a bank, identical in colour to Napoleon's sarcophagus in Les
Invalides. Lustgarten is employed at this point by the U.S. Army in graves
registration, much occupied with cemeteries and monuments. Lustgarten
also survives a car crash, an event which associates him with Mosby's

fantasy self and with survival guilt. Prosaically, Lustgarten laments his survival (163) because his life insurance would at least have covered the financial losses of his mother, uncle, and brother—all ruined by the crash. Survival here is more reminiscent of the unkillable clown than of some sinister ghostly double.

If Bellow ascribes his own political errors satirically to Lustgarten, it is none the less striking that Lustgarten is allowed to expiate them. After his fiasco as would-be capitalist Lustgarten gives Marxism one more chance and departs for Yugoslavia, "a candidate for resurrection" (165) for what he assumes is a "V.I.P. deal" (165) as a foreign observer, with seminars in dialectics to boot. "I really believe Tito may redeem Marxism by actually transforming the dictatorship of the proletariat" (165), he proclaims. He returns emaciated, sun-blackened, sick, and embittered from what has turned out to be a forced labor brigade. Lustgarten may not have experienced the actual horrors of the Holocaust, but as a member of a chain gang in Dalmatia he has been thoroughly punished for his errors. Abused by fate, battered and ragged, Lustgarten remains a clown in the Chaplinesque mode. Tellingly his wife shares his clownishness—they are a fool pair—and it entails an image of doubleness:

> Trudy too was funny, however. What a large belly she had. Since individuals are sometimes born from a twin impregnation, the organism carrying the underdeveloped brother or sister in vestigial form . . . Mosby often thought that Trudy had a little sister inside her. And to him she was a clown. (172)

Even Trudy's face registers self-division—the left eye wanders (159). For all his amusement, Mosby is now, however, reminded of several uncomfortable facts—his own adultery with Trudy for example. Like any good double, Mosby had come between Lustgarten and the object of his affections, with disastrous consequences: "his vision of Lustgarten as a funny man was transmitted to Trudy. She could not be the wife of such a funny man" (172). If Lustgarten fulfils one comic purpose, that of the fool who survives everything and the expiatory comedian, Mosby (who makes fun of Lustgarten in his misery) fulfils that of the joking partner, the counter-irritant.

Up to this point it may appear that Mosby's strategy has worked rather well. The tale of the Lustgartens, undeniably comic, holds the reader's attention and (as Mosby remarks) has a certain symmetry. "There was a coda: The thing had quite good form" (168). Lustgarten is glimpsed once more on his way to the offices of *Fortune* Magazine, prosperous, remarried, and happy. Predictably, he is on the wrong elevator for *Fortune*, the story of his life as opposed to Mosby's secure place in the public eye. At the close of the tale, however, as the reader leaves the joking partner behind to return to the frame tale in Mexico, the story reverses its aspect and turns back upon itself. ("There was a coda: The thing had quite good form.") By allowing Lustgarten to take over the story, Mosby allows him to become a threat to his identity rather than a means of defense. Essentially Lustgarten's counterexample reveals the extent of Mosby's social death. Unmarried, friendless, childless, Mosby has suppressed all human ties— unlike Lustgarten, a keen father and uxorious husband. Ruled by his intellect, Mosby's concern with rationality and objectivity has been absolute. Mosby had declared during the war that the Germans were winning because their managerial revolution had come first (151). He went on to assert that "however deplorable the concentration camps had been, they showed at least the rationality of German political ideas" (151–52). To adopt Mosby's cold rationality would be akin to killing the dead all over again. Mosby scorns Lustgarten's tears ("Such unmastered emotion was abhorrent" [163]) and restricts his comment on Lustgarten's passionate fatherhood to the supercilious statement that "for Plato, this childbreeding is the lowest level of creativity" (169). For all his clever political-historical pronouncements, Mosby has no actual connection to society at all.

At the close of the tale, Mosby sets off to tour the monuments of Mitla. The tour begins with the tree of Tule, an image of continuity in community between the living and the dead: "A world in itself! It could contain communities . . . [recalling] a primal tree, occupied by early ancestors" (170). Mosby's fantasy of death-in-life recurs at this point, immediately before he enters the final tomb. His own self-division has now become overt, as the language of the story becomes that of Beckettian clowning. A textual double act is staged in his memories:

> At this time, Mosby had been making fun of people.
> "Why?"
> "Because he had needed to."
> "Why?"
> "Because." (172–73)

Entering the tomb, dyed red, Mosby contemplates the horrors of human sacrifice—an image of the loss of the heart which has made him a Zapotec man in a way in which Lustgarten never was. Around him he admires the precision of the cut stone, the geometrical masses and the mathematical perfection of the masonry. As Dan Fuchs has argued, the precision, calculation, and sacrifice of the human all align Mosby with the tomb. H. Porter Abbott comments that the Mexican sepulchre is an image of the tomb which Mosby has constructed for himself—and called his life. Contemplating the tomb he reflects on the contrast between foolish Lustgarten, "who didn't have to happen" (173), and historically important Mosby, a complete and finished product. "He had completed himself in this cogitating, unlaughing, stone, iron, nonsensical form" (173). Nonsensical, but unlaughing, Mosby is a fool, but not an unkillable one. Mosby had intended the Lustgarten digression as "the correction of pride by laughter" (167), a means of maintaining human interest in an inhuman story. Where kings have jesters for purposes of ritual insult and self-revelation, Mosby has Lustgarten. But Lustgarten is the jester who betrays Mosby into a real confrontation with death. By creating a third-person self, Mosby dehumanizes and depersonalizes himself to the point of extinction; Lustgarten steps into the character vacuum. All Mosby's efforts to defer death, to fantasize it away, now founder on the logic of his own belief in precision, objectivity, and reason. In the tomb he is seized with horror:

> His heart was paralysed. His lungs would not draw. Jesus! I cannot catch my breath! To be shut in here! To be dead here! Suppose one were! Not as in accidents which ended but did not quite end existence. Dead-dead. (174)

In the last scene the typical forgery of memory in the memoirs is corrected. As in Bellow's encounter with death in Mexico (Trotsky), the scene registers the fact that death is inevitable, for all Mosby's intellectual historicizing. The reader will also note that in the face of the finality of death Mosby reverses from third to first person ("His heart . . . his lungs . . . I cannot"), no longer split between his two selves. Stooping, he emerges from the tomb, at last a penitent survivor.

If "Mosby's Memoirs" allows Lustgarten to expiate previous errors, Mosby (the writer, the wit, the thinker about history) does not get off so lightly. And nor, perhaps, does Bellow's audience. For if Mosby is doubled, so are we. As an audience to "Mosby's Memoirs" we read of the imaginary audience for which Mosby is providing the comic relief which we are enjoying, comic relief which also takes us to the edge of the tomb. Like Mosby in Mitla, we are placed in an ambiguously liminal position, simultaneously within two tales, two audiences and two locations. The form of "Mosby's Memoirs" thus duplicates its theme. In the face of death Bellow multiplies the number of characters and readers, establishing a convergence between story theme and narrative environment, as inset tale and frame tale coalesce into one. At the end Mosby is restored to his individual self and comes back from the death-in-life which has been his. As Kiernan notes, "to his surprise the reader ends up respecting a man he suspects he should loathe" (135). Arguably the reader's empathy results from the uneasy sense that he too has been doubled and fooled. Reading "Mosby's Memoirs" is uncomfortable, offering an experience of both solace and aggression. If Lustgarten's expiation reassures, Mosby's fate offers no such relief. The tale also constitutes a thorough investigation of the writer's activity. It is a mark of the seriousness of Bellow's exploration of the issues posed by the Holocaust that, as a comic writer, he implicitly interrogates his own practice. Is comedy a form of denial of death, an evasion? Alternatively, is the comic writer a "guerrilla" whose comedy merely enlarges the field of slaughter? Arguably, Bellow's comedy—dark as it is—provides a necessary counterirritant in an extended ritual of mourning, insisting upon the vital role of the imagination in maintaining the social relation to the dead.

Notes

1. Elsie Clews Parsons's work on the sacred clowns of American native peoples, and among the Zapotecs in Mitla, is also relevant to the tale. See Parsons, 1934 and 1936.
2. Bellow's second published story, "The Mexican General," draws upon this experience.

Works Cited

Abbott, H. Porter. "Saul Bellow and the 'Lost Cause' of Character." In *Saul Bellow in the 1980s: A Collection of Critical Essays*, edited by Gloria L. Cronin and L. H. Goldman, 113–36. East Lansing: Michigan State University Press, 1989.

Barley, Nigel. *Dancing on the Grave: Encounters with Death*. London: John Murray, 1995.

Bellow, Saul. *It All Adds Up: From the Dim Past to the Uncertain Future, A Non-Fiction Collection*. London: Secker and Warburg, 1994.

———. "The Mexican General." *Partisan Review* 9 (May–June 1942): 178–94.

———. *Mosby's Memoirs and Other Stories*. Reprint, London: Penguin, 1971. New York: Viking , 1968.

———. *The Victim*. Reprint, London: Penguin, 1966. New York: Vanguard, 1947.

Dutton, Robert R. *Saul Bellow*. Revised edition. Vol. 181 of Twayne's United States Author Series. New York: Twayne, 1982.

Fuchs, Daniel. *Saul Bellow: Vision and Revision*, 43–49. Durham: Duke University Press, 1984.

Hyland, Peter. *Saul Bellow*. Modern Novelists Series. New York: St. Martin's Press, 1992.

Kiernan, Robert F. *Saul Bellow*. New York: Frederick Ungar, 1989.

Leslie, Charles M. *Now We Are Civilized: A Study of the World View of the Zapotec Indians of Mitla, Oaxaca*. Detroit: Wayne State University Press, 1960.

Malinowski, Bronislaw, and Julio de la Fuente. *Malinowski in Mexico: The Economics of a Mexican Market System*. Edited and with an introduction by Susan Drucker-Brown. Boston and London: Routledge & Kegan Paul, 1985.

Miller, Arthur G. *The Painted Tombs of Oaxaca, Mexico: Living with the Dead*. Cambridge: Cambridge University Press, 1995.

Newman, Judie. "Bellow's Ransom Tale: The Holocaust, *The Victim*, and The Double." *Saul Bellow Journal* 14, no. 1 (Winter 1996): 3–18.

———. "Saul Bellow and Social Anthropology." In *Saul Bellow at Seventy-five: A Collection of Critical Essays*, edited by Gerhard Bach, 137–49. Tubingen: Gunter Narr Verlag, 1991.

———. "Saul Bellow and Trotsky." *Saul Bellow Journal* 1.1 (1981): 26–31.

Parsons, Elsie Clews. *Mitla: Town of the Souls and Other Zapoteco-Speaking Pueblos of Oaxaca, Mexico*. Chicago: University of Chicago Press, 1936.

———. "The Sacred Clowns of the Pueblo and Mayo-Yaqui Indians." *American Anthropologist* 36, no. 4 (October–December, 1934): 491–514.

Rank, Otto. *The Double: A Psychoanalytic Study*, translated and edited by Harry Tucker, Jr. Chapel Hill: University of North Carolina Press, 1971.

Verrill, Hyatt, and Ruth Hyatt. *America's Ancient Civilizations*. New York: G. P. Putnam's Sons, 1953.

Whitecotton, Joseph W. *The Zapotecs: Princes, Priests and Peasants*. Norman: University of Oklahoma Press, 1978.

Willeford, William. *The Fool and His Sceptre: A Study in Clowns and Jesters and Their Audience*. Evanston, Ill.: Northwestern University Press, 1969.

The Achievement of Saul Bellow's
Seize the Day

RALPH CIANCIO

If the short novel *Seize the Day*[1] is not the central story of our time, as one critic has commented, it is Saul Bellow's supreme achievement so far and, I think, a masterpiece of the first order. To be sure, it cannot lay claim to what is perhaps especially memorable about several of his full-length and more popular novels—the intellectual weight and lavish treatment of scene in *Herzog;* the rich variety of experience and linguistic range of *The Adventures of Augie March;* the comic and sweeping inventiveness of *Henderson the Rain King*—and its impact perhaps is not as immediately powerful. But its impact endures, and ultimately it is more satisfying because it derives from the achievement of perfect form. By this I do not mean to suggest that the book's content is more tractable because slighter in scope and less probing; that the difference between *Seize the Day* and Bellow's longer novels, in other words, can be reduced to a simple matter of purpose and the comparative freedom these dissimilar genres allow. Certainly its content is compressed, but one would hardly want to call it a thin or less complex story for that. To the contrary, its content, enlarged as well as intensified by metaphor, is far reaching indeed: ostensibly an indictment of contemporary urban society, the story also encompasses religious and, ultimately, metaphysical issues. Nor, of course, do I mean to suggest that Bellow's longer novels are without discipline, the prime example to the contrary being *The Victim.* But as Leslie Fiedler has stated, the tight organization of *The Victim* represents only one tendency of Bellow's diverging styles; the tendency toward looseness and release, as in *Augie March,* is the other. Only in *Seize the Day* are both tendencies counterpoised, and to great effect, so as to produce a low-keyed but

Reprinted by permission of the *James Joyce Quarterly* from *Literature and Theology.* Vol. 7 of the University of Tulsa Department of English Monograph Series, edited by Thomas F. Staley and Lester F. Zimmerman, 49-80. Tulsa, OK: University of Tulsa, 1969.

passionate "perilous rest,"[2] a tragic-comic tension and balance, Fiedler might have added, which is precisely the stylistic correlative to reality as Bellow's fiction explores it. In this respect alone, it is his most completely realized work.

In fact, *Seize the Day* coheres like a poem. "I . . . think that the novel has imitated poetry far too much recently," Bellow has said. "In its severity and style and devotion to exact form."[3] He ought to know: by his statement Bellow meant to explain his adoption of the picaresque form in *Augie*, but by then he had already written *Seize the Day*. The aim of the analysis below, which hopefully will give to this remarkable work some measure of its due,[4] is to explain its unity, how it holds together as a "poem" in conjunction with its meaning.

I

The story's controlling idea is propounded by Dr. Tamkin, a beguiling humbug sage posing as a psychologist and a friend in order to bilk Tommy Wilhelm, the protagonist, of his last seven hundred dollars.

> In here, the human bosom—mine, yours, everybody's—there isn't just one soul. There's a lot of souls. But there are two main ones, the real soul and a pretender soul. (70)

Every man wants to live and to be loved, Tamkin argues, but because he lacks confidence in his real soul—what nature has made of him, the source of life—and the wisdom to comply with its strict demands, he finds nothing in himself to love and consequently seeks the approval of others as justification for self-approval; he turns his energies outward. In doing so, he activates the pretender soul, a false, theatrical self whose "interest . . . is the same as the social life, the society mechanism"—namely, vanity and the acquisition of financial power, the only value and criterion of success society honors—and the individual thus pursues money feverishly to prove his distinction. But he does so at the price of extinction, says Tamkin. To begin with, the pretender is sadistic; money-making is nothing but a disguised form of aggression:

> People go to the market to kill. They say, 'I'm going to make a killing.' It's not accidental. Only they haven't got the genuine courage to kill, and they erect a symbol of it. The money. They make a killing by a fantasy. (69)

Misdirected by the pretender, the individual's love turns to hate, his passion for life to a passion for death; and when the real soul, victimized and maimed by its own energy, is laid to rest, the individual suffers a dehumanized, death-in-life existence. This is not all. After a time, enfeebled by efforts to overreach itself and scarred with guilt from having lived a falsehood, the real soul rebels and becomes masochistic:

> The true soul is the one that pays the price. It suffers and gets sick, and it realizes that the pretender can't be loved. Because it is a lie. The true soul loves the truth. And when the true soul feels like this, it wants to kill the pretender. The love has turned to hate. Then you become dangerous. A killer. You have to kill the deceiver. (71)

The paradoxical corollary to this internecine and inward strife is twofold: every man is his own best lover and at once his own worst enemy, and all suicide is murder and all murder suicide.

Yet life is hardly meant to be so grave, as the affirmative and complementary side of Tamkin's philosophy stresses. The essence of it he writes out in a prescriptive poem, "Mechanism vs Functionalism [,] Ism vs Hism," the hero of which, the doctor says, is "sick humanity" in general and Wilhelm in particular. A ludicrous piece of doggerel, the poem nonetheless makes its humanistic point. Man is the center of all things; his eternity and rightful due, his cradle to joy and ecstasy rests with him. But it rests in the here-and-now and not in some future or transcendent state, "at the foot of Mt. Serenity" and not at the top; and it derives from his share in the brotherhood of man, in his common humanity rather than in his uncommonness as an individual. The poem thus urges man to put a halt to his strivings, to accept creation as it is given, the holiness of nature, "earth-moon-sea, the trinity," and his eminent place in its scheme; it urges man to know and to accept himself as he is, the limitations of his blessings as well as the blessings of his limitations; it urges man to seize the day and amen:

> Seek ye then that which art not there
> In thine own glory let thyself rest.
> Witness. Thy power is not bare.
> Thou art King. Thou art at thy best. (75)

Perhaps we should remark from the very start that Tamkin's ideas are the gauge of Bellow's primary interest, spiritual landscape, and in turn the gauge of his dramatic method, the fusion of the symbolic and the naturalistic, of metaphor and material image; to speak of one is to speak of the other. And whereas they perhaps seem conventional enough stated boldly and summarily, Tamkin's ideas cannot be separated either from his corny expression of them or from his motives as a confidence man: he obviously uses them as part of his pitch, he means to seize the day himself. Indeed, Tamkin's ambiguous character not only gives vitality and depth to his ideas but also is axial to both the structure of the story and to Wilhelm's fate; we shall have to ponder him at length. But the irony notwithstanding, and however commonplace, what is necessary to see first is that he in fact utters the truth, and a truth of considerable magnitude. What begins with the schizoid estrangement of the individual and his authentic self begets the estrangement of father and son, the individual and the contemporary urban world, the Jew and his spiritual heritage, the individual and humanity—issues which Bellow manages to encompass in the short breadth of his novel by focusing squarely on the plight of his protagonist and expanding centrifugally, as it were, the antagonism between the real and pretender souls according to Tamkin's diagnosis.

The perfect schlemiel, a failure at middle-age, Wilhelm enters the scene a desperate man on the day before Yom Kippur. He has lost his job with the Rojax Company; he is separated from his children and mercilessly hounded for alimony by Margaret, who refuses to give him a divorce; he is skeptical of his future with Olive, the woman from Roxbury he adores; and he is fearful that he will lose the money he has invested with Tamkin. In short, he faces the total ruination of his life. For all this he is largely to blame; he is the victim of his own blunders, a series of mistakes perpetrated even though he knew they would bring on disaster:

> This was typical of Wilhelm. After much thought and hesitation and debate he invariably took the course he had rejected innumerable times. Ten such decisions made up the history of his life. He had decided that it would be a bad mistake to go to Hollywood, and then he went. He had made up his mind not to marry his wife, but ran off and got married. He had resolved not to invest money with Tamkin, and then he had given him the check. (23)

His feelings, the instinctual and the irrational, even the desire to fail, it is suggested, have governed Wilhelm's life. In everything, in fact, in all his habits as well as in all his endeavors, he is radically immature, emotionally a case of arrested development. Like the proverbial schoolboy, he stuffs his pockets with junk—packets of pills, strings of cellophane, pennies, and crushed cigarette butts—and affectionately humanizes his dog, Scissors, his one-time companion; he whines with self-pity and looks to Coca-Cola bottles for security, sucking one after the other during the day; and he is indifferent to the neglect of his run-down and dirty car, not to mention the wall-to-wall slovenliness of his room. Further, for the same reason that the sight of children playing potsy and hopscotch eases his anxieties, we can assume that, before his improvident falling out with the boss, his moderate success with the Rojax Company derived from his feeling at home with its products—"Kiddies' furniture. Little chairs, rockers, tables, jungle gyms, slides, swings, seesaws" (35).

But if Wilhelm's feelings account for his failure, he at least *has* feelings, he at least evinces an eagerness for life, and in this sense his failure is also the measure of his human worth. If as willful and perverse as a child, he is also honest and direct as a child; if he allows people like Tamkin and Maurice Venice to dupe him, the reason is that he is trustful as well as naive. For everyone, in fact, he shows sympathy, compassion, love. When he hears that Venice was jailed for pandering, he grieves and wishes to express his sorrow in a letter; for the sake of his children, and even for the predaceous Margaret, he wants desperately to meet his alimony payments; and for reviling his father he suffers deep remorse. Being radically immature, in other words, Wilhelm is also radically innocent; indulgent with his own, "he would never willingly hurt any [other] man's feelings" (29).

Or, as Tamkin would have it, Wilhelm's feelings are the inescapable source of his humanity as well as his inhuman adversary. Experience has made him aware that "he had been slow to mature, and he had lost ground, and so he hadn't been able to get rid of his energy, and he was convinced that his energy had done him the greatest harm" (7), but he has yet to learn that it has done him the greatest harm not because it propels him against his will but because, although primordial and necessary, in itself it is not enough. His feelings need to be tempered by the acidity of hard facts and hard luck, the unpredictable in life and the consecrated if contingent clues to his identity as a human being—time, fallibility, death; they need, in short, to become integral with and guided by reality. Reality, however, Wilhelm deliberately shuns. Implicit to his behavior is the romantic assumption that he is above or below, in one way or another beyond, the travails that assail the common lot of man. For example, sporadically, during the day, a glimmer of the truth comes forth from his real soul—

> he received a suggestion from some remote element in his thoughts that the business of life, the real business—to carry his peculiar burden, to feel shame and impotence, to taste these quelled tears—the only

important business, the highest business was being done. Maybe the making of mistakes expressed the very purpose of his life and the essence of his being here (56)

—but he lets the truth go, preferring instead to regard even his burdens and suffering as extraordinary. He must be different; he must prove his uniqueness; he must remain apart.

All "Ism," in other words, he has courted the pretender's interest to his own detriment. Although still alive, although his real soul has not yet been crushed, he has allowed the pretender to scatter his energy outward and so far has defeated his own end. The salient example is his pseudonym, Tommy, which he adopted at the age of twenty while seeking fame and quick success in Hollywood, the land of make-believe—an attempt, he has come to see, to gain liberty from family ties, which is to say from his identity. And that he still hopes to redeem himself according to the ethos of cash-and-carry is shown in his investment with Tamkin, another bid for freedom initiated by "Tommy" and at the most precarious time of his life. This, too, Wilhelm faintly surmises, but it is a truth that neither his pride nor his guilt will permit him to believe in his heart. Again, he would rather believe that he is "a fool" and "a chink" by nature, that the aspect of his personality he calls "Wilky" is his real soul, whereas "Wilky," to the contrary, denotes what "Tommy" has made of him, his own victim, and is another rationalization that blurs his true identity all the more. Rather, the name of his real soul is Velvel (evidence of this I shall present below), the name by which his grandfather called him; and until, amidst all this confusion, he begins to conceptualize the truth he is instinctively attuned to and to control the tropism of his feelings in accord with reality, his real soul will remain undiscovered in limbo and he a potential killer and suicide. For Wilhelm "is a visionary sort of animal. Who has to believe that he can know why he exists. Though he has never seriously tried to find out why" (39). The events of the day, all of which take place within ten to twelve hours, are calculated to bring him unswervingly, shockingly to the answer.

But unfortunately Wilhelm has more to combat than just himself, and before the events of the day come to a close, his confusion is knotted over several times, which enlists our sympathies for him. Victimized from within, on the one hand, he is victimized from without, on the other hand, and ironically by the identical power, the externalization and metaphor of the same inhuman limits which bound his real soul and which he refuses to acknowledge in himself, the pretender interest. In other words, his external conflicts parallel the inner drama of his self-estrangement, amplifying his quest for identity and stifling further his growth as a human being.

Of a piece dramatically as well as metaphorically, these external conflicts unfold in dissolving view. But to take them in the order of their prominence, the first consists of his estrangement from his father, Dr. Adler, an affluent and retired diagnostician in whom the pretender has obviously usurped command. An eagle by name (the German and Yiddish meaning of "Adler") and description ("round-headed . . . with . . . feather-white, ferny hair"), he remains aloof from Wilhelm's anguish, stiff-backed and proud, unsullied, self-sufficient. A specialist in internal medicine, he knows nothing about the heart and its affections. He pockets rather than wears his hearing aid, having tuned out the human race. Even his clothes, the flamboyant shirts and vests he buys at a college haberdashery, betray at once his values—theatricality, hypocrisy, a concern for furbelows—and his obsession with death, the prospects of his dying in a year or two, the dread of which he suffers in silence, with style; a youthful facade, we see, to conceal his age and to arrest time, as if scream-ing colors might delay the entelechy of nature's juices. "And not only is death on his mind," Wilhelm notes, "but through money he forces me to think about it, too" (56). This expresses succinctly the terms as well as the stakes of their bloody feud, life or death. On the one hand, Dr. Adler refuses to save his son from financial ruin because, by the perverse logic of his standards, Wilhelm is practically impoverished to begin with, not the kind of son a vainglorious father can boast of, not at all the right kind of Jew. On the other hand, Dr. Adler repudiates his son because Wilhelm threatens to drag him into the turmoil of life as he would drag Wilhelm into the grave.

This is the quirk of his obsession—it derives more basically from a fear of life than of death, and in fact he, even more than Wilhelm, cowers in the face of reality. To Dr. Adler, life and death are synonymous; to him, the whole of life resides on the outskirts of time: in the future, with thoughts of his own death, and in the past, on the basis of which he condemns Wilhelm—on the basis of his son's dead mistakes. By thus objectifying death, he conveniently suspends the present, the here-and-now, the actual domain of human activity and the real stuff of life—struggle, defeat, suffering and, if struggle and defeat and suffering can be met with it—joy. Joy Dr. Adler has no affinity with; the rest he wishes to suppress at all costs. In contrast, Wilhelm at least senses that "if he didn't keep his troubles before him he risked losing them altogether, and he knew from experience that this was worse" (43). Dr. Adler has his legitimate complaints and miseries, to be sure, but he clings to them; they are death's miseries, moreover, not life's; abstract and cerebral, not concrete, not the flesh-and-blood miseries that accompany existential life.

From such he has paid the price of immunity, he believes, by coming up the hard way, through aggressive entrepreneurism, and now is entitled to die in peace. Wilhelm is a blight in his eyes, then, because he lays his confusions and pains at his father's feet, begging him to flex his stiff carriage and pick them up. To accept the challenge is unthinkable: "You want to make yourself into my cross. But I am not going to pick up a cross. I'll see you dead, Wilky, by Christ, before I let you do that to me" (110). Seated on a table in the hotel's massage room as he lets fly his final renunciation, Dr. Adler appropriately "gathered over him a sheet," his shroud.

Wilhelm's second external conflict consists of his estrangement from the contemporary urban world, the collective soul of which Dr. Adler, pampered and "idolized by everyone," epitomizes. The setting is the Upper West Side of Manhattan—a world of shops and restaurants with gilded fronts and huge, baroque, mausoleum-like hotels, whose clients—aged, decrepit, gaudily dressed businessmen—are waiting to die; a world of stock markets and electronic bookkeeping machines that cancel "you out automatically" (74); a world, as Wilhelm observes, that caters to the likes of the cruel and otiose Mr. Rappaport, a millionaire who has acquired his fortune in the chicken-killing industry and an obvious death-figure (he hardly has flesh enough to keep his trousers on) who clicks and clacks rather than talks when Wilhelm addresses him. And no wonder, still throbbing with life, Wilhelm is an alien to the city, an intruder, the violator, in fact, of its first taboo: he bewails his troubles before all, clamoring with anguish and operatic gestures in a society dedicated to spiritual suffering but, as if by tacit oath, to keeping its suffering buried. Mr. Perls's biological ailments, his clubfoot, for example, cannot be hidden, but about his flight from Germany and obscure tragedies not one illuminating word is mentioned; the business of the somnolent, droopy-eyed stock market manager, the overseer of daily catastrophe, is "to conceal his opinion"; and "the great weight of the unspoken" leaves Wilhelm and Reuben, a hotel clerk who suffers, like Wilhelm, marital and pecuniary problems, "little to talk about." Mum's the word, we see; no one dares articulate his genuine feelings lest he rattle society's bones. And yet Reuben, like the stock market manager, "knew and knew and knew"; the truth too is made to endure a subterranean life. Meantime, as Bellow's metaphors make clear, the world above rams on aggression and humanity bleeds; to suffer a loss on the market is to be "hit," to buy and sell is to "strike"; Mr. Perls, whose geniality is as artificial as the color of his hair, pierces Wilhelm with his questions and "thrusts with his cane" when he walks, a man with "fish teeth," "pointed crowns" of "stainless steel, or a kind of silver," which liken him to the piranha fish that devour a Brahma

Bull in a movie Wilhelm later recalls; and Wilhelm himself "hemorrhaged money," at various times feeling "battered" and ridden on "with hoofs and claws" and torn "to pieces." Savage, mechanical, and blood-soaked, filled with grotesque creatures only faintly animate—in all, the world Bellow delineates resembles the apocalyptic visions of Hieronymus Bosch.

The third of Wilhelm's external conflicts consists of his struggle to regain his Jewish heritage and the spiritual values of his race. When Dr. Adler introduces him to friends and says, "I uphold tradition. He's for the new"; of course the opposite is true. To be sure, Wilhelm does not go to synagogue, he cannot even translate into English the meaning of common Hebrew prayers. But in contrast to a society composed largely of assimilated Jews who pay homage to the bitch goddess and only lip service to the Hebraic God—the man Wilhelm pays to pray for his mother at the cemetery wants to be tipped for intoning *El molai rachamin*; and after the custom of theatrical performances people must purchase and reserve seats for Yom Kippur, the cost of atonement—Wilhelm "often prayed in his own manner" (86) and "would occasionally perform certain devotions, according to his feelings." If not by the letter of the law, he lives by the spirit of the Law. Moreover, Wilhelm visits his mother's grave each year in keeping with Jewish custom, whereas Dr. Adler has forgotten even the year that she died; and when, outraged by the incident, Wilhelm learns that vandals have split in two the bench between her and his grandmother's grave and tells his father about it, Dr. Adler is unmoved and refuses to have it replaced. In one trenchant image, that of the broken bench, Bellow symbolizes simultaneously the loss of Wilhelm's consolations (another of his havens, like his children, is taken away from him); the power (money, needed to replace the bench) that alienates him from the succor of the past (the bench joins one generation to the next, his mother's grave to his grandmother's); and, more to the point here, Dr. Adler's denial of familial ties, traditional values, and the traits of his race—"sensitive feelings, a soft heart, a brooding nature, a tendency to be confused under pressure" (25), traits which Mrs. Adler shared with her ancestors, and indeed with all humankind, and which Wilhelm has inherited from her. More profoundly than he suspects, then, Wilhelm is right when he declares to his father that Mrs. Adler's death marked "the beginning of the end," the end of their spiritual kinship as well as, potentially, the end of Jewish history.

The very fact that Dr. Adler fails in the least to comprehend his son's words confirms their acuteness. For like Wilhelm's distant and pretentious sister, who takes after her father and whose Philistine paintings convey meaning to neither Jews nor Gentiles (she has adopted Phillipa as a professional name!), and like society as a whole, which Wilhelm likens to the Tower of Babel, Dr. Adler has disavowed himself of a heritage nourished by the experience of humanity, in the permanence, universality, and continuity of which rests the *logos*, and hence he speaks an alien language. Wilhelm speaks from the heart, he from the glands—"voodoo," he says of Wilhelm's problems, and for therapy recommends steam. Consequently, he can be of no real help, for more urgently than money Wilhelm needs and seeks spiritual guidance, an authoritative, patriarchal word: "'Father, listen! Listen'" is his first and final plea. The cynical and solipsistic injunction he gets as advice—"Carry no one on your back!"— makes a mockery of Moses' farewell to the Jews:

> Remember the days of old;
> Consider the years of many generations,
> Ask your father and he will inform you.

With good reason, therefore, Wilhelm prays for deliverance, in Psalm-like cadences if in colloquial idiom—

> Oh, God, . . . Let me out of my trouble. Let me out of my thoughts, and let me do something better with myself. For all the time I have wasted I am very sorry. Let me out of this clutch and into a different life. For I am all balled up. Have mercy. (26)

—for he lives in a fallen world, "a kind of purgatory [*sic*]," as Tamkin says, a world besieged by "plague."

Of these religious references "plague" is the most apt dramatically, as I shall explain in a moment. But first let me indicate that these and other religious references function only as one aspect of Jewish culture and are meant to crystallize the estrangement of the contemporary Jewish community not from orthodox Judaism or the Hebraic God but from the humanistic thrust of its spiritual past in secular terms, which in turn functions as the veil or projection of modern man's estrangement from humanity, from the Life Force—the last of Wilhelm's external conflicts against the suffocating grip of the pretender, to keep alive and to preserve his identity as a human being. It is in this secular and symbolic sense that plague of a biblical kind is given form in the novella. It is in this sense, too, as part and parcel of his estrangement from his real soul, his father, the urban world, and his Jewish consciousness, relating organically the furthest reach of Bellow's theme to the novella's controlling idea, that Wilhelm's total crisis comes down to a struggle against damnation.

All this Bellow manages through water imagery, which pervades the book from start to finish, in conjunction with variant expressions of one subsuming metaphor, the Waters of Life, the Stream of Humanity. According to its rationale, the Life Force originates in both an external and internal source, from Nature, the Fountainhead of the Human Spirit conceived of as God, and in man, whose real soul partakes of Nature. The holy life, therefore, the genuinely human life, consists of man living in organic unity with God and, as Tamkin observes, "rolls the waters of the earth." Now the urban world has fallen into damnation because it has sundered its attachment to God, the humanizing energy the Jewish religion has thrived on in the past, and at once denied the flow of its real soul, or vice versa. But more than this, as we have seen, the urban world has converted its human energy into inhuman energy; it has, according to Bellow's metaphor, drained its real soul from within and rechanneled the Life Force against its purpose, against God. Hence, as if by the wrathful God of Creation, it has brought upon itself a deluge, wholesale death by water reminiscent of the Flood, the symbolic form plague assumes in the story: the Ansonia Hotel looks "like the image of itself reflected in deep water, white and cumulous above, with cavernous distortions beneath" (5); people cross "the tide of Broadway traffic" (77); "in full tumult the great afternoon current raced toward Columbus Circle" (100). The entire urban world, Bellow wants us to see, is inundated, a wasteland of plenitude, as it were.

Or, to sum up Wilhelm's total crisis as it is dramatized symbolically, against the pretender and damnation he struggles to keep himself from drowning: "The waters of the earth are going to roll over me" (77). Instinctively he thus recoils from the "swirling green," "wall-locked and chlorinated" (107, 43) waters of the hotel pool in which the clean and immaculate Dr. Adler daily immerses himself and from the "brackish tidal river smell . . . the smell of mop water" (106) that rises high above the city from the Hudson River, whose currents separate him from New Jersey and from his children, who reside there. But his ordeal is more complicated than this. Although society has defiled the waters of life and makes it difficult for him to exist without sinking beneath them, they are nevertheless inherently holy, and this, as we have seen in another context, he has not yet acknowledged; he is right to say no to the pretender but yet must learn to say yes to the sacred fount of experience which alone can purify and make him a whole person, those brute realities he continues to oppose although floundering through life like a "hippopotamus"(55) and soaking wet with them. In brief, his fear of drowning is inextricable from his fear of life: he uses "an electric razor so that he didn't have to touch water" and usually wears "his coat collar turned up as though he had . . . to go out in the rain" (16). Thus resisting reality and a potential plague-carrier himself—he "smelled the salt odor of tears in his nose"—he has become vulnerable to the pretender and ironically swells the very tide he would escape by frantically following its inclinations: on the day he invests his money in the stock market, a rainy, "weeping day," the water dribbles over his hat and transparent raincoat. And although he does not "wash his hands in the morning" (36), significantly the commodity he invests in is lard, the rudimentary but essential ingredient of soap and hydrotherapy—hydrotherapy being what Dr. Adler grotesquely prescribes for Wilhelm's traumas, in particular the steam baths located at the very bottom of the Gloriana Hotel, below sea level, where an attendant passes out soap and where Dr. Adler damns him to death rather than listen to his miseries in their climactic encounter; a situation, if we wish to follow the tug of associations still further, that parallels what Wilhelm recollects of a movie in which the heroine Annie Laurie pleaded and "wrung" her hands before the Laird as he ordered the bagpipers "to drown her out" (89). Once caught up in the cash nexus, in other words, Wilhelm's fate is set—"By and by, you'll get the drift'" (69), Tamkin assures him! He begins to vacillate like a "seaweed" in what Tamkin calls the "money-flow" of business transactions, the same deadly flow, we can assume, that has battened the fish-toothed Mr. Perls (his very name links wealth with the sea), who has a "drippy mustache," and made him successful. And finally, feeling the loss of his self-control, likened to "a ball in the surf washed beyond reach" (53); having taken barbiturates throughout the day, with each Phanaphen capsule swallowing "a long gulp of water" (70); filled with "unshed tears" and looking "like a man about to drown" and recalling lines from "Lycidas"—finally Wilhelm sinks "beneath the wat'ry floor" (13).

But not entirely. What begins in a paradox, the self-antagonism between the real and pretender souls, ends in a paradox. Wilhelm drowns insofar as, in the end, the pretender leads him to financial and social bankruptcy. But in the concluding scene, a scene, like "Lycidas," at once elegiac and redemptive, his resurrection is born of his defeat, he survives the waters, his real soul intact. For his salvation and, in the qualified sense I have just stated, his death, one man is largely responsible, the enigmatic Tamkin, to whom we are now prepared to turn.

II

As the prototype for Wilhelm's characterization is the schlemiel, so that of Tamkin's is the schnorrer, the professional mendicant and swindler of

Jewish humor. He not only strikes us as a conspicuous imposter, he means to beat Wilhelm at the confidence game, of all deceptions the most befitting for the pretender soul. He wears flashy clothes, the meretricious trappings of the pretender; and although he proclaims that psychology is his first interest, his dealings with the stock exchange preoccupy his mind and obviously go back a long way. There "all the branch managers knew" him (8); there the urge to make a killing brings out his fangs: "His face turned resolute, and on either side of his mouth odd bulges formed under his mustache" (75) Most telling of all, he actually looks like a bird of prey, like some old vulture:

> His figure was stocky, rigid, short in the neck, so that the large ball of the occiput touched his collar. His bones were peculiarly formed, as though twisted twice where the ordinary human bone was turned only once, and his shoulders rose in two pagoda-like points. At mid-body he was thick. He stood pigeon-toed. . . . The skin of his hands was aging, and his nails were moonless, concave, claw-like, and they appeared loose. (62)

In brief, about this peculiar bird we know from the start what Wilhelm only later suspects, "that Tamkin hadn't made [his ideas] his own" (82).

The irony, however, is more complex than the relatively simple duplicity of outright fraudulence. For whereas Tamkin's life seems to be propelled exclusively by the pretender, he speaks the truth, as we have seen, and the pretender knows not the truth. Even the passage I have cited above, the description of Tamkin as a vulture, suggests something more complex: his looks are ludicrously exaggerated, even caricatural, the implication being that Tamkin's appearance and the real man are in some sense are askew. The same duality is implicit in Tamkin's pitch. I refer especially to his proliferous and preposterous claims, which are so outrageously false, so absurdly inept that they deceive no one, not even so ingenuous a person as Wilhelm. In addition to being a practicing psychologist, a poet, and an entrepreneur, as Tamkin says of himself, he is also a scientist, an inventor, and a teacher of Greek. He has worked for Eastman Kodak in Rochester, as the head of a mental clinic in Toledo, as a television consultant in, presumably, New York; at various prestigious jobs in Hollywood and Chicago, and as psychiatrist in attendance at the villa of a royal family in Egypt. He even hints that once he was a fugitive at large in the underworld, a member of the Detroit Purple Gang! And finally, counter to first impressions again, for a man who haunts and makes a study of the stock market, Tamkin's acumen as a speculator is nil. It is true that Wilhelm falls prey to his inane use of jargon and silly, oversimplified formulae for success, and for this reason we tend at first to regard Tamkin's ignorance as the ploy of a smooth operator who knows his victim. But in the end his as well as Wilhelm's stocks collapse, and we are hardly surprised. Far from being simply a case of hard luck, Tamkin, like Wilhelm is, by implication, a habitual failure; if Wilhelm's investment costs him his last seven hundred dollars, Tamkin's costs him his last three hundred. "He sweated blood when he signed that check" (77), Wilhelm later reflects.

Blood indeed. Tamkin dies. This is the symbolic import of his disappearance at the end of the story. It also is a clue to his true identity—or, rather, to his identities—and to his affinities with Wilhelm as well. For self-evidently, before he is liquidated, Tamkin is very much alive, a man flailing for air in a world flooded with blood partly his own, and therefore he is not entirely to be identified with the world of the dead and the likes of its keepers, Dr. Adler. Indeed, he speaks the truth even in death; the quirk of his demise is not simply that he "hadn't made [his ideas] his own" (82) but that he destroyed himself exactly as his ideas prophesy.

The fact is that Tamkin cannot escape the truth, just as Wilhelm cannot escape his feelings. The difference is that Tamkin acutely, painfully, and tragically too late, knows this. As he himself confesses, his destiny by nature, his

> real calling is to be a healer. I get wounded. I suffer from it. I would like
> to escape from the sicknesses of others, but I can't. I am only on loan
> to myself, so to speak. I belong to humanity. (95)

Not, of course, that Tamkin willfully gives allegiance to his calling; we can be sure that he intends to swindle Wilhelm. And in this sense, to the extent that he deceives others, what he says here is sheer humbug, another aspect of his pitch. But *only* to this extent; that he does not believe what he says, or that what he says about himself is false, does not necessarily follow. Quite simply, the crux of the irony, the source of all Tamkin's ambiguities, comes down to this: although he has consciously renounced his real soul, his real soul has not renounced him. For as long as he fights to stay alive, he draws upon the energies of his real soul, from which the will to live derives and in which his feelings and the truth, the stuff of his calling, dwell; and therefore the innocent and natural expression of his real soul cannot be repressed entirely. Despite his will to power, the truth will out and will qualify his intentions in all he attempts. This explains not only the naivete of his ludicrous claims and the parody he makes of financial expertise, it also explains his absurd doggerel and even so trivial a matter as his handwriting, which is "monstrous" but also childlike, like the unintelligible scrawl of a "fourthgrader." And similarly, to come back to the quotation cited above, here, as in other declarations about himself, Tamkin speaks the truth, despite the fraudulent use he intends to make of it. As for what is suspect about its tone, its ebullient and hyperbolic quality, this trait is perfectly coeval with the whole man. Consistent with the self-dramatic expansiveness of innocence, it is also consistent with the self-dramatic egotism of the pretender. It renders at once the two prongs of his inner divergences and the dilemma, indeed the very peril, of self-betrayal—innocence driven to desperation and choking at the throat by its own hand.

As Wilhelm literally seizes his own throat—as if to strangle himself in front of Dr. Adler, that is—so Tamkin too is his own victim. For like Wilhelm he is as immature as he is innocent, as unwilling to accept reality as he is contemptuous of his true self. We hear the plaintive exasperation of his own transcendent yearnings even as he would incite Wilhelm's, and the echo of his guilt as well: "I get so worked up and tormented and restless, so restless! I haven't even been able to practice my profession" (9). In keeping with the novella's key metaphor, the waters of life, certain of his tales also betray the truth about him, as when he laments the death of his supposed wife who supposedly drank too much and supposedly drowned herself in Cape Cod; when he boasts of having worked on an "unsinkable ship" (67) with a Polish inventor; and when, by report, he claims to have invented an "underwater suit" (41) that makes it possible for a man to survive at the bottom of the Hudson River during an atomic attack. Not only naive, we see, his tales are fantasies, the inflated sham of a deflated ego afraid of life and yet anxious to stamp the world with its impression—fantasies wholly in accord, by the way, with his hydrophobic habits: a foul-smelling man, Tamkin refrains from bathing much. And this, we can infer, has been the story of his life. Rather than compromise his fanciful and emotional image of himself, he capitulated to the pretender long ago, growing more impatient and more desperate with each failure, and now, having cornered himself in a messy "box of a room" (106) at the Gloriana, he has no exit. When Wilhelm enters that room at the pitch of his own desperation, he notices among the heaped-up symbols of a botched-up life, the mirror of his own, "bottles of pills" (107) and the *Wall Street Journal* hanging "in separate sheets from the bed-table under the weight of the *silver water jug*" (106, italics mine). Having resisted the waters of life, in other words, Tamkin has consumed the waters of plague, and finally, like his supposed wife, he drops out of sight and into damnation.

But at the same time, since his innocence protrudes, gets in the way, and trips him up, so to speak, it qualifies his failure. Like Wilhelm's, it attests to his humane impulses as much as to his pretenses. He fails as a confidence man for the same reason Wilhelm fails as an actor; he cannot conceal his emotions, and subtlety and the knack of subterfuge elude him. Since aggression is also alien to his nature, he is out of his sphere at the stock market and consequently flops there. As he rightfully comments again, "I am at my most efficient when I don't need the fee. When I only love" (66). All this is to say obversely that the urban world has brought to bear upon Tamkin the same pressures that portend Wilhelm's dehumanization and is as much to blame for his tragedy as the errant urges that have thrust him wayward from within; a prophet crying in a cynical wilderness, in a world where "everyone was supposed to have money" (30), his essential being has not been permitted to flourish. The otherwise supercilious Mr. Perls adumbrates the point when he says that Tamkin "could be both sane and crazy. In these days nobody can tell which is which"(41); that is, since the same guileless spirit that undercuts Tamkin's pitch also infuses his ideas, society won't buy him as a healer either. Just as Dr. Adler regards Wilhelm's problems as voodoo and tunes him out, so the truth spills from Tamkin's throat with such simplicity to seem either simple-minded or extraordinarily slick, with such unaffected emotion as to seem like incontinent rant to a society so long masked in falsehood that it is no longer capable of recognizing the face of truth. No wonder he understands "what it is when the lonely person begins to feel like an animal. When the night comes and he feels like howling from his window like a wolf" (67).

And this, of course—to consider finally the significance of their relationship—is the reason that Wilhelm and Tamkin are singularly attracted to each other, despite the pretenses that come between them. On the side of life, they stand two together against the dead, schlemiel and schnorrer, outcasts both, united in failure and bound by the reciprocities of their real souls. Better still, they are compelled toward each other. Wilhelm puts his fate in bogus hands not solely because Tamkin seemingly provides a solution to his financial emergency but also and primarily because he is drawn instinctively to the truth he needs; if he is naive enough to believe that Tamkin is a wizard of finance—"Otherwise he could not make it sound so simple!" (9)—he is also naive enough to perceive the wizardry of Tamkin's insights—"True, true . . . I believe what he says. It simplifies much—everything!" (99). Likewise, Tamkin concentrates his energies on Wilhelm because he finds in him an audience and the potential fulfillment of his destiny as well as an easy victim. As Wilhelm correctly fathoms him: "Maybe he wished to do good, maybe give himself a lift to a higher level, maybe believe his own prophecies, maybe touch his own heart" (82). As Wilhelm is incomplete without Tamkin, so Tamkin is incomplete without Wilhelm, their humanity being consubstantial.

From this, by symbolic extensions, it becomes quite clear that Tamkin, a doctor of the soul, rather than Dr. Adler, a doctor of the body, is Wilhelm's spiritual and real father. The point suggests itself again and again once we have remarked the double-edgedness of Bellow's irony, as when, for example, Wilhelm makes such statements as "My Dad is something of a stranger to me" (93). Not as succinctly but somewhat more directly, the "father-and-son case" Tamkin relates to Wilhelm makes the same point: having learned that his wife had committed adultery, the father in the case is no longer certain of his son's identity and has peremptorily disowned him. This is another of Tamkin's apocrypha, but nevertheless it illumines Wilhelm's estrangement from Dr. Adler and, in this sense, as Tamkin insists, it is "a true case history" (65). For like the man in the story, Dr. Adler reduces his son's identity to a matter of genes; he has no spiritual affinities with Wilhelm whatsoever, and hence he too disowns his son. Also relevant is Wilhelm's response to the story. He immediately detects it is false because it violates his own paternal instincts; as he said to Dr. Adler earlier, "You ought to know your own son" (52). No wonder, then, that he turns to Tamkin, who knows him better than he knows himself—"no matter what he said or did it seemed that Dr. Tamkin saw through him" (61)—and who shepherds Wilhelm's inner life with true paternal feelings. He lectures him on the fundamental nature of life, consoles him with truth, and even, if only sporadically, frees Wilhelm of worry: "His face became warm and pleasant, and he forgot his father, his anxieties" (65). But even more essential to their familial relationship, unlike Dr. Adler, who makes of his unwillingness to carry his son on his back a way of life, Tamkin, because they are his own, identifies with and assumes the weight of Wilhelm's problems. As Wilhelm observes, "I am on his back—his back" (96). Later, to be sure, he observes that he "was the man beneath; Tamkin was on my back" (105). But this does not negate his first observation; both are partial truths, the whole truth being that each is the burden and back of the other, that like father and son they are united by the blood of the human spirit and they either stand or fall together. Tamkin says as much when he appears to be reconciling Wilhelm to Dr. Adler: " 'You should be proud of such a fine old patriarch of a father. It should give you hope. The longer he lives, the longer your life-expectancy becomes' " (62).

Finally, extending further the symbolic significance of their common humanity in keeping with his secular use of religious allusion, Bellow also compares the relationship of Tamkin and Wilhelm to that of the zaddik, the teacher and leader of the Hasidic community, and his disciple. The parallel is obscure but implicit from the start in the derivation of Tamkin's ideas. Although the thinking of Freud and Erich Fromm, and David Riesman's concept of inner-and outer-directedness, come to mind immediately as possible sources, and indeed may have played some part in their amplification,[5] Tamkin's ideas more directly are founded upon the principles of Hasidism: upon the joyful and mystical affirmation of life; upon compassion, love, and charity; upon democracy and the economic brotherhood of man; upon the holiness of each individual person. More specifically, the polar forces Tamkin categorizes as "Mechanism" and "Functionalism" correspond respectively to *perud*, "separation" or "detachment" and the first of Hasidic sins, and *yihud*, the synthetic unity of man and his essential self with God and the world; the antagonism between the real and pretender souls corresponds to the eternal clash between the *yetzer hatob*, the inclination to do good, and the *yetzer hara*, the relative and abused passion underlying all human activity inclined toward evil; and, finally, the doctrinal injunction to seize the day, the idea that serenity and one's redemption come from one's acceptance of his nature and station in life, corresponds to the *madregah* or belief that the Hasid more assuredly reaches the top of Jacob's ladder and God by enjoying to the fullest life at his teleological "rung" and serving God there. In fact, so steeped in Hasidism is Bellow's fiction that the reader who would make a serious study of his art and mind, as far reaching as it is, is well advised to begin there.[6] More than simply any one or any number of its principles, he finds especially congenial to his vision the essential moral spirit of the Hasidic way, what Martin Buber, the foremost proponent of Neo-Hasidism in our time, isolates as its most vital and enduring belief:

> Man cannot approach the divine by reaching beyond the human; he can approach Him through becoming human. To become human is what he, this individual man, has been created for. This, so it seems to me, is the eternal core of Hasidic life and of Hasidic teaching.[7]

And we can be sure that Bellow specifically had Buber in mind when he wrote *Seize the Day*. Perplexed by the meaning and clap-trap of Tamkin's poem and pressed for an opinion, Wilhelm says, "I'm trying to figure out who this Thou is." "Thou?" replies Tamkin. "Thou is you" (76). Clearly this is a reference to Buber's famous I-Thou dictum.

That Bellow means for us to identify Tamkin as a zaddik is unmistak-able in light of the qualities Hasidism has traditionally ascribed to the zaddik and his dealings with his people. In the synopsis below, which is based primarily on readings in Buber[8] and Samuel H. Dresner,[9] I have restricted the zaddik's qualities to those which are pertinent to Tamkin's characterization and relations with Wilhelm, but not, I trust, with oversimplified damage to the total Hasidic view of this sacred institution. Again, the prime difference is that Bellow has secularized the parallel.

As the term denotes, the zaddik is first of all a righteous man, a proven or perfected man, "the foundation of the world." He is righteous because the *Shekhinah* (God's Presence) dwells within him as he dwells within it. He stands between heaven and earth serving his people in a mediatory capacity; through him the Hasid is raised to and united with God in *yihud.* Yet he is not endowed with supernatural powers, however mysterious and mystical his ways, or even with special learning in a scholas-tic or sophisticated sense; indeed, the Hasidim have traditionally shunned elegant oratory and writing as the show of insincerity. The zaddik teaches primarily through parable, anecdotes as well as serious tales, his example, and the emotional intensity of his words and commitment. He does not "land" the truth to his disciples but prefers instead to help them find themselves through engagement and self dialogue, often compounding their problems and exacerbating their need of him before solacing them. Nor does he preach from on high—historically, the separation and aloofness of the Jewish leaders from the people in fact gave impetus to the Hasidic movement. In this respect the salient quality of the zaddik is his concern for the people; he mixes with them, if need be descending even into the mire with them, into the midst of their uncleanliness and polluting himself with sin, so that he can better understand their guilt and the trials of being human. And yet, paradoxically, although he would seem "to die" through such transgressions, he retains his holiness all the same:

> Transgression may come to the zaddik by virtue of his *finite nature.* No man is perfect, not even the zaddik. Every man is a "rising and falling creature," inferior to the angels in that angels never fall, but superior to them in that angels never rise. The angels are static; man is dynamic. And when the zaddik falls into a lower spiritual state, as all men do, he must not despair, but turn his falling into a creative act.
>
> The guilt of the zaddik . . . may be a guilt of *complete fiction,* an imaginary guilt, which he claims to find after searching his inner self in his desire to cast his lot with the people. He is guilty in his own eyes, but in the eyes of God he is innocent. It is a guilt which in fact does not

exist at all. But there are times when the zaddik must go beyond what is just and in love accept the plight of the people as his own, though no fault of his own is involved. God wants it so and sometimes tries him to see if he is worthy.[10]

Also pertinent is the tradition by which the Hasid will give to the zaddik a sum of money in payment for his instruction, "ransom" for his soul. And last of all, the zaddik is not always recognized as such. Existing now as always are thirty-six "hidden *zaddikim*" (readers familiar with André Schwarz-Bart's *The Last of the Just* will know the legend) who wander homelessly in the guise of common laborers and who, when their people are threatened by disaster, step forward unobtrusively to succor them and then vanish for fear of being exposed.

Tamkin is one of the hidden *zaddikim*. The point about the zaddik's fictive guilt explains how he can deceive himself and others as charlatan on one level of his existence and simultaneously cleave to his humanity and identification as a zaddik on another level; his symbolic death, his disappearance at the end of the story, represents the termination of his pretender soul, his life as a fraud, but in his role as a zaddik he and his real soul live on. Consider further the indubitable significance of Tamkin's strange name. In Hebrew, which Bellow knows, the word "tam" means righteous; it is predicated of Noah in its first biblical appearance. Quite obviously, then, Tamkin is "kin" to the righteous. Moreover, his hazy background and odd ways are imbued with an aura of mystery suggestive of his saintliness. He has extraordinarily powerful eyes, which coincides with his resemblance to a vulture, of course, but it also suggests that he has extraordinary vision. And if he has not wandered the globe in actuality, he at least seems to be acquainted with, and to show concern for, everyone, from the downtrodden to the rich, from foreigners to spinsters. "What kind of privileged life did this man lead," Wilhelm ponders. "Everybody came under his care, no one could have secrets from him" (73). Just so, he seems to know when Wilhelm needs him most and, as mysteriously as he disappears later, he suddenly stands before him as if out of nowhere. I refer to the description of his first entrance, which is worth quoting for other reasons. Wilhelm has just quarreled with Dr. Adler and is ruminating:

> If he was poor, I could care for him and show it. The way I *could* care, too, if I only had a chance. . . . He'd put his hands on me and give me his blessing. (56-57)

Someone in a gray straw hat with a wide cocoa-colored band spoke to Wilhelm in the lobby. The light was dusky, splotched with red underfoot; green, the leather furniture; yellow, the indirect lighting.

"Hey, Tommy. Say, there."

"Excuse me," said Wilhelm, trying to reach a house phone. (57)

But this was Dr. Tamkin, whom he was just about to call. In addition to Tamkin's timely, seemingly telepathic entrance, his "dusky" or concealed identity and the abrupt transition from "blessing" to the impersonal "someone" all contribute to the impression of his sanctity. And most indicative of all is his hat, symbolically a kind of *yarmulke* with a halo—the cocoa-colored band. With what might be called truly divesting irony, Tamkin removes his hat when he enters the stock exchange, the temple of unholiness, and only then does he look like a vulture, when the irreverent, pretender side of his character predominates and he seems to become "a different man" (78). It is his hat, specifically the cocoa-colored band, that Wilhelm spies in a crowd and zeroes in on as he pursues Tamkin in the end, that leads him as if by the nose to the funeral parlor and to his salvation, to the truth he has been looking for all day. All this is anticipated in lines that follow almost immediately the ones quoted above: "The sight of Dr. Tamkin brought his quarrel with his father to a close. He found himself flowing into another channel" (57). In the presence of Tamkin, Wilhelm moves from plagued to pure waters. Not only revelatory with respect to Bellow's subsuming metaphor, however, the term "channel" (*sheveel*) is another appellation by which the zaddik is known to the Hasid, a term denoting his function as an intermediary.[11]

To sum up this section, the brilliance with which Bellow delineates Tamkin consists not so much in the simultaneous rendering of his multiple identities as in the organic relevance of his characterization to Wilhelm's quest for identity and the structure of the novella as a whole. In Tamkin all the antinomial forces, the tensions of both content and form, converge and are balanced. On the one hand, as charlatan, as victimizer, and the tragic victim of himself, he is the pretender incarnated, symbolically all that threatens to dehumanize and suck Wilhelm under, inwardly and outwardly. On the other hand, insofar as Tamkin vies against his pretender soul and is victimized by the urban world, as the comic and ebullient schnorrer, he is Humanity incarnated, symbolically all that the pretender has estranged Wilhelm from—his real soul, his father, his Jewish heritage, and his humanity. More than simply Everyman, we see, Tamkin represents the totality of all there is, the efflux and influx of life and death, of comedy and tragedy; he represents the Life Force. Wilhelm meets him outwardly as he meets himself inwardly, at the core of his being, in an existential encounter with his total self, the axial center of his quest for identity and the structure of the novella. He moves resolutely toward life and death simultaneously as their relationship deepens, toward the death of his pretender soul and the life of his real soul, the second being dependent on and concomitant with the first; he must die in order to live; he must kill the pretender and bring to quietus his suicidal investment on the stock market. Tamkin's fate is somewhat more complex. As the pretender, insofar as he invests Wilhelm's money and hastens his bankruptcy, he is an accomplice to the murder of Wilhelm's pretender soul; but as Humanity he brings on his own bankruptcy and kills his own pretender soul, at the same time replacing Wilhelm's money with the truth upon which the survival of Wilhelm's real soul depends. As Humanity, in other words, the final quirk of Tamkin's failure is that he must drown himself in order that Wilhelm may be buoyed up.

III

This brings us to the resolution of Wilhelm's quest which, as I have intimated, builds in momentum with his loss of hope. He gets closer to his real soul the deeper he sinks into the caverns of his despair, and by late morning, his true feelings already stirred to foam, he is more quick to seize the purport of Tamkin's truths and more quick to reject the falsehoods. He also becomes more openly critical of Tamkin's person. Whereas earlier he had laughed off Tamkin's lies as the eccentricity of a gifted man and even defended him against Dr. Adler's sneers and charges, now he becomes hostile and assertive, he begins to show the enmity of the real soul for the pretender:

> "Damn it, Tamkin! . . . Cut that out. I don't like it. Leave my character
> out of consideration. Don't pull any more of that stuff on me" (88);

then, "Now look here. . . . Just lay off!" (98). And again, when he wants to return to the brokerage in a hurry and Tamkin lingers over his watermelon, "Never mind that. You've had enough to eat. I want to go back" (98). Fearing the worst, Tamkin is stalling for time; and when they arrive at the brokerage and meet the blind Mr. Rappaport, who wants someone to escort him to a cigar store, he takes the opportunity to dodge Wilhelm and siphons him off to the death figure with this ironical valediction, not the least acute part of which is the clinching sentence:

"He wants you. Don't refuse the old gentleman. . . . This minute is another instance of the 'here and now.' . . . Don't think of the market. It won't run away. Show your respect to the old boy. Go ahead. That may be more valuable." (100)

Wilhelm returns soon after and learns that he has been wiped out, the first of a quick series of blows that strip him of his pretenses: Tamkin seems to have skipped the scene, Dr. Adler refuses to pay even his hotel bill, and Margaret is hot upon him for overdue alimony.

Barely able to contain himself, his feelings and tears together welling up to the surface *de profundis*, Wilhelm begins to find himself at this point. Like Tamkin, who already in his life has felt the aching and ferocious loneliness of a hungry animal in the night, he too begins to act like a "wolf," the Yiddish meaning of the name *Velvel* and the signification that he at last has come into naked and uninhibited contact with his real soul. "I won't stand to be howled at," says Margaret during their talk over the telephone; and when she hangs up, he tries

to tear the apparatus from the wall. He ground his teeth and seized the black box with insane digging fingers and made a stifled cry and pulled. (114)

His real soul can no longer bear the suffering, the lies, the hypocrisy; he has become a killer; he must slay the deceiver. But rather than direct his hatred inward, he vents his feelings against Tamkin, Dr. Adler, Margaret, and the "Ism" he sees on every face among the fragmented crowd of people in the street; and even yet, even at this stage of his self-discovery, he will not surrender his pretender soul and admit to his innate limitations. He still harbors hopes of fleeing to Olive and making a new start, this being the last refuge of his pride.

As we shall see in a moment, his thoughts of Olive lead Wilhelm to the final phase of his quest and the final scene of the book. Before turning to that scene, however, I should like to return first to the very beginning of the story, for it will show to best advantage, I think, the discipline and formal consciousness with which the resolution was conceived and with which, in keeping with my first purpose, the novella as a whole is executed. There, in the very first paragraph, the story's central theme, its crucial events, its major issues and symbolism—all that I have elaborated on—are anticipated, and the story's conclusion prepared for as well. Here is the opening paragraph:

When it came to concealing his troubles, Tommy Wilhelm was no less capable than the next fellow. So at least he thought, and there was a certain amount of evidence to back him up. He had once been an actor—no, not quite, an extra—and he knew what acting should be. Also, he was smoking a cigar, and when a man is smoking a cigar, wearing a hat, he has an advantage; it is harder to find out how he feels. He came from the twenty-third floor down to the lobby on the mezzanine to collect his mail before breakfast, and he believed—he hoped— that he looked passably well: doing all right. It was a matter of sheer hope, because there was not much that he could add to his present effort. On the fourteenth floor he looked for his father to enter the elevator; they often met at this hour, on the way to breakfast. If he worried about his appearance it was mainly for his old father's sake. But there was no stop on the fourteenth, and the elevator sank and sank. Then the smooth door opened and the great dark red uneven carpet that covered the lobby billowed toward Wilhelm's feet. In the foreground the lobby was dark, sleepy. French drapes like sails kept out the sun, but three high, narrow windows were open, and in the blue air Wilhelm saw a pigeon about to light on the great chain that supported the marquee of the movie house directly underneath the lobby. For one moment he heard the wings beating strongly. (3)

The hotel, ironically named the Gloriana, is a microcosm of the urban world. It is, first of all, a dead world, "dark, sleepy," tomblike. Built on and chained to a "movie house," it also relies on the skeleton of reality for support—theater, make-believe, pretense—and hence it also is an unauthentic world. Accordingly, "knowing what acting should be" and using his cigar and hat as props, Tommy Wilhelm attempts to hide his troubles as he enters the scene. His very name, the pseudonymous coupling of two first names, rings with Hollywood spuriousness (John Gilbert, John Wayne, William Holden). In all this he belongs to this world, but not entirely: "If he worried about his appearance it was mainly for his old father's sake." Besides, he is too self-conscious, too obviously ill at ease and incapable of faking his emotions, as evidenced by his ludicrous pose, the caricature, as it turns out, of the spy within our midst; all he lacks is a trenchcoat. As in Hollywood, so in New York; he was not really an actor, merely an "extra," which is to say superfluous, not needed and not akin, a marginal figure contending for his life in the territory of the dead. That both his father, who shares the values of the urban world by implication, and society will reject him is prefigured when the elevator fails to stop at his father's floor; instead, it "sank and sank." And with this last metaphor the crucial symbolism of the novella is introduced. A deluge, we see, engulfs the lower regions of the hotel, and Wilhelm is about to go under: "the red uneven carpet that covered the lobby billowed toward Wilhelm's feet." The waters that threaten to submerge this world are "red" with the blood of its victim, humanity. But much more is suggested. The Red Sea comes to mind; and certainly the story of the Flood and Noah's Ark, which the phrases "drapes like sails" and the "pigeon about to light" unmistakably point to. Like the dove, the pigeon signifies hope: "For one moment he heard the wings beating strongly." And on this his Day of Judgment, hope for Wilhelm rests with Tamkin (later, when he rushes to Tamkin's room, he hears the "sounds of pigeons on the ledges" outside) but not, as we know, in the way he imagines, not with their mutual investment. In this respect, Tamkin is comparable to Noah's raven (a sagacious, quick-sighted, and, like the vulture, carnivorous bird that feeds on the dead), which led Noah to believe that the saving shores were in sight when in fact they were not. In other words, the allusion to the story of the Flood anticipates Tamkin's ambiguous role—he is both raven and dove, deceiver and savior—and the novella's central irony: looking to be rescued in a social and, unknowingly, false sense by Tamkin's promise of profits, Wilhelm is saved in a spiritual, real sense by Tamkin's truths and guidance. Further, like Noah, Wilhelm is a righteous man in his generation. He also has his failings, but this does not weaken the parallel—Noah has his failings, too, according to the symbolic interpretation of his character set forth by the Hasidim, knowledge of which, I think, is crucial to a full understanding of the story's conclusion. Voiced by Rabbi Yaakov Yosef, the Hasidic charge against Noah is that basically, out of selfishness, he was concerned with his own spiritual welfare and, out of pride that he had been chosen, not at all concerned for his people; unlike Abraham later, who walked "*before* God" (Gen. 17:1) and among the people, Noah "walked *with* God" (Gen. 6:9) on high, secluded from the people.[12] The Hasidic interpretation of the Ark also differs from the conventional view: it was created by God not for Noah's protection but for his punishment, as a prison and the symbol of his self-imposed isolation.[13] Wilhelm is no leader, of course, but he is guilty of Noah's sin: aloofness from the human condition. And he suffers in the urban world as Noah suffered in his Ark, for the purpose of his atonement, so that he might be restored to the brotherhood of man as Noah was restored to God.

We return, then, to the final phase of Wilhelm's quest and the story's conclusion, which begins, as I have said, with his thoughts of Olive. The not-so-common name of Wilhelm's love was obviously chosen with care, purposely with the story of Noah in mind and with the intention of linking the conclusion to the beginning. Wilhelm looks to Olive for peace as Noah looked to the augury of his dove, which reappeared after its second flight with an olive leaf, the sign that the waters had abated and his deliverance was at hand. But more than this, Bellow makes it clear through Wilhelm's thoughts that Tamkin is decidedly Wilhelm's savior, ultimately dove rather than raven. This he accomplishes through stress, by first having Wilhelm repeat Olive's name five times in quick succession, drawing our attention to it, and then, through an abrupt transition, by interrupting and juxtaposing Wilhelm's thoughts of Olive and peace with the sight of Tamkin, or at least what Wilhelm thinks to be Tamkin:

> "I'll have to go on my knees to Olive and say, 'Stand by me a while. Don't let her [Margaret] win. Olive!'" And he thought, I'll try to start again with Olive. In fact, I must. Olive—
>
> Beside a row of limousines near the curb he thought he saw Dr. Tamkin. (115)

But again, Wilhelm must die in order to be saved, and Tamkin, who seems to be "talking with a solemn face" to someone in front of a funeral parlor and "gesticulating with an open hand," beckons him to his death. Moreover, this is a "huge funeral," and not solely Wilhelm's; all humanity is dead, the urban world as a collective body, and this includes Tamkin in his role as the pretender. "Funny, he never mentioned he had a funeral to go to today" (116), thinks Wilhelm, after "the pressure of the crowd" makes it easier for him to follow Tamkin into the funeral parlor's chapel. But meantime Tamkin has fled, he is nowhere in sight; having led Wilhelm to his salvation, like Noah's dove he disappears, never to return again.

So compact and replete with limning metaphor and irony are the last three pages that I wish I could quote them in toto. Inside the chapel, as the organ begins to play, Wilhelm walks beneath the Star of David etched in stained glass, the indication again that the dead being mourned is not one man but the entire Jewish community, and at once a reminder that this is the eve of Yom Kippur, the Jewish Day of Atonement, and the beginning of a new year, anticipating Wilhelm's rebirth. To the same effect and at the same time, in the same paragraph, the Noah parallel is reinforced, linking Wilhelm's need to atone with his quest for identity, his struggle to keep afloat: he wipes the "salt itch" from his forehead and crosses the "cork floor." Presently caught up among the mourners who move in a line past the coffin, "the beating of his heart anxious, thick, frightening, but somehow rich" (116), he stops in turn and gazes at the face of the middle-aged but gray-haired man with a "splash of heart-sickness" and "nodded and nodded"; whereas the other mourners, who gaze at the corpse with "veiled looks," observe only the opulent and cosmetic artifice of the pretender—the formal clothes, the silk lapels, the powdered cheeks—and move on, Wilhelm perceives the corpse to the dark and hollow core of its real soul and acknowledges the truth of Tamkin's wisdom: he sees in the dead man the remnants of a wasted humanity. He begins to cry out of sorrow for the man in the coffin, for his father and Tamkin and the Jewish community at large, for all the people and forces that have besieged him during the day; he makes his *Yiskor*—prayers for one's father and the Jewish dead, a service preparatory to Yom Kippur— and at once his amends with the external world. But soon and at the same time he cries "from deeper feelings," from having gazed at the dead man with the shock of self-recognition; and no longer able to resist reality and the "devil" who wants his life, he surrenders himself in bursts of irrepressible wracking sobs.

> The source of all tears had suddenly sprung open within him, black, deep, and hot, and they were pouring out and convulsed his body, bending his stubborn head, bowing his shoulders, twisting his face, crippling the very hands with which he held his face and wept. He cried with all his heart. (117)

Reducing him to utter humility, his tears geyser up from his love of life, from "the source of all tears"; they are purgative tears, an outpouring of universal mourning that cleanses his real soul from within, his *Ereb Yomtob*, a ritualistic bath performed by Jews in preparation for Yom Kippur so as to appear pure in soul before God. And by virtue of this act of love, his identification with the brotherhood of man, he opens himself to the ecstatic waters of life, which rush into him from without.[14] This is the substance of the last paragraph, in which the water of his tears and that of the "sea-like-music"—the swelling sound of the organ—merge to symbolize the organic unity of Wilhelm's inner being and the external world, and his reconciliation with life:

> The flowers and lights fused ecstatically in Wilhelm's blind, wet eyes, the heavy sea-like music came up to his ears. It poured into him where he had hidden himself in the center of a crowd by the great happy oblivion of tears. He heard it and sank deeper than sorrow, through torn sobs and cries toward the consummation of his heart's ultimate need. (118)

That ultimate need is self-knowledge, through which he transcends his social death and, like Noah, is redeemed. The difference, of course, is that whereas Noah was removed from the waters and delivered unto God, Wilhelm immerses himself in the waters, "in the center of a crowd," and is delivered unto Humanity. With lasting impact he experiences again his evanescent joy of a few days back, when deep below sea level, in a crowded subway and in a subterranean "blaze of love," he identified himself with his imperfect "brothers and sisters" and the "larger body" of humankind. As for his destitution and the bearing of the book's title on his naturalist situation, the title obviously is ironical; having lost all he owns and having no one to turn to, he can hardly hope to seize the day socially. But the point is that ultimately all he or any of us can "bank" on is reality and the truth about oneself without a sense of which meaningful life is impossible. Wilhelm has no need to seize the day in society's terms; the day has seized him.

Notes

1. Saul Bellow, *Seize the Day*. New York: Viking Press, 1956.
2. "Saul Bellow," *Prairie Schooner* 31 (Summer 1957): 109.
3. In Harvey Breit, *The Writer Observed* (New York: World Publishing Company), 273.
4. Most reviewers—Leslie Fiedler, Alfred Kazin, and Herbert Gold among them—praised the book highly for its integrity (the reviews are conveniently listed by Harold W. Schneider, "Two Bibliographies: Saul Bellow and William Styron," *Critique* 3, no. 3 [1959]: 71–86); and criticism directed to it since then has been of the same mind and, as deep as it goes, perceptive. But with the exception of a study by Daniel Weiss ("Caliban on Prospero: A Psychoanalytic Study on the Novel *Seize the Day*, by Saul Bellow," *American Imago* 19 [Fall 1962]: 277–306), the criticism in all does not go deep enough; in deference to Bellow's longer works, it is either too short of breath or too general to indicate the superior quality of the book's art.
5. Cf. David Riesman, *Individualism Reconsidered* (Glencoe, Ill.: The Free Press, 1954), 59–60: "This [the social victimization of the individual] is also a fate that, both in its economic and its psychological aspects has overtaken vast numbers of the less 'successful' classes in our new society, and condemned them to 'alienation.' For them, as for Jews, the relative security of a social role fixed by skill, family, age, and sex has vanished. One must now 'show one's stuff' in a competitive market, and one's stuff is one's 'personality,' an externalized part of the self, and not primarily one's matter-of-fact skill. . . . In other words, it is not the genuine self that is put, or the market in the race for success, or even economic survival, but the 'cosmetic' self, which is free of any aroma of personal, non-marketable idiosyncracy as it is free of 'B. O.' or last year's waistline. If this artificial self succeeds, then doubts may be temporarily quieted. However, since self-evaluation has been surrendered to the market, failure in the market, or even

fear of failure, is translated into self-contempt. (The market in this sense includes all spheres of life—business, politics, art, love, friendship.)"

6. Chester E. Eisinger makes a similar but much more modest claim in *Fiction of the Forties* (Chicago: University Press, 1963), 343.

7. Martin Buber, *Hasidism and Modern Man: The Origin and Meaning of Hasidism*, trans. Maurice Friedman (New York: Horizon Press, 1958), 42–43.

8. Martin Buber, *Hasidism and Modern Man*, trans. Maurice Friedman (New York: Horizon Press, 1960). See also the helpful glossaries in *The Early Masters*, vol. 1, *Tales of the Hasidism*, edited by Martin Buber and trans. Olga Marx (New York: Schocken Books, 1947), and vol. 2, *The Late Masters* (1948); *The Hasidic Anthology: Tales of the Hasidim*, trans. and edited by Louis I. Newman (New York: Schocken Books, 1963); *A Treasury of Jewish Folklore*, edited by Nathan Ausubel (New York: Crown Publisher, 1948), pp. 104, 204, 320, 448.

9. Samuel H. Dresner, *The Zaddik* (New York: Abelard-Shurnan, 1960).

10. Dresner, 200–201.

11. Dresner, 125.

12. Dresner, 104–5.

13. Dresner, 106.

14. Cf. the last paragraph and reconciliation between Rogin, the protagonist, and his wife in Bellow's short story "A Father-to-Be," which is included among the works collected with *Seize the Day*, 133: "But there's absolutely nothing wrong with you," she said, and pressed against him from behind, surrounding him, pouring the water gently over him until it seemed to him that the water came from within him, it was the warm fluid of his own secret loving spirit overflowing into the sink, green and foaming, and the words he had rehearsed he forgot, and his anger at his son-to-be disappeared altogether, and he sighed, and said to her from the water-filled hollow of the sink, "You always have such wonderful ideas."

Works Cited

Ausubel, Nathan, ed. *A Treasury of Jewish Folklore*. New York: Crown Publisher, 1948.

Bellow, Saul. *Seize the Day*. New York: Viking Press, 1956.

Breit, Harvey. *The Writer Observed*. New York: World Publishing Company, 1956.

Buber, Martin. *Hasidism and the Modern Man*. Translated by Maurice Friedman. New York: Horizon Press, 1958.

———. *The Origin and Meaning of Hasidism*. Trans. by Maurice Friedman. New York: Horizon Press, 1960.

Buber, Martin, ed. *The Early Masters*. Vol. 1. *Tales of the Hasidism*, translated by Olga Marx. New York: Schocken Books, 1947.

———. *The Late Masters*. Vol. 2. *Tales of the Hasidism*, translated by Olga Marx. New York: Schocken Books, 1948.

Dresner, Samuel H. *The Zaddik*. New York: Abelard-Shurnan, 1960.

Eisinger, Chester E. *Fiction of the Forties*. Chicago: University Press, 1963.

Fiedler, Leslie. "Saul Bellow." *Prairie Schooner* 31 (Summer 1957): 109.

Newman, Louis I., ed. *The Hasidic Anthology: Tales of the Hasidism*, translated by Louis I. Newman. New York: Schocken Books, 1963.

Riesman, David. *Individualism Reconsidered*. Glencoe, Ill.: Free Press, 1954.

Schneider, Harold W. "Two Bibliographies: Saul Bellow and William Styron." *Critique* 3, no. 3 (1959): 71–86.

Weiss, Daniel. "Caliban on Prospero: A Psychoanalytic Study on the Novel *Seize the Day*, by Saul Bellow." *American Image* 19 (Fall 1962): 277–306.

Seize the Day: Intimations of Anti-Hasidic Satire

S. LILLIAN KREMER

Saul Bellow is an artist of the caliber T. S. Eliot described in "Tradition and the Individual Talent," one who makes profound use of and contribution to the literary heritage. Bellow persistently demonstrates the historic sense that "impels a man to write not merely with his own generation in his bones, but with a feeling that the whole of literature . . . has simultaneous existence and composes a simultaneous order."[1] Intelligent application of the materials and techniques of Jewish literature infuses the content and style of Bellow's allegoric novella *Seize the Day*.[2] Set in New York City's decaying West Side, the narrative deals with a multileveled conflict including, on an allusive plane, the historic antagonism between Hasidim and their Jewish opponents. Bellow's use of historic *misnagdic* and *maskilic* opposition to the Hasidic way, heretofore ignored by critics and explicators, justifies the dramatic function of the novella's minor actors and, more important, clarifies the paradoxical nature of Dr. Tamkin's character.[3] A solution to the Tamkin enigma lies in analysis of Bellow's masterful juxtaposition of Hasidic-*maskilic* perspectives, especially in Tamkin's modern secular correspondence to the corrupt spiritual leader of Joseph Perl's nineteenth-century satire, *Megallah Temirim (Revealer of Secrets)*.

Literary critics have speculated at length on the perplexing nature of Bellow's holy conman. Addressing Dr. Tamkin's ambiguous role, Ralph Ciancio argues that "he is both raven and dove, deceiver and savior—the novella's central irony."[4] Clinton Trowbridge agrees that there is duality in Tamkin's role, characterizing him as "one of Bellow's strongly ambivalent seers . . . a savior and destroyer."[5] Despite Tamkin's assistance to the

Reprinted with permission from *MJS Annual IV*: Special Publication of *Yiddish* 4.4 (Winter 1982): 32-40.

protagonist, Trowbridge views him essentially as "a destroyer of the soul. . . the touch of death, not life, . . . a false image of salvation."[6] Sarah Blacher Cohen contends that Tamkin fulfills his spiritual function as a "trained comedian of ideas,"[7] whereas his secular function remains that of "diabolic confidence man whose physical characteristics immediately suggest that he may be the devil in disguise."[8] At worst, Tamkin is perceived by J. C. Levenson as "an extraordinary villain . . . [a] purveyor of all the false or questionable or merely specious cures for what ails Wilhelm."[9] Bellow's sinner–saint is better understood in the context of Jewish literature, specifically in the line of anti-Hasidic satire and parody.

Requisite to understanding the novelist's rendering of Tamkin's pernicious attributes, attributes that confound his role as spiritual leader, is an examination of Bellow's delineation of the Jewish context of the spiritual quest. To this end, we are obliged to unravel the secular pastiche of Yiddish character constructs that forms the provocative alliance of schlemiel/Hasid (Wilhelm) and schnorrer/zaddik (Tamkin). Analysis of Tamkin's character is further complicated because he is a composite of two antagonistic visions: the venerated charismatic guide of Hasidic persuasion, and the incompetent and fraudulent zaddik of *misnagdic* and *maskilic* interpretation.

On the narrative level, Tamkin and Wilhelm are analogous to the schnorrer and schlemiel of Yiddish literature. Unlike many of his noble quest antecedents in English literature, Bellow's schlemiel–protagonist behaves in a manner characteristic of the stock comic figure in Yiddish literature and drama; he is an awkward bungler, behaving in a foolhardy manner, accruing mishaps as he drifts from situation to situation.[10] As a middle-aged failure, separated from his wife and children, estranged from his mistress, a college dropout, failed actor, and unemployed salesman, Wilhelm fulfills the essentials of his character type by missing opportunities and sabotaging his own chances for success and happiness.

Wilhelm's facility for self-recrimination is appropriate to his dual role as schlemiel–penitent. The novella's final purgation scene is anticipated in Wilhelm's early prayer. Despite the vernacular slang of Wilhelm's supplication, it is nevertheless composed of the traditional elements of worship: contrition for a wasted life, petition for forgiveness and mercy, and expression of hope.

> "Oh God," Wilhelm prayed. "Let me out of my trouble. Let me out of my thoughts, and let me do something better with myself. For all the time I have wasted I am very sorry. Let me out of this clutch and into a different life. For I am all balled up. Have mercy." (26)

As a secular schnorrer, Dr. Tamkin relieves Wilhelm of his funds, thereby stripping him of his security in order to prepare Wilhelm to accept him as spiritual mentor. The traditional schnorrer, who lived by facility for repartée and ability to disburden the fortunate of their wealth, was a learned man, versed in Torahic and Talmudic law, who engaged his benefactor in theological discussion.[11] The schnorrer contributed to the ethical well-being of the Jewish community by helping Jews to discharge the commandments related to charity. Therefore, the schnorrer did not demean himself, cringe, cower, or beg in an apologetic manner; on the contrary, he demanded his due. A concealed saint,[12] at this juncture of the novella, Bellow's secular schnorrer does not concern himself with religious rationale in the traditional style of Israel Zangwill's hero-beggar in *The King of the Schnorrers*.[13] Instead, Tamkin's appeal for funds is stylistically representative of the scholarly, self-assured beggar of Judaic tradition. Endowed with the vanity, arrogance, and chutzpah of the Zangwill hero, Tamkin impresses Wilhelm with his wisdom, while fleecing the schlemiel of his meager capital. Wilhelm yields to Tamkin's psychological persuasion as Jewish philanthropists have historically succumbed to Talmudic and Maimonidean argument regarding charitable behavior. "For all his peculiarities," Wilhelm believed, Tamkin "spoke a kind of truth and did some people a sort of good" (70). Dazzled by Tamkin's wit and apparent goodwill, Wilhelm invests his last $700, more than twice the amount of Tamkin's share, in what was to have been an equal venture. Furthermore, the schlemiel also entrusts the physician of the soul with power of attorney. Thus, in secular America, financial failure becomes the catalyst for spiritual recovery.

Allusions to Renaissance and Hasidic spiritual dramas are effectively fused in the novella's setting. Hotel Gloriana, symbolic of America's materialism, is evocative of Renaissance palace and Hasidic court and serves also as backdrop for an assimilated Jew's spiritual renewal. In a manner reminiscent of Spenser's Red Cross knight receiving the blessing of Queene Gloriana prior to his journey, the contemporary quester is encouraged by his mentor, Dr. Tamkin. Tommy Wilhelm's arrival at the Hotel Gloriana in the Yom Kippur[14] season to seek spiritual consultation parallels the East European custom of high holiday pilgrimage to the Hasidic leader's court for religious study, worship, and celebration.[15] Allegoric intent is suggested in the Decalogue reference of Wilhelm's Yom Kippur eve elevator descent from the hotel's twenty-third to the fourteenth floor, and reinforced in the crucial Times Square epiphany scene. Thus the quasireligious setting of the hotel qua Hasidic court serves as the appropriate starting place for a religious quest that concludes with the spiritually renewed protagonist praying beneath the symbolic shield of Israel in a Jewish chapel.

It is at the hotel newsstand, in conversation with the attendant Rubin, that Wilhelm first speaks of his anxieties; it is here too that he takes his initial step toward salvation. Playing the traditional role of *gabai*,[16] assistant to the zaddik, Rubin listens attentively to Wilhelm's story, informs him of Tamkin's spiritual assistance to other hotel guests, and advises him to seek Tamkin's aid. Rubin's interview with Wilhelm corresponds to the historic *gabai*'s interrogation of the Hasid prior to his audience with the zaddik. Wilhelm notes that "Rubin was the kind of man who knew, and knew, and knew" (10), a fitting assessment of the *gabai* figure, whose function as an intermediary required that he take the equivalent of the supplicant's case history for the zaddik's review. In Bellow's secular morality drama, the *gabai* performs dual dramatic roles of assistant to the healer and choral commentator.

On the thematic level, Tamkin and Wilhelm, guide and disciple, interact as zaddik and Hasid.[17] Bellow parallels Wilhelm's role as unconventional religious quester to Tamkin's role as unconventional religious guide. Although Tamkin appears to be a charlatan, leading Wilhelm to financial ruin, he is in reality a revealer of metaphysical truths. Although he adopts the guise of pretender-psychologist, Tamkin triumphs as an authentic physician of the soul. His role is to serve as spiritual father to Tommy Wilhelm, whose biological father, Dr. Adler, physician of the body and fallen Jew, has abandoned his son in time of spiritual and emotional crisis.

To the secular role of psychologist, twentieth-century guide to the perplexed, Tamkin adds the zaddik's characteristic commitment and personal involvement with the disciple. Like the selfless Hasidic zaddik who devoted himself to the service of the needy, Tamkin believes that he belongs to humanity, explaining that he is "a radical in the profession" (72), that he shares the wounds and suffering of his patients and is unable to detach himself from the sickness of the world. Wilhelm responds positively to Tamkin's personal concern: "That the doctor cared about him pleased him. That was what he craved, that someone should care about him, wish him well. Kindness, mercy, he wanted" (80). Furthermore, like the true zaddik for whom charitable behavior toward others is its own reward, Tamkin claims disinterest in financial compensation for his work: "I am at my most efficient when I don't need the fee. When I only love. . . . The spiritual compensation is what I look for" (73).

That Tamkin departs from conventional psychological methodology is evident. His unprofessional disclosure of case histories recalls the zaddik's instruction via parable and anecdote. More concerned with his patient's ethical conduct than is the secular psychologist, Tamkin instructs Wilhelm about the necessity for postponing personal gratification and exercising his moral obligation to assist people in need. In diction reminiscent of his poem, "Mechanism vs. Functionalism, Hism vs. Ism," Tamkin advises:

> This minute is another instance of the here and now. You have to live
> in this very minute, and you don't want to. A man asks you for help.
> Don't think of the market. . . . Show your respect to the old boy. . . .
> That may be more valuable. (109)

In this manner Tamkin counsels his patient in Judaic ethics: first, in the traditional obligation to discharge charity and social justice sooner rather than later; second, in the religious import of every action and instant of one's life.

In the prescriptive poem "Mechanism vs. Functionalism, Hism vs. Ism," Tamkin celebrates the holiness of life, the here and now, advising Tommy to abandon his pretender soul, the construct designed in society's valued image, and charging him to be true to his real soul, to "seize the day." Tamkin's poem echoes the Hasidic interpretation of classic Judaic principles honoring God's creation. In "poetic" diction evocative of the prose of Martin Buber, the foremost modern interpreter of Hasidic philosophy, Tamkin celebrates the sanctity of the individual.

Writing of the importance of the individual in the Hasidic way, Buber states: "Every single man's foremost task is the actualization of his unique, unprecedented and never-recurring potentialities."[18] Buber's assertion of the individual's responsibility to develop his potential spiritual being reverberates in Tamkin's praise of individuality:

> If thee thyself could'st only see
> Thy greatness that is and yet to be,
> Thou would feel joy–beauty–ecstasy. (82)

Buber contends that Hasidim believe "what a man does now and here with holy intent is [a] no less important, no less true . . . link with the divine being than the life in the world to come."[19] Tamkin reverses only the master's word order in advising his disciple to live a holy life in the present: "You should try some of my 'here and now' mental exercises. . . . You must go along with the actual, the Here and Now, the glory. . . . Be in the present. Grasp the hour, the moment, the instant" (97–98).

Yet Bellow's saint is not the righteous saint of traditional Hasidic literature. In the imagination of the twentieth-century artist, writing in a secular age, the zaddik has become more complex, a composite figure of good and evil, a charismatic eccentric viewed from polar perspectives of adherents and opponents of the Hasidic institution of *zaddikim*. Wilhelm's assessment of Dr. Tamkin parallels that of ardent Hasidim. The disparaging censure of Dr. Adler and Mr. Perls, however, corresponds to views of the opposition.

At the heart of Bellow's richly allusive treatment of Dr. Tamkin's specious nature are historic *misnagdic* and *maskilic* criticisms of the Hasidic movement. *Misnagdim*, orthodox and rabbinic traditionalists, and *maskilim*, Enlightenment and rabbinic progressives, denounced the authority of the zaddik, who, irrespective of Torahic knowledge, provided religious leadership.[20] The Jewish opposition argued against Hasidic exaltation of the zaddik as a "living Torah," convinced that Hasidic devotion to this human authority would diminish Torahic authority.[21] Furthermore, they viewed "veneration of the Hasidim for the zaddik as the vessel whereby God's grace and blessing is transmitted to man"[22] as a serious departure from Jewish belief that no one requires a mediator between himself and God. In addition to this essential variance, both traditionalists and liberals viewed with horror the Hasidic tendency to characterize *zaddikim* as wonder-workers and to establish dynastic houses. In utter frustration, the Orthodox hierarchy invoked the institutional weapon of excommunication against Hasidim.

In addition to suffering separation from the Orthodox community, Hasidim found themselves the object of *maskilic* satire and parody. Tamkin, who has intrigued readers and critics, is a direct, albeit secular, offspring of Joseph Perl's corrupt zaddik. Bellow acknowledges his debt to the *maskilic* literary heritage via allusions, using the surnames of two celebrated *maskilim*, Joseph Perl and Judah Lob Rapaport, for key minor figures. The fictional Perls and Rappaport function as secular *maskilim*, frequently passing judgment on Tamkin and Wilhelm.

Foremost among *maskilic* literary satirists was Joseph Perl, who published his parody, *Megallah Temirim (Revealer of Secrets)*, in epistolary form in 1819.[23] Mimicking the corrupt Hebrew of the self-styled zaddik, the lax grammar, and the indiscriminate intermingling of Yiddish, Hebrew, Russian, and Polish, Perl effectively lampooned the Hasidic linguistic style.[24] Remaining true to Perl's technique, Bellow secularizes and modernizes it, substituting fractured English syntax to suggest the imperfect Hebrew of the corrupt zaddik and replacing the nineteenth-century religious dialogue with twentieth-century psychological and economic jargon. Perl's zaddik used a talisman to make himself invisible in order to observe the habits and manners of his disciples and then recorded his observations. Analogous to his predecessor's method is Tamkin's predilection for revealing the secrets of the patients he claims to have attended. In the role of traditional Hasidic zaddik, Tamkin seeks troubled individuals in order to help them even before they seek him out. In the polar capacity of satirical zaddik, Tamkin's clandestine observation of Wilhelm resembles Perl's corrupt zaddik who secretly watched his subjects. Wilhelm is offended when he discovers that he is the object of Tamkin's professional concern. He wonders, "What right had Tamkin to meddle without being asked? What kind of privileged life did this man lead? . . . Everybody came under his care. No one could have secrets from him" (80). This is but one of Bellow's devices for rendering the delicate balance of antagonistic Hasidic and *maskilic* elements in Tamkin's richly complex character. Albeit secular and modern, Tamkin is clearly the legitimate heir of both Hasidim and *maskilim*.

Evidence of the fictional Perls's correspondence to the historic satirist is found in Bellow's delineation of his character's physical attributes, attributes suggestive of his critical function: his sharp teeth, which are compared to stainless steel; his sharp voice and heavy cane, accouterments evocative of the acerbic and mordant wit of the cynic. Analogous to the *maskilic* and *misnagdic* reservations regarding the religious legitimacy and scholarly standards of the *zaddikim* are Mr. Perls's and Dr. Adler's qualms about Dr. Tamkin's credentials. In an exchange that is the equivalent of a *misnagdic* attack on the zaddik's Torahic competence, Perls entreats Dr. Adler to be wary of Tamkin. Responding to Adler's query, "I wonder if he is really a medical doctor?" (45), Mr. Perls avoids affirmation, remarking only that Tamkin has convinced others of his professionalism, that he counsels patients and prescribes courses of treatment. In another passage reflective of *maskilic* condemnation of wonder-working *zaddikim*, Mr. Perls derides Tamkin's design of an underwater suit for escape from nuclear attack. Perls concludes with an observation suggestive of the contradictory evaluation of Hasidim in the larger Jewish community: "He could be both sane and crazy. In these days nobody can tell for sure which is which" (46).

Tamkin's acquaintance, Mr. Rappaport, an elderly, nearly blind gentleman of the stock exchange, corresponds to the historic Rabbi Judah Lob Rapaport, a contemporary of Joseph Perl.[25] Perl's satire, *Megallah Temirim*, was for a time ascribed to his *maskil* associate, Judah Lob Rapaport,[26] who commented on the authenticity of Perl's Hasidic portraits.[27] In the context of the brokerage house scene, Mr. Rappaport instructs Tommy Wilhelm to think about Yom Kippur observances and reminds him of the need to say *Yiskor*, the traditional memorial prayer. In Tommy's meditation on Mr. Rappaport's advice, Bellow repeats the phrase "life to come" three times in a single paragraph, emphasizing the religious concept of salvation. In the Hasidic context of *Seize the Day*, however, it will not be the *maskil* correspondent of poor vision who will lead the quester to purgation. Instead, it is dramatically consistent and thematically logical to allow Dr. Tamkin to lead Tommy Wilhelm from financial bankruptcy to spiritual recovery.

Thus we see that the Judaic religious and literary heritages have been skillfully integrated by Bellow on symbolic and allusive levels to delineate the spiritual return of a mid-twentieth-century assimilated Jew. Though staged before a secular, materialist backdrop, the morality drama of *Seize the Day* draws its spiritual and literary values from the Hebraic context. As Wilhelm wanders about the New York wasteland contemplating his troubles, he reads graffiti evocative of the ancient Hebraic command-ments: "Sin No More," and "Do Not Eat the Pig" (92). At this juncture, Tommy experiences spiritual renewal manifested as an outpouring of love for humanity. Juxtaposition of spiritual return with universal love and a reference to the dietary laws suggests confirmation of the protagonist's return to his ancestral heritage. The quester, who began the period of atonement in a mood of self-indulgence, has progressed from need for spiritual supervision to undirected compassion; he is now capable of love for others and prepared to be united with strangers whom he recognizes as "brothers and sisters" (92). Tommy's comprehension of the human bond is reinforced by Tamkin's advice that he delay self-gratification in order to help Mr. Rappaport. In the novella's denouement, Tommy's cathartic tears shed for a dead stranger symbolize his redemption.

In the guise of secular physician of the soul, Dr. Tamkin has fulfilled his mediatory function and guided Wilhelm to an understanding of his Jewish soul, and thereby to union with God. In the tradition of hidden saints, those who intentionally assumed the identity of commoners in order to operate secretly, Dr. Tamkin delivers his disciple to the scene of salvation and then disappears.

Apropos of the novella's purification and redemption themes, the final resolution scene is in a Jewish chapel. In the season of spiritual renewal, the quester affirms his Judaic identity. Tommy had begun this day of self-examination by considering his history of error and contemplating the Yom Kippur spirit of forgiveness. "You had to forgive. First to forgive yourself, and then general forgiveness" (30). He concludes the day in the honored tradition of contrition and spiritual return. Standing beneath the Star of David, a symbol long identified with the Jewish people and their cause, the quester finds "consummation of his heart's ultimate need" (128) in worship suggestive of Hasidic intensity and devotion.

Postscript

My 1982 analysis of Bellow's borrowings from Joseph Perl's *Revealer of Secrets* was based on my reading of Israel Davidson's description of Perl's satire. In 1997, the first English translation of *Revealer of Secrets* appeared in *Joseph Perl's Revealer of Secrets: The First Hebrew Novel*, trans. introduction and notes by Dov Taylor (Boulder, CO: Westview Press, 1997). In light of the recent translation, I must correct my initial attribution of manipulative invisibility to a corrupt *tzaddik* in Perl's text and note that the technique is, in fact, used by Perl's editor/narrator. This figure is a *maskil* masquerading as a devout Hasid to spy on the Hasidic spiritual leaders who are the targets of his satire and to facilitate collection of their correspondence. In the Prologue, the narrator justifies his chicanery as serving the higher good of revealing Hasidic secrets withheld from the public. Dov Taylor argues that adoption of this convention allows Perl "to strengthen the credibility of his hoax that [*Revealer of Secrets*] was actually an authentic hasidic work" (Taylor, xxix).

Notes

1. T. S. Eliot, "Tradition and the Individual Talent," in *Selected Essays 1917–1932* (New York: Harcourt, Brace, and World, 1950), 4.
2. Saul Bellow, *Seize the Day* (Greenwich, Conn.: Fawcett, 1956). Subsequent citations will be from this edition and appear in the text in parentheses.
3. Jewish critics of the Hasidic movement, known as *misnagdim* and *maskilim*, objected to attitudes and practices of Hasidim including Hasidic exaltation of their leaders whose authority stemmed from personal charisma irrespective of rabbinic ordination or scholarship; emphasis on the doctrine of immanence rather than the traditional Judaic balance between immanence and transcendence of God; establishment of separate synagogues; and dominant use of the Lurianic worship.
4. Ralph Ciancio, "The Achievement of Saul Bellow's *Seize the Day*," in *Literature and Theology*, edited by Thomas F. Staley and Lester F. Zimmerman (Tulsa, Okla.: University of Tulsa Press, 1969), 76. I am indebted to Ciancio, who identified the Hasid–zaddik relationship between Wilhelm and Tamkin.
5. Clinton Trowbridge, "Water Imagery in *Seize the Day*," *Critique* 9 (Summer 1967): 68.
6. Ibid.

7. Sarah Blacher Cohen, *Saul Bellow's Enigmatic Laughter* (Urbana: University of Illinois Press, 1974): 103.

8. Ibid., 105.

9. J. C. Levenson, "Bellow's Dangling Men," *Critique* 3 (Summer 1960): 9.

10. Nathan Ausubel, ed., "Introduction to *Schlemihls* and *Schlimazls*," in *A Treasury of Jewish Folklore* (New York: Crown, 1948), 343–44.

11. Ibid., "Introduction to *Schnorrers* and Beggars," 267–68.

12. The hidden saints conceal their true identities behind a mask of boorishness, poverty, and ignorance. The thirty-six hidden saints of Jewish legend, referred to as *Lamed-Vav Zaddikim*, serve the Jewish people in anonymity in periods of danger. See ibid., 204.

13. Israel Zangwill, *The King of the Schnorrers* (New York: Dover, 1965).

14. Yom Kippur, the Day of Atonement, is the culmination of a ten-day period of repentance that begins with Rosh Hashanah, the Day of Judgment. This season is characterized by reflection, moral and ethical self-examination, repentance, and spiritual regeneration. The Hebrew term for "repentance," *teshuvah*, signifies return to God and should not be confused with external manifestations of penitence or penance.

15. For a discussion of the operation of the East European zaddik's court, see Mark Zborowski and Elizabeth Herzog, *Life Is with People: Culture of the Shtetl* (New York: Schocken, 1962), 170.

16. Ibid., 172.

17. As spiritual leader of the Hasidic community, the zaddik functions as teacher and counsellor. The Hasid consulted the zaddik on matters of religion, economics, and familiar and social relationships. According to Martin Buber, "One of the great principles of hasidism is that the zaddik and the people are dependent on one another. . . . Their relationship is compared to that between substance and form in the life of the individual, between body and soul." Buber, *Tales of the Hasidim: Early Masters* (New York: Schocken, 1947), 7.

18. Martin Buber, *Hasidism and Modern Man*, edited by and trans. Maurice Friedman (New York: Horizon Press, 1958), 140.

19. Ibid., 174.

20. The zaddik is neither elected nor appointed by the community. Unlike the rabbi, he requires no ordination. His authority comes from his followers who believe in his mystical communion with God. He need not be, but frequently is, a man of scholarship.

21. Bernard Martin, *A History of Judaism: Europe in the New World* (New York: Basic Books, 1974), 2:184.

22. Ibid.

23. Joseph Perl (1774–1839), an Enlightenment figure, was convinced that only intellectual enlightenment, exposure to nonsacred Western thought, could change the difficult position of European ghetto Jews. In an effort to counteract Hasidim, who maintained separation from others, Perl was active in religious and social reform. In addition to *Megallah Temirim*, which was published under a pseudonym, Perl also published "Dibre Zaddikim" and "Bohen Zaddik," both in the satiric vein.

24. Israel Davidson, *Parody in Jewish Literature*, no. 2 of Columbia University Oriental Studies (New York: AMS Press, 1966), 60.

25. Judah Lob Rappaport (1790–1867) was an Austrian rabbi who published scholarly articles, translations, criticism, and poems. In 1837, Rappaport was appointed rabbi of Tarnapol through the efforts of Joseph Perl and his associates among the *maskilim.*

26. *Jewish Encyclopedia* (New York and London: Funk and Wagnalls, 1925), 9: 641.

27. Davidson, *Parody in Jewish Literature,* 62.

Works Cited

Ausubel, Nathan, ed. "Introduction to *Schlemihils* and *Schlimazls.*" In *A Treasury of Jewish Folklore,* 343–44. New York: Crown, 1948.

——. "Introduction to *Schnorrers* and Beggars." In *A Treasury of Jewish Folklore,* 267–68. New York: Crown, 1948.

Bellow, Saul. *Seize the Day.* Greenwich, Conn.: Fawcett, 1956.

Buber, Martin. *Hasidism and Modern Man,* edited and translated by Maurice Friedman. New York: Horizon Press, 1958.

——. *Tales of the Hasidim: Early Masters.* New York: Schocken, 1947.

Ciancio, Ralph. "The Achievement of Saul Bellow's *Seize the Day.*" In *Literature and Theology,* edited by Thomas F. Staley and Lester F. Zimmerman, 76. Tulsa, Okla.: University of Tulsa Press, 1969.

Cohen, Sarah Blacher. *Saul Bellow's Enigmatic Laughter.* Urbana: University of Illinois Press, 1974.

Davidson, Israel. *Parody in Jewish Literature.* No. 2 of Columbia University Oriental Studies, 1966.

Eliot, T. S. "Tradition and the Individual Talent." In *Selected Essays 1917–1932,* 4. New York: Harcourt, Brace, and World, 1950.

Jewish Encyclopedia. Vol. 9. New York and London: Funk and Wagnalls, 1925.

Levenson, J. C. "Bellow's Dangling Men." *Critique* 3 (Summer 1960): 9.

Martin, Bernard. *A History of Judaism: Europe in the New World.* Vol. 2. New York: Basic Books, 1974.

Trowbridge, Clinton. "Water Imagery in *Seize the Day.*" *Critique* 9 (Summer 1967): 68.

Zangwill, Israel. *The King of the Schnorrers.* New York: Dover, 1965.

Zborowski, Mark, and Elizabeth Herzog. *Life Is with People: Culture of the Shtetl.* New York: Schocken, 1962.

Atonement in Bellow's *Seize the Day*

GAYE McCOLLUM SIMMONS

As a precaution to those who would read Judaism into Bellow's work, L. H. Goldman reminds the readers of Bellow's fiction that Bellow has "consistently rejected the category 'Jewish-American writer' for himself," though she allows that Bellow is not rejecting his Jewishness but the category, "which he views as a limiting factor" ("Saul Bellow and the Philosophy of Judaism," 57). If it is well to keep in mind that Bellow is writing more than an apologetic for a specific community, however, it is undoubtedly the case that Saul Bellow has internalized the Jewish tradition out of which he comes. And while Judaism is an explicit text in most of his novels, the tradition's influence is never so keenly felt as it is in *Seize the Day*.

Ironically, with critics cautiously avoiding the locus of Judaism, the readings of *Seize the Day* have been especially limited. And while it is true that all readings are necessarily partial, to ignore the Jewish influence is to introduce unnecessary silences into the critical corpus on this work.[1] Additionally, "Jewish tradition" is itself problematical in that there are so many expressions of it. A noncredal religion, Judaism is best thought of as a 6,000 year-old conversation, contentious and philosophically rich, with an impulse toward the open and contingent and an impulse away from the closed and dogmatic. There is an ethos, nevertheless, that cuts across these multiple conversations. Ethical monotheism requires a constant care of the self in its relation to God *and* a constant care of the self in relation to the entire human community. It is this ethos that interests Bellow as an artist; it is what Goldman calls "Bellow's urgent desire to restore a balance to man's existence" (Goldman, "Saul Bellow and the Philosophy of Judaism," 58).[2]

To restore this balance, what then does ethical monotheism require but acts of loving kindness (*hesed*) toward both the self and the

Reprinted from *Saul Bellow Journal* 11, no. 2 & 12, no. 1 (Double Issue 1993): 30-53.

community? *Seize the Day* is a novella about Tommy Wilhelm's mostly unarticulated desire to restore a balance to his own existence; it is about his own experience of *hesed,* and the lack thereof. While Tommy begins as one of Bellow's "dangling men," it is an incomplete reading that sees him as ending merely as another of this century's alienated fragments. I suggest that the proclivity to see Wilhelm as finally and irrecoverably alienated is a mistake predicated upon not recognizing just how strong the pull of culture is in disrupting full assimilation as well as in interrupting the universalizing tendencies of assimilationist readings. Indeed, Goldman cautions against the misapplication of such "negative qualities" as alienation and exile to Bellow's work (*Saul Bellow's Moral Vision,* xii). Here I would quibble with Goldman and with Robert Alter, whom she quotes. Exile and alienation are not the same thing, and to treat them as such is to lose the tension that a tradition in exile creates. Whereas alienation suggests a complete separation and loss of identity, exile suggests a residual ethnicity, a particular ethic that provides a situation out of which one might know and a narrative by which one might understand oneself anew.[3] In fact, what is in place in Tommy's alienated and fragmented world is a tradition that is so strong that even the dead have a part in it. Through that tradition, Judaism takes stock of itself during the Days of Atonement (Rosh ha–Shanah through Yom Kippur) and, as such, this tradition is the means by which even fully assimilated Jews are reminded of their bond with Judaism and of the necessity for an ethical bond with humankind.

With the exception of L. H. Goldman's work, the critical work on *Seize the Day* has all but ignored the Judaic tradition in favor of an admittedly fruitful discussion of American Romanticism and the dangling existential man.[4] This silence is especially odd given that Tommy's day in New York is Yom Kippur (86). While I certainly do not expect in such a short space to tease out all the complexities of what it might mean to be Jewish in America, or even to be Jewish in America with a particular "affirmativist" view of the human condition,[5] I do mean to ask that we consider further Jewish readings alongside both the American Romantic and the American existentialist readings of *Seize the Day* (both readings seem to be complicated by Christian assumptions) and to recommend that we take another look, this time through texts that are peculiar to Judaism.[6] I will be using S. Y. Agnon's *Days of Awe* (1948), a very rich synopsis of the ritual and traditions surrounding the high holy days. In addition, I will be drawing upon the *Yoma* tractate of the Talmud for the rabbinic discussions about the importance and the requirements surrounding these days. And, finally, from the *Pesikta Rabbati,* I will bring the rabbinic homilies to bear upon what I see to be Tommy Wilhelm's decidedly Jewish experience of atonement.

Christian atonement is accomplished by proxy—Christ's blood—and is final and unrepeatable. For Jews, atonement is ultimately a very different process, requiring no extraordinary mediation between the human and the divine. Metaphorically speaking, the tradition itself mediates insofar as it creates a space, annually, in which a person might see himself in relation to others and not despair. Just as the light of day was sustained for thirty-six hours during the "first day of the world," the days for repentance are "like the beginning of [God's] work" and in those days "the light is prolonged for [humanity's] sake in order not to distress [it]" (*Pesikta*, 46.1). The high holy days are like that prolonged light and provide a time to respond to the imperative to "Remake yourselves by repentance during the ten days between" as well as for the realization of the promise that "on the Day of Atonement I will hold you guiltless, regarding you as a newly made creature" (*Pesikta*, 40.2). So, in a Jewish reading, we should expect to see Tommy Wilhelm as a man struggling with his past and pleading for help and, in the end, we should expect to see Wilhelm aware of his common human lot and out of that awareness returning his soul to those around him.

Seize the Day insists that we "put nothing human from us" by placing us firmly in New York, "with its complexity and machinery" (83). Judaism does not teach hatred for the chaotic, fragmented world of New York (or anywhere else, for that matter); on the contrary, it requires an acknowledgment of complicity in and an acceptance of fellow human suffering and joy. Agnon cites the question from *Yesod ha-Teshuvah*, "Why was the Confession composed in the plural, so that we say, 'We have sinned,' rather than 'I have sinned'?" He follows with Rabbi Isaac Luria's answer: "We are all responsible for one another when we sin . . . and despite the fact that one has not committed [an] iniquity, one must confess to it. For when one's fellow has sinned, it is as though one has sinned oneself" (Agnon, 220). Such an acknowledgment of complicity initiates an atonement with a messy and conflicted humanity.

As we shall discover in reviewing the work's seven episodes, *Seize the Day* does not replicate the religious service on the Day of Atonement (Yom Kippur) as a full-scale allegory might, though there is something allegorical about the process. There are few exact correspondences to the traditional rituals and prayers. As Goldman observes, however, "although Bellow's ethical monotheism is devoid of all Jewish ritual on the protagonist's part, it remains in his memory" ("Saul Bellow and the Philosophy of Judaism," 54). These traces are sufficiently present to allow us to assert that Tommy finally manages to seize the day.

It may be argued that Tommy is not strong enough to take control of his life even for one day, but it is the losers, the weak, and the self-centered who are returned to the community and called into a relationship with the Father, whose mercy is made manifest by just such a reconciliation. A mental inventory of the Hebrew scriptures should confirm my point. Rabbinic tradition, too, has made provision for the inclusion of even the weakest individuals:

> Consider the parable of a prince who was far away from his father—a hundred days' journey away. His friends said to him: "Return to your father." He replied: "I cannot: I have not the strength." Thereupon his father sent word, saying to him: "Come back as far as you can according to your strength, and I will go the rest of the way to meet you." (*Pesikta,* 44.9)

Out of a modern sense of diaspora, Tommy Wilhelm observes the day as a Jew in exile cut off from his father, who is himself a Jew in exile. It is highly unlikely that Tommy would be able to articulate his experiences in traditional terminology and, as there is no narrator translating his experiences into theological terms, we must find our own way through Tommy's confusion and muddled point of view.

Let us begin with Tommy Wilhelm's condition. Standing in the mezzanine of the Hotel Gloriana, Tommy is introduced in the lengthy first episode as a perfect example of modern alienation. He is completely cut off in space and time. There is no community of which he is a part, and he is so unsynchronized as to be in some sense living *in* borrowed time. His "home," the Gloriana, is completely given over to those well past the age of retirement (4), and Tommy, who is in his midforties but looks "much younger than his years" (6), is obviously an anomaly. Yet he attempts to place himself in time and space by asserting that he is "doing all right" and by "following a daily course" of rising early and getting out, "which had in itself become the chief business" (4). He is a man going through the motions of keeping up appearances and getting by on charm and a Jack Fagman shirt.

In direct contrast to Tommy's contrived appearance, we get a glimpse through his own eyes of his "inescapable self" (25). We see thereby that he has always been pitching himself headlong into chaos. Tommy's plight is that of the modern man who tosses himself from place to place and between past and future in a kind of self-inflicted, self-maintained exile. Ever since Tommy walked away from his family, making "his first great mistake" (17) by exchanging his name for a chance at stardom, he has chosen to separate himself again and again from any kind of community. In leaving his family (mother, father, sister, wife, and sons) and walking away from both college and a job, Tommy has abandoned any opportunity to find a place within a community of fellow human beings.

Further, Tommy separates himself not only from others but from himself; that is, he suffers from a kind of psychic alienation. Believing that he can become an extraordinary individual only by isolating himself from his family, Tommy chooses against his own sound judgment and leaves home.

> This was typical of Wilhelm. After much thought and hesitation and debate he invariably took the course he had rejected innumerable times. Ten such decisions made up the history of his life. He had decided that it would be a bad mistake to go to Hollywood, and then he went. He had made up his mind not to marry his wife, but ran off and got married. He had resolved not to invest money with Tamkin, and then had given him a check. (23)

It's not that Tommy's judgment is poor; rather, he betrays his own good sense with the choices he ultimately makes. His remaining alternative is to create fictions to cover up his mistakes. Though Tommy is aware that he tells lies out of "charity to himself" (15), lying becomes a habit of mind he can no longer control. It may be true that Tommy "could still separate what he had invented from the actual happenings" (15), but the continual and necessary fragmentation precludes any integrated experience. Before finishing the first episode, the reader knows that on this morning in the Gloriana mezzanine "the smooth door [of the elevator] opens" upon a man alone and disintegrating (3).

Bellow does not leave the reader with this vision of an alienated and drifting Tommy for very long, however. By the end of the first page, the novella's water imagery promises a change. Appearing almost bloodlike, "the great dark-red uneven carpet . . . billows toward Wilhelm's feet" (3). The mixed imagery, blood and water, is our first allusion to the ritual of atonement. During the two periods of Jewish temple worship, blood was spilled to atone for sins. After the destruction of the second temple (70 C.E.), weeping and prayer substituted for sacrifice. Yet the conditions for the spilling of sacrificial blood are carefully delineated in the Rosh ha-Shanah tractate and form a part of the lore surrounding the days of repentance (*Rosh ha-Shanah* 28b). Even though the reason behind the imagery may escape us at first, the general point is clear. Something new awaits Tommy. He intuits that his "routine [is] about to break up and he senses that a huge trouble long presaged but till now formless [is] due" (4). His charitable lies have created the delusion that "he was more capable than the next fellow when it came to concealing his troubles" (14). When Tommy and Rubin, who "knew, and knew, and knew" (6), gaze across the street at the Ansonia, they see something that could very well be emblematic of Tommy, "the image of [himself] reflected in deep water, white and cumulus above, with cavernous distortions underneath" (5). When Tommy's routine is finally broken apart, it will reveal the distortions, the lies within. Those lies, the formless chaos of his soul, will be given form. When Tommy can name his sins and recognize what he really needs, he will have made an accounting and created order out of chaos. Recognizing the disarray of the amorphous soul, the Morning Prayer of Yom Kippur asks that one's life be given substance, pleading, "My God, before I was formed, I was of no worth, and now that I have been formed, it is as if I had not been formed. I am dust in my life" (*Yoma* 87b). Thus, on Yom Kippur, in order to become substantial (formed) while remaining within the messiness of human experience, form out of formlessness is due.

The sense that something is due is one of the major unifying themes of *Seize the Day*. "Due" could mean in this context either "expected" or "owed." Eventually, however, the reader discovers that Bellow means to imply both meanings, and he creates from the pun on the word *due* his accounting or reckoning metaphor. In the first sense, "expected," Tommy is going to know "before evening," and what he will know is his "heart's ultimate need" (118). While Goldman is partly correct in assuming that Tommy sees his heart's ultimate need as "a rightful place in the familial structure" (*Saul Bellow's Moral Vision*, 73), the morning prayer, which begins "Master of the universe, fill the needs of our heart *for our good*" (emphasis added), allows for something other than what an individual might think is his or her ultimate need. In a religious context, such a disjuncture between what a person prays for and what a person gets as a result of that prayer points to the omniscience of the divine. In a secular context, the same disjuncture points to the limits of human knowledge and, as such, is a critique of abstract individualism. That is, apart from what Bellow calls the "imperfect and lurid-looking people" (84) and apart from a communal ethos, the individual cannot know what he needs, especially what he ultimately needs.

Aware that he is lacking something, Tommy is able to wrinkle his brow to form a "comprehensive bracket sign ([ ]) upon his forehead" (6), a sign that in accounting denotes an account in arrears—a loss. Tommy is a loser, not because he fails to live the American dream, but because he lacks integration. Tommy sees the fallibility of individualism and the search for success, yet he cannot overcome the losses they have brought into his own life. These losses estrange him from himself, his family (or community), and God. In fact, Tommy's characterization of his losses serves as a metaphor for sin. Sin, in the Jewish tradition, is "shortcoming due to error and thoughtlessness" (Sperling, 218). With sin, as with his losses in the gin game, "Tommy couldn't afford to lose any more. . . . And while the losses were small they weren't gains, were they? They were losses. He was tired of losing" (7).

Tommy would like to turn his losses to gains. He attempts this by alternately seeking reconciliation with his own father and by turning to Dr. Tamkin as a surrogate. It is important in this context to discuss the fathers briefly, because money in both relationships becomes a metaphor for the indebtedness between fathers and sons, which in turn becomes a metaphor for the indebtedness between the human and the divine. Tommy needs more from his father, Dr. Adler, than money to pay his rent. Tommy remarks that if he could "speak his mind or ease his heart" to his father, he wouldn't turn to Tamkin (11). But Dr. Adler cannot abide his son's shortcomings, and Tommy's indebtedness to him for past slights as well as Tommy's inability to pay his rent at the Gloriana stand between any kind of reconciliation between father and son. By contrast, while Dr. Adler deals in the past, Dr. Tamkin deals in the future—in futures, to be exact. Tommy has mortgaged his future to Tamkin through his investment in lard, or schmaltz. Dr. Adler, "idolized by everyone" (11), is not God, and Dr. Tamkin, scandalized by everyone and looking a great deal like Satan himself, is only a charlatan and not the devil. That neither doctor can cure anything is a part of rabbinic lore surrounding the days given to repentance. To get the full impact of the analogy, I include the entire parable:

> Israel may be likened to a man who had a swelling which a physician opened up. Now when the man with the swelling saw that the swelling was not healing, he began to go about to other physicians, but they could find no healing for him. Then he was told: You keep going to one physician after another, but they have no way of healing you because they do not know what kind of a swelling you have. If you want to be healed, go back to him who first opened you up and he will heal you.
> (*Pesikta*, 33.7)

Turning in disappointment from Adler to Tamkin and back again, Tommy next turns in desperation to the Father who can redeem the debts of both the past and future, to "him who first opened [him] up" (*Pesikta*, 33.7). Believing that the "pathetic day when the sin [of changing his name] was committed was past and dead" (25), Tommy turns and prays, "Oh,

God. Let me out of my trouble. Let me out of my thoughts, and let me do something better with myself. For all the time I have wasted I am very sorry. Let me out of this clutch and into a different life. For I am all balled up. Have mercy" (26). With this prayer, which accomplishes two things at once, Tommy has done enough to redeem himself. First, prayer is thought to be greater than repentance, more efficacious, in that it is uttered by one in distress, by one who cannot, because of that distress, possibly know exactly of what he must repent. Second, "a man's dire distress may be the cause of his being redeemed," for "in thy distress, when all these things are come upon thee, at the end of the year. . . . He will not forget the covenant with thy fathers" (*Pesikta* 47.1, 44.9, 40.2; Deut. 4:30). Again, tradition draws the individual into itself, insofar as Tommy is drawn into the promises of the covenant and the ethos of the fathers. By evening, Tommy will know that his prayer has been answered. Indeed, the prayer is a final turning that concludes the novella's first episode and sets in motion the fulfillment of Tommy's ultimate need.[7]

With the prayer at the end of episode one, *Teshuvah* has begun. *Teshuvah* is the Hebrew word for repentance, and it literally means "to turn." Among other things, *Seize the Day* is a story about turning and returning, affirming movement toward community and the possibility for human wholeness. In *Days of Awe*, Agnon emphasizes the connection between *Teshuvah* and community: "We must still fulfill a great principle of *Teshuvah*, which is the acceptance of the commandment 'Thou shalt love thy neighbor as thyself' . . . [from this] unification of our souls to love our neighbors will follow" (Agnon, 206). Tommy's remark to Tamkin, that "a man is only as good as what he loves" (10), anticipates such a unity.

Episodes two through six cover the period from breakfast to early afternoon. During breakfast, Tommy attempts to come to some kind of understanding with his father, Dr. Adler. During late morning and lunch, he comes to understand Dr. Tamkin. In the early afternoon, Tommy returns to his father and leaves knowing himself and Dr. Adler better. The water imagery is concentrated in these five episodes and appears to divide itself into two forms—the glasses of water and the Lycidas/Jonah allusions. The glasses of water serve to define the relationship between Tommy and his father and ultimately to say something about atonement with the Father. The Lycidas/Jonah allusions clarify Tommy's relationships with others, relating first to Tamkin and then later to all of humanity, and emerge as the controlling image of Tommy's atonement with the community.

As we have already seen, Dr. Adler refuses to redeem Tommy from his indebtedness. Tommy's filthy exterior and chaotic interior are repugnant to his father. Likewise, Tommy's messy emotional life confounds his father, who dismisses Tommy's anguish by keeping his "sympathy for the real ailments" (42). Dr. Adler recommends "water and exercise" (45) as a cure for Tommy's problems, but of course Tommy is right to insist on more than a bath and a walk. We sense that Tommy's exterior reflects his impoverished, chaotic interior. In episode one, when we first meet Tommy, we are aware of the difficulties Tommy has had to make himself look "passably well" (3). In fact, Tommy continually berates himself for his disheveled appearance, but his messy soul is unable to exert any control over his messy body. It is as if Tommy's soul, though weak, is ashamed of his "clunky" body. The *Yoma* tractate cautions the observers of Yom Kippur that "it is forbidden to wash part of the body, as [it is forbidden] to wash the whole body" (*Yoma* 77b). Agnon makes the point that on the Day of Atonement one should not wash because "*the soul is not supposed to be at home in the body*" as it is atonement that "removes all manner of filth" (195–96; emphasis added). Granted, Tommy is not thinking about keeping the provisions of Yom Kippur when he does not wash this morning (or any other morning). Nevertheless, if we agree that Tommy's soul and body are both filthy and at war with one another, then we can see that Dr. Adler's cure will not make Tommy's soul comfortable in his body.

Tommy ultimately needs neither money nor advice from his father—he needs acceptance. In episode three, Tommy's pleadings and his father's refusals intensify, widening the chasm between them. When "the doctor opened his small hand on the table in a gesture so old and so typical that Wilhelm felt it like an actual touch upon the foundations of his life" (44), the reader sees the possibility for something more between father and son. Yet Tommy and Dr. Adler remain separate, like the two glasses of water on the table at breakfast. The "small hoops of brilliance . . . cast by the water glasses" (31), though not joined in their reflections, offer an image that prepares the reader for the expanded vision of individuals poured out into humanity developed later in episode five.

Turning from his father, Wilhelm struggles in episodes four, five, and six with his father–son relationship with Dr. Tamkin. Tamkin is the philosophical opposite of Dr. Adler, but the paternal equivalent. While Dr. Adler is concerned with appearances and with pragmatism, Tamkin says that he is concerned with the soul and with idealism. While Adler is concerned with washing Tommy's body, Tamkin is concerned with washing Tommy's soul. Neither father can fulfill Tommy's need. The unctuous Tamkin preaches his "mishmash" (75) as a corrective for the ills of Tommy's soul. Were Tommy to listen to the "real soul" rather than the "pretender soul" and to give in to his "own glory" (75), he would be well. Tamkin confides, "The past is no good to us. The future is full of anxiety. Only the present is real—the here-and-now," and he advises Tommy to "seize the day" (66).[8] As both Tommy and the reader know, there is something not quite right about Tamkin. Someone who lauds the here-and-now while he speculates in futures and manipulates the facts of the past cannot be trusted. Tamkin, "the confuser of the imagination," urges Tommy into fierce individualism and further away from union with others. When he tells Tommy to seize the day, Tamkin intends for Tommy to see himself as a king who should rest in his own glory (75). Though Tamkin is not Satan, something Satanic resonates from his being:

> What a creature Tamkin was . . . gull's nose . . . deceiver's brown eyes. . . . His bones were peculiarly formed, as though twisted twice where the ordinary human bone was turned only once. . . . He stood pigeon-toed, a sign perhaps that he was devious or had much to hide. The skin of his hands was aging, and his nails were moonless, concave, clawlike, and they appeared loose. There was a hypnotic power in his eyes. (62)

The resonance is made stronger through an allusion to *Paradise Lost*. Both Tamkin and Tommy are talking about their estrangement from their fathers. Tamkin, who confuses Tommy's imagination, has just completed a fabrication about his own father; Tommy now speaks of his own confusion as "chaos and old night" (93; *Paradise Lost* I, 543).

Not only does Tamkin mortgage Tommy's financial future, but in the most sinister sense he tries to cheat Tommy of his spiritual future as well. If he were to follow Tamkin's tempting advice, Tommy would remain an isolated individual, believing in the division of the psyche (pretender and real souls) and the kind of possibility for success that comes only to one who can ignore the individual's responsibility toward his fellow human beings. As weak as Tommy is, he is able to resist Tamkin's alluring message. Perhaps experience has taught Tommy that extreme individualism is the cause of his own alienation and fragmentation. An eighteenth-century story embedded in the sermon before *Kol Nidre* (the evening of Yom Kippur) helps us to understand, according to tradition, the impotence of Tamkin's advice:

> [Yom Kippur] is like the story about the son of a lord, on whom one of the officers used continually to inform. Once the informer left the city; at once the son ran to his father and cried and supplicated before

him, saying that he regretted the evil he had done and was ready from that time on to leave his evil way. At once his father's compassion was moved, and he drew the son near to himself and rejoiced greatly over him. The reference is evident [the rabbis say]: "On Yom Kippur, Satan has no permission to act as accuser." (Agnon, 205)

Further, Tamkin tells Tommy that his father and his wife are wrong to "marry suffering" and that Tommy should not "play [his wife's] game" (98). Such advice drives a deeper wedge into Tommy's relationships. Though Tamkin would separate Tommy from his family, Tommy knows the cost and realizes with anguish that he is deprived of his children (98).

Tommy also realizes that he "is trying to stay alive and work[ing] too hard at it" (99). This working too hard defeats its own end. Trying to put together his own life is just as futile as Tommy's efforts in the commodities market. In fact, both are speculations in the future. On this day, as on the Day of Atonement, Tommy's day of reckoning, "any work will come to naught" (Agnon, 198). Tamkin's advice is schmaltz and his investment is lard—when rendered, both come to naught. As in the parable above, once Tamkin leaves the city, Tommy's atonement will be completed.

As Tommy comes to see the truth about Tamkin, his impression grows that he is drowning and that "the waters of the earth [are] going to roll over him" (77). Early in episode four, where the reader is introduced to Dr. Tamkin and his philosophy, Tommy establishes the relationship between atonement and his sense of drowning. After feeling that his chest is constricted, "he smell[s] the salt odor of tears in his nose" (56). This experience is immediately connected with the following insight:

> But at the same time, since there were depths in Wilhelm not unsuspected by himself, he received a suggestion from some remote element in his thought that the business of life, the real business—to carry his peculiar burden, to feel shame and impotence, to taste these quelled tears—the only important business, the highest business was being done. (56)

Tommy follows this insight with a misappropriation of a line from *Lycidas*. He accepts the fact that he will "finally sink beneath that watery floor" (56). He feels that he is being drowned by the demands of others; his problems are all awash in his "unshed tears [which] rose [until] he looked like a man about to drown" (140). But the Miltonic line is anything but pessimistic; "sunk though he be beneath the wat'ry floor" promises deliverance from a watery grave. A biblical allusion completes the Miltonic promise of resurrection. The story of Jonah is considered by Jews to be a story of resurrection. Sent by God to Nineveh to preach repentance to the community there, Jonah chooses to go his own way instead. God dumps Jonah overboard where he is swallowed by a large fish (not a whale), remaining there until he repents. God hears the penitent even "in the uttermost parts of the sea" and redeems him from his suffering (Agnon, 262–64). Jonah's repentance and that of the entire community of Nineveh are inextricably linked. The Book of Jonah is read during the afternoon service of Yom Kippur to remind those who are making *Teshuvah* of the mercy of God (Agnon, 188, 262–64).

Bellow varies the image of the fish and the sea and makes a further allusion to Yom Kippur. As Tommy thinks of his father and mother, "there was a great pull at the very center of his soul. When a fish strikes the line you feel the live force in your hand. A mysterious being beneath the water, driven by hunger, has taken the hook and rushes away and fights, writhing" (92). Tradition reminds the Jew during Yom Kippur "that we are like so many fish caught unawares in the net of judgment and justice." This awareness should impel us to sincere "repentance" (Sperling, 229). Clearly, the tug at the very center of the soul signals a need for reconciliation. "The mysterious being beneath the water" is that which hinders peace in the soul.

As Nineveh was for Jonah, so New York is for Tommy. It is also a "Tower of Babel in paint" (32), a place "where every other man [speaks] a language entirely his own" (83). Tommy is not calling its inhabitants to repentance, but he does become one with them, recognizing something that the strong often do not recognize—human complexity and his complicity in humanity. Recalling from episode three that the glass of water image stands for the isolated individual, we must consider that glass of water further. Tommy laments that to "talk about a glass of water, you had to start back with God creating the heavens and the earth; the apple; Abraham; Moses and Jesus; Rome; the Middle Ages; gunpowder; the Revolution; back to Newton; up to Einstein; then war and Lenin and Hitler" (83). In such a catalog, Tommy traces the history of his people, the Jews. He is right when he says that "after getting [the history] all straight you could proceed to talk about a glass of water" (83). One is indeed bound to one's ancestry. The individual is not worth discussing without his tie to his people; the tie broken, he has to reiterate continually what at one time would have been assumed. Tommy is again correct in his judgment that "it was the punishment of hell itself not to understand or be understood" (84). Communication is impossible without the community.

In the subway a few days earlier, Tommy envisioned "a larger body, from [which] you cannot be separated. The glass of water fades out" (84).

Today, on "his day of reckoning," Tommy wants to return to that feeling. It was "something very big. Truth, like":

> On the walls between the advertisements were words in chalk: "Sin No More," and "Do Not Eat the Pig." And in the dark tunnel, in the haste, heat, and darkness . . . all of a sudden, unsought, a general love for all these imperfect and lurid-looking people burst out in Wilhelm's breast. He loved them. One and all, he passionately loved them. They were his brothers and sisters. He was imperfect and disfigured himself, but what difference did that make if he was united with them by this blaze of love? (85)

Together in their disfigurations and imperfections, humanity suffers and loves, and the individual leaves aside alienation and fragmentation as he or she joins the community of humans. During Yom Kippur, "every place where suffering weeps, the Jew weeps," for no one is redeemed outside of the community (Agnon, 220).

At the beginning of episode seven, "the hoary old fiddler [again] points his bow at Wilhelm, [but] Wilhelm . . . denies his omen" (105). Though Tommy denies the omen, thus denying that he has accounts to reckon, his prayer early that morning has set the process in motion. He has two people with whom he must settle: his father Dr. Adler and his wife Margaret. Though in both cases he seeks initially to clear up his financial indebtedness, he ends up pleading for mercy from each. First, Tommy hurries to see Dr. Adler, who is bathing in the hotel spa. Initially, Tommy ignores the business of atonement in order to seek his father's help in settling his business account, now depleted by Tamkin. His father refuses, so Tommy makes a second plea. To his father, Tommy complains that his "chest is all up—[he] feels choked," and he then stares at "his father's nakedness" (109). A crucial moment between father and son, this scene allows Tommy to see his father for what he is, while it alludes to Noah's son, cursed by his father for looking upon his nakedness. Dr. Adler, sensing the importance of the recognition, "was making an effort to keep his temper. He was on the verge of an explosion" (109). This time, Tommy is not standing before his father pleading for money to save him, for "it isn't all a question of money" (109). He has returned to ask for a blessing: "'one word from you, just a word . . . there are other things a father can give to a son'" (109). Unfortunately, Tommy's recognition and his "look of suffering appeal stir his father even more deeply against him" (109), and Tommy receives not a blessing but a curse: "'You want to make yourself into my cross. But I am not going to pick up a cross. I'll see you dead,

Wilky, by Christ, before I let you do that to me. . . . Go away from me now. It's torture for me to look at you, you slob'" (110).

Next, though he has not intended to call his wife, Tommy is compelled to do so by the seeming urgency of a phone message she has left for him. When he does call, he discovers that she is only asking that he pay her the alimony he owes. Relieved that his sons are all right, he pleads with Margaret to "go easy on [him for he is] suffocating" (113). She refuses and hangs up on him—her way of cursing him. At this point, Tommy has completed the requirements of *Teshuvah*. He has no further responsibility for his sins (shortcomings and thoughtlessness) against his father and his wife. In Judaism, "for transgression of things between man and his fellow man, the Day of Atonement does not bring atonement to a man unless he makes peace with his fellow man" (*Yoma* 8.9), but if his fellow man refuses and "holds on to his arrogance, no remission will be granted him" (*Pesikta*, 38.1).

In the first half of episode seven, *Teshuvah* is completed; in the second half, atonement is achieved. On Broadway, Tommy experiences the "larger body" (84) in "the great crowd, the inexhaustible current of millions of every race and kind pouring out, pressing round, of every age, of every genius, possessors of every human secret antique and future" (115). Calling after someone he supposes is Tamkin, "Wilhelm [is] moved forward by the pressure of the crowd" into a chapel where a Jewish funeral is taking place. As he looks down into the coffin, all the tears that had been choking him come forth. Agnon tells us that as one "engages in the study of the death of these righteous, it will be accounted for you as though you were sacrificing on this day and it will make atonement for you" (Agnon, 231). Further, the penitent offers proof by letting "his tears fall for [those who have died]" (Agnon, 232). Agnon explains why the tears for the dead atone for the living: "The mention of death breaks a man's heart and subdues his inclination to evil. This is particularly true when the deaths of the beloved and pleasant men who sanctified the name of heaven in their lives and in their deaths are mentioned" (Agnon, 237).

As Tommy weeps for "a man—another human creature" (117), he joins himself to that man's suffering and can now weep for his own situation. Tommy is "soon past words, past reason, coherence" (117). His grief is complete. Sorrow has come with tears that "convulsed his body, bending his stubborn head, bowing his shoulders, twisting his face," so that "he gave in utterly and held his face and wept" (90, 118). Tommy's prayer of this morning has been answered. He has been "let out of his thoughts" and "let out of this clutch" (26). God has been merciful.

Not only has Tommy found atonement with the dead, he has found it with the living as well. Moments before he is pressed into the chapel,

Tommy captures the vision he has had two days earlier in the dark subway. This time he experiences the "something very big. Truth, like" in the sunlight (85):

> And the great, great crowd, the inexhaustible current of millions of every race and kind pouring out, pressing round, of every age, of every genius, possessors of every human secret, antique and future, in every face the refinement of one particular motive or essence—*I labor, I spend, I strive, I design, I love, I cling, I uphold, I give way, I envy, I long, I scorn, I die, I hide, I want.* (115)

Tommy recognizes that the "particular essence," the "I," is a part of "the great, great crowd" and that the "I" is his own striving and desiring, his own loving and upholding. He understands that he is part of the "larger body, from [which he] cannot be separated" (84). It is a recognition by a particular and historically located individual that he or she has an investment in the ongoing life and health of the larger community. This, too, is at the heart of the Jewish ethos. In this case, *tikkun olam*, repairing the world, is accomplished by this recognition, as expressed in the following homily on community and atonement:

> On New Year's Day the entire world stands for judgment before the Holy One, blessed be He. Although the world deserves extermination because its creatures are soiled by transgressions, nevertheless the Holy One, blessed be He, declares His world to be free of guilt. So you may conclude that on New Year's Day it is as though the world were created anew. (*Pesikta*, 40.5)

Paradoxically, a bystander remarks about the improbability of Tommy's brotherhood with the dead man: "they're not alike at all. Night and day" (118). By such an observation, Tommy is transformed into a distinct individual, "a possessor of every human secret" (115). As episode seven concludes, Tommy's alienation and fragmentation also end. The comic difference between the corpse and Tommy is that Tommy is alive— truly a difference between night and day. On Yom Kippur, one is thankful to God "who has kept us alive" and "waked us from a terrible dream" (Agnon, 215). Once grieving and atonement are complete, the rabbis declare, "let all the tears we shed on this day be tears of joy—we who are alive every one of us this day. For weeping on this day will not avail if there is sadness in it" (Agnon, 207). As the people weep in joy, "light is sown"

(Agnon, 209). So it is for Tommy, when the light and the music "poured into him where he had hidden himself in the center of a crowd by the great and happy oblivion of tears. He heard it and sank deeper than sorrow, through torn sobs and cries toward the consummation of his heart's ultimate need" (118).

Tommy's tears join the tears first of sorrow and then of joy. By releasing what he has been holding back, he becomes a member of humanity. He is no longer merely a single glass of water casting hoops of brilliance but part of the heavy, sea-like music of the great crowd. As Tommy grieves over his sins and unites his suffering with that of others, he at last can "understand and be understood" (83–84). Finally, his are tears of joy, for "the soul is not in pain at the end of the Day" (Agnon, 275).

Weeping is a peculiar sign, a kind of sacrifice joined with prayer to effect atonement. Tommy has turned from his past, first by giving it form, naming each shortcoming, each thoughtlessness, and then by forgiving himself and others. He has prayed for mercy, however feeble and desperate his prayer, and has received it. He has offered the sacrifice of prayer and weeping. He has, in truth, seized the day. That morning, he knew something long presaged awaited him and that "to [have] forfeit[ed] the Day [would have been] an irrecoverable and irreplaceable loss" (*Pi-Shenayim, Tallit Aheret*, quoted in *Encycl. Judaica* 6:1384). By sundown, it is completed.

Whether Tommy takes hold of his life after this experience is not a relevant question. The novella is over. It leaves the reader at the edge of the abyss knowing that most of us are wont to blink now and again. As Goldman tells us, "the cleavage" between an increasingly nihilistic world and Bellow's optimism "is caused in the main by [his] indebtedness to Jewish philosophers and possibly the influence of their writings on Christian thinkers with whom Bellow is familiar." This optimism asserts that "if life is sacred, then survival is a moral obligation." And while I concur with Goldman's subtle distinction between the search for an identity and the "quest for a significant existence that would embrace [an] identity, such as it is" ("Saul Bellow and the Philosophy of Judaism," 53, 54, 58), I would add that a "significant existence" depends upon both the sanctity of the private self and the constant care of the community, which may, in turn, depend upon hearing the particular cultural resonances out of which a private self might emerge. Insofar as Bellow expects to awaken the reader from the anesthesia of assimilation on one hand and of abstract individualism on the other, *Seize the Day* is a piece of conversion poetics, calling the reader to become a *mensch* in a world seeking to reduce all to a faceless and characterless universal humankind.

Notes

1. Gloria Cronin, in her introduction to *Saul Bellow in the 1980s*, celebrates what she calls the "second wave" of Bellow criticism for its attention to cultural particulars. According to Cronin, L. H. Goldman's work on Bellow's Jewish sources exemplifies this "second wave." See Goldman's "The Philosophy of Judaism" in *Saul Bellow in the 1980s* for Bellow's indebtedness to Jewish philosophers, from Moses ben Maimonides to Leo Baeck and, ultimately, to the Hebrew Scriptures.

2. When the artist seeks to make peace or to repair the world (*tikkun olam*), art becomes an act of loving kindness (*hesed*) by pointing out both human frailty and potential through anecdote and narrative. In this, the artist enters the tradition of the parabalist. See *Pesikta* 50.6: "Come and see how great is the reward of him who makes peace between man and man." For the Christian counterpart, see John Freccero's introduction to *Dante: A Collection of Critical Essays* in which Freccero observes that "Dante considered his poem to be a relationship between his experience and the experience of his readers, not simply a literary object"; furthermore, the poem is "an attempt at unification of the self" (2–4). See also Freccero's *Dante: The Poetics of Conversion*.

3. Gerhard Bach, in his "The Dean Who Came in from the Cold," observes that "there is a strong gravitational force pulling mankind away from itself into a collective stupor" (304) and cites from *The Dean's December* that "unless you pass [the world] through your own soul you can't understand it" (305). I agree with Bach, but, as souls are made up out of material effects, I would particularize the soul and would prefer to talk about the mind in this context. Here I find Donna Haraway's "Situated Knowledges" compelling in her discussion of the effects of culture and cultural traces on the mind. Recalling Haraway's caveat that "all is not to be done from scratch," I agree that "vision is *always* a question of the power to see . . . . We are not immediately present to ourselves. Self-knowledge requires a semiotic-material technology linking meanings and bodies." Without being a single influence, Judaism, as any critical positioning might, provides a "semiotic-material technology" out of which Bellow's characters can gain an epistemic purchase on both the self and the world. What Haraway says of the self can be applied readily to Tommy Wilhelm: "The knowing self is partial in all its guises, never finished, whole, simply there and original; it is always constructed and stitched together imperfectly, and *therefore* able to join with another, to see together without claiming to be another" (192–93).

4. See Gloria Cronin's introduction (*Saul Bellow in the 1980s*) in which she credits L. H. Goldman for having corrected this partial view. In *Saul Bellow's Moral Vision*, Goldman discusses Tommy Wilhelm's frustrated desire to be accepted by his father; she does this in the context of the parent–child relationship and its importance to the survival of Jewish life.

5. According to Gerhard Bach, the first and second generations of Bellow scholars concerned themselves with Bellow's "affirmativist humanism." The third generation, L. H. Goldman among them, "reconsiders such classifications." While the earlier work on Bellow seemed eager to counter the nihilism of the "collective stupor" of modernity with an equally modernist and universal, abstract humanism, the third generation entertains several postmodernist approaches, among them a "situatedness" that allows for a discussion of particulars grounded

variously in experience and culture, as well as in continental philosophy. See Gerhard Bach's "The Dean Who Came in from the Cold: Saul Bellow's America of the 1980s" and, for a fuller treatment of this issue, his *The Critical Response to Saul Bellow* (Westport, Conn.: Greenwood Press, 1995).

6. It should not surprise postmodern readers that what are taken to be universals proliferate in Christian assumptions. While redemption, as an architectonic for reading, is readily available, almost unconsciously, it is necessary to see that there are differences in redemptive strategies in different cultures and traditions. It is even more difficult to tease out those differences in the all-too-often hyphenated Judeo-Christian experience. For example, most of Bellow's first and second generation of critics agree that it is through baptism that Tommy Wilhelm finds his heart's ultimate need. Patrick Costello sees this need as "communion with the Father" which is preceded by "the turning of the heart" and achieved through "the tears which Wilhelm finally sheds [that] become a baptism, a conversion." Robert Dutton, likewise, argues that the ending "depicts a kind of baptism as the setting for Tommy's rebirth," and John Jacob Clayton agrees that "if the final scene is symbolic drowning, it is also a symbolic rebirth out of water." The problem here is that the language of baptism necessitates a Christian reading and precludes a Jewish one. To deconstruct the hyphenated Judeo-Christian experience is especially perplexing in Bellow's case, as he himself is thoroughly influenced by such writers as James Joyce, whose *Ulysses* combines Christian and Jewish senses of redemption, and Wilhelm might be seen as a modern-day conflation of Daedalus/Bloom in a New York "Bloomsday." See Patrick Costello, "Tradition in *Seize the Day*" (128–29); Robert Dutton, *Saul Bellow* (89); and, for a treatment of humanism itself as redemptive, see John Jacob Clayton's *In Defense of Man* (4, 129).

7. L. H. Goldman remarks that "Tommy shows evidence of having had some Jewish education. He recalls certain blessings and commandments and uses them accordingly. As an assimilated Jew, Tommy has equivocal Jewish values" (*Saul Bellow's Moral Vision*, 62). While such a prayer may bring divine intervention, I think of the prayer as Tommy's first step in piecing together enough fragments of his heritage to make meaning for himself. In that gesture, he is like the artist who will make form out of formlessness; his redemption will be the product of his own making.

8. Goldman says that "Bellow's use of the term 'seize the day' appears to be ironic" (*Saul Bellow's Moral Vision*, 62). Indeed, there is a tension in the imperative "seize the day." In one sense, Tamkin means for Wilhelm to seize the opportunity to realize the American Dream by a damn-the-cost individualism. In another, which I shall attribute to Bellow, Tommy is urged, as is the reader, to take stock of his relationship with the self and the world, to awaken from the "collective stupor. "

Works Cited

Agnon, S. Y. *Days of Awe*. New York: Schocken Books, 1948.

The Babylonian Talmud: Seder Mo'ed, Tractate *Rosh ha-Shanah*.

The Babylonian Talmud: Seder Mo'ed, Tractate *Yoma*.

Bach, Gerhard. *The Critical Response to Saul Bellow*. Westport, Conn.: Greenwood Press, 1995.

———. "The Dean Who Came in from the Cold: Saul Bellow's America of the 1980s." In *Saul Bellow in the 1980s*, edited by Gloria L. Cronin and L. H. Goldman, 297–313. East Lansing: Michigan State University Press, 1989.

Bellow, Saul. *Seize the Day*. 1956. Reprint, London: Penguin, 1975.

Braude, William G., trans. *Pesikta Rabbati*. Vol. 2. New Haven: Yale University Press, 1968.

Clayton, John Jacob. *In Defense of Man*. 2d ed. Bloomington: Indiana University Press, 1968.

Costello, Patrick. "Tradition in *Seize the Day*." *Essays in Literature* 14, no. 1 (Spring 1987): 117–31.

Cronin, Gloria. "Introduction." In *Saul Bellow in the 1980s*, edited by Gloria L. Cronin and L. H. Goldman, 1-19. East Lansing: Michigan State University Press, 1989.

Dutton, Robert. *Saul Bellow*. Revised edition. Boston: Twayne, 1982.

Encyclopedia Judaica. Jerusalem: Macmillan, 1971.

Freccero, John. *Dante: The Poetics of Conversion*. Cambridge: Harvard University Press, 1986.

———, ed. "Introduction." In *A Collection of Critical Essays*. Englewood Cliffs, N.J.: Prentice-Hall, 1965.

Goldman, L. H. "Saul Bellow and the Philosophy of Judaism." In *Saul Bellow in the 1980s*, edited by Gloria L. Cronin and L. H. Goldman, 51–66. East Lansing: Michigan State University Press, 1989.

———. *Saul Bellow's Moral Vision: A Critical Study of the Jewish Experience*. New York: Irvington, 1983.

Haraway, Donna. "Situated Knowledges." In *Simians, Cyborgs, and Women: The Reinvention of Nature*. New York: Routledge, 1991.

Sperling, Rabbi Abraham Isaac. *Reasons for Jewish Customs and Traditions*, translated by Rabbi Abraham Matts. New York: Bloch, 1968.

Trowbridge, Clinton W. "Water Imagery in *Seize the Day*." *Critique* 9, no. 3 (1987): 62–73.

Some Versions of the Real:
The Novellas of Saul Bellow

MICHAEL K. GLENDAY

I

> One of my themes is the American denial of real reality, our devices
> for evading it, our refusal to face what is all too obvious and palpable.[1]

So, in a discussion of his latest novel, *The Dean's December* (1982), Saul
Bellow speaks of an abiding concern in his fiction—the escapism of
Americans, their refusal to face squarely the "real reality" upon which
national and individual life, as he sees it, must be founded. He has always
stressed this escapist tendency as a worrisome hallmark of the national
psyche, a trait the narrator of *The Dean's December* calls nothing less than
"the American moral crisis." Given the crisis, "the first act of morality [is]
to disinter the reality, retrieve reality, dig it out from the trash."[2] And
"retrieving reality" is nowhere more sharply present as a concern than in
his two early novellas *Dangling Man* (1944) and *Seize the Day* (1956) and in
his return to the form with "What Kind of Day Did You Have?" (1984).

Perhaps the very intensity and concentration of the novella form
accentuates Bellows concern in this regard, especially since, as critics have
noted, his longer fiction is occasionally weakened by his "metaphysical
garrulity."[3] Though his eminence has tended to rest upon full-length
fictions such as *Augie March* (1953) and *Herzog* (1964), Bellow has always
given notice that he has been adept in the art of short fiction as his
collection *Him with His Foot in His Mouth and Other Stories* (1984) testifies. As
Bellow observed in the 1950s, the business of the writer is not only to take

Reprinted with permission of St. Martin's Press, Incorporated, from *The Modern American
Novella*, edited by A. Robert Lee, 167-77. New York: St. Martin's Press, 1989.
Copyright © Robert Lee (ed.).

the nature of reality as theme and subject, but also to use the art of fiction as a tool to cut through, toward ultimate recognition of that subject:

> to find enduring intuitions of what things are real and what things are important. His business is with these enduring recognitions which have the power to recognize occasions of suffering or occasions of happiness, in spite of all distortions and blearing.[4]

The novella, in Bellow's hands, then, serves as a tool with an especially sharp cutting edge, one that enables him to discover those "enduring recognitions" of reality with fewer impediments, without the "distortions and blearing" which sometimes encumber the expression of the same theme in parts of his longer fiction. His use of the shorter form allows him to exploit the localizing incident more effectively, and the plenitude of ideas—often predominating the novels to the detriment of plot and story—is subordinate to the dramatic capacity of such incidents. In the account which follows I want to focus essentially on two novellas, *Seize the Day* and "What Kind of Day Did You Have?"—early and late works respectively—to pursue Bellow's preoccupation with "obvious and palpable" reality and the devices of "distortion and blearing" which too often come between Americans and this fundamental recognition "of what things are real."

To discuss "reality" in connection with fiction is, to be sure, to enter a loaded literary minefield. For what else has been at the center of its concerns, form, philosophy, or very purpose? But in Bellow's case, so often and explicitly has he made it the actual *theme* of his work that it assumes an even greater importance than usual. Reality, in one key sense, is not at all problematic for him: it is there, "obvious and palpable." Also, there is very little in Bellow's work to show any trace of that philosophical skepticism about the nature of reality which has so characterized the postmodern literary aesthetic over recent years.[5] There have been few modern American writers quite so vigorous, or persistent, in getting it down upon the page—for all his reputation as an "ideas" writer Bellow is still a sturdy, unremitting and circumstantial "realist." I have said that he uses the novella as a form of fiction that cuts through toward such reality. As a realist, a large part of his own self-appointed brief has been to reflect contemporary data in all its barbarism, the urban killing fields of Chicago—"many, many square miles of civil Passchendaele or Somme"[6]—to make "the real world realer" and to confront its perversities.[7]

But Bellow, in his Nobel Prize address, acknowledges also that the writer must go beyond documentation, must penetrate toward the essentially real: "Only art penetrates what pride, passion, intelligence, and habit erect on all sides—the seeming realities of this world."[8] In the embrace of these "seeming realities" Americans, above all, have tended to become chronically unmoored, adrift with nothing solid to cling to. Or as Larry Wrangel in "What Kind of Day Did You Have?" puts it:

> The created souls of people, of the Americans, have been removed. The created soul has been replaced by an artificial one, so there's nothing real that human beings can refer to when they judge any matter for themselves.[9]

II

Wedged between the stylistic extroversions of *The Adventures of Augie March* and *Henderson the Rain King*, as Marvin Mudrick has observed, *Seize the Day* still tastes like "the real pastrami between two thick slices of American store bread."[10] The members of the Royal Swedish Academy evidently shared Mudrick's taste when they singled out the novella for special mention in Bellow's Nobel Prize citation. Even the Bellow-baiting Norman Mailer grudgingly threw a bouquet in the direction of the book as a tribute to its "surprisingly beautiful ending," the "first indication for me that Bellow is not altogether hopeless on the highest level."[11]

A good deal of critical debate has, perhaps understandably, centered upon the final scene of *Seize the Day*, with some critics arguing that the tears shed by Tommy Wilhelm are ones that signify a new enlightenment for him.[12] Others have contended that the rhetorical flourish of the novella's ending cannot disguise Bellow's inability to solve narrative tensions satisfactorily.[13] My own view is that the ending is perfectly compatible as a response to, and a culmination of, Bellow's searing condemnation of American "reality"—the subject of *Seize the Day*. It also provides a perfect example of Bellow's skill in the novella form, his use of the dramatic incident as a means of heightening and intensifying thematic concerns. The reader has been led, from the very start, to anticipate a climactic ending, a resolution to suspenseful elements of the narrative:

> [H]e was aware that his routine was about to break up and he sensed that a huge trouble long presaged but till now formless was due. Before evening, he'd know.[14]

Bellow uses the brevity of the novella to embody these tensions, to lead inexorably toward Tommy's convulsive *cri de coeur*. His fiction is full of anguished and heart-torn individuals, but surely none so full of anguish and heartache as Tommy. One of the main reasons for this must be due in large part to the sharp and unremitting awfulness of Tommy's "day," undiluted in novella medium. The reader is as permanently conscious of Tommy's suffering as Tommy himself; the third-person narrator maintains that intimacy, refusing the reader any remission at all.

This narrator stresses throughout the horrific price Tommy pays for his physical appearance ("fair-haired hippopotamus"), his gaucherie, his failure in the business world, and his lack of emotional reserve. Mainstream reality in America is still—as Joseph of *Dangling Man* puts it in the first paragraph of Bellow's first novel—dominated by "hardboiled-dom." According to this regimen one has to be a tough guy, possessed of a mind defined by Henry Adams more than a century ago as "a cutting instrument, practical, economical, sharp and direct."[15] The narrator mocks Tommy's efforts to keep up appearances of capability, telling us that Tommy

> had once been an actor—no, not quite, an extra—and he knew what acting should be. Also, he was smoking a cigar, and when a man is smoking a cigar, wearing a hat, he has an advantage; it is harder to find out how he feels. (7)

Tommy knows the ground rules, knows how he is expected to behave, having been taught by his father how, despite "bad luck, weariness, weakness, and failure" he must still affect a low-key tone, must "sound gentlemanly, low-voiced, tasteful" (15). He knows also the rules that govern American reality, but always loses the game.

> I am an idiot. I have no reserve . . . I talk. I must ask for it. Everybody wants to have intimate conversations, but the smart fellows don't give out, only the fools. (43)

Dr. Adler's repudiation of his son is justified to some extent. Indeed Bellow has carefully prepared a case for the doctor's perception of Tommy as a slob, a miscreant, a maladroit bungler with an unerring talent for taking the wrong road. Dr. Adler, then, as has been argued, "is right, when his slovenly, failure-ridden son comes on his knees, begging, to both feel and articulate his disgust. He is right but not human."[16]

And this is Bellow's subject in *Seize the Day*: not Tommy's pathos but all those, such as his father and Tamkin—the primary "reality-instructor"[17] of the novel—by whose example he seems such a misfit. Such a reality, as

Martin Amis has recently pointed out in connection with Bellow's fiction, "is not a given but a gift, a talent, an accomplishment, an objective."[18] Whereas Joseph of *Dangling Man* sets out in knowledgeable defiance of a prime commandment of American reality—"if you have difficulties grapple with them silently"[19] —Tommy's pathos derives from his unexamined acceptance of this axiom. His tears at the end are an expression of his inability to live within a reality that is contemptuous of their shedding.

In one of his acute culture-readings in *In the American Grain*, William Carlos Williams denunciates the "coldness and skill" which serve as an accepted part of American manners:

> Who is open to injuries? Not Americans. Get hurt; you're a fool. The only hero is he who is not hurt. We have no feeling for the tragic. Let the sucker who fails get his. What's tragic in that? That's funny! To hell with him. He didn't make good, that's all.[20]

Years after the publication of *Seize the Day*, Bellow spoke in an interview of his belief in the necessity of emotional display and of the hardboiled American ethos that condemns such emotional release:

> Is feeling nothing but self-indulgence? . . . When people release emotion, they so often feel like imposters. By restraining themselves, they claim credit for a barren kind of honesty. . . . Nothing is gained by letting yourself go among people who hate such letting go.[21]

Tommy Wilhelm is by far the most vulnerable of Bellow's major characters. Whereas other Bellow heroes such as Albert Corde, Moses Herzog, and Charlie Citrine[22] realize the prudence of closing the valves of feeling in public, Tommy has neither the intelligence nor the guile to develop any strategies of concealment. He is the "sucker who fails," and *Seize the Day* is the story of how America sends him to hell, how he "gets his" from America's hardboiled and heartless.

In the novella's final scene, Bellow's stress falls upon Tommy "hidden" in the center of a crowd of mourners. Though it is true that Tommy cries openly, he is in the most crucial sense as concealed as ever, "protected by the occasion"[23] of the funeral rite so that the onlookers are never truly aware of the nature of his grief. Instead of being outraged, embarrassed, or moved by that grief, these onlookers are merely curious or, more significantly, envious—"'It must be somebody real close to carry on so.' 'Oh my, oh my! To be mourned like that,' said one man . . . with wide, glinting, jealous eyes" (125). In a culture in which real feeling has apparently atrophied, the generous tears of Tommy Wilhelm turn him into a bizarre celebrity.

Ironically, too, Tommy is made to seem a dramatic embodiment of Bellow's idea that "when people release emotion, they so often feel like imposters," as one mourner wonders whether Tommy was "perhaps the cousin from New Orleans they were expecting" (125). So this final scene demonstrates not "the possibility of communion," not Tommy's newly found connections with the city's crowd, but rather his awful isolation, his emotional release figured as a sinking downward "deeper than sorrow" toward extravagant oblivion. The oblivion is "great and happy" because it serves simultaneously as both an expression and extinction of self. American reality has broken him, denied him, hounded him, and fleeced him. Finally ("Wilhelm was moved forward by the pressure of the crowd . . . carried from the street into the chapel") it brings him face to face with the look of death. But Tommy sees beyond the reality of appearances:

> Now at last he was with it, after the end of all distractions, and when his flesh was no longer flesh. And by this meditative look Tommy was so struck that he could not go away. . . . On the surface, the dead man with his formal shirt and his tie and silk lapels and his powdered skin looked so proper; only a little beneath so black, Wilhelm thought, so fallen in the eyes. Standing a little apart, Wilhelm began to cry. (124–25)

Tamkin is in some ways the major character of the novella,[24] no less than a prototype in Bellow's fiction. He also bears a striking resemblance to the protean Rinehart of Ralph Ellison's *Invisible Man* or the adaptive Milo Minderbinder of *Catch-22*, not to mention numerous similar figures in Thomas Pynchon's fiction. He is also the forerunner of Valentine Gersbach in *Herzog* and Dewey Spangler in *The Dean's December*, as well as of Victor Wulpy in "What Kind of Day?" Like Gersbach, Tamkin comes over as the self-proclaimed poet who also "put himself forward as the keen mental scientist" (67). Both Dr. Adler (described as "a fine old scientist") and Tamkin, who gambled "scientifically," are associated with an anti-humanistic rationalism which will reappear in Bellow's fiction in increasingly nasty forms until given its baleful apotheosis in *The Dean's December*. There, we are told by Bellow's narrator, we may indeed have reached a stage wherein "science had drawn all the capacity for deeper realizations out of the rest of mankind and monopolized it. This left everyone else in a condition of great weakness."[25] Like Spangler and Wulpy, Tamkin is a rhetorician who has no purpose "except to talk" (99).

And just as Albert Corde makes the mistake of unburdening himself to Spangler in Budapest, Tamkin finds Tommy willing prey. Following his rejection by his father, Tommy stumbles into Tamkin's orbit, feeling that there at least he would find one who could "sympathise with me" and try "to give me a hand" (14).

It is of course Tamkin who voices the novella's carpe diem ethos; he is the successful predator, perfectly adapted to the jungle of the American metropolis, "the end of the world, with its complexity and machinery, bricks and tubes, wires and stones, holes and heights" (89). Amidst this frightening perplexity, Tommy prays that Tamkin will show him the way, "give him some useful advice and transform his life" (78). But like Wulpy's mistress Katrina ("an average Dumb Dora"), Tommy knows he is "a sucker for people who talk about the deeper things of life" (74). Tamkin, however, for all his rhetorical composure, is not in truth that complex a being. Bellow's narrator allows us to see Tamkin in much the same way as we eventually see Gersbach of *Herzog*—"not an individual, but a fragment, a piece broken off from the mob."[26] We feel, too, the underlying terror that buoys up Tamkin's masquerade as well as the slightest bit of sympathy for the very real sense in which Tamkin is as much the prey of "the world's business" (41) as Tommy:

> [H]is face did not have much variety. Talking always about spontaneous emotion and open receptors and free impulses he was about as expressive as a pincushion. When his hypnotic spell failed, his big underlip made him look weakminded. Fear stared from his eyes, sometimes, so humble as to make you sorry for him. Once or twice Wilhelm had seen that look. Like a dog, he thought. (104–5)

The remote but detectable resemblance to the eyes of the dead man in the final scene ("on the surface . . . so proper; only a little beneath so black, Wilhelm thought, so fallen in the eyes") is a chilling touch, for Tamkin of course has no being, no personality, no soul. He succeeds because of his protean capacities ("Funny but unfunny. True but false. Casual but laborious, Tamkin was" [71]) and because of his fake profundity which creates a reality beyond comprehension, so that

> listening to the doctor when he was so strangely factual, Wilhelm had to translate his words into his own language, and he could not translate fast enough or find terms to fit what he had heard. (73)

But in Bellow's trenchant vision of American reality as nightmare, this confusion of language and meaning is one that extends to embrace the entire gamut of knowledge, and knowledgeability, to lead modern America toward the vortex reality of absolute unintelligibility where solipsism alone reigns:

> You had to translate and translate, explain and explain, back and forth, and it was the punishment of hell itself not to understand or be understood, not to know the crazy from the sane, the wise from the fools, the young from the old or the sick from the well. The fathers were no fathers and the sons no sons. You had to talk with yourself in the daytime and reason with yourself at night. Who else was there to talk to in a city like New York? (89–90)

Tamkin is at once creator, beneficiary, and victim of this state of affairs. He feeds without scruple on the likes of Tommy. Bellow's physical description of Tamkin emphasizes the animal in him as well as the deceiver, and there are insinuations too of Mephistophelian grossness and carnality.[27] The image of Tamkin's twisted anatomy may be the analogue of his perversion of the natural which is his stock-in-trade. "If you were to believe Tamkin . . . everybody in the hotel had a mental disorder, a secret history, a concealed disease . . . every public figure had a character-neurosis" (69). And commensurate with the suggestion that Tamkin embodies a kind of barely concealed, devilish bestiality is his view of reality as hell, an infernal pit of pain and suffering:

> Wilhelm said, "But this means that the world is full of murderers. So it's not the world. It's a kind of hell."
> "Sure," the doctor said. "At least a kind of purgatory. You walk on the bodies. They are all around. I can hear them cry *de profundis* and wring their hands. I hear them, poor human beasts. I can't help hearing." (77)

In its depiction of dissociation and dissolution, of Dr. Adler's well-dressed affability and heartlessness triumphing over his son's despair, of Tamkin's high-powered mountebankery exploiting that despair, *Seize the Day* warns of the crisis afflicting American reality. Wilhelm's "reality" is made up of despair, confusion, loneliness, and failure; this is his "real reality," the bottom line, "obvious and palpable" in the suffering it inflicts upon him. Because they cannot, or will not, take account of this reality, having built up defenses of "seeming realities," those who could have taken the elementary moral, human step—his father, his sister, family and friends—hasten Tommy's demise. As Larry Wrangel in "What Kind of Day Did You Have?" remarks: "What's really real is the unseen convulsion under the apparitions" (113). Perhaps this is the kindest view to take of all those who deny Tommy's "real reality," to say that they simply do not see it. But the price for such blindness is the highest people can pay, a Faustian price— their souls removed, to be "replaced by an artificial one, so there's nothing real that human beings can refer to when they try to judge any matter for themselves" (114).

That all of these thematic concerns are carried within the novella format is a tribute to Bellow's ability to make that format more capacious than its slender frame would seem to imply. The tribute is the greater when we consider that unlike Hemingway in *The Old Man and the Sea*, or James in *The Beast in the Jungle*, Bellow does not rely upon symbolical properties to give narrative depth. Instead the profundity and intensity of his themes are carried in and through such things as the immaculately rendered linear plot—enhanced in terms of suspense and drama by its diurnal span—and here the novella's brevity makes it a propitious vessel; this novella also contains some of Bellow's best writing: succinct, lyrical, evocative, and in these ways a revelation to all those readers put off by the prosiness of the longer fiction.

III

"What Kind of Day Did You Have?," Bellow's latest novella, consolidates his vision of American reality as I have been seeking to describe it. Again, Bellow chooses to give this novella the time-scale frame of a single day, an apparently climactic day in the lives of the two central characters. Yet the tale is clearly late-Bellow in many ways. Structurally, and even within the constraints imposed by the form, it is more diffuse, even ending in deliberate anticlimax. One feels the ending might have been more pointedly accomplished, especially after a consideration of the virtues of *Seize the Day*, yet the conclusion of the later novella contains muted epiphanies which perhaps required the understated ending. Victor Wulpy, the character who towers over the story, amounts to one of Bellow's most biting satirical portraits of the American intellectual. Though Tamkin is his antecedent, Wulpy is physically and mentally more formidable, "a kind of tyrant in thought" (96). Fortunately, the novella's concision imposes its own discipline upon that tyrannical display, though Wulpy is, in the course of the story itself, forced to consider the nature of his tyrannical thoughts.

Wulpy's character had been predicted in Bellow's novels of the '60s; Herzog, for instance, has been a witness to man's preparation for assuming the mantle of his "future condition," a condition of amoral automatism "free from human dependency."[28] Artur Sammler, too, faces up to the same dehumanized projection of the race, knowing that the day of the "old-fashioned sitting sage"[29] is over. The day of Wulpy, the shuttle-intellectual, has arrived. His very name, Victor, confirms his peerless command—"such a face, such stature; without putting it on, he was so commanding that he often struck people as being a king" (65).

Into his kingdom comes Katrina, who "had been raised to consider herself a nitwit" (66). Her home life is in a mess; she is in the middle of an "ugly" divorce, and her two young daughters are the subject of a custody wrangle. This broken family and its anomie give us the damning backdrop against which the events and relationships of the novella are played out. As with *Seize the Day*, Bellow exploits the timespan to good effect. The narrative opens with Katrina about to leave her Chicago home and two daughters and closes with her return to it after traveling back from Boston with Wulpy. Again the brevity of the novella enhances this pattern. We are, for instance, always aware of the maternal responsibilities Katrina has left behind her in Chicago; indeed this particular abdication of duty becomes a central aspect of the novella's moral design.

What Katrina desires is what middle-America desires: significance, gravitas, a piece of the action, however vicarious or compromising. In a 1975 interview Bellow spoke of this rage for significance in American life:

> Life . . . has become very current-eventish. People think they are polit-
> ical when they are immersed in these events—vicariously. . . . Society is
> monopolising their brains, and taking their souls away from them by
> this interest, by the news, by spurious politics[30]

Wulpy is Katrina's way in to this reality. She signs up with him, a babble-king who can connect her to the current of current events. She needs this like a drug to relieve herself of the boredom of all that her home life entails, since "when the current stopped, the dullness and depression were worse than ever" (116). By trading in her family for Wulpy she can now share a room with "the Motherwells and Rauschenbergs and Ashberys and Frankenthalers and . . . leave the local culture creeps grovelling in the dust" (66). The frame of departure and return allows Bellow to use this novella so as to meaningfully enmesh form and subject. We are able to view the object of Katrina's Bostonian flight, to see Wulpy perform his tyrannies (and here it is interesting to note that Bellow needed the extra wordage to do justice to Wulpy's Olympian bearing—the effect could not have been achieved within the smaller compass of a short story), and to receive the challenge posed by the Larry Wrangel character. Thus we are able to see what she has sacrificed, and what she has sacrificed it for.

The moral design of "What Kind of Day Did You Have?" is similar to that of *Seize the Day*. It is one in which the realities of public life—represented and interpreted by Wulpy—here a kind of Tamkin empowered—are seen to bear down upon, and to be inimical to, the imperatives of personal ethics. In this context, Katrina's children are wordless witnesses of their neglect, hovering in the far background of the story (in the domestic overviews comprising the "frame" of the story's beginning and end; so in the far background in terms of their mother's "day" but not at all minimalized by Bellow's narrator, who makes their silent presence so eerily indicting in the important frame areas), "silent Pearl, wordless Soolie" are forced to ponder their mother's unseemly departure from their wintry Chicago home to Boston and Wulpy's bed.

As we see so often in Bellow's fiction,[31] family ties are an index to the probity of his characters. Because Wulpy is wholly devoid of a moral nature, "categories like wife, parent, child never could affect his judgement. He could discuss a daughter like any other subject submitted to his concentrated, radiant consideration" (107). However, Victor "didn't like to speak of kids. He especially avoided discussing her children" (89). He has a daughter whom he calls "a little bitch." Her more recent claims to that title have included "giving her mother sex advice" together with "the address of a shop where she could read some passages on foreplay" (106). Of course Wulpy never considers the extent to which his own neglect of parental responsibilities have contributed to these violations of the natural, only that such "facts" seem to him to "add up to an argument for abortion" (106–7). For Wulpy, "insofar as they were nothing but personal, he cared for nobody's troubles" (95). His grotesque blindness to the elemental duties of fatherhood is compounded by Katrina's willingness to accept Wulpy as "the child . . . which not even my own kids will be with me" and by her acknowledgment that "as a mother I seem to be an artificial product" (104).

The latter remark as noted earlier anticipates that of the novella's co-star, Larry Wrangel. He correctly exposes the inhumanity of Wulpy's idea-mongering mentality:

> You always set a high value on ideas, Victor. I remember that. Well, I've considered this from many sides, and I am convinced that most ideas are trivial. A thought of the real is also an image of the real; if it's a true thought, it's a true picture and is accompanied by a true feeling. Without this our ideas are corpses. (114)

This confrontation between Wrangel and Wulpy marks the center point of the tale. He is the only character able to challenge Wulpy, and he does so successfully as Wulpy himself later seems to concede ("there may have been something in what Wrangel said" [147]). His attack is aimed at the inhuman abstraction of Wulpy's thinking; in peddling abstractions Wulpy is a "caricaturist," his shorthand representations causing human beings, in reduction, to be "represented as *things*" (137). Like Albert Corde, Wrangel argues that this tendency toward abstraction both contributes to and results from the flight from "real reality":

> We prefer to have such things served up to us as concepts. We'd rather have them abstract, stillborn, dead. But as long as they don't come to us with some kind of reality, as facts of experience, then all we can have instead of good and evil is . . . concepts. Then we'll never know how the soul is worked on. Then for intellectuals there will be discourse or jargon, while for the public there will be ever more jazzed-up fantasy.[32]

For Bellow, a writer renowned for the intellectual appetite of his work, the above seems an extraordinary indictment of intellectual process. The attack, however, is more properly seen as one leveled at what passes for a moral use of such process. Instead of an intellectual response based upon "facts of experience," minds such as Wulpy's, trained to entertain rather than edify, can only add to the rift between an authentic reality and its public travesty. Bellow's point is that the development of a moral sense depends upon this correspondence between intellect and experience, and that without it there can be only a degeneration of the moral life.

As I noted earlier, there is a subdued epiphany for Katrina at the close of the narrative. But unlike *Seize the Day*, this novella aims more at representing the unleavened slice of life, a life that will continue to be lived—certainly by Wulpy, probably by Katrina—in the way of the narrative's day. Still, even Victor fleetingly realizes—as the small plane carrying them back to Chicago seems about to plummet into Lake Michigan—the force of Wrangel's criticisms and the truth that "of all that might be omitted in thinking, the worst was to omit your own being" (156). But Bellow is quick to stress the momentary nature of this insight, and the last we see of Wulpy is the picture Katrina has of him "in the swift, rich men's gilded elevator rushing upward, upward" toward his next public address—"pressed for time . . . all that unfinished mental business to keep him busy forever and forever" (159).

But it is in Katrina's return home that Bellow proves his mastery of the novella form. For it is only at that point that the reader realizes the importance of this territory, and realizes, too, that the narrative had been bound to return there, with its neglected children waiting—and certainly not for the first time—for Katrina's brief interludes of motherhood. The relative brevity of the novella means we have not forgotten their environment, though since leaving it at the beginning of the narrative we have seen how odious is the personality and the lifestyle for which they have been sacrificed. Katrina finds her house empty and though her initial fear that her children have been taken away by their father proves to be unfounded, there is a terrible irreducible reality—unsullied by any abstraction—in their renunciation of the maternal tie, in their alien self-sufficiency:

> They didn't say, "Where have you been, Mother?" She was not called upon for any alibis. Their small faces communicated nothing. They did have curious eyes, science-fiction eyes, that dazzled and also threatened from afar . . . Emissaries from another planet, grown from seeds that dropped from outer space, little invaders with iridium in their skulls. (162–63)

Like Tommy Wilhelm, these innocents are the misfits, without reality in a world of distorted forms—"the fathers no fathers and the sons no sons." Katrina, self-confessedly an "artificial" mother, has perpetuated the breed, the nothingness of response and the remoteness in her daughters' eyes being a chilling cause to reflect again upon Wrangel's theory that "the created souls . . . of the Americans have been removed."

Both novellas are powerful examinations of the extent to which Americans collaborate in this process. And the fact that they are novellas shows how well Bellow is able to explore the potentialities of this bantam form, using its brevity to create effects—of suspense, and of subtle thematic control—not possible in novel or short story. "To have a soul, to *be* one—that today is a revolutionary defiance of received opinion,"[33] Bellow remarked in a recent interview. In such a climate these novellas suggest that the reality of American lives will be one of increasing artificiality, increasing inhumanity.

Notes

1. Matthew C. Roudané, "An Interview with Saul Bellow," *Contemporary Literature* 25 (1974): 270.

2. Saul Bellow, *The Dean's December* (New York: Harper & Row, 1982), 123.

3. Tony Tanner, *Saul Bellow* (Edinburgh: Oliver & Boyd, 1965), 111.

4. Saul Bellow, "The Writer and the Audience," *Perspectives* 9 (Autumn 1954): 12.

5. For a concise and lucid exposition of the postmodern aesthetic and its distinctive literary expression, see David Lodge, *The Modes of Modern Writing: Metaphor, Metonymy, and the Typology of Modern Literature* (London, 1977), 220–45.

6. Saul Bellow, *The Dean's December*, 205.

7. Martin Amis, "The Moronic Inferno," in *The Moronic Inferno and Other Visits to America* (London: J. Cape, 1986), 10.

8. "The Nobel Lecture," *American Scholar* 46 (1977): 321.

9. Saul Bellow, *Him with His Foot in His Mouth and Other Stories* (London, 1984), 114. All further references are to this edition and will be given after quotations in the text of the essay.

10. Marvin Mudrick,"Who Killed Herzog? Or, Three American Novelists," *University of Denver Quarterly* 1 (1966): 78.

11. Norman Mailer, *Advertisements for Myself* (London, 1965), 402.

12. See, for instance, M. Gilbert Porter, "The Scene as Image: A Reading of *Seize the Day*," in *Saul Bellow: A Collection of Critical Essays*, edited by Earl Rovit (Englewood Cliffs, N.J., 1975), 70; Clinton W. Trowbridge, "Water Imagery in *Seize the Day*," *Critique* 9, no. 3 (1967): 62–73; and Malcolm Bradbury, *Saul Bellow* (London, 1982), 55–56.

13. See Andrew Waterman, "Saul Bellow's Ineffectual Angels," in *On the Novel*, edited by B. S. Benedikz (London, 1971), 228.

14. Saul Bellow, *Seize the Day* (Harmondsworth, 1966), 7. All further references are to this edition and will be given after quotations in the text of the essay.

15. Henry Adams, *The Education of Henry Adams: An Autobiography* (London, 1919), 181.

16. Gerald Nelson, "Tommy Wilhelm," in *Ten Versions of America* (New York, 1972), 135.

17. Saul Bellow, *Herzog* (London, 1965), 125.

18. Martin Amis, "Saul Bellow in Chicago," in *The Moronic Inferno*, 208.

19. Saul Bellow, *Dangling Man* (London, 1946), 9.

20. William Carlos Williams, *In the American Grain* (London, 1966), 180.

21. Maggie Simmons, "Free to Feel: A Conversation with Saul Bellow," *Quest* (February/March 1979), 32.

22. Of *The Dean's December* (1982), *Herzog* (1964), and *Humboldt's Gift* (1975) respectively.

23. Ray B. West, "Six Authors in Search of a Hero," *Sewanee Review* 65 (1957): 505.

24. Bellow has said (Simmons, 31) that "it isn't Tommy Wilhelm . . . that interests me but that crook and phony, Dr. Tamkin."

25. Saul Bellow, *The Dean's December*, 141.

26. Saul Bellow, *Herzog*, 258.

27. See the description of Tamkin on pages 67–68.

28. Bellow, *Herzog*, 265.

29. Bellow, *Mr. Sammler's Planet* (London, 1970), 74.

30. Robert Boyers et al., "Literature and Culture: An Interview with Saul Bellow," *Salmagundi* 30 (Summer 1975): 11. And as early as 1963 Bellow was casting doubt even upon the resistance of the stoutest minds when confronted by

such omnipresent foes; he wrote then that "public life, vivid and formless turbulence, news, slogans, mysterious crises, and unreal configurations dissolve coherence in all but the most resistant minds, and even to such minds it is not always a confident certainty that resistance can ever have a positive outcome" ("Recent American Fiction," *Encounter* 21 [November 1963]: 23).

31. Apart from Tommy's neglect by his father, one remembers Herzog's desertion by his wife, Madeleine, and the breakdown of family ties in the relationship between Asa Leventhal and his in-laws in *The Victim* (1947), Henderson and his family in *Henderson the Rain King* (1959), and Joseph and his wife and family in *Dangling Man* (1944).

32. Bellow, *The Dean's December*, 243.

33. Rockwell Gray, Harry White, and Gerald Nemanic, "Interview with Saul Bellow," *TriQuarterly* 60 (Spring/Summer 1984): 14.

Works Cited

Adams, Henry. *The Education of Henry Adams: An Autobiography*. London, 1919.
Amis, Martin. "The Moronic Inferno." In *The Moronic Inferno and Other Visits to America*. London: J. Cape, 1986.
———. "Saul Bellow in Chicago." In *The Moronic Inferno and Other Visits to America*. London: J. Cape, 1986.
Bellow, Saul. *Dangling Man*. London, 1946.
———. *The Dean's December*. New York: Harper & Row, 1982.
———. *Herzog*. London, 1965.
———. *Him with His Foot in His Mouth and Other Stories*. London, 1984.
———. *Mr. Sammler's Planet* (London, 1970), 74.
———. "The Nobel Lecture." *American Scholar* 46 (1977): 321.
———. *Seize the Day*. London: Harmondsworth, 1966.
———. "The Writer and the Audience." *Perspectives* 9 (Autumn 1954): 12.
Boyers, Robert, et al. "Literature and Culture: An Interview with Saul Bellow." *Salmagundi* 30 (Summer 1975): 11.
Bradbury, Malcolm. *Saul Bellow*. London, 1982.
Gray, Rockwell, Harry White, and Gerald Nemanic. "Interview with Saul Bellow." *TriQuarterly* 60 (Spring/Summer 1984): 14.
Lodge, David. *The Modes of Modern Writing: Metaphor, Metonymy, and the Typology of Modern Literature*. London, 1977.
Mudrick, Marvin. "Who Killed Herzog? Or, Three American Novelists." *University of Denver Quarterly* 1 (1966): 78.
Mailer, Norman. *Advertisements for Myself*. London, 1965.
Nelson, Gerald. "Tommy Wilhelm." In *Ten Versions of America*. New York, 1972.
Porter, M. Gilbert. "The Scene as Image: A Reading of *Seize the Day*." In *Saul Bellow: A Collection of Critical Essays*, edited by Earl Rovit. Englewood Cliffs, N.J., 1975.
Roudané, Matthew C. "An Interview with Saul Bellow." *Contemporary Literature* 25 (1974): 270.

Simmons, Maggie. "Free to Feel: A Conversation with Saul Bellow." *Quest* February/March 1979), 32.

Tanner, Tony. *Saul Bellow*. Edinburgh: Oliver & Boyd, 1965.

Trowbridge, Clinton W. "Water Imagery in *Seize the Day*." *Critique* 9, no. 3 (1967): 62–7.

Waterman, Andrew "Saul Bellow's Ineffectual Angels." In *On the Novel*, edited by B. S. Benedikz. London, 1971.

West, Ray B. "Six Authors in Search of a Hero." *Sewanee Review* 65 (1957): 505.

Williams, William Carlos. *In the American Grain*. London, 1966.

HIM WITH HIS FOOT
IN HIS MOUTH
AND OTHER STORIES

◆

Farcical Combat in a Busy World

CYNTHIA OZICK

A concordance, a reprise, a summary, all the old themes and obsessions hauled up by a single tough rope—does there come a time when, out of the blue, a writer offers to decode himself? Not simply to divert, or paraphrase, or lead around a corner, or leave clues, or set out decoys (familiar apparatus, art-as-usual), but to kick aside the maze, spill wine all over the figure in the carpet, bury the grand metaphor, and disclose the thing itself? To let loose, in fact, the secret? And at an hour no one could have predicted? And in a modestly unlikely form? The cumulative art concentrated, so to speak, in a vial?

For Saul Bellow, at age sixty-eight, and with his Nobel speech eight years behind him, the moment for decoding is now, and the decoding itself turns up unexpectedly in the shape of a volume of five stories, awesome yet imperfect, at least one of them overtly a fragment, and none malleable enough to achieve a real "ending." Not that these high-pressure stories are inconclusive. With all their brilliant wiliness of predicament and brainy language shocked into originality, they are magisterially the opposite. They tell us, in the clarified tight compass Bellow has not been so at home in since *Seize the Day*, what drives Bellow.

What drives Bellow? The inquiry is seductive because Bellow is Bellow, one of three living American Nobel laureates (the only one, curiously, whose natural language is English), a writer for whom great fame has become a sort of obscuring nimbus, intruding on the cleanly literary. When *The Dean's December* was published in 1982, it was not so much reviewed as scrutinized like sacred entrails: Had this idiosyncratically independent writer turned "conservative"? Had he soured on Augiesque America? Was his hero, Albert Corde, a lightly masked Saul Bellow? Can a

Reprinted from *New York Times Book Review*, 20 May 1984, 3.

writer born into the Jewish condition successfully imagine and inhabit a WASP protagonist? In short, it seemed impossible to rid Bellow's novel of Bellow's presence, to free it as fiction.

In consequence of which, one is obliged to put a riddle: If you found *Him with His Foot in His Mouth and Other Stories* at the foot of your bed one morning, with the title page torn away and the author's name concealed, would you know it, after all, to be Bellow? Set aside, for the interim, the ruckus of advertised "models"—that Victor Wulpy of "What Kind of Day Did You Have?" has already been identified as the art critic Harold Rosenberg, Bellow's late colleague at the University of Chicago's Committee on Social Thought; that the prodigy–hero of "Zetland: By a Character Witness" is fingered as the double of Isaac Rosenfeld, Bellow's boyhood friend, a writer and Reichian who died at the age of 38. There are always anti-readers, resenters, or recanters of the poetry side of life, mean distrusters of the force and turbulence of the free imagination, who are ready to demote fiction to the one-on-one flatness of photojournalism. Omitting, then, extraterritorial interests not subject to the tractable laws of fiction—omitting gossip—would you recognize Bellow's muscle, his swift and glorious eye?

Yes, absolutely; a thousand times yes. It is Bellow's Chicago, Bellow's portraiture—these faces, these heads!—above all, Bellow's motor. That he himself may acknowledge a handful of biographical sources—"germs," textured shells—does not excite. The life on the page resists the dust of flesh, and is indifferent to external origins. Victor Wulpy is who he is as Bellow's invention; and certainly Zetland is. These inventions take us not to Bellow as man, eminence, and friend of eminences (why should I care whom Bellow knows?), but to the private clamor in the writing. And it is this clamor, this sound of a thrashing soul—comic because metaphysical, metaphysical because aware of itself as a farcical combatant on a busy planet—that is unequivocally distinguishable as the pure Bellovian note. "The clever, lucky old Berlin Jew, whose head was like a round sourdough loaf, all uneven and dusted with flour, had asked the right questions" (93-94). If this canny sentence came floating to us over the waves, all alone on a dry scrap inside a bottle, who would not instantly identify it as Bellow's voice?

It is a voice demonized by the right (or possibly the right) questions. The characters it engenders are dazed by what may be called the principle of plentitude. Often they appear to take startled credit for the wild ingenuity of the world's abundance, as if they had themselves brought it into being. It isn't that they fiddle with the old freshman philosophy course conundrum, why is there everything instead of nothing? They ask rather:

What is this everything composed of? What is it preoccupied with? They are knocked out by the volcanic multiplicity of human thought; they want to count up all the ideas that have ever accumulated in at least our part of the universe; they roil, burn, quake with cosmic hunger. This makes them sometimes jesters, and sometimes only sublime fools.

"What Kind of Day Did You Have?," the novella that is the centerpiece of this volume, and also its masterpiece, gives us a day in the life of "one of the intellectual captains of the modern world" (75)— Victor Wulpy, who, if love is sublime and lovers foolish, qualifies as a reacher both high and absurd. Reaching for the telephone in a Buffalo hotel, Victor calls his lover, Katrina Goliger, in suburban Chicago, and invites—commands—her to fly in zero weather from Chicago to Buffalo solely in order to keep him company on his flight from Buffalo to Chicago. "With Victor refusal was not one of her options" (64), so Trina, sourly divorced, the mother of two unresponsive young daughters, acquiesces. Victor's egotism and self-indulgence, the by-blows of a nearly fatal recent illness and of a powerfully centered arrogance, are as alluring as his fame, his dependency, his brilliance, his stiff game leg "extended like one of Admiral Nelson's cannon under wraps" (103), his size sixteen shoes that waft out "a human warmth" when Trina tenderly pulls them off.

Victor is a cultural lion who exacts, Trina surmises, $10,000 per lecture. In Buffalo his exasperating daughter, a rabbinical school dropout who once advised her decorous mother to read a manual on homosexual foreplay as a means of recapturing Victor's sexual interest, hands him her violin to lug to Chicago for repairs; it is Trina who does the lugging. Victor is headed for Chicago to address the Executives Association, "National Security Council types," but really to be with Trina. Trina suffers from a carping angry sister, a doting hanger-on named Krieggstein who carries guns and may or may not be a real cop, and the aftermath of a divorce complicated by psychiatric appointments, custody wrangling, greed. She is also wrestling with the perplexities of a children's story she hopes to write, if only she can figure out how to extricate her elephant from his crisis on the top floor of a department store, with no way down or out. At the same time Victor is being pursued, in two cities, by Wrangel, a white-furred Hollywood plot-concocter, celebrated maker of "Star Wars"–style films, a man hot with ideas who is impelled to tell Victor that "ideas are trivial" and Trina that Victor is a "promoter."

Meanwhile, planes rise and land, or don't take off at all; there is a bad-weather detour to Detroit and a chance for serendipitous sex in an airport hotel, and finally a perilous flight in a Cessna where, seemingly facing death in a storm, Trina asks Victor to say he loves her. He refuses, they touch down safely at O'Hare Airport, the story stops but doesn't exactly end. Wrangel has helped Trina dope out what to do about the trapped elephant, but Trina herself is left tangled in her troubles, submissively energetic and calculating, and with no way up or out.

What emerges from these fluid events, with all their cacophonous espousal of passion, is a mind at the pitch of majesty. The agitated, untamable, yet flagging figure of the dying Victor Wulpy, a giant in the last days of his greatness, seizes us not so much for the skein of shrewd sympathy and small pathos in which he is bound and exposed, as for the claims of these furious moments of insatiable connection:

> Katrina had tried to keep track of the subjects covered between Seventy-Sixth Street and Washington Square: the politics of modern Germany from the Holy Roman Empire through the Molotov–Ribbentrop Pact; what surrealist communism had really been about; Kiesler's architecture; Hans Hofmann's influence; what limits were set by liberal democracy for the development of the arts. . . . Various views on the crises in economics, cold war, metaphysics, sexaphysics. (93)

Not that particular "subjects" appear fundamentally to matter to Bellow, though they thrillingly engage him. The young Zetland, discovering *Moby Dick*, cries out to his wife: "There really is no human life without this poetry. Ah, Lottie, I've been starving on symbolic logic" (186). In fact he has been thriving on it and on every other kind of knowledge.

> What were we here for, of all strange beings and creatures the strangest? Clear colloid eyes to see with, for a while, and see so finely, and a palpitating universe to see, and so many human messages to give and receive. And the bony box for thinking and for the storage of thought, and a cloudy heart for feelings. (184)

It is the hound of heaven living in the bony box of intelligence that dogs Bellow, and has always dogged him. If the soul is the mind at its purest, best, clearest, busiest, profoundest, then Bellow's charge has been to restore the soul to American literature.

The five stories in *Him with His Foot in His Mouth* are the distillation of that charge. Their method is to leave nothing unobserved and unremarked, to give way to the unprogrammed pressure of language and intellect, never to retreat while imagination goes off like kites.

These innovative sentences, famous for pumping street smarts into literary blood vessels, are alive and snaky, though hot; and Bellow's quick-witted lives of near poets, as recklessly confident in the play and intricacy of ideas as those of the grand Russians, are Russian also in the gusts of natural force that sweep through them—unpredictable cadences, instances where the senses appear to fuse ("A hoarse sun rolled up," [89]); single adjectives that stamp whole portraits, portraits that stamp whole lives (hair from which "the kink of high vigor had gone out," [232]), the knowing hand on the ropes of how-things-work, the stunning catalogues of worldliness ("commodity brokers, politicians, personal injury lawyers, bagmen and fixers, salesmen and promoters," [263-64]), the boiling presence of Chicago, with its "private recesses for seduction and skulduggery" (233).

A light flavoring of Jewish social history dusts through it all: Victor Wulpy reading the Pentateuch in Hebrew in a cheder on the Lower East Side in 1912; or Zetland's immigrant father who, in a Chicago neighb orhood "largely Polish and Ukrainian, Swedish, Catholic, Orthodox, and Evengelical Lutheran" (168), "preferred the company of musical people and artists, bohemian garment workers, Tolstoyans, followers of Emma Goldman and of Isadora Duncan, revolutionaries who wore pince-nez, Russian blouses, Lenin or Trotsky beards" (172).

What this profane and holy comedy of dazzling, beating, multiform profusion hints at, paradoxically, is that Bellow is as notable for what isn't in his pages as for what is. No preciousness, of the ventriloquist kind or any other; no carelessness either (formidably the opposite); no romantic aping of archaisms or nostalgias; no restraints born out of theories of form or faddish tenets of experimentalism or ideological crypticness; no Neanderthal flatness in the name of cleanliness of prose; no gods of nihilism; no gods of subjectivity; no philosophy of parody. As a consequence of these and other salubrious omissions and insouciant dismissals, Bellow's detractors have accused him of being "old-fashioned," "conventional," of continuing to write a last-gasp American version of the nineteenth-century European novel; his omnivorous "Russianness" is held against him, and at the same time he is suspected of expressing the deadly middle class.

The grain of truth in these disparagements takes note, I think, not of regression or lagging behind, but of the condition of local fiction, which has more and more closeted itself monkishly away in worship of its own liturgies—of its own literariness. Bellow, however, seeing American writing in isolation from America itself, remembered Whitman and Whitman's cornucopia, in homage to which he fabricated a new American sentence. All this, of course, has been copiously remarked ever since *Augie*

March; but these five stories say something else. What Bellow is up to here is nothing short of a reprise of Western intellectual civilization. His immigrants and children of immigrants, blinking their foetal eyes in the New World, seem to be cracking open the head of Athena to get themselves born, in eager thirst for the milk of Enlightenment. To put it fortissimo: Bellow has brain on the brain, which may cast him as the dissident among American writers.

But even this is not the decoding or revelation I spoke of earlier. It has not been enough for Bellow simply to have restored attention to society—the density and entanglements of its urban textures, as in "A Silver Dish": "He maintained the bungalow—this took in roofing, painting, wiring, insulation, air-conditioning—and he paid for heat and light and food, and dressed them all out of Sears, Roebuck and Wieboldt's, and bought them a TV which they watched as devoutly as they prayed" (218). Nor has it been enough for Bellow to have restored attention to the overriding bliss of learning:

> Scholem and I [of "Cousins"], growing up on neighboring streets, attending the same schools, had traded books, and since Scholem had no trivial interests, it was Kant and Schelling all the way, it was Darwin and Nietzsche, Dostoyevsky and Tolstoy, and in our senior year it was Oswald Spengler. A whole year was invested in 'The Decline of the West'. (269)

To this thickness of community and these passions of mind Bellow has added a distinctive ingredient, not new on any landscape, but shamelessly daring just now in American imaginative prose. Let the narrator of "Cousins" reveal it:

> We enter the world without prior notice, we are manifested before we can be aware of manifestation. An original self exists, or, if you prefer, an original soul. . . . I was invoking my own fundamental perspective, that of a person who takes for granted distortion in the ordinary way of seeing but has never given us the habit of referring all truly important observations to that original self or soul. (267-68)

Bellow, it seems, has risked mentioning—who can admit to this without literary embarrassment?—the Eye of God.

And that is perhaps what his intellectual fevers have always pointed to. "Cousins" speaks of it explicitly: "As a man is, so he sees. As the Eye is formed, such are its powers" (268). Yet "Cousins" is overtly about "the observation of cousins" (267) and moves from cousin Tanky of the rackets to cousin Seckel, whose "talent was for picking up strange languages" (255), to cousin Motty who, "approaching ninety, still latched on to people to tell them funny things" (263). All this reflects a powerfully recognizable Jewish family feeling—call it, in fact, family love, though it is love typically mixed with amazement and disorder.

The professor-narrator of "Him with His Foot in His Mouth"—the title story—like cousin Motty is also a funny fellow, the author of a long letter conscientiously recording his compulsion to make jokes that humiliate and destroy, putdowns recollected in tranquillity. But the inescapable drive to insult through wit is equated with "seizure, rapture, demonic possession, frenzy, Fatum, divine madness, or even solar storm" (57), so this lambent set of comic needlings is somehow more than a joke, and may touch on the Eye of Dionysus.

"A Silver Dish," with its upside-down echo of the biblical tale of Joseph's silver cup, concerns the companionable trials of Woody Selbst and his rogue father, the two of them inextricably entwined although the father has abandoned his family; all the rest—mother, sisters, aunt and ludicrous, immigrant uncle—are Jewish converts to evangelicalism. Woody, like Joseph in Egypt, supports them all. The Eye of God gazes through this story too, not in the bathetic converts but in the scampish father, "always, always something up his sleeve" (222). Pop had "made Woody promise to bury him among Jews" (193)—neglected old connections being what's up that raffish sleeve. It is Woody's "clumsy intuition" that "the goal set for this earth was that it should be filled with good, saturated with it" (220). All the same, the commanding image in this narrative is that of a buffalo calf snatched and devoured in the waters of the Nile, in that alien country where Joseph footed the family bills and his father, Jacob, kept his wish to be buried among Jews up his sleeve almost to the end.

The commanding image of this volume—the concordance, so to speak, to Bellow's work—turns up in the reflections of one of the cousins, Ijah Brodsky:

'To long for the best that ever was': this was not an abstract project. I did not learn it over a seminar table. It was a constitutional necessity, physiological, temperamental, based on sympathies which could not be acquired. Human absorption in faces, deeds, bodies, drew me toward metaphysical grounds. I had these peculiar metaphysics as flying creatures have their radar. (232)

This metaphysical radar (suspiciously akin to the Eye of God) "decodes" Saul Bellow, and these five ravishing stories honor and augment his genius.

Works Cited

Bellow, Saul. *Him with His Foot in His Mouth and Other Stories*. New York: Harper, 1984.

Artist-by-Artist (De)Construction: Mediated Testimony in Bellow's "Zetland: By a Character Witness"

PHILLIP A. SNYDER

"Yes, I knew the guy."
—Unnamed Narrator of "Zetland"

"Invocation of the truth is a sign of lying."
—Tzvetan Todorov

Introduction: Character Witness Discourse

In courtroom proceedings character witnesses traditionally function as substitutes or supplements for concrete exhibits, direct eye-witness information, or expert testimony. Whatever they have to say relates only indirectly to the case in question as they strive to set the defendant's character and behavior in a context broad enough to bring into doubt the likelihood of specific criminal deviation from the established pattern of general goodness: "For over ten years I've known so-and-so to be a hard-working, law-abiding citizen who would never even contemplate the commission of a crime such as this one. It would be totally out of character." They offer subjectivity in a forum distinguished by its preoccupation with objectivity as they attempt to convince judge and jury of the defendant's credibility through a direct demonstration of their own: "Being a fine, upstanding citizen myself, as you can all plainly see by my dress and comportment on the stand, I recognize so-and-so to be a fine, upstanding citizen as well. To believe me is to believe the defendant."

Reprinted from *Saul Bellow Journal* 11, no. 2 & 12, no. 1 (Double Issue 1993): 66-79.

Character witnesses thus operate in the space between evidence and impression, privileging the testimonial over the empirical and filling any evidentiary absence with their narrative presence. As courtroom mediators they "stand in" for the defendant and, like public relations specialists, (re)present their client, the defendant, to the public by creating a positive double persona of self-client they trust the public will accept in the either/or choice between guilt and innocence, a binary into which every word of their testimonies becomes circumscribed. Unlike most narratives, the testimonies of character witnesses depend on their audience-readers, rather than on themselves as speaker-authors, to supply the final word of narrative closure as well as the interpretation and evaluation that precedes it. Consequently, until the verdict of judge or jury, these testimonies remain inherently open, subject to infinite (re)vision; indeed, even after the verdict is rendered, their cases can be opened again on appeal in an endless cycle of narrative performance.

As an exemplary model of testimonial narration, Saul Bellow's short story "Zetland: By a Character Witness" (re)presents well the complexities and incongruities of this kind of discourse, existing as it does in the gap between binaries such as fact/fiction or guilt/innocence. "Zetland" depicts a particular instance of character witness testimony, a kind of memoir Mikhail Bakhtin calls *apomnemoneumata*, or recollections, and describes as "transcripts based on personal memories of real conversations among contemporaries; characteristic, also, is the fact that a speaking and conversing man is the central image of the genre" (24). Here the unnamed narrator recounts his Chicago and New York memories of Max Zetland, his boyhood friend, especially his impressions of Zetland's education, philosophy, and family relationships.

Yet it is a dramatic monologue whose context remains mysterious, beyond the reader's power of decisive inference, because it is told without introduction or conclusion and raises in our minds some significant contextual questions: Is Zetland actually on trial here? If so, then with what has he been charged? What "truth" about Zetland's "character" is being pursued in the narrative? What is his importance? And why should we be interested in him at all? Because the unnamed narrator's motivation, purpose, audience, and attitude cannot be determined definitively, they must be provided by the readers, who thus occupy a powerful dual position with regard to the narrative, both inventing its rhetorical stance and then responding to it. Our frame-of-*reference* depends almost exclusively on our frame-of-*inference* and complicates our attempts to bring closure to the narrative by determining Zetland's guilt or innocence. Further, because Bellow dramatizes the distance between character (*sujet de l'énoncé*, or spoken subject) and witness (*sujet de l'énonciation*, or speaking subject), signified in the story's title by the colon separating the two, and demonstrates the mediated "discourse of absence" typical of character witness narration, which offers a metonymic substitution of witness for character, we are forced to engage Zetland through a third-party narrator and render a verdict at least several steps removed from the defendant and the "facts" of his case. In the tradition of Conrad's Marlow or Fitzgerald's Gatsby, Zetland exists only as a character in another character's narrative; he cannot speak for himself. Nevertheless, however effaced these narrators appear to be, they always occupy the center stage of the narrative performance, on which the credibility of their character constructions depend, and mediate virtually everything in the text according to the selected cultural codes of their narrative discourse. The narrator of Zetland constructs his character witness testimony after the traditional developmental pattern of the *bildungs-künstlerroman*, emphasizing especially Zetland's initiation into multiple philosophical and literary modes of being.

Narrator: Mechanics of Mediation

Like all language constructions, "Zetland" turns on the signifier, deferring the signified, within the infinite play (*jeu*) of the text and the pluralistic activity of its production, so it (dis)plays only textual "traces" of the absent signified, Max Zetland.[1] As a "historical" document, however, one that purports to (re)present the events of the past, it desires to minimize the pluralistic production of that (dis)play by the authority of its performance to shirt our attention from *récit* (variously associated with or defined as "narrative," "plot," or "subject") to *histoire* (variously associated with or defined as "event," "story" or "fable").[2] In other words, it desires to be mimetic instead of diegetic, or "show" rather than "tell." To satisfy this mimetic desire, "Zetland" depends on "realistic effects," which are details designed to give readers the impression of a "true picture" governed by the "reality" of the past and not by the narrator's mediating power of narration in making such choices as the inclusion/exclusion or the extension/reduction of narrative events. Gerard Genette calls these details "connotators of mimesis" and notes that they constitute an illusive aspect of narrative performance which is still inevitably diegetic:

> All [narrative] can do is tell [the story] in a manner which is detailed, precise, "alive," and in that way give more or less the illusion of *mimesis*—which is the only narrative mimesis, for this single and

sufficient reason: that narration, oral or written, is a fact of language, and language signifies without imitating. (164)

In short, everything is "tell." Despite any illusion of "show" through such narrative techniques as the domination of scene or the transparency of narrator (Genette, 166), for example, "Zetland" remains essentially diegetic. Like every other narrative, it functions from within a specific instance of narration, or discourse, which simply means that the basic communication model consists of two people actually talking to each other in a particular time and place and making specific choices in their dialogic exchange according to their rhetorical stances and ideological agendas (Bakhtin, xx). Emile Benveniste clarifies the difference between the speech-acts of discourse and story in the following definitions:

> [Discourse involves] any speech-act supposing a speaker and listener, and in the speaker an intention to influence the listener in some way. . . . [Story involves] the presentation of phenomena which occurred at a certain moment of time without any intervention on the part of the speaker of the story. (qtd. in Todorov, 25)

But because any knowledge of story comes indirectly through the intermediary of discourse, a story cannot mean anything outside its performative context, for "language, when it means, is somebody talking to somebody else" (Bakhtin, xxi). Or, as Genette points out, "[narrative] lives by its relationship to the story that it recounts; [discourse] lives by its relationship to the narrator that utters it" (29). The following formulas differentiate between mimetic and diegetic narrative discourse as analogues to the notions of *histoire* and *récit*, respectively:

Mimesis = maximum information + minimum informer (*histoire*)
Diegesis = minimum information + maximum informer (*récit*)

Within the (dis)play of the text, mimesis can be recognized and distinguished further as "reported" discourse and diegesis as "narratized" discourse (Genette, 169–70). The following passages from "Zetland" illustrate the difference between the two:

> Reported (mimetic): "He wanted me to be a John Stuart Mill," said Zet. "Or some shrunken little Itzkowitz of a prodigy—Greek and calculus at the age of eight, damn him!"

Narratized (diegetic): Zet believed he had been robbed of his childhood, robbed of the angelic birthright. (173)

As an example of an I-witness, first-person, testimonial narrative, "Zetland" cannot conceal the mediation of its narrator by the camouflage of mimetic literary devices or hide behind the authority of the narrator's performance designed to provide his narrative with the illusion of disinterested omniscience. "Zetland," despite the unclear context of its *énonciation*, remains situated as a dialogic production requiring the interested participation of both narrator and reader in a specific communication situation. The narrator cannot escape his multiple mediating functions within the text—categorized by Genette as narrative (storytelling), directing (text manipulation), communication (situation control), testimonial (information attestation), and ideological (action justification) (256–57)—just as readers cannot escape their role in engaging that narrator within the text. Indeed, Marie Maclean describes the text as a locus for the confrontation of narrator and reader in a struggle for "meaning":

> Through a narrative text I meet *you* in a struggle which may be cooperative or may be combative, a struggle for knowledge, for power, for pleasure, for possession. The meeting is manifest in the course of the narrative performance in which the performer, whether human or textual, undertakes to control the audience by words or signs alone, while they, the partners in the act, use their power as hearers to dictate the terms of the control. If you tell me a story, I can refuse to listen, but if I become a listener, even a forced listener, I can also remind you that words, in the last resort, can only mean what my mind allows them to mean. I, too, am constantly performing. (xxii)

In "Zetland" the testimonial performance of its narrator must be matched by the interpretive-evaluative performance of its readers. According to Roland Barthes, when readers operate in this "writerly" mode, they actually create the text themselves: "the writerly text is *ourselves writing*" (*S/Z*, 5). Bakhtin adds that the text is a site for heteroglossia, or the dynamic interaction of opposing forces, described by his editors as a "struggle at the heart of existence, a ceaseless battle between centrifugal forces [more powerful and ubiquitous] that seek to keep things apart, and centripetal forces [less powerful and complex] that strive to make things cohere" (xviii). This struggle cannot be reduced to a simple binary setup, however, because "all transcription systems . . . are inadequate to the multiplicity of the meanings they seek to convey" (Bakhtin, xx). The control of "Zetland," then, must be shared by all the forces, including its narrator and readers, that contribute to its "multiplicity of meaning." As testimonial discourse "Zetland" attempts to move toward the closure of a verdict, but the infinite complexity of the forces contributing to its production make that closure impossible, deferring that verdict by keeping the deliberating jury of readers sequestered indefinitely.

Character: Codes of (De)Construction

The narrator of "Zetland" may create a "unique" character portrait—as his wife, Lottie, says, "There's no one in the world like Zet" (178)—but his particular utterance (*parole*) depends on the larger sign-system of language (*langue*) for the codes, or conventions, that make that utterance possible. As Maclean notes, "Linguistic performance implies an active and variable relationship between sender and receiver, as well as between the collective social and cultural forces controlling the language and the individuals putting it into practice" (xi). The pervasive influence of this controlling language opens to question the very existence of purely "unique" utterances made by wholly "integrated" selves, complete and individually determined. In fact, there may be a multitude of "Zets" in the world. "Zetland" is, at once, a production of both *parole* and *langue*, or, in Bakhtinian terms, of dynamic centripetal and centrifugal forces that keep it in a perpetual state of dialogic flux:

> Every utterance participates in the "unitary language" (in its centripetal forces and tendencies) and at the same time partakes of social and historical heteroglossia (the centrifugal, stratifying forces). The authentic environment of an utterance, the environment in which it lives and takes shape is dialogized heteroglossia, anonymous and social as language, but simultaneously concrete, filled with specific content and accented as an individual utterance. (272)

"Zetland," as a construction of individual utterance or self, is also a (de)construction of individual utterance or self, because language, in signifying without imitating, belongs to a realm outside any notion of "natural" fixity; further, because language always "lays bare the device" of its construction, it also always makes implicit its (de)construction. In other words, every construction carries the seeds of its own (de)construction. Generically, "Zetland" belongs to the tradition of the *bildungs-künstlerroman*, or development-artist novel, which provides it with the stabilizing centripetal forces against which the destabilizing centrifugal forces collide, and may be (de)constructed according to the following aspects of *bildungs-künstlerroman* discourse: developmental patterns of Western initiation convention, literary codification of the self, and multivocalic self-assertion.

The Western tradition of the *bildungs-künstlerroman* pattern of initiation and development depends on the possibility of individual self-determination through educational, social, and other cultural experience. It is a tradition that pretends to be a mimetic description of the self-construction undergone "naturally" by the typical Western male but which exists primarily as a diegetic prescription that is "culturally" codified and imposed. The standard narrative structure includes the following:

•Protagonist, a child of sensibility, grows up in the country or a provincial town.
•Protagonist experiences constraints, especially from the family and the father in particular.
•Protagonist's schooling is inadequate.
•Protagonist leaves repressive atmosphere and goes to the city.
•Protagonist's real education begins.
•Protagonist has two love affairs, one which debases and one which exalts.
•Protagonist begins soul searching and accommodating the self to the modern world.
•Protagonist leaves adolescence and finds maturity, the initiation complete.
•Protagonist returns home and demonstrates newfound maturity.[3]

"Zetland" features many of these characteristics but emphasizes Zetland's repressive home life, particularly his domineering father, and his educational pursuits. The narrator, for example, describes Zetland as being from the "sticks" (178) and portrays his move from Chicago to New York as a move to a place where it is "normal to be human" (181). The repression from which Zetland flees with Lottie stems from his sense of having been "cheated of his childhood . . . the lost paradise" (173), a result of both his serious childhood illness (167–68) and his father's ambitious immigrant ethic of cultural capitalism (170 ff), which manifests itself most pointedly in his desire to make his son a *"wunderkind"*: "Old Zet would be the *man* of the family and young Zet its *genius*" (173). Combined with a lack of parental approval (174), Old Zet's ambition has the effect of setting up his son as a binary contrary to himself, involving them in an Oedipal complex manqué which features an absent mother whose place in the triangle is occupied by Lottie, whom misogynistic Old Zet blames for "ruining his son" and calls after her as their train for New York departs: "'You wait! I'll get you. Five years, ten years, but I'll get you. . . . You bitch—you nasty cunt'" (180–81).

It is doubtful Old Zet makes good on his threat because, according to the narrative, Zetland and Lottie remain in New York, so they do not complete the initiation circle which would have culminated in a triumphant return to their Chicago community. This incomplete cycle in "Zetland" reflects the pattern of the *künstlerroman,* which rarely attempts to bring its protagonists to full closure but usually concludes with them on the threshold of their artistic apprenticeships, just ready to separate themselves from their old communities. In Zetland's case, this threshold is never crossed, partly because he changes apprenticeships not long after moving to New York and entering Columbia's graduate program in philosophy. As a result of his (re)experiencing his childhood illness and subsequent resurrection while reading Herman Melville's *Moby Dick,* Zetland, the "disinterested intellectual parvenu" philosopher (174), becomes reborn as Zetland, the American romantic in the "bohemian avantgarde" (187). The narrator describes Zetland's epiphanic rebirth in these terms:

> So Zet laid aside his logic books. They had lost their usefulness. . . . He said to Lottie, "What other books are there?" He stopped her at *Moby-Dick,* and she handed him the large volume. After reading a few pages he knew that he would never be a Ph.D. in philosophy. . . . He had reached a bad stage of limited selfhood, disaffection, unwillingness to be; he was sick; he wanted *out.* Then he read this dazzling book. It rushed over him. He thought he would drown. But he didn't drown; he floated. (185)

The romantic power of the imagination engaged through Melville's text transports Zetland from his dingy New York studio apartment to Atlantic ocean settings far beyond the rational systems of the logicians he had been studying. He trades his quest after a "resemblance theory of universals" for a quest after a "comprehensive vision" of life (185–86).

Self-construction in "Zetland" depends on *bildungs-künstlerroman* literary codes as a kind of language into which the narrator and his character, Zetland, enter. In the text their "real life" and narrative experiences are translated into this code, their extensive knowledge of which also demonstrates their personal credibility and narrative authority. Continental philosophy, for example, functions as the "logical" initial translation code, being replaced later by the "visionary" code of literature as represented by *Moby Dick*. Nevertheless, while the codes change, the general construction pattern remains the same and depends on a similar concept of the self and the world based on post–1750 philosophical and literary writing, a concept from which the whole notion of *bildungs-künstlerroman* develops. "Zetland" mentions every important post–1750 continental philosopher from Voltaire to Tarski, a total of more than fifty names, including other political, literary, and musical figures as well.[4] Robert C. Solomon describes continental philosophy as the story of a "self-image" which invokes a "transcendental pretence":

> [Continental philosophy is] the dramatic story of the European self-image, in which science and knowledge play an important role but only alongside the romantic imagination, unprecedented cosmic arrogance, continual reaction and rebellion, and the ultimate collapse of a bloated cosmopolitan self-confidence. . . . The self becomes not just the focus of attention but the entire subject-matter of philosophy. The self is not just another entity in the world, but in an important sense it creates the world, and the reflecting self does not just know itself, but in knowing itself knows all selves, and the structure of any and every possible self. The ramifications of this view constitute the transcendental pretence. (3, 6)

Solomon's description here applies to Melville as easily as it does to Kant or Nietzsche. Zetland, with his "natural, universal, gorgeous power" (178), then, becomes archetypically ordinary in his *bildungs-künstlerroman* development, even as a nonpareil modern philosopher and man of letters, in a world of "high culture" (172) that comes from literary rather than "real life" sources: "All this [Zetland's theory on the creation, prehistory, and history of the world] Zetland got out of books" (167). By experiencing the world primarily through books, his life is vicarious in the extreme: "He did not go to the woods, was not taught to shoot, nor to clean a carburetor, nor even to play billiards or to dance. Zet concentrated on his books . . ." (173). Like a Chinese box assembly, Zetland thus (re)presents a literary (re)presentation of a literary (re)presentation, the center-origin of which is found to be empty when the final box is opened: he is more device than substance.

Zetland's pseudo-mimetic, modernist self is undermined by his postmodernist self, disunified, complex, and articulated in the *bildungs-künstlerroman* tradition as multifaceted and multivoiced.

As Maclean notes:

> One must remember that through the speaking subject is heard not just the voice of the teller but the voices of language, of narrative tradition, of ideology, of the whole social context. In the spoken subject we have the whole range of voices of the tale itself and its various actors. (7)

In "Zetland" this self as spoken subject is (dis)played by the speaking subject as an actor in various roles, a supreme mimic who becomes caught up in the language into which his self enters in his multiple modes of self-invention. "Playing parts" (177), Zetland acts out the "real life" roles of son, lover, husband, friend, student, logician, critic, musicologist, and so forth while adding other roles and voices as supplements to them in his imitative performances which are clearly reminiscent of stand-up comedy routines:

> Zet entertained . . . with his charades, speeches, jokes, and songs. He was a laundry mangle, a time clock, a tractor, a telescope. He did *Don Giovanni* in all the parts and voices. . . . To follow up he might do Stalin addressing a party congress, a Fuller brush salesman in German, or a submarine commander sinking an *amerikanische* freighter. (175)

This "stage" motif appears throughout the narrative. For example, Zetland often talks of "scenes" (170) and "dramas" (174) being played out and seems to be attracted to Lottie at least partly because she is "theatrical" (177). Their mutual awareness of romantic conventions and their individual willingness to act out their respective parts characterize their relationship and, in addition, ensure their happiness in it: "After being separated for five minutes [on their wedding day], Zet and Lottie ran the whole length of the corridor, embracing, trembling, and kissing. 'Darling, suddenly you weren't there!' 'Sweetheart, I'm always there. I'll always be there'" (178). The narrator, in one of the only places in the narrative where he makes his presence explicit, mentions his "testiness" with Zetland's preoccupation with "practicing his feelings on everyone," in this instance grieving as if the stillborn kittens of his cat were his own, and describes their subsequent argument: "I said he exaggerated everything. He accused me of a lack of sensibility. . . . We were a laughable pair of university high-brows who couldn't have a spat without citing William James and Karl Marx, or Villiers de l'Isle-Adam or Whitehead" (176). Zetland and his narrator both speak in voices that are not theirs exclusively but are omnipresent within their discourse community available to anyone willing to enter and (de)cipher the cultural language codes.

Conclusion: (Mis)Trials of Memory

The narrator depends on Zetland's memory as well as his own in (re-)creating the events depicted in the narrative; they don't become friends until they are fourteen, so much of the narrative depends on Zetland's memory entirely. Memory, however, is one of the most unreliable sources of *histoire*, itself having become mediated within the *récit* of the mind almost as soon as it becomes translated from experience. As Genette explains:

> Nothing is more explicitly mediated, avouched as memory. . . . It cannot be said that this narrator here lets the story tell itself, and it would be too little to say that he tells it without any care to efface himself before it: what we are dealing with is not the story but the story's "image," its trace in a memory. But this *trace*, so delayed, so remote, so indirect, is also the presence itself. (167–68)

Through the textual "trace" that constitutes "Zetland" as a narrative presence marking the absence of Zetland, the character witness creates a portrait of the artist, but as Zetland's (re)presentative, the narrator becomes an artist himself by virtue of his effective narrative performance. Thus "Zetland" functions as an artist-by-artist (de)construction, mediated by eyewitness testimony and codified by the *bildungs-künstlerroman* tradition. In "Zetland" the "hearsay" of memory becomes the "heresay" of the text, but as readers we are forced to declare "Zetland" a (mis)trial of memory. Zetland will never be sentenced because the judge will keep the case under constant advisement while the jury deliberates infinitely, never coming in with its verdict. With narrative performance there are no supreme courts of final interpretative-evaluative appeal; even if there were, every definitive reading would be declared unconstitutional and a violation of textuality's first amendment, free speech rights. Paradoxically, while the narrator's character witness testimony promises to keep Zetland from being imprisoned within a verdict of closure, it also guarantees him an open court date that stretches on like a series of life-sentences running consecutively, one after the other, into the eternity of the text.

Notes

1. For more information on the concept of "textuality," see Roland Barthes, "From Work to Text," especially 157–59.

2. For further discussion of *histoire, récit*, and their analogues, see Tzvetan Todorov, especially 25–26.

3. For more information on the *bildungs-künstlerroman*, see Maurice Beebe, Jerome H. Buckley, and Randolph Shaffner.

4. Bacon, Balzac, Beethoven, Borodin, Breton, Carnap, Casanova, Chaliapin, Cohen, Dewey, Dickens, Dietrich, Dostoyevsky, Duncan, Einstein, Esterhazy, Feigl, Frederick the Great, Galli-Curci, Goldman, Haggard, Haydn, Hegel, Heine, Hitler, Hume, Itzkowitz, l'Isle-Adam, James, Kant, Keats, Leibnitz, Lenin, Marx, Melville, Mill, Nietzsche, Prokofiev, Roland, Rousseau, Russell, Santayana, Schubert, Schuschnigg, Stalin, Tarski, Tolstoy, Trotsky, Tzara, Voltaire, Warwick, Whitehead, Wittgenstein.

Works Cited

Bakhtin, Mikhail. *The Dialogic Imagination: Four Essays*, edited by Michael Holquist, translated by Caryl Emerson and Michael Holquist. Austin: University of Texas Press, 1981.

Barthes, Roland. "From Work to Text." In *Image-Music-Text*, translated by Stephen Heath. 155–64. New York: Noonday, 1977.

———. *S/Z: An Essay*, translated by Richard Miller. New York: Hill and Wang, 1974.

Beebe, Maurice. *Ivory Towers and Sacred Founts: The Artist as Hero in Fiction from Goethe to Joyce*. New York: New York University Press, 1964.

Bellow, Saul. "Zetland: By a Character Witness." In *Him with His Foot in His Mouth and Other Stories*. 165–87. New York: Harper, 1984.

Buckley, Jerome H. *Season of Youth: The Bildungsroman from Dickens to Golding*. Cambridge: Harvard University Press, 1974.

Genette, Gerard. *Narrative Discourse: An Essay in Method*. Trans. Jane E. Lewin. Ithaca, NY: Cornell UP, 1980.

Maclean, Marie. *Narrative as Performance: The Baudelairean Experiment*. London: Routledge, 1988.

Shaffner, Randolf. *The Apprenticeship Novel: A Study of the Bildungsroman as a Regulative Type in Western Literature with a Focus on Three Representatives by Goethe, Maugham, and Mann*. New York: Peter Lang, 1984.

Solomon, Robert C. *Continental Philosophy Since 1750: The Rise and Fall of the Self*. Oxford: Oxford University Press, 1988.

Todorov, Tzvetan. *The Poetics of Prose*, translated by Richard Howard. Ithaca, N.Y.: Cornell University Press, 1977.

Self and Transcendence in
"A Silver Dish"

DIETER SCHULZ

First published in 1978 in *The New Yorker* and later included in *Him with His Foot in His Mouth* (1984), "A Silver Dish" has been praised as one of Saul Bellow's finest stories. Much of this enthusiasm stems no doubt from the joy of recognition. The story reassembles a number of motifs, themes, and figures familiar from Bellow's earlier work (Clayton). Much like the hero of *Henderson the Rain King*, the protagonist, a successful Chicago businessman by the name of Woody Selbst, combines elements of American modernity with a larger, more spiritual realm. Although fully immersed in the business of buying and selling, with a keen relish for facts and figures, widely traveled and a reader of magazines that offer "real information" (192), "fleshy and big, like a figure for the victory of American materialism" (203), Woody nevertheless possesses "a secret certainty that the goal set for this earth was that it should be filled with good, saturated with it" (220). The cen tral plot element—the encounter of Woody with his father—recalls the numerous male relationships from *Dangling Man* to *Humboldt's Gift*, a line one could extend to such later works as *More Die of Heartbreak* and *The Bellarosa Connection*. Even where the male encountered by the protagonist is not technically the father, he embodies features of a father figure; more specifically, he represents the principle of reality as opposed to the wishes and dreams of the son.

In this sense Woody's father, too, serves as a "reality instructor," teaching his son a lesson or two about the ways of the world. These ways include a lusty enjoyment of life's physical pleasures—"Horses, cards, billiards, and women were his lifelong interests, in ascending order" (198)—as well as sharp business dealings including petty thievery and fraud. The core episode of the story involves the theft of a silver dish engineered by Pop and helplessly connived at by the son, with the result that Woody is kicked out of a Christian seminary and forced to launch his own career in business. Ironically, the father initiates his son into disrespect for the law, the latter being equated with Christian hypocrisy and sham, while reality in volves the ruthless fight for survival. In a hilarious twist of the father-as-authority motif, this father teaches his son not to trust anybody, least of all his own father.

The opposition of idealist son and realist father reaches its climax in physical struggle as Woody tries to take the stolen silver dish away from his father. The attempt has to be unsuccessful, for obvious practical and symbolic reasons (Knight, 42). The dish is tucked away in Pop's underpants where Woody cannot reach it even after he has jumped Pop and pinned him to the ground. Thus Woody, as it were, falls in line with the many defeated or failed sons from Joseph in *Dangling Man* and Tommy Wilhelm in *Seize the Day* to Kenneth Trachtenberg in *More Die of Heartbreak*. Moreover, the wrestling scene parallels similar physical encounters in Bellow's earlier fiction, where the plot typically involves a climactic embrace or struggle (Opdahl, 24–28).

It seems worth recalling the continuities of "A Silver Dish" with the rest of Bellow's oeuvre partly because the success of the story, as the success of many of Bellow's novels, derives to a considerable degree from powerful psychological themes and motifs. One need hardly point to Freud to perceive the basic Oedipal pattern in Woody's failed attempt to wrest the stolen dish from Pop. Moreover, across cultures and ages, contests between fathers and sons have formed an important part of nitiation rites marking the transition of the youth from adolescence to adulthood (Ong, 85; Friedrich, 173–74). The initiation pattern, in turn, acquires special urgency in American culture, which emphasizes the separation of the son from the father as a prerequisite for selfhood; as Benjamin Franklin, the paradigmatic American, illustrates in his career, one has to reject one's father in order to become a self-made man. The American is the Prodigal Son who makes his fortune by failing to return (Fliegelman).

In dramatizing themes that have a strong psychological or mythic appeal, Bellow, one could argue, could hardly have failed, and one may feel reminded of Edgar Allan Poe's censure of James Fenimore Cooper and other novelists who, in picking such topics as the wilderness and the West, almost automatically ensure popular success for their works given the interest everybody takes in their subject matter (Poe, 479–80). Yet such considerations should prompt us to take a closer look at "A Silver Dish."

If Woody Selbst, as his very name appears to suggest, embodies representative traits, his central gesture of mourning implies a resistance to the dynamics of modern American life. Although immersed in "the ways of Chicago" (199), which epitomize contemporary civilization, he holds on to a notion of transcendence that counters the push and pull of materialism, his own as well as that of his environment. The wrestling scene in the middle of the story is counterpointed by the concluding scene of the son embracing his dying father in an effort to keep him warm and prolong his life. The image of protective nurturing offers a stark contrast to the hypermasculinity inherent in capitalist society and to the forces of disintegration characteristic of modern civilization.

Such resistance to modern fragmentation, of course, is vintage Bellow. What makes "A Silver Dish" such an astonishing feat is the fusion of technique and theme. The structural frame of the story is an extended act of mourning and meditation. According to Bellow, the ability to meditate is the imaginative person's and notably the artist's antidote to the frantic pace of life under the auspices of possessive individualism and the culture industry. Imaginative vision tries to capture "impulses from a human hinterland unacknowledged by our modern enlightenment and its psychology" ("Summations," 196); it creates a "significant space"—"a place where the human being really has removed to, with all his most important spiritual possessions" (Brans, 63; Riese, 114). This space constitutes a "quiet zone," a refuge where significant speech may emerge from the din of official jargon and gibberish ("Nobel Lecture," 321; Riese, 116). If there is hope in a world of noise and bustle, it resides in moments of stillness. From this per spective, "A Silver Dish" can be read quasi-allegorically as the temporary triumph of imaginative man over a world "in a state of distraction, even of frenzy" ("A World Too Much with Us," 6). The setting of the story marks off a space that makes meditation and mourning possible and allows the emergence of a voice that prevails against the meaningless chatter of a fallen world.

By the same token, the protagonist transcends the limitation of the ego-oriented self imprisoned in a civilization dedicated to the pursuit of wealth and a commitment to existing in the present alone. As Woody Selbst mourns the death of his father and recalls major incidents in their rela tionship, the ego-self—what Meister Eckhart called *eigenschaft*—gives way to a gesture of reaching out which culminates in the recollection of the final embrace that involves neither aggression nor possession but relinquishing. With Pop's escape into death, Woody becomes aware, once again, of his father's otherness and elusiveness. This insight combines a sense of loss with feelings of gratitude; Woody's admiration for a man who could never be pinned down sums up the Emersonian recognition that we are most enriched by what we cannot possess.

"A Silver Dish" is divided into three clearly marked sections. The centerpiece—the account of Pop's and Woody's fundraising trip and the theft of the silver dish—is flanked by an introduction to Woody's biography and a coda offering further insights into his character and concluding with the final struggle or embrace between father and son. The tripartite structure is underscored by shifts in narrative technique. While the central section dramatizes the theft of the dish by means of scenic narration, sections one and three alternate between showing and telling, with emphasis on reflection and summary.

Despite the heterogeneity of its parts, the story has considerable coherence. Among the factors contributing to unity, the most important is narrative voice. As in all of his works with the exception of a few early pieces written in straightforward first-person monologue, Bellow employs a persona whose point of view overlaps with that of the protagonist without coinciding with it. Long segments seem to be written from inside Woody's mind, yet all the time we sense the presence of an authorial figure editing and controlling his main character's flow of ideas and sensations.

The opening of the story—"What do you do about death—in this case, the death of an old father?"—hits the reader with the full weight of an authorial figure firing point-blank at him. As the following remarks reveal, the same question is also on Woody's mind, although he probably would not have phrased it in such universal terms. From the beginning, then, we feel we are being addressed by a voice that comes from the protagonist *and* goes beyond the limitations of an individual consciousness in assuming an authorial role.

If one prefers to discuss Bellow's narrative craft in terms of voice rather than point of view, it is because this is precisely the impression one has from most of his writing. Bellow himself has called his novels "'voice' books (as distinguished from 'eye' books)," and the same is true of his shorter pieces (Fuchs, 234; Friedrich, 169–84). Despite a wealth of visual details, especially in the central section, the overall effect of "A Silver Dish" is that of a speaker addressing an audience (as in the first paragraph) or talk ing to himself with the hope perhaps of being overheard.

The narrative voice is particularly important in the first section in which the reader would be in danger of being overwhelmed by a welter of data were not for the reassuring continuity of the speaker's presence. Within a few paragraphs, after learning of Pop's death, we receive information about Woody's education and travels, episodes from his life, his daily occupations, and the way he manages to look after an extended family of father, mother, two sisters, wife, mistress, and his father's mistress. Woody's large family in turn serves as a microcosm of the United States with its ethnic and religious diversity. Pop is an irreligious Jew, his mistress a devout Catholic, while Woody, who along with his mother and sisters converted to Protestantism, now considers himself an agnostic. Matters are further complicated by Bellow's telescoping of three different time levels. Forty years ago, "in 1933," Woody, who at the time attended a seminary run by Protestant fundamentalists committed to the conversion of Jews, was talked into a borrowing scheme by Pop that led to the stealing of the silver dish and the wrestling match between father and son. Less than a week ago, "last Tuesday," Pop died fighting in Woody's arms. Now, on Sunday morning, Woody reviews his life with the wrestling episodes standing out as particularly striking illustrations of his relationship with Pop. Biography, personal recollections, reflections on death and life, glimpses of America as melting pot and of Chicago as epitome of America, thumbnail sketches of several characters in addition to Woody and Pop: what prevents the reader's head from spinning is primarily the continuous murmur of the narrative voice blending with the flow of the protagonist's reminiscences.

A second unifying factor is provided by the setting of the story. After several days of suppressing his grief, Woody finally sits down "to reflect" (195). Prompted by the clanging of the church bells all over town, he no longer evades the unpleasantness or the triviality of death; instead, he pon ders the meaning of his relationship with Pop and the possible significance of his father's dying. Throughout the story, the reader remains aware of Woody sitting in his apartment on top of his warehouse and musing on his past life. Even the scenic account of the fundraising trip is sprinkled with occasional editorial comments reminding us that we are privy to a Sunday morning meditation whose apparent randomness is tied to the situation of a man swamped by memories:

> Bell-battered Woodrow's soul was whirling this Sunday morning, indoors and out, to the past, back to his upper corner of the warehouse, laid out with such originality—the bells coming and going, metal on naked metal, until the bell circle expanded over the whole of steel-making, oil-refining, power-producing mid-autumn South Chicago, and all its Croatians, Ukrainians, Greeks, Poles, and respectable blacks heading for their churches to hear Mass or to sing hymns. (198)

More subliminally, despite the whirl of memory pieces, the reader's attention is aided and focused by a number of recurrent ideas and motifs organized around sets of opposites. A cluster of ethical polarities centers around the conflict between Woody's mother and Pop. Mother, the Christian convert, stands for middle-class respectability and piety; she and her Christian friends warn Woody not to associate with his father. In the minister's words, Pop is "a dangerous person . . . leading a life of vice" (197). From Pop's perspective, these people are a bunch of hypocrites. His own philosophy has no patience with such "foolishness," and the lessons he teaches his son are intended as demonstrations "on behalf of real life and free instincts, against religion and hypocrisy" (197). Woody's character from his youth on is marked by a discrepancy between his mother's religion and his father's recklessness. Interestingly, these elements do not constitute an inner conflict; rather, they coexist in him without friction. Without qualms, Woody testifies in church and picks the lock of the storeroom. Going from lovemaking to studying New Testament Greek, he leads "a double life, sacred and profane" (197). Woody performs such shifts "without inconsistency" (199); even while he pimps for his clients at the Century of Progress World's Fair, he has religious visions of a world filled with love. The ease of Woody's code-switching recalls the chameleonlike adaptability of Augie March and other picaresque heroes. Perfectly capable of conforming to standards of piety and respectability, he is also a con man and trickster who gets a kick out of taking risks and of sinning "on a boy level" (197).

If Pop and Mother fight over Woody's soul, the result is a personality that combines their different sets of values without conflict. Nevertheless, Pop eventually gains the upper hand and wins the "war with Mother" (218). Almost from the outset, parallels and affinities with Pop abound to the point where one can argue that "A Silver Dish," far from dramatizing a conflict between father and son, actually presents a story of male bonding. Both Woody and Pop are introduced as "vital and picturesque," both relish "risk and defiance" (192), both are "common, thick men" (200). Pious Aunt Rebecca has a case when she lumps father and son together in a remark she repeats at Woody's dismissal from the seminary: "You're a little crook, like your father" (200, 216).

Woody and Pop, then, are very close from the beginning, and their relationship deepens over the years. Yet there is also in Woody a spiritual yearning that ties him to the Christian associates of his mother. Although he sides with Pop in rejecting their hypocrisy and cant, the vision of a world filled with God's love stays with him, and much of his behavior evinces a pull toward transcendence.

The opening paragraphs of the story introduce a polarity that draws on but also goes beyond the terms of the war between Mother and Pop. At stake is the ability to mourn amidst the pressures of modernity. In an age when international terrorism and mindless shootings are the order of the day, what could be the point of mourning "an octogenarian father, nearly blind, his heart enlarged, his lungs filling with fluid, who creeps, stumbles, gives off the odors, the moldiness or gassiness, of old men"? (191). Mourning appears senseless "against a contemporary background," particularly for a successful, experienced, and widely traveled businessman from Chicago. Yet Woody does mourn. At the funeral, he insists on performing "the final duty of a son" (194) by shoveling dirt on the coffin. Such filial piety ties in with an equally outmoded sense of family responsibility. Practically half his week is dedicated to members of his extended family—wife, mistress, mother and sisters, and (when he was alive) Pop. Woody does their shopping, provides funds, medical care, and entertainment. This is quite a feat, as all of them live in separate locations.

Throughout his career, Bellow has projected protagonists who, however tentatively and precariously, counter the fragmentation of modern life with at least a residual sense of family. From this perspective, "A Silver Dish" illustrates a shift from the nuclear to the extended family that is most noticeable in the novella "Cousins" and has continued in his later writings. On the one hand, the nuclear family has fallen apart; in "A Silver Dish," Pop contributed his share to its disintegration when he abandoned his wife and children when Woody was fourteen years old. Woody, on the other hand, reassembles the dispersed members. In an earlier manuscript fragment of the story, Bellow depicts a household where people of different religious persuasions "peacefully live together, caring for one another" in "a regular Utopia" (Friedrich, 78). The remark points to the utopian as well as the retrospective dimensions of the family theme in Bellow's writing. The narrator of *The Bellarosa Connection* is "preoccupied with feelings and longings, and emotional memory" (3). Family feelings offer glimpses of trans cendence, a way out of the prison-house of selfishness and the constrictions of the present, by pointing toward a future utopia of a community ruled by love as well as to a network of relationships extending across generations to the past (Schulz). This is where Woody differs most strikingly from Pop. Over the years, the two men have grown more and more alike: "Pop was no worse than Woody, and Woody was no worse than Pop." But although Woody identifies with his father's position—"a jolly, hearty, natural, likeable, unprincipled position"—he nevertheless suffers from a "weakness": he is "unselfish." As Pop remarks critically, "You take too much on yourself" (217).

Woody's mourning reflects a sense of family commitment that reaches beyond the confines of the ego-self. This is a profoundly human gesture that advances man beyond the level of brutes who—as the thrice-remembered incident of the buffalo calf caught by a crocodile suggests—are incapable of grief. More important, Woody's grief marks him as endowed with a soul that has not fully succumbed to the rat race. His heartbreak, like that of Benn Crader in *More Die of Heartbreak*, fails to make sense "against a contemporary background," but it is a sign of true humanity. The soul is an anachronism. Moses Herzog calls himself "a family type" and refers to his emotional makeup as "archaic" (265), and in the words of a character in *Mr. Sammler's Planet*, memories are necessary to "keep the wolf of insignificance from the door" (174).

Section one of "A Silver Dish" establishes a narrative voice, a local and temporal setting, and a set of moral coordinates that guide the reader through the barrage of memory bits flooding the protagonist's mind. Even when the reader may feel whirled around by a multitude of data and impressions, such a strategy prepares the "quiet zone" from which moral authority emerges. When the church bells stop clanging, Woody's emotional turmoil subsides and gives way to moments of pure vision.

Paradoxically, some of the most dramatic incidents of the story occur in these moments of mental rest. Section two offers a delightful piece of fast-paced picaresque narrative. The account of the fundraising trip is saturated with physical details and sensory impressions. The color and noise of the streetcars, the fury of a Chicago blizzard, the elegance of the Skoglund residence in the midst of Depression poverty, the stove in front of which Woody and Pop wrestle over the silver dish, the posturing of the crook-father and his unwilling accomplice-son vis à vis the dignified Christian ladies: the whole section manifests tremendous narrative drive and visual power. Moreover, it offers any amount of situational comedy and a hilarious portrait of Pop as both con man and moral authority. Even the son's agony appears amusing rather than distressing. If Woody gets thrown out of the seminary as a result of his collaboration with Pop, one tends to applaud Pop's assessment of the incident as a victory of honesty and life over hypocrisy and a kind of living death. The sheer energy of the sentence flow, the zest of the narrative, and the effortless brilliance of the writing suggest the Bellow of *Augie March*: an author in love with the exuberant vitality of his characters and the vibrancy of the scene they confront in their shady activities.

Technically, apart from a few editorial comments, showing has replaced telling in part two, dialogue alternates with description, and some of the descriptive paragraphs—as for instance the remarks on Western

Avenue (202)—resemble Whitmanesque catalogues. Only toward the end of the section, after the scene of Woody's dismissal from the seminary, does the narrative voice reemerge with some force as Woody ponders the moral implications of his adventure: "Pop had carried him back to his side of the line, blood of his blood, the same thick body walls, the same coarse grain. Not cut out for a spiritual life. Simply not up to it" (217). Written in free indirect speech, these observations mark the transition to section three, which begins after a final bit of dialogue with further remarks on "Pop's war with Mother" and ends with the scene depicting Woody's struggle with Pop on his deathbed.

The concluding section offers an interpretation of the foregoing episode and refines earlier remarks on the strife between Pop and Mother in Woody's psyche. On the face of it, Pop, who "took his stand on realism," has won out over Mother, who "represented the forces of religion and hypochondria" (218). Woody becomes a successful tile contractor, as shrewd and reckless an American as his father. Yet he also acts as a "dutiful and loving son and brother" to his ailing and aging relatives, fixing their homes, paying for electricity and food, and assisting them in their various educational and business projects. Unlike his macho father, Woody is a family type with a talent for such "feminine" virtues as caring and nurturing. Indeed, in his final gesture in the hospital, as he hugs Pop and tries to keep him from removing the intravenous needles, he crosses gender boundaries and assumes the duties of a mother and nurse. The impact of the scene derives to a considerable degree from its contrast with the wrestling match in Mrs. Skoglund's house. The fight over the silver dish had strong overtones of an Oedipal struggle, with the son trying to assert his masculine autonomy over the father's authority. At the hospital, in contrast, Woody's embrace not only lacks all elements of male self-assertion, it also marks the high point of a career of "feminine" unselfishness that has always accompanied and counterpointed his business career.

As in *Humboldt's Gift* and elsewhere in Bellow's fiction, such crossing of gender boundaries does not involve the acceptance or integration of actual women; the literal feminine remains outside the protagonist's quest (Cronin, 108–9). Mother and sisters deteriorate into "welfare personalities" without "individual outlines" (218), and as he hugs Pop in the hospital bed, Woody motions the nurses out of the room. Nevertheless, even at the price of such misogynist exclusions, Woody's sensibility and the sense of self hinted at in his last name achieve a wider range than his father's personality would allow. Just as his jogging is not merely a physical activity but in cludes spiritual moments, his vision of life transcends the selfish ego. If he was unable to identify with the Christian fundamentalists' concept of the Second Coming, he nonetheless clings to "a secret certainty that the goal set for this earth was that it should be filled with good" (220). For Woody, such a notion is no more than a "clumsy intuition," but it has immediate practical consequences in his many acts of kindness that climax in his attempt to preserve Pop's life. In his own way, one could argue, he contributes his share to the Second Coming; God's Kingdom, as a close examination of the relevant biblical passages shows, should not be envisaged as a distant and cataclysmic epiphany but rather as an emerging event that takes shape in acts of generosity right here and now (Welker). In this sense, as an ethical imperative with a strong pragmatic tinge, Woody's visionary bent opposes the destructive dynamic of a civilization dominated by greed and selfishness.

At the level of discourse, Woody's ethos translates into strategies of mourning and meditation. Even the highly dramatic money-raising sequence is framed by the posture of a person engaged in thoughtful recollection: "When the tolling stopped, Woody didn't notice that a great lake of quiet had come over his kingdom, the Selbst Tile warehouse. What he heard and saw was an old red Chicago streetcar" (201). Emerging as they do from moments of stillness, Woody's reflections provide an analogue to the task of the artist. The "great lake of quiet" in Woody's warehouse corresponds to the "quiet zone" Bellow stipulates in his Nobel lecture as the area from which significant speech and writing originate in an age of debased, inflationary language. Along similar lines, in the face of postmodernism with its emphasis on the free play of signifyers, Bellow remains committed to realism—not in the sense of simplistic mimesis, but as responsible exploration of character. As the earlier manuscript fragments reveal, in writing "A Silver Dish," Bellow started out with character sketches modeled, perhaps, after real-life people (Friedrich, 77). In the process of composition toward the final version, he develops the narrative voice that weaves in and out of the central character's consciousness in an effort to come to grips with its ethical core. After all, character in the Aristotelian sense means *ethos*—the set of motives, habits, and values that accounts for personality. The distinctive attitude of the Bellovian voice is meditation; such meditation, as the speaker in *Humboldt's Gift* explains, strives to "work your way behind the appearances," and to succeed in this endeavor, "you have to be calm" (163). What the voice might achieve is not the Second Coming so much as its ethical correlative: the flow of moral power. In this sense, as an activity and a moral force, the narrative voice in Bellow's fiction claims authority (Riese, 119–22).

The form of "A Silver Dish" befits its theme. The "regular utopia" of people caring for each other and the story-as-threnody belong together. The themes of family and mourning reinforce each other; both create a space in which love can circulate without impediment. Hence the note of triumph on which the story ends. As in the previous wrestling scene, Woody finds himself defeated by Pop, but his reaction is a far cry from the "bad feelings" and "groveling emotions" (213) he suffered then. Instead, in reviewing the hospital scene, he admires Pop's final feat of slipping away into death and formulates an epitaph that reads more like a paean than an expression of grief: "You could never pin down that self-willed man. When he was ready to make his move, he made it—always on his own terms. And always, always, something up his sleeve. That was how he was." The last sentence points both toward Woody's mourning and Bellow's commitment to character as a central feature of realism. Much like Sherwood Anderson, whose narrative art circles around and respects the mystery of character, the concluding note of Bellow's speaker signals a letting go; the artist's probing into personality reaches a point where all that can be said is "that was how he was." By the same token, Woody's work of mourning succeeds inasmuch as he can relinquish Pop and accept "his terms" instead of trying to absorb him into his emotional sphere.

"A Silver Dish" illustrates an insight forcefully developed in Ralph Waldo Emerson's essay "Experience." Prompted in part by the death of his son, Emerson begins by expressing his sense of bewilderment at not being more deeply touched: "In the death of my son, now more than two years ago, I seem to have lost a beautiful estate,—no more. I cannot get it nearer to me" (473). In economic metaphors that might appeal to the author of *Humboldt's Gift* and *A Theft*, Emerson goes on to develop the implications of loss and gain and possession, until he realizes that what looked like a cause for despair may be converted into an asset: grief cannot touch him because the boy was not his to begin with but a gift that could never be incorporated into his property. We are only enriched by what we fail to possess. Beginning in gloom, "Experience" ends in affirmation as Emerson welcomes the dark forces— "the lords of life" (491)—that resist our desires and foil us ever. Their very alienness helps us toward our humanity, for our wealth lies in what is not ours.

The ending of "A Silver Dish" follows this pattern. Pop's final maneuver becomes a source of joy for a son who recognizes the identity of an other that literally eludes him. Neither an act of self-assertion nor of possessiveness, Woody's embrace of his father succeeds because it fails. In making contact with a will that resists his own, he transcends the limits of his ego. He can appreciate the gift of a father who was a boon by always being himself.

Works Cited

Bellow, Saul. *The Bellarosa Connection.* New York: Penguin, 1989.

——. *Herzog.* New York: Viking Press, 1964.

——. *Humboldt's Gift.* New York: Viking Press, 1975.

——. *Mr. Sammler's Planet.* New York: Viking Press, 1970.

——. "The Nobel Lecture." *American Scholar* 46 (1977): 316–25.

——. "A Silver Dish." In *Him with His Foot in His Mouth and Other Stories,* 191–222. London: Secker & Warburg, 1984.

——. "Summations." In *Saul Bellow: A Mosaic,* edited by L. H. Goldman, Gloria L. Cronin, and Ada Aharoni. Vol. 3 of *Twentieth-Century American Jewish Writers,* edited by Daniel Walden, 185–99. New York: Peter Lang, 1992.

——. "A World Too Much with Us." *Critical Inquiry* 2, no. 1 (1975): 1–9.

Brans, Jo. "Common Needs, Common Preoccupations: An Interview with Saul Bellow." In *Critical Essays on Saul Bellow,* edited by Stanley Trachtenberg, 57–72. Boston: G. K. Hall, 1979.

Clayton, John. "A Rich Reworking." *Saul Bellow Journal* 6 (1987): 19–25.

Cronin, Gloria L. "The Quest for the Feminine Poetic in *Humboldt's Gift.*" In *Saul Bellow at Seventy-five: A Collection of Critical Essays.* Vol. 9 of Studies & Texts in English, edited by Gerhard Bach, 93–112. Tübingen: Gunter Narr, 1991.

Emerson, Ralph Waldo. "Experience." In *Essays and Lectures,* 471–92. New York: Library of America, 1983.

Fliegelman, Jay. *Prodigals and Pilgrims: The American Revolution against Patriarchal Authority, 1750–1800.* Cambridge: Cambridge University Press, 1982.

Friedrich, Marianne M. *Character and Narration in the Short Fiction of Saul Bellow.* Vol. 5 of *Twentieth-Century American-Jewish Writers,* edited by Daniel Walden. New York: Peter Lang, 1995.

Fuchs, Daniel. *Saul Bellow: Vision and Revision.* Durham, NC: Duke University Press, 1984.

Knight, Karl F. "The Rhetoric of Bellow's Woody Selbst: Religion and Irony." *Saul Bellow Journal* 8 (1989): 35–43.

Ong, Walter. *Fighting for Life: Contest, Sexuality, and Consciousness.* Ithaca, NY: Cornell University Press, 1981.

Opdahl, Keith. "'Stillness in the Midst of Chaos': Plot in the Novels of Saul Bellow." *Modern Fiction Studies* 25 (Spring 1979): 15–28.

Poe, Edgar Allan. Review of *Wyandotté,* by Cooper. In *Essays and Reviews,* 479–90. New York: Library of America, 1983.

Riese, Utz. "The Authority of Representation and the Discourse of Post-Modernity: *Humboldt's Gift.*" In *Saul Bellow at Seventy-five: A Collection of Critical Essays.* Vol. 9 of Studies & Texts in English, edited by Gerhard Bach, 113–23. Tübingen: Gunter Narr, 1991.

Schulz, Dieter. "'Family' in Bellow's *More Die of Heartbreak.*" In *Saul Bellow at Seventy-five: A Collection of Critical Essays.* Vol. 9 of Studies & Texts in English, edited by Gerhard Bach, 151–62. Tübingen: Gunter Narr, 1991.

Welker, Michael. "The Reign of God." *Theology Today* 49 (1992): 500–515.

Saul Bellow's "Him with His Foot in His Mouth": Why Bellow (and Other Writers) Matter

ANDREW FURMAN

S aul Bellow contends,

> When you open a novel—and I mean of course the real thing—you
> enter into a state of intimacy with its writer. You hear a voice or, more
> significantly, an individual tone under the words. This tone you, the
> reader, will identify not so much by a name, the name of the author, as
> by a distinct and unique human quality. It seems to issue from the
> bosom, from a place beneath the breastbone. It is more musical
> than verbal, and it is the characteristic signature of a person, of a soul.
> ("Distracted," 168)

Ah, the soul. Bellow is one of the few writers these days bold enough to
champion the soul, not to mention the writer's role in illuminating its
truths. As Cynthia Ozick notes (alluding, like Bellow does above, to the
mere aesthetic "thrills" of postmodernism), "Bellow's charge has been to
restore the soul to American literature" (238). Such an endeavor, to most
contemporary academics, smacks of an unsavory moral didacticism from
yet another aging, if not dead, white male. But Bellow refuses to waver in
his views of the writer's moral role in society. At the 1987 international
Saul Bellow Conference in Haifa, he remarked, "Readers . . . expect
authors to be instructive, informative, edifying, revelatory, even prophetic,
and writers put themselves out to meet these expectations"
("Summations," 185). In an earlier interview, Bellow also contended that

the writer "should perform a moral function . . . should provide emotional, spiritual stuff—those are rather old fashioned ideas, but I don't think that people have really given up old fashioned ideas—they just scoff at them, while in reality they continue to live by them" (qtd. in Boyers, 7).

I would only qualify Bellow's prescient view of the writer's role in society by asserting that they are not nearly as old-fashioned as Bellow concedes. For outside of the increasingly insular world of academics, readers still unabashedly rely on literature to illuminate truths about the soul. A book reviewer in the popular magazine, the *New Republic*, could still depend upon the empathy of his readers when he mused recently, "Imagine our collective consciousness without what we learned about the human soul from *Crime and Punishment*" (Baranczak, 37). The contention caught my eye since I have been trained of late (dare I say indoctrinated) to challenge its principal assumptions: that there exists a truly "collective" consciousness, a "human" soul (i.e., one common to us all), that any work of literature can access these upper-case "T" Truths. Moreover, the sentence captured my attention since it embodies what literature still means to many of us, and what it still should mean.

It is in the spirit of this reviewer's remark—that the soul exists and that the best literature pierces our collective consciousness with a greater knowledge of this human essence—that I undertake this examination of Saul Bellow's story, "Him with His Foot in His Mouth." As pointedly as any other story in Bellow's canon, "Him with His Foot in His Mouth" bespeaks the writer's indefatigable persistence in engaging the individual's quest for a higher spirituality than that afforded by America's credo of anarchic individualism and rampant materialism. The story revolves around an aging musicologist, Herschel Shawmut; his profession suggests, straight away, that he aspires toward a higher spirituality. Bellow has repeatedly insisted upon the power of classical music to tap the wellspring of our inmost self. What composers have in common with other artists (like writers), Bellow insists, "is the soul to which their appeal is made, whether it is barren or fertile, empty or full, whether the soul knows something, feels something, loves something" ("A Matter," 77). In a more recent essay, "Mozart: An Overture," Bellow reflects upon Mozart's power to speak to us "(beyond words) . . . about the mysteries of our common human nature" ("Mozart," 14). Shawmut, as one might expect, wafts himself away to the sublime when he conducts Mozart or Handel (60–61). Like Bellow himself, Shawmut believes in the common human soul and the epiphanic power of classical music to move us at this most essential level.

It comes as little surprise that this contemplative, soulful sort would be inclined to brood over matters when he receives word from an old colleague, Eddie Walish, that an insensitive retort he made to a college librarian some thirty-five years ago traumatized her for life (after the librarian told Shawmut that a hat he was wearing made him look like an archaeologist, he fired back mercilessly, "And you look like something I just dug up" [9]). Racked by guilt, Shawmut decides to make amends with the retired librarian, Carla Rose, by writing her an extended letter in which he explains his unfortunate predilection for insulting people. The story, "Him with His Foot in His Mouth," represents the first draft of this letter to the long-suffering Carla Rose.

To be sure, Shawmut has some very real problems of his own with which to occupy himself. Early on in the letter he lets Rose know that he was in poor shape when Eddie Walish's accusatory letter arrived:

> I have to swallow all sorts of pills. I take Inderal and quinidine for hypertension and cardiac disorders, and I am also, for a variety of psychological reasons, deeply distressed and for the moment without ego defenses. . . . To the disorders aforementioned I must add teeth with cracked roots, periodontia requiring antibiotics that gave me the runs and resulted in a hemorrhoid the size of a walnut, plus creeping arthritis of the hands. (3–5)

To add to these physical and psychological ailments, serious legal problems dog Shawmut (more on the specifics later), who ill-advisedly fled to British Columbia but faces extradition to the United States. Burdened by such palpable *sores*, one wonders why Shawmut frets so over one insensitive joke he made years ago. Shawmut, however, writes the letter to heal himself every bit as much as he writes it to relieve the questionable suffering of Carla Rose. Shawmut's italicized note early on in the story—"*I will say it all and then revise, send Miss Rose only the suitable parts*"—reveals that he must "say it all" for himself; then he might revise the letter for Rose (4). Like several of the letters in Bellow's *Herzog*, one cannot even be sure that he will send the letter. Rather, it serves the brainy, contemplative Shawmut as a medium through which to scrutinize the past events in his life, his honorable and dishonorable actions, to glean whatever insight into his soul he possibly can. Eugene Goodheart aptly characterizes the story as a "confession of sin, an attempt at purgation, so that he can hear words of ultimate seriousness" (153).

Given the alienation and nihilism to which the archetypal modernist heroes succumb, their rejection of the human community (e.g., Nick Adams's flight to the backwoods), and the virtual absence of a tangible human community in the more avant-garde postmodern work of, say,

Donald Barthelme, Robert Coover, and John Barth, Bellow stakes out highly unusual territory when he creates a protagonist sensitive to his capacity to injure another with the spoken word, a protagonist who broods about his inner life, the state of his soul. What is more, Bellow's Shawmut does not represent a creative departure for Bellow at all, only a fresh set of circumstances and a fresh pair of eyes through which Bellow explores his enduring artistic concerns. As Daniel Walden notes, Bellow has proposed throughout his career that "genuine (real) freedom comes only by accepting the fact that life can only proceed by reviewing itself and by acknowledging that such review is continual and necessary. . . . Bellow beckons us to live by discovering the inner self" (60). Indeed, Shawmut's agonizing efforts to reach "the right state, the state of vision [he] was meant or destined to be in" (55) parallel the effort of a younger Augie March to "come back to these axial lines" where "He will be brought into focus" (*AAM* 454–55); or Moses Herzog's attempt to *"figure out what's what"* so that he might *"exert a positive influence"*(*Herzog*, 128); or, finally, Artur Sammler's efforts to condense what he knows about the human soul into one single statement—"Short views, for God's sake!"—before he concludes his "earth business" (*MSP*, 148). Like these quintessential Bellovian protagonists, Shawmut, through his introspection, affirms the individual's connectedness to and responsibility for the larger human community. Specifically, Shawmut must discern "Why does anybody *say* such things as I said to [Carla Rose]" (28), he must achieve this "state of vision," since he knows that he "must assume responsibility for the unhappiness others suffer because of [his] disorientation" (55).

To orient himself, so to speak, Shawmut begins his letter by reflecting upon his years at Ribier College as a young Music History professor, fresh out of graduate school; he returns to the scene of the crime. Through Shawmut's reminiscences, Bellow takes pains to emphasize Shawmut's youthful innocence and awkwardness:

> Fresh from Chicago and from Bloomington, Indiana, where I took my degree, I had never seen birches, roadside ferns, deep pinewoods, little white steeples. What could I be but out of place? It made me scream with laughter to be called 'Dr. Shawmut.' I felt absurd here, a camel on the village green. I am a high-waisted and long-legged man, who is susceptible to paradoxical, ludicrous images of himself. (7)

Even the undergraduates at Ribier find Shawmut hopelessly unsophis ticated. "A girl to whom I was assigned adviser," he tells Rose, "asked for another one because I haven't been psychoanalyzed and can't even begin to relate to her" (8). In a *New York Times* Op-Ed piece entitled, "Ethnic Pop and Native Corn" (Sept. 19, 1988), Philip Roth sheds some light upon Shawmut's predicament when he alludes to one reason why Michael Dukakis would not defeat George Bush in the 1988 presidential election. Dukakis, drawing upon his immigrant roots to court popularity, simply could not command the authority of a "Native Corn" Bush, whose family has spoken unaccented English "for more than a mere 50 or 60 years— they have spoken it forever" (Roth, A23). Granted, Shawmut's Eastern European immigrant roots manifest themselves in his "Russian church art" features, distinct from Michael Dukakis's Mediterranean visage. But one might as well substitute Shawmut's bald pate for Dukakis's unruly, dark mop. What they both do *not* look like—in a word, "American"—is more significant than what they do look like. Shawmut, like Dukakis, cannot pass for Native Corn. Amid the meticulously manicured grounds of a New England private college, he looks (and feels) not a whit more natural than Dukakis in a tank. He broods, "I don't even look like an American. . . . I might have come straight from Kiev. . . . I am tall but I slouch, my buttocks are set higher than other people's" (27).

Shawmut's backwardness and "un-Americaness" contrast interestingly to the hipness of his accuser, Eddie Walish. Where Shawmut is naive, unfinished, crude, Walish is sophisticated, refined, polished—"Early Hip with a Harvard background" (8). Or so Walish would like others to believe. As Shawmut probes deeper into Walish's character and background, he remembers that Walish was not nearly so "establishment" as he let on. "[H]e's not a real Yankee," Shawmut discloses to Rose: "His father, a second-generation American, is a machinist, retired, uneducated." One of the old man's letters reads, "Your poor mother—the doctor says she has a growth on her virginia which he will have to operate. When she goes to surgery I expect you and your sister to be here to stand by me" (9). To add to the indignities of Walish's upbringing, Shawmut recalls that "one of Walish's longstanding problems was that he looked distinctly Jewy. Certain people were distrustful and took him with gratuitous hostility, suspecting that he was trying to pass for a full American. . . . A taste of persecution made him friendly to Jews, or so he said" (17–18).

Shawmut has good reason to suspect Walish's proclaimed sympathy for the Jews; Walish's belated personal attack on Shawmut aside, he did everything he could, Shawmut remembers, to align himself with the Eastern Establishment and dissociate himself from the only ones below him, blacks and Jews. For example, he made sure to marry a woman above him socially, and cultivated a front of intellectual confidence and physical health. In sharp contrast to Shawmut, who accepts his physical awkwardness, Walish "would not act the cripple despite his spiral back. Even though he slouched and walked with an outslapping left foot, he carried himself with style. He wore good English tweeds and Lloyd & Haig brogans" (13). Walish also incorporated his mother's maiden name into his signature to affect a more blue-blooded identity.

Insofar as Walish's humble family origins resemble Shawmut's own, Walish's attempts to liberate himself from these origins offer Shawmut insight into the toll of such assimilatory strategies. Walish, who embraced the distinctly American code of the self-made man, lost all sense of self. Shawmut recognizes that Walish succumbed to the pressures of being avant-garde: "To be avant-garde means to tamper with yourself, to have a personal project requiring a histrionic routine—in short, to put on an act" (24). Walish "*seems* all sorts of things" to Shawmut, but what he actually is, even Walish apparently did not know (14). Indeed, his psychiatric problems indicate the emotional cost of his effrontery that, in the end, fooled no one anyway. Though Walish may have talked the establishment talk, he, ultimately, could not walk the walk. Despite natty clothes and his refusal to use a cane or an elevated shoe, Walish cut a far more ridiculous figure than even Shawmut:

> One of the campus ladies suggested that I urge him to shave his ears. . . . He has a sort of woodwind laugh, closer to oboe than to clarinet, and he releases his laugh from the wide end of his nose as well as from his carved pumpkin mouth. He grins like Alfred E. Neuman from the cover of *Mad* magazine, the successor of Peck's Bad Boy. (13–14)

Here, Bellow demonstrates his unsurpassed precision in rendering a character's physical details to reveal the essence of that character. Even Brent Staples, who recently took Bellow to task for his ugly depictions of African-Americans, admires Bellow's penchant for creating such vivid human beings. Says Staples, "Bellow's people leaped more vividly from the page than any I'd encountered. Often he reduced them to a single bodily feature that carried their entire person in its wake" (217–18). Staples may have been thinking of Bellow's depiction of Walish above when he goes on to observe, "He sometimes snatched bodies whole, but mainly he cannibalized them, taking only the choicest parts. He stole from himself as well, giving his characters his own enormous eyes and unflatteringly spaced teeth" (218). To be sure, Bellow "cannibalizes" Walish (perhaps modeling the jack-o-lantern mouth after his own) to expose the salient, and pitiable, element of Walish's character. Through emphasizing Walish's grotesque physical form which undermine his airs of inbred gentility,

Bellow reveals (to Shawmut and to the reader) the wrongheadedness of such affectation.

Walish's efforts to court the establishment would seem to contrast sharply with Shawmut's code of behavior. Shawmut, at any rate, peppers his recollections of his colleague's buffoonery with a healthy dose of critical detachment. That said, Shawmut cannot help but recognize a disconcerting element of Walish in himself. Indeed, Walish represents an exaggerated manifestation of Shawmut's own efforts to escape the meanness and poverty of his past. Why, after all would Walish's letter pull Shawmut to pieces if he did not suspect a grain of truth in his colleague's accusation that he played the assimilation-game, so to speak, himself? Walish, specifically, accuses Shawmut of cannily promoting his musical textbook to earn a fortune. He compares Shawmut to Kissinger, "a Jew who made himself strong in the Establishment, having no political base or constituency but succeeding through promotional genius" (25). Shawmut cannot reject these accusations out of hand. He remembers that he gravitated toward Walish, in the first place, since he wanted to learn about the mores of the Eastern Establishment. Walish's bitterness toward Shawmut can be attributed to the fact that Shawmut learned from him all too well and managed to assimilate himself even more effectively into the mainstream—hence Shawmut's textbook in all the libraries and his popular musicology programs on public television.

Shawmut's backward glance at Walish's exaggerated airs of sophistication, then, offers him insight concerning his own phoniness, inextricably linked to his drive to insult. He intuits that he lashes out at others to preserve whatever shred of selfhood he can amid an establishment which demands that he suppress his true feelings. As he explains to Rose,

> I came to believe for a time that I couldn't get on in life until I, too, had a false self like everybody else and so I made special efforts to be considerate, deferential, civil. And of course I overdid things and wiped myself twice where people of better breeding only wiped once. But no such program of betterment could hold me for long. I set it up, and then tore it down, and burned it in a raging bonfire. (11)

The particular insults that Shawmut meditates upon through the course of the story bear out his explanatory logic above. He offends a professor who espouses Alexander Pope's thesis of the "unreality of evil" with the sarcastic retort, "Do you mean that every gas chamber has a silver lining?" (19); he startles guests at a party when he exclaims that he would be "happy" to write the obituary for an arrogant professor who worries that no one will be learned enough for the task (29); "Will you use a typewriter or an adding machine?" he snidely asks a wealthy benefactress who confides in him her plans to write her memoirs (33). Shawmut cannot suppress such "seizures," as he calls them. His distinct sensibilities burst through his veneer of cordiality. Importantly, he developed these distinct sensibilities, not from the university, but from his Jewish upbringing. Though Shawmut cultivates a genteel enough English, the brutal frankness and honesty of Yiddish provokes his outbursts. "Yiddish is severe and bears down without mercy," he tells Rose (19). "If there is a demiurge who inspires me to speak wildly," Shawmut continues, "he may have been attracted to me by this violent unsparing language" (19). One senses that Walish suffers from clinical depression since he stifles the angst that Shawmut regularly vents through Yiddish-inspired insults. A language which likens faces to slop jars has little patience for genteel phoniness.

Shawmut, then, seems to have all the answers early on in the story. Assimilation into the mainstream threatens to diminish one's identity, as it diminished Walish's. To preserve one's soul one must resist the temptation to court the establishment with phony airs. The rub, however, is that Shawmut's expression of his true self—saturated with deep and abiding family feelings—cannot carry the day in America. Shawmut, after all, listened to his heart's most sincere yearnings when he decided to go into business with his brother, Philip:

> What affected me was that my brother and I should be really associated for the first time in our lives. . . . I was unreasonably stirred by emotions that had waited a lifetime for expression; they must have worked their way into my heart at a very early age, and now came out in full strength to drag me down. (40–41)

As Shawmut suggests in the final line of the passage, his decision to heed the yearnings of his soul did him in. Philip, strategically cooing Shawmut with Yiddish endearments, took advantage of his brother's filial longings to lure him into investing $600,000 into a huge auto wrecking center in Texas. He picked Shawmut up by his "trustful affections as one would lift up a rabbit by the ears" (52). Unbeknownst to Shawmut at the time, Philip used credit established by his brother's money to dabble in fraudulent real estate schemes. The law eventually caught up to Philip who fled to Mexico to escape incarceration, leaving a hapless Shawmut to face the angry creditors. As I mentioned above, Shawmut fled to Canada upon bad legal advice from his brother-in-law, yet another unsavory lawyer in Bellow's oeuvre.

Having rejected Walish's code of phoniness to embrace the stirrings of his inner self, it perplexes Shawmut that things did not simply turn out better. He muses to Rose, "[W]hat sort of act was it to trust a close relative who turned out to be a felon, or to let my late wife persuade me to hand over my legal problems to her youngest brother?" (24). Shawmut realizes that he may have been better off had he suppressed his soul's deepest yearnings. He, however, (like Bellow) believes in the soul. More to the point, Shawmut possesses a Jewish immigrant consciousness enraptured by the promise of a boundless America to unshackle the human soul. In Walt Whitman's introduction to *Leaves of Grass*, he gives voice to the dream of America shared by a whole generation of Jewish immigrants:

> The United States themselves are essentially the greatest poem. . . . Here is not merely a nation but a teeming nation of nations. Here is action untied from strings necessarily blind to particulars and details magnificently moving in vast masses. Here is the hospitality which forever indicates heroes. . . . Here are the roughs and beards and space and ruggedness and nonchalance that the soul loves. (Whitman, 5)

Of course, a scarce few Jewish immigrants in the late-nineteenth-and early-twentieth-century had the opportunity to read American Transcendentalist literature. Shawmut, however, knows his Whitman and alludes to some of the lines above: "The United States is destined to become one of the great achievements of humanity, a nation made up of many nations. . . . The U.S.A. itself is to be the greatest of poems, as Whitman prophesied" (26). He hopefully anticipates the fulfillment of Whitman's prophecy but, as one might expect, the painful episode involving his brother complicates his Whitmanesque vision. Something about America—something Whitman never fathomed—squeezes both Shawmut and his brother from its northern and southern borders and Shawmut must get to the bottom of it.

Shawmut scrutinizes the fiasco with his brother and looks down the maw of a ruthless and sterile America. For Philip, Shawmut realizes, embraced what can only be a distinctly American code of materialism and self-centered individualism when he married a rich gentile woman and moved into her mansion in the suffocating heat of Texas. "[H]e was thoroughly Americanized" Shawmut tells Rose (39). Bellow's depiction of the sprawling estate evokes its complete lack of human warmth. Perhaps most tellingly, Philip's wife, Tracy, breeds ferocious pit bulldogs that bare their teeth at Shawmut and horrify him:

> They are the most terrifying of all dogs. . . . they attack all strangers, kids as well as grownups. As they do not bark, no warning is given. Their intent is always to kill, and once they have begun to tear at you they can't be called off. . . . In the pit, the dogs fight and die in silence. Aficionados bet millions of dollars on the fights (which are illegal, but what of it?) (41–42)

The people at the estate may not wish, like the dogs, to rip Shawmut to pieces, but they treat him with an icy indifference:

> For breakfast, if I called the kitchen persistently, I could have freeze-dried coffee and a slice of Wonder bread. They were brought to my room by a black person who answered no questions. Was there an egg, a piece of toast, a spoonful of jam? Nothing. It wounds me desperately not to be fed. (47–48)

Bellow, a painstaking craftsman, chooses his details carefully. The freeze-dried coffee and Wonder bread evoke, tersely and precisely, the coldness and sterility of America itself. Philip may live on a virtual state park, with prize-winning gardens and Portuguese linens in the bedroom, but Shawmut recognizes that a spiritual impoverishment bears down upon the estate like a plague. Whether self-consciously or not, Bellow depicts a contemporary House of Pride (the other deadly sins—idleness, gluttony, lechery, avarice, envy, and wrath—all make their appearances as well). The apparent majesty of the estate awes Shawmut at first, but he soon recognizes that it sits on a foundation of sand. It may be cosmetically wondrous, but it is only eye candy, so to speak.

The utter lack of human warmth at Philip's Texas mansion provokes Shawmut's nostalgia for their childhood home. Despite the dinginess and downright poverty of their home in Hammond, Indiana, something about the Roosevelt Road neighborhood pierces Shawmut's consciousness in Texas through the din of pit bulldog barks and blaring American rock music. He remembers the "chicken coops stacked on the sidewalks, the Talmudist horseradish grinder in the doorway of the fish store," and "the daily drama of the Shawmut kitchen" (39). He thinks of their father, a carpet-peddler, who couldn't earn enough for the rent during the Depression, and their mother who managed defiantly to feed all of them, regardless: "She cooked tubs of stuffed cabbage and of chop suey. . . . Mother shopped, peeled, chopped, boiled, fried, roasted, and baked, served and washed" (47). Tracy might have a degree from the cordon bleu (as Philip boasts), but her kitchen lacks the most essential ingredient, love.

Still, Shawmut recalls that Philip refused to recognize the emotional richness of their childhood. He turned a deaf ear to Shawmut's persistent efforts to remind him of their rich past—in Philip's view, their "dreary origins" (39). Philip, like Eddie Walish, cares not a fig about the past. He cannot erase it, but he can try his best to forget it. "Family sentiment was not his dish," Shawmut laments to Rose, and continues, "All that he had was for the new family; for the old family, nix. He said he couldn't recall Hammond, Indiana. . . . he was aware that there were two departed sisters, but their names didn't come to him" (45). While Shawmut recognizes that his brother did not belong at the Texas estate any more than he himself did, he remembers that Philip could not have been happier with his new "American" life in Texas: "His greatest satisfaction was that everything was so American. It was, too—an all-American production" (47). Philip, ultimately, winds up in a Texas prison and dies of a massive heart attack while doing push-ups. Philip, Shawmut laments, paid dearly for his myopia: "Philly had put himself into Tracy's hands for full Americanization. To achieve this (obsolete) privilege, he paid the price of his soul" (50).

One should not be misled by Bellow's almost surreal depiction of Philip's life in Texas. For Philip's story, Bellow suggests, is all too real in America. Importantly, Bellow does not depict his ethos of avaricious materialism and ruthless individualism as atypical. Rather, it is the new American ethos that even Shawmut's mother adopts. At her nursing home, decorated with plastic ferns and light, synthetic furniture (Bellow bombards us with images of an ersatz, plastic America), she boasts about her "millionaire" son, Philip, and does not even recognize Shawmut, the only one who visits her. "My mother," Shawmut reflects in his letter to Rose, "two-thirds of her erased, and my brother . . . had both been true to the present American world and its liveliest material interests. Philip therefore spoke to her understanding. I did not" (60). That Shawmut's mother—the embodiment of love and selflessness—embraces the new American code which gives short shrift to these values proves devastating to Shawmut.

The story, however, does not culminate in the absolute triumph of the new American ethos. Shawmut, throughout the story, searches for an alternate code that will give meaning to his life, that will give meaning to human life, in general. He briefly considers Allen Ginsberg's artistic vision. Ginsberg's code of unfettered eroticism appeals to Shawmut insofar as it shouts "no" at the American code of ruthless capitalism. But Shawmut, himself, cannot say yes to Ginsberg's brand of "sincerity and authenticity" that, in his view, "overvalue[s] the erotic life" (27). Instead, Shawmut affirms what can only be called a religious vision. Ultimately, the spiritual convictions of Shawmut's neighbor, an elderly Canadian woman, speak to him more profoundly than either Ginsberg's eroticism or the highbrow intellectualism proffered by Ginsberg's cohorts at the American Academy of Arts and Letters:

> Intellect, worshiped by all, brings us as far as natural science, and this science, although very great, is incomplete. Redemption from *mere* nature is the work of feeling and of the awakened eye of the Spirit. The body, she says, is subject to the forces of gravity. But the soul is ruled by levity, pure. . . . I listen to this and have no mischievous impulses. (69–70)

Through deep and prolonged introspection, then, Shawmut achieves a good bit of self-knowledge and at least a modicum of peace. He tells Rose, "the writing of this letter has been the occasion of important discoveries about myself" (67). Practically all of Bellow's protagonists make these important discoveries and Bellow's essentially religious vision earmarks his protagonists as his own. Often exceedingly brainy, Bellow's heroes recognize, in the end, the limits of straight intellectualism and accept their "human contract" with God. Reflecting upon the breadth of Bellow's work, Robert Alter notes that he "repeatedly raises questions about what we are and why we are here, and his ability to combine racy realism and philosophic reflection is one of his greatest strengths" ("Mr. Bellow's Planet," 35). I suppose that many contemporary readers continue to admire Bellow's "racy realism," but feel they could just as well do without the "philosophical reflection."

Saul Bellow has always believed that literature matters, that it matters, perhaps, more so now in our dicey spiritual moment than ever: "The powers of soul, which were Shakespeare's subject (to be simple about it) and are heard incessantly in Handel or Mozart, have no footing at present in modern life and are held to be subjective. Writers here and there still stake their lives on the existence of these forces" ("Writers" 113). "The concern of tale-tellers and novelists," Bellow asserts in a separate recent essay, "is with the human essences neglected and forgotten by a distracted world" ("Distracted," 169). We are "distracted," Bellow insists, by the flurry of information that bombards us from, to name one source, the seemingly ubiquitous media. Certainly, Bellow—a child of Russian immigrants—would be the first to extol the virtues of a free press; but he also recognizes that the wealth of information in, say, the Sunday edition of the *New York Times* offers little by way of true (which is to say, "inner") knowledge. Alternatively, the best literature drowns out the deafening hum of our information age to express one simple heart's truth. These are essences which writers must continue to tap if they are to assert their relevance in our modern world. For these are the essences in which most of us still believe and about which literary theorists and critics have exceedingly little to say. To his credit, Saul Bellow seems to have known this all along.

Works Cited

Alter, Robert. "Mr. Bellow's Planet." Review of *Him with His Foot in His Mouth and Other Stories*, by Saul Bellow. *New Republic*, 11 June 1984, 33–37.

———. *The Pleasures of Reading in an Ideological Age*. New York: Simon & Schuster, 1989.

Baranczak, Stanislaw. "The Gambler." Review of *Dostoevsky: The Miraculous Years, 1865–1871*, by Joseph Frank. *New Republic*, 15 May 1995, 35–40.

Bellow, Saul. *The Adventures of Augie March*. New York: Viking, 1953. Noted parenthetically as *AAM*.

———. "The Distracted Public." In *It All Adds Up: From the Dim Past to the Uncertain Future*, 153–69. New York: Viking, 1994.

———. "Him with His Foot in His Mouth." In *Him with His Foot in His Mouth and Other Stories*, 1984. 3–70. New York: Simon & Schuster, 1985.

———. "A Matter of the Soul." In *It All Adds Up: From the Dim Past to the Uncertain Future*, New York: Viking, 1994. 73–79.

———. "Mozart: An Overture." In *It All Adds Up: From the Dim Past to the Uncertain Future*, 1–14. New York: Viking, 1994.

———. *Mr. Sammler's Planet*. New York: Viking Press, 1970. Noted parenthetically as *MSP*.

———. "Summations." In *Saul Bellow: A Mosaic*, edited by L. H. Goldman, Gloria L. Cronin, and Ada Aharoni, 185–99. New York: Peter Lang, 1992.

———. "Writers, Intellectuals, Politics: Mainly Reminiscences." In *It All Adds Up: From the Dim Past to the Uncertain Future*, 98–114. New York: Viking, 1994.

Boyers, Robert T. "Literature and Culture: An Interview with Saul Bellow." *Salmagundi* 30 (1975): 6–23.

Goodheart, Eugene. "Parables of the Artist." Review of *Him with His Foot in His Mouth and Other Stories*, by Saul Bellow. *Partisan Review* 52, no. 2 (1985): 149–53.

Ozick, Cynthia. "Farcical Combat in a Busy World." In *Saul Bellow*, edited by Harold Bloom, 235–41. New York: Chelsea, 1986.

Roth, Philip. "Ethnic Pop and Native Corn." *New York Times*, 19 Sept. 1988, sec. A, p. 23.

Smith, Dinitia. "Still Writing, Walking and Celebrating New York." *New York Times*, 11 May 1995, sec. B, p. 3.

Staples, Brent. "Mr. Bellow's Planet." In *Parallel Time: Growing Up in Black and White*, 191–242. New York: Pantheon, 1994.

Walden, Daniel. "Saul Bellow's Paradox: Individualism and the Soul." *Saul Bellow Journal* 12, no. 2 (1994): 59–71.

Whitman, Walt. *Leaves of Grass*. 1855. New York: Penguin, 1986.

Bellow's "Cousins": The Suspense of Playing It to the End

KARL F. KNIGHT

A principal theme in Saul Bellow's "Cousins" is the effort to hold things together against the forces of dissolution. Ijah Brodsky, the protagonist, has an apocalyptic sense of the struggle, but avoids despair by working for continuity within his family, by being a responsive and responsible cousin. But the story suggests too that responsibility to the larger society may at times take precedence over loyalty to a particular cousin; indeed, the term "cousins" comes to mean the universal human family.

Dissolution for Brodsky first of all means death, for the old values fade with the deaths of old cousins, such as Shana Metzger, who "clothed and bathed and fed" the Brodskys, fresh immigrants from Europe (242). That kind of cousinly sense of responsibility has given way to modern hedonism, which Brodsky associates with the decay of the American Dream:

> Odd that *it* should begin to roll towards oblivion just as we were perfecting ourselves in this admirable democracy. . . . Being an American always has been something of an abstract project. You came as an immigrant. You were offered a most reasonable proposition and you said yes to it. You were *found*. With the new abstractions you were *lost*. They demanded a shocking abandonment of personal judgment. . . .You could say, for instance, "Guilt has to die. Human beings are entitled to guiltless pleasure." (282)

Brodsky thinks of collapse also in terms suggesting the loss of the harmony of the spheres: "a different, barbarous music" has replaced "an unheard music which buoyed [humanity] . . . , gave it flow, continuity,

Reprinted from *Saul Bellow Journal* 5, no. 2 (1986): 32-35.

coherence"; "the cosmic orchestra sending out music has suddenly canceled its performance" (245–46).

Brodsky's evidences of deterioration also include the breaking of family ties (his own failed marriage; his brothers, who no longer keep in touch; Cousin Eunice's daughter, who is too busy to see her mother; Cousin Miltie, who left his wife and ran off with a switchboard operator); mob violence and slayings, and corruption in high office ("the Hoffa school—in more than half its postulates virtually identical with the Kennedy school," [237]).

Brodsky feels too that the debasement of language signifies general deterioration. Traditionally weighty words are exploited by advertising and public relations: "Nowadays 'We Care' is stenciled on the walls of supermarkets and loan companies" (227). Pseudo-scientific jargon is too available: "These psychological terms lying around, tempting us to use them, are a menace. They should all be shoveled into trucks and taken to the dump" (280–81). And closer to home are complex, disturbing misuses of language. Cousin Eunice was forced to "donate" $50,000 to a medical school to secure her daughter's admission, half paid initially, the remainder due before graduation. But Eunice evaded the second payment, guaranteeing it "as a person of known integrity." Although Brodsky recognizes that the donation is a kind of extortion and that Eunice could be bankrupted by a recurrence of cancer, he thinks, "All the words were up for grabs. . . . I didn't like to see the word 'integrity' fucked up" (250–51).

Despite Brodsky's devotion to the purity of language ("the defense of poetry," [251]), he also misuses it. In pleading with his friend Judge Eiler for special consideration for Cousin Tanky, a convicted mobster, Brodsky knows that he is writing "pure malarkey," typical of "the low language of high morals—payola letters." He rationalizes that the judge can "read between the lines" (242–43).

Faced with such evidences of decay, Brodsky is caught in "the *suspense*" of "whether we are preparing a new birth of spirit or the agonies of final dissolution" (253). The story then becomes largely an elaboration on his related question, "And where, with regard to the cousins, does that leave us?" (246). Brodsky's answer is "Once under way, these relationships have to be played to the end" (261).

Brodsky is reminded of his responsibility to Cousin Motty, who at almost ninety has pneumonia as a complication from a car wreck. Brodsky recoils from the prospect of witnessing the humiliation of Motty, who has to be strapped upright in a chair to keep fluid from building up in his lungs. Regardless of the immediate feelings of Brodsky or even of Motty, the old-fashioned relationship requires that Brodsky visit Motty:

I had . . . claimed Motty's affection, given him my own, treated him with respect, observed his birthdays, extended to him the love I had felt for my own parents. By such actions, I had rejected certain revolutionary developments . . . , the contempt for parents. . . . The very masses are turning their backs on the family. (260–61)

Bellow uses Cousin Tanky to show that there are limits to what one is obliged to do in the name of family loyalty. Tanky is the cousin gone bad, a convicted racketeer awaiting sentencing. When he and his sister Eunice ask Brodsky to use his influence with the judge, Brodsky writes, urging a light sentence. He does it not so much for Tanky, however, but for memories of Tanky's family: Cousin Metzger, who had a "tic" and loved "Neapolitan ice cream," and Cousin Shana, with her "ruddy hair" and with her "bare feet . . . as she mopped the floor. . . . It was also for Cousin Eunice's stammer" (241–42). And for family loyalty he writes a second letter, requesting special medical attention and diet. But finally Brodsky's sense of rightness forbids him to write a third letter. This limitation to what one can do out of family loyalty is emphasized by Bellow's contrast between Tanky, the herald of collapse, and Cousin Scholem, who may represent the "new birth of spirit" that Brodsky hopes for.

Scholem, a philosophy student, volunteered for World War II; fought at the Elbe River, where American and Russian soldiers met and pledged friendship and peace; drove a taxi in Chicago for twenty years while writing his grand philosophical synthesis. Out of parasitic luxury and decadence, Tanky offered society corruption and violence. Out of a terrible war, poverty, self-discipline, and the turmoils of Chicago traffic, which might have caused his cancer (276), Scholem offers three lofty gestures: his manuscript, work with the United Nations to arrange an international gathering of cab drivers in Paris to commemorate the ideal of brotherhood in World War I, and a plan to be buried at Torgau on the Elbe as a symbol of reconciliation between East and West. Whether or not Scholem's gestures will have impact, Brodsky sees his efforts to "bless mankind" as traditional, representative of "the classical norm for Jews of the diaspora" (276). Bellow heightens the contrast between Tanky and Scholem by having Brodsky refuse to write that third letter while he is in Paris waiting to see Cousin Scholem.

After doing as much as conscience would allow for Tanky, Brodsky dedicates himself to Scholem's causes. He gets money from a family trust administered by Cousin Mendy, money which will allow the burial at Torgau, while Brodsky himself will pay for processing and evaluating Scholem's manuscript.

Cousin Scholem and the assembled taxi drivers from all over the world suggest hope. They remind Brodsky of the simple lessons in cousinhood he learned as a schoolboy: "We were not guineas, dagos, krauts; we were cousins" (292). Physically wasted by cancer, Scholem paradoxically suggests youth, rebirth: "the tightening of the skin brought back his youthful look. . . . There seemed a kind of clear innocence about him. The size of his eyes was exceptional—like the eyes of a newborn infant" (293).

Bellow rounds out his story with an additional optimistic touch. Becoming "bizarrely weak in the legs," Brodsky at first wants to reject the proffered arm of Cousin Scholem's daughter, but "[i]nstead I passed my arm through hers and she led us down the corridor" (294). The event suggests that Brodsky accepts the inevitability of his own decay and his need to lean on others. The image of youth helping age down the symbolic corridor is a promise that the tradition of cousinly responsibility will continue. Further, the meaning of playing relationships "to the end" is clarified, suggesting to the mortal end of cousins, to the end of one's own life, and to whatever end the apocalyptic struggle brings. Although "Nobody—nobody at all—can say how it's going to turn out" (237), Brodsky knows that his best hope and the world's lies in cousinly responsibility.

Works Cited

Saul Bellow. "Cousins." In *Him with His Foot in His Mouth and Other Stories*, 225–94. New York: Harper & Row, 1984.

Saul Bellow's Fiction of Contemplation and "What Kind of Day Did You Have?"

JAY L. HALIO

"There is that poem about the nightingale singing that humankind
cannot stand too much reality. But how much unreality can it stand?
Do you follow? You understand me?"
—Henderson the Rain King

S aul Bellow is not a storyteller, certainly not in any recognized,
conventional sense. His fiction, long or short, is more interested in
matters other than the usual kinds of narrative, concerns such as we find
in the stories of O. Henry or, closer to home, many of Isaac Bashevis
Singer's stories. In "The Gentleman from Krakow," for example, its
significant symbolism and moralism notwithstanding, the narrative builds
with considerable suspense to a climax in the destruction of Frampol and
the bitter despair of its inhabitants. Like a typical short story, "The
Gentleman from Krakow" focuses on a single major incident, to which
character and other aspects of the story are properly subordinated. It is
quite otherwise in Saul Bellow's short fiction.

To readers and critics of his later novels, this will come as no surprise.
Written in the same time period as the stories in *Him with His Foot in His
Mouth*, *The Dean's December* has at best a rudimentary plot, or rather two
rudimentary plots—vehicles, merely, for what Bellow is much more
concerned with. And he is concerned with a great deal—above all the
nature of reality and our apprehension of it. In a review in the *Southern
Review* of *The Dean's December* and other contemporary novels, I had
occasion to cite Joyce Cary's comment on the function of the novel, which
was, in his view, "to make the world contemplate and understand itself"

Reprinted from *Saul Bellow Journal* 11, no. 2 & 12, no. 1 (Double Issue 1993): 124-32.

(203). I was pretty sure that was what *The Dean's December* was doing, and had I a mind, I might have coined the term "novel of contemplation" to parallel Louis Martz's term "poetry of meditation." But the substance of Bellow's fiction and its aims—not literary nomenclature—were, and are, more to the point.

In *The Dean's December*, Albert Corde, that "earnest, brooding, heart-struck, time-ravaged person," ponders what is happening to "the American idea: liberty, equality, justice, democracy, abundance." In whatever ways he can, he tries to prevent that idea from "being pounded into dust," as appears to be happening in one of our great American metropolises, Chicago (123). For this reason, he writes a pair of articles for *Harper's* to reveal conditions in that city in the hope that through his exposé people will begin to perceive—really perceive—and thus experience the reality that is properly theirs. Only then could they begin to apprehend events.

But "facts were covered from our perception" both by an increase in consciousness—particularly "false consciousness"—and by "a peculiar kind of confusion" (123). Corde blames the increase in theories and discourse for the distortions of public consciousness and other strange forms of blindness. The need then is "to disinter reality, retrieve the reality, dig it out from the trash, represent it anew as art would represent it" (123). Reality does not exist "out there"; it begins to be real only when the soul finds its underlying truth. "In generalities there was no coherence—none," Corde believes. "The generality-mind, the habit of mind that governed the world, had no force of coherence, it was dissociative. It divided because it was, itself, divided. Hence the schizophrenia, which was moral and aesthetic as well as analytical" (265–66).

The increase in theories and discourse Corde (and through him, Bellow) complains of has much to do with the kinds of evasion people are presently addicted to. We prefer "concepts" to reality, as Corde remarks (243). Abstractions evade the reality of good and evil; they eventuate in the discourse or jargon of intellectuals, and for the public "ever more jazzed-up fantasy" (243). Here Bellow is at one with the ideas and attitude of Martin Buber who, in *I and Thou*, warns against our abstracting tendency and argues for the need to commune with concrete reality, to get into genuine relation. This is precisely what Corde and Bellow's other heroes (insofar as they are heroes) try to do. And this is what Bellow, through them, tries to do: represent reality anew, "as art would represent it," so that we may perceive and commune with it, not merely engage in "theories and discourse." Through the disinterment of reality, the direct apprehension of events, we can recover coherence and again become whole human beings.

Like *The Dean's December*, the stories in *Him with His Foot in His Mouth* achieve these goals, to a greater or lesser degree. The kinds of realities that Bellow deals with are complex and significant. Many of them focus on human relationships, the nature of which becomes increasingly important, especially as they help the main characters understand themselves and others better. Though often the stories seem to digress interminably, the digressions are never beside the point; usually, they *are* the point. "Cousins," for example, seems to move from one digression to another, but actually through these seeming digressions Ijah Brodsky finds a greater understanding of himself and his interest in his extended family—the realities this story is mostly (but not exclusively) about. Moreover, the digressions are linked, as the episode involving Cousin Mordecai (Motty) leads to one involving Cousin Scholem Stavis and the final episodes of the story in Paris. The paragraphs devoted to Ijah reading the series of reports of the Jessup Expedition in Siberia are not merely excursions into the exotic; they reveal a good deal about Ijah and the kinds of entertainment that he, a solitary individual, requires.

If a rigorous self-examination of his motives and emotions, and the ways they are aroused, leads Ijah to one kind of reality, analysis of his encounters with cousins and other relatives, including his ex-wife, helps him to uncover other related realities. Together, these analyses build a new coherence in his life, or rather a new apprehension of what his life has been and now is. The ending of the story brings these facts sharply into focus: "I had remembered, observed, studied the cousins, and these studies seemed to fix my own essence and to keep me as I had been. I had failed to include myself among them, and suddenly I was billed for this oversight" (294). Presented with the bill, Ijah becomes "bizarrely weak in the legs." But he does not reject the debt for, as the story shows, he has actually been paying it right along. Sudden awareness, the blinding illumination, is what causes him to go weak in the knees, just as similar awareness astonishes others among Bellow's protagonists. Daniel Fuchs is surely right, then, in arguing that our interest in this "lyrical" story lies "not so much in what happens but in the contemplative consciousness of the central character" (7).

Woody Selbst in "A Silver Dish," for all his toughness and maturity, "a modern person, sixty years of age, and a man who's been around" (191), is astonished not by himself so much as by the apprehension, the recognition, of his father's mortality, specifically the way he died. In the title story "Him with His Foot in His Mouth," Shawmut astonishes himself by apologizing for the first and only time in his life for an insulting, half-witted remark delivered thirty-five years ago to "Miss Rose," a spinster lady who had done nothing to deserve his slur. His apology goes on for more than fifty printed pages, but in the process of contemplating his actions, Shawmut discovers more about himself and his relations with others than he has ever done before. In the longest story in the volume, "What Kind of Day Did You Have?," a middle-class housewife and mother, Katrina Goliger, contemplates reality at the knee (and other bodily parts) of her lover, Victor Wulpy, a world-class art historian and intellectual. But it is not only Katrina who learns.

In every sense that matters, Katrina is a surrogate for many humble but earnest individuals who find ordinary life—the life they seem to have been born to—distinctly dissatisfying. Extramarital affairs may be one form of escape, as it was for Madame Bovary and as it was briefly for Katrina, who is wrongly referred to by her sister, Dorothea, as a reincarnation of the Flaubertian heroine (94). But by the time she encounters Victor Wulpy, Katrina has passed beyond the mere excitement of an extramarital affair and is intent on matters of more importance, such as the world of art and ideas. She is also intent on learning more about herself and the nature of her relationships—with Victor, yes, but also with her sister, another suitor (Lieutenant Krieggstein), her estranged husband, and her two small children. If her affair with Victor is the main vehicle for this education, it is not only she who learns. Victor, too, acquires some unexpected, even unsought-after knowledge about himself and others. But it is Katrina who consciously conceives herself as his student. "She had been admitted to his master class," she says to herself. "Nobody else was getting such instruction" (75). Enrolled as Wulpy's only pupil, "she paid her tuition with joy" (94).

The story begins with a midnight telephone call from Victor summoning Katrina in the dead of winter from Evanston, Illinois, to join him in Buffalo, where he has just given a lecture, and return with him to Chicago, where he is booked the next evening for another one. Why Victor wants her to come all that way (at considerable inconvenience and some risk—her husband is suing for custody of their children) she does not fathom, but she obeys, appearing for a while as the dutiful slave-mistress of the distinguished Wulpy. We soon learn, however, that it is a mistake to regard Katrina thus. An individual in her own right, she emerges throughout the story as someone of much greater stature and humanity. Physically clumsy as she is—and Bellow repeatedly emphasizes her clumsiness—she is not intellectually as clumsy as she seems. Under Wulpy's tutelage, her self-awareness grows, and she becomes a person of much greater stature than either he—or we—may have recognized.

Victor Wulpy is by no means a "reality-instructor" of the sort Philip Roth satirizes in *The Anatomy Lesson* any more than Katrina is someone mysteriously afflicted like Nathan Zuckerman in that novel. Although Victor does undertake, willy-nilly, to teach Katrina a few things, he is not about becoming her mentor. His interest in her lies elsewhere—in her life-giving warmth, for instance. Recalling Beaudelaire's poem, he believes "she did in fact have the touch that brought back the dead" (105). And it was only a few months ago in fact that he did almost die. At the same time, being who and what he is, Victor cannot help but increase Katrina's consciousness of herself and her world—a world that seems to expand each time she is in Victor's company. Although his world remains nearly light years away from hers, by the end of the story we recognize that she is no longer quite what she once was, nor is her apprehension of her world what it was. Although she "had been raised to consider herself a nitwit" (66) and has been largely treated as such, she is none, and she knows it. She understands fully her relationship to Victor, for example, vis-à-vis Beila, "the presiding woman, the wife," who maintains her rights like her self-respect with tremendous dignity (106). Katrina does not fool herself about this: she "really did know the score" (106).

Nor is she incapable of following Wulpy's thoughts on a wide variety of interests—art, civilization, politics. Their pillow talk is not the typical utterance of lovers (they are hardly typical lovers). Stimulated by sex, Victor becomes a talker, not stopping to explain himself:

> Abed, Victor and Katrina smoked, drank, touched each other (tenderness from complicity), laughed; they thought—my God they thought! Victor carried her into utterly foreign spheres of speculation. He lived for ideas. And he didn't count on Katrina's comprehension; he couldn't. But . . . when he was wicked she understood him well enough. He wasn't wasting his wit on her. (77)

As further testimony of their intellectual compatibility, when they meet in Buffalo, Katrina asks Victor to resolve the apparent paradox of his Marxism and his conviction that Communism has failed. Far from putting her off as someone who could not understand, he seems to welcome the question and responds accordingly. He had trained his mind on "hard Marxist texts" and was permanently influenced. He is convinced, furthermore, that Marx had America's present number:

When wage earners, the middle class, the professions, lose track of their true material interests, they step outside history, so to speak, and then nonclass interests take over, and when that happens society itself collapses into neuroses. An era of playacting begins. Vast revolutionary changes are concealed by the trivialities of the actors. Clowns and ham actors govern, or seem to. Superficially, it looks like farce. The deeper reality is anything but. (103)

If Victor regards Katrina as his "manifest Eros" (104), she is much more. Having "that touch that brought back the dead," in Beaudelaire's phrase, she "kept him going" (105), but in more than in a physiological or sexual sense. As the conversation about Marxism demonstrates, Katrina knows how to stimulate Victor in other ways as well. The conversation revives him, and he looks more like himself (104). Of this Katrina is fully aware. And increasingly, so is Victor. Near the end of the story he recognizes that if he cannot explain Katrina's sexual drawing power, "the Eros that (only just) kept him from disintegrating," she is, nevertheless, "as a subject for thought," the least trivial of ideas (156).

More than anything else, trivial ideas—such as those Wrangel formulates when he talks with Victor in Buffalo and later in Detroit while Katrina and he are temporarily grounded—infuriate Victor. Insofar as he may be Bellow's spokesperson, the point is not to be taken lightly. A maker of science fiction films, Wrangel is an intellectual lightweight, but not without pretensions to something greater. As Katrina recognizes, Victor is not above using such people for trivial purposes, like getting a good lunch in the airport's restaurant, but he has a very limited tolerance for their pretensions. By contrast—and as testimony to her greater humanity, perhaps—Katrina is more tolerant and understanding, though she too "uses" Wrangel to help her with a children's story she is trying to write. But she is entirely conscious of what is happening, both between Victor and Wrangel and between Wrangel and herself. She appreciates Wrangel's willingness to stand up to Victor, and she is not afraid to criticize Victor's treatment of the man (113, 138). But Victor has his standards of behavior, too, and will not compromise them. Still higher are his standards of intellectual conversation.

Victor's anger at Wrangel is occasioned, as he later explains to Katrina, by hearing "a California parody of things I had been thinking myself." What was parodied was the idea that "a true thought may have a true image corresponding to it" (147). If, as Victor also says, "in our real thoughts . . . alert persons recognize what is happening" (147), Bellow here imagines—presents concretely the image of—a couple who are certainly alert and comprehending. When Victor lay desperately ill in Massachusetts, Katrina knew what her position was, as did Beila, who allowed her moments of privacy with Victor. "It wasn't just another adultery," Katrina understands. "She wasn't one of his casual women. . . . Her suffering was conceded its rights. Their relationship was certified" (153). These thoughts pass through Katrina's mind during the flight from Detroit to Chicago in very rough weather, when she and Victor are both concerned that the plane might crash. He has similar thoughts, wondering why she lived the life she lived—a wicked question, as he recognizes, even with its "tinge of comedy." But the question exposes him to a difficult judgment, one that—however painful—he does not shirk from. Although by comparison to his own life, which had "caused significant intellectual and artistic innovations," hers was not serious, still . . . he had to concede that "the obscurest and most powerful question, deeper than politics, was that of an understanding between man and woman" (155–56). If he could not entirely figure out Katrina's power over him, what kept them together and plunged them into danger like this, yet he knew that she was important in his life. He knew, also, that "of all that might be omitted in thinking, the worst was to omit your own being" (156).

As part of her tutelage, Victor had earlier given Katrina Céline's *Journey to the End of Night*. At first Katrina does not fully understand why he wanted her to read the book, horrifying as it was, its ideas "truly terrifying" (150). She is especially struck by the episode at the end when the adventurer Robinson refuses to tell a woman that he loves her, whereupon she shoots him dead. Although she recognizes that Victor, as always, wants her to "face the destructive facts. No palliatives" (151), its true significance for her and the reader comes later, during the plane ride from Detroit. Fearing death, Katrina similarly asks Victor to say he loves her, and he refuses. Like Robinson, he will not say the words, but they are not really necessary, as she later realizes. After all, it is for her sake that he traveled from home in the first place (161).

In a world of "fucked-up consciousness," such as Wrangel has contributed to, Victor has little time for people or ideas that are not "serious" (137). That is why he rejects Wrangel. Katrina is something else again, not only serious but open, receptive to genuine ideas. She sees in Victor "a mine of knowledge, a treasury of insights in all matters concerning the real needs and interests of modern human beings" and finds in him a release from all the junk that has hitherto filled her life (73). Although her sister, Dorothea, cannot grasp this and sees Victor only as an aging man who finds in Katrina the one person who can turn him on, she misses what their relationship really is, just as she fails to understand what her sister is and what she is becoming under Victor's instruction. Others also cannot see: Ysole, her housekeeper, for instance; her two small children; and Wrangel, for all his courteous behavior toward her. But Wrangel at least knows something about Victor Wulpy. He knows that Victor knows "what the real questions are," that "without art we can't judge what life is, we can't sort anything out at all" (134). Finally, as Victor himself tells Katrina, apropos of his contempt for people in private life who, unlike him, have no "power-stir," "You get as much truth as you have the courage to face" (146–47).

In the stories collected in *Him with His Foot in His Mouth*, as in his novels, Bellow offers us as much truth as we may have the courage to face, especially in "What Kind of Day Did You Have?" His disdain of simple narratives, his difficult, measured style, above all his confrontation of the real issues of contemporary human experience elevate his fiction to the highest order. Reading it, one naturally falls into a contemplative mode, precisely as one should, given the subject matter and its presentation. Everywhere beset with the temptation to maintain "the *mauvais foi*, the false description of your personal reality" (148), one is warned not to yield, not to lie to oneself. The realities may be hard to bear, but the opposite course, Bellow demonstrates, leads not only to intellectual decay, but to moral and spiritual death as well. Katrina has taken a far different path; and although Victor is physically dying, in every other way that matters, he is far from dead.

Works Cited

Bellow, Saul. *The Dean's December*. New York: Harper & Row, 1982.
———. *Him with His Foot in His Mouth and Other Stories*. New York: Harper & Row, 1984.
Fuchs, Daniel. "On *Him with His Foot in His Mouth and Other Stories*." *Saul Bellow Journal* 5, no. 1 (Fall/Winter): 3–15.
Halio, Jay L. "Contemplation, Fiction, and the Writer's Sensibility." *Southern Review* 19, no. 1 (Winter 1983): 203–18.

Recent Adventures of Saul Bellow: Reflections on "What Kind of Day Did You Have?"

ALAN LELCHUK

There is a moment in "What Kind of Day Did You Have?" when Victor Wulpy, the seventy-year-old-plus protagonist, a man with gruff charm, is reflecting on the difference between charm and style:

> For the moment, Victor was being charming. "Most people know better than to lack charm," he had once told Katrina [his girlfriend]. "Even harsh people have their own harsh charm. Some are all charm, like Franklin D. Roosevelt. Some repudiate all charm, like Stalin. When all-charm and no charm met at Yalta, no-charm won hands down." Victor in his heart of hearts dismissed charm. Style, yes; style was essential; but charm tended to blur your thoughts. (129)

A charming statement? Or something more important? Certainly this last credo and distinction are interesting, coming from a writer who has made his lasting mark, in significant part, by means of his literary style, a style as memorable as any we've seen in American literature. Let me, briefly, consider that style, analyzing what it is composed of and how it serves, or fulfills, Bellow's meaning.

An immediate example of that style may be seen in a physical description of character, in this case the formidable Wulpy. What is rather perfunctory filling-in in most writers' hands becomes, with Bellow, a more important detailing, and investigating:

Reprinted with permission from *Saul Bellow: A Mosaic*. Vol. 3 of Twentieth-Century Jewish Literature, edited by L. H. Goldman, Gloria L. Cronin, and Ada Aharoni, 59-71. Series editor, Daniel Walden. New York: Peter Lang, 1992.

In the old Mediterranean or in Asia you might have found examples of Victor's physical type. He towered. He also tilted, on account of the leg. Katrina had never determined exactly what was the matter with it, medically. For drainage it was punctured in two places, right through the flesh. Sometimes there was a deposit around the holes, and it was granular, like brown sugar. That took getting used to, just a little. He made jokes about his size. He said he was too big for the subtler human operations. He would point out the mammoths, they hadn't made it, and he would note how many geniuses were little guys. But that was just talk. At heart he was pleased with the way he was. Nothing like a mammoth. He was still one of the most dramatic-looking men in the world, and besides, as she had reason to know, his nervous reactions were very fine. A face like Victor's might have been put on the cover of a book about the ancient world: the powerful horizontal planes—forehead, cheekbones, the intelligent long eyes, the brows kinky with age now, and with tufts that could be wicked. His mouth was large, and the cropped mustache was broad. By the way the entire face expanded when he spoke emphatically you recognized that he was a kind of tyrant in thought. His cheekbones were red, like those of an actor in makeup; the sharp color hadn't left him even when he was on the critical list. It seemed a mistake that he should be dying. Besides, he was so big that you wondered what he was doing in a bed meant for ordinary patients, but when he opened his eyes, those narrow visual canals, the message was, "I'm dying!" Still, only a couple of months later he was back in circulation, eating and drinking, writing critical pieces—in full charge. A formidable person, Victor Wulpy. Even the way he gimped was formidable, not as if he was dragging his leg but as if he were kicking things out of the way. All of Victor's respect was reserved for people who lived out their idea. For whether or not you were aware of it, you had one, high or low, keen or stupid. He came on like the king of something—of the Jews perhaps. By and by, you became aware of a top-and-bottom contrast in Victor; he was not above as he was below. In the simplest terms, his shoes were used up and he wore his pants negligently, but when his second drink had warmed him and he took off the corduroy coat, he uncovered one of his typical shirts. It resembled one of Paul Klee's canvases, those that were filled with tiny rectilinear forms—green, ruby, yellow, violet, washed out but still beautiful. His large trunk was one warm artwork. After all, he was a chieftain and pundit in the art world, a powerful man; even his oddities (naturally) had power. Kingly, artistic, democratic, he had been around forever. (95–97)

In this single extended paragraph, we learn about Victor's vast size and physical infirmity, his ancient-world looks and modern Klee-like shirts, his tyranny of thought and his near-death. And at the center of the portrait is the *idea* of Victor: his power. "He came on like the king of something—of the Jews perhaps." In other words, Victor the intellectual is a modern David or, perhaps, Solomon. The entire energy of the paragraph is guided by this aim—namely, that every person had an idea to fulfill or live out, if only he or she would, and Victor had lived out his: to rule by his prodigious intellectual power. Indeed the paragraph is a little drama of its own, built as it is on fact, sense, and feeling and culminating in idea, inseparable from and embodied in Victor Wulpy. It is important to understand, when reading Bellow, that the paragraph is a crucial unit, much like the line in poetry; and its rich economy of culture and biography, dazzling description, and striking idiom force one to read and reread it to appreciate its full flavor.

Let me look at another, longer example of the Bellow poetry-in-prose, which appears a little later in the text. The pair of lovers, Victor and Katrina, have been stranded in the Detroit airport on the way to Chicago, where Victor is to deliver a lecture, and are waiting for a private Cessna to pick them up. The point of view switches, as it does throughout the tale, between Katrina and Victor. While Katrina tries her best to figure out how to break her long-term writer's block on her elephant story for children—the elephant is stuck in the department store, and Katrina, after months of deliberation, still can't figure out how to get him out—Victor also meditates, for three long paragraphs of revery and memory.

> Victor's mind was also at work, although you couldn't say that he was thinking. Something soft and heavy seemed to have been spread over his body. It resembled the lead apron laid over you by X-ray technicians. Victor was stretched under this suave deadly weight and feeling as you felt when waking from a deep sleep—unable to lift your arm. On the field, in the winter light, the standing machines were paler than the air, and the entire airport stood in a frame of snow, looking like a steel engraving. It reminded him of the Lower East Side in—oh, about 1912. The boys (ancients today, those who were alive) were reading the Pentateuch. The street, the stained pavement, was also like a page of Hebrew text, something you might translate if you knew how. Jacob lay dreaming of a ladder which rose into heaven. *V'hinei malachi elohim*— behold the angels of God going up and down. This had caused Victor no surprise. What age was he, about six? It was not a dream to him. *Jacob*

was dreaming, while Victor was awake, reading. There was no "long ago." It was all now. The cellar classroom had a narrow window at sidewalk level, just enough to permit a restricted upward glance showing tire escapes under snow, the gold shop sign of the Chinese laundry hanging from the ironwork, and angels climbing up and down. This did not have to be interpreted. It came about in a trance, as if under the leaden weight of the flexible apron. Now the plane was starting its takeoff run, and soon the No Smoking sign would be turned off. Victor would have liked to smoke, but the weight of his hands made any movement impossible.

It wasn't like him to cherish such recollections, although he had them, and they had lately been more frequent. He began now to remember that his mother had given him the windpipe of a goose after drying it in the Dutch oven of the coal stove, and that he had cut a notch in the windpipe with his father's straight razor and made a whistle of it. When it was done, he disliked it. Even when dry it had kept its terrible red color, and it was very harsh to the touch and had left an unpleasant taste in his mouth. This was not exactly Marx's nightmare of history from which mankind had to be liberated. The raw fowl taste was nasty. The angels on the fire escape, however, were very pleasing, and his consciousness of them, while it was four thousand years old, had also been exactly contemporary. Different ideas of time and space had not yet been imposed upon him. One comprehensive light contained everybody. Among the rest—parents, patriarchs, angels, God—there was yourself. Victor did not feel bound to get to the bottom of this; it was only a trance, probably an effect of fatigue and injury. He gave a side thought to Mass. General, where a tumor had been lifted out of a well of blood in his belly, and he reminded himself that he was still a convalescent—reminded himself also that Baudelaire had believed the artist to be always in a spiritually convalescent state. (This really was Baudelaire Day; just a while ago it had been the touch that brought the dead to life.) Only just returned from the shadow of death, the convalescent inhaled with delight the close human odors of the plane. Pollution didn't matter, the state of a convalescent being the state of a child drunk with impressions. Genius *must* be the recovery of the powers of childhood by an act of the creative *will*. Victor knew all this like the palm of his hand or the nose on his face. By combining the strength of a man (analytic power) with the ecstasy of a child you could discover the New. What God's Revelation implied was that the Jews (his children) would obstinately will (with mature intelligence) the divine adult promise. This would earn them the hatred of the whole world.

They were always archaic, *and* they were always contemporary—we could sort that out later.

But now suppose that this should not be convalescence but something else, and that he should be on the circuit not because he was recovering but because he was losing ground. Falling apart? This was where Katrina entered the picture. Hers was the touch that resurrected, or that reunited, reintegrated his otherwise separating physical powers. He asked himself: That she turns me on, does that mean that I love her, or does it simply mean that she belongs to the class of women that turn me on? He didn't like the question he was asking. But he was having many difficult sensations, innumerable impressions of winter, winters of seven decades superimposed. The winter world even brought him a sound, not for the ear but for some other organ. And none of this was clearly communicable, nor indeed worth communicating. It was simply part of the continuing life of every human being. Everybody was filled with visions that had been repressed, and amassed involuntarily, and when you were sick they were harder to disperse. (117–19)

Well, there is prose and there is prose.

Starting with the basic image of a lead apron laid over Victor's body, an image suggesting the swooning but lucid trance spreading over his consciousness, Bellow proceeds to roam through the thick jungle of memories, thoughts, incongruous worlds. From his boyhood in the cellar basement in the Lower East Side, to reading the Bible and learning about Jacob and his dream of the angels climbing on the ladder (just before the jet takeoff); from the dry windpipe of a goose given to him by his mother and made over into a whistle, leading, of course, to Marx's nightmare of history; and from Victor as a convalescent in Mass. General, we move to Baudelaire's idea of the artist in a permanently spiritual convalescent stage, to a definition of a genius, God's revelation and the Jews; to the sexual impulse and Katrina; to the sounds and impressions of seven decades of winter, and visions, repressed involuntary visions of all citizens.

A revery of genius, it is enough stuff to stop average readers, make them hold up, make the soft-brained call a halt altogether. This is controlled, dense, heavily textured prose, to be digested slowly, like some fine French meal or twenty pages of Proust. Slowly. It moves by association, sometimes drastic, from childhood memory to present predicament to collective vision. The sense of childhood and its regenerative powers, and its alignment with creative energy, strikes a Wordsworthian chord. The mingling of idea with tactile image, of high thought with everyday detail, is essential Bellow. The prose altogether urges, coerces the reader to think and feel simultaneously, to follow steadily the cultural allusiveness and associative play, or risk losing the train of consciousness, that central control tower of consciousness that so flavors Victor and so distinguishes Bellow.

That consciousness is an instrument of rather delicate and complex assemblage, making the new IBMs look like the old Philco radios, flashing the intimate moments of his own boyhood alongside the grand ideas of adult history. The intimacy of family is lined up alongside the history of ideas, both authentically felt, both equally weighty. Unlike many current writers, for whom craft means something detached from moral will and style means using pretty words strung together for the sake of appearance, style here is composed of sensibility and knowledge, character and idea, feeling and moral vision.

Of course, the consolidating unity amidst the teeming variety of details is Victor Wulpy and the dramatic power of his mind. This mind is a presence, here and throughout, and is given further linguistic credibility by the subtle weaving of the narrative voice. Both in language and syntax, we are moved imperceptibly back and forth between the interior Victor speaking—the "I" voice—and the exterior narrator observing or speaking—the voice of the third person. This careful track-switching enables Bellow to move back from an identification with Wulpy's perception, to a position of distance, even at times to a position of some irony—a calling of old Wulpy's bluff, if you will.

With Bellow's unique economy, where paragraphs work like short stories to reveal whole characters and chunks of history, it is no surprise that the novella, in Bellows hands, reads like a much longer work. Novellas such as *Seize the Day*, "The Old System," "What Kind of Day Did You Have?" stay put in the reader's mind long after he or she has put the book down. Like the novella masterpieces of the nineteenth-century Russians—Gogol, Turgenev, Dostoyevsky, Tolstoy, and Chekhov—the short novels of Bellow extend their shadows far beyond their compact size.

Now, another aspect. Most traditional writers would agree that a great novel depends on character and plot, not merely on style. This is true of the short novel as well. Besides style, to which I will return later, there are the incidents, or plot, and "What Kind of Day Did You Have?" characters. Once again, Bellow proceeds on his original literary paths. He does not shape his story or plot his material in the traditional linear movement from point A to point B leading, say, to climax point C, and so on. Rather, there is a hovering and circling movement, a widening and deepening of character strung along a few slender incidents.

In other words, by ordinary standards, there is not much plot to "What Kind of Day Did You Have?" Victor Wulpy, on his way from Buffalo to Chicago to give his culture talk, invites his girlfriend Katrina to join him for the trip. She does. The weather turns bad. They are grounded temporarily in Detroit before being picked up by a private plane that takes them into Chicago. On the way, the small Cessna jolts frighteningly in the turbulent weather before landing safely. That's the story. And nothing is really different at the end from the beginning—no solving of a problem, no new revelation of the past or striking resolution for the future, no major change in the relationship. In place of the traditional dependence on incident to move the story along, we have a focusing in on the protagonists, a closer look and intensifying inside feel for their lives, a deeper sense of their incongruous togetherness.

This deceptive, radical way of proceeding should not be confused with those arch, antistory experiments produced so vigorously in France a few decades ago and imitated, so feebly still, in America today, boldly pronounced as forms of the new novel but that are, in fact, exercises in literary boredom. With Bellow, the readers are never shortchanged: they are not held hostage in sly contempt or capricious amusement by a teasing or bluffing writer but rather are considered full partners in the literary task. That is, they are asked to read with an energy and alertness that begin to match the power and subtlety of the writing.

Certainly no one in recent literature produces characters as memorable and deep as Bellow, and the figures here are no exception. Victor Wulpy, a "cultural monument," a heavyweight intellectual in the arts and letters for some fifty years, fits Trotsky's description of Tolstoy: "a colossal human fact." Reminiscent of a breed of intellectuals that is quickly vanishing, such as Rosenberg and Rahv, Trilling and Wilson, Schapiro and Arendt, Victor Wulpy stands for the life of ideas and serious devotion to art and literature. At seventy in the novella, he is celebrated everywhere, proving that the intellectual has "made it" in America by his invitations to corporate headquarters to give lectures.

But Wulpy is also an old, wounded man, a kind of Greek hero via Greenwich Village, struggling against his physical infirmities but armed still with sensual appetite, facing death squarely every day but refusing to cop out from truth-telling. He is, indeed, like Oedipus at Colonus, to whom he is likened, wounded and in exile of sorts, still sought after for his wisdom. Tyrannical, fierce, prideful, and narcissistic, Victor is also a man in great need: he takes up with dizzy-headed Katrina from a lower petit-bourgeois world and, through various stages, truly falls for her. After passion, for example, "they rested on the edge of the bed, legs hanging. He took Katrina's hand, kissed her fingers. He was a masterful cynical man, but with her at times like these he put aside his cynicism. She took it as a sign— how much he cared for her" (146). By means of their lopsided relationship, he of the great mind and she of the right sensual mix ("grace-in-clumsiness" Victor terms it), Bellow portrays Wulpy's wounds, his vulnerabilities, his selfish follies, his humors and warts.

All this substantiates Victor Wulpy, turns him from a flat, mental creature of easy construction into a complex, convincing man. Near dying, he is more intensely alive than most. Despite his cerebral powers, his relentless will for historical understanding, and his penchant for the grand ideas, Victor remains too smart, too honest, and too instinctive not to recognize that the greatest mystery, the "most powerful question, . . . was that of an understanding between man and woman" (156).

This deepness, this mystery, is dramatized throughout—perhaps especially in a fantastic Gogolian sequence, in which Victor is driving around trying to locate a nursing home for his decaying mother, whom he locks in the car at each stop because of the dangerous neighborhoods, at the same time yielding to his fantasy of Katrina following them in her car, dressed in an Aquascutum raincoat and nothing else. "Intimations of helplessness" run alongside the deep erotic urges. Oh, life is rich, life is dark, life is chaotic and secretive, Wulpy seems to say, too, and Bellow portrays this deep rich stir in all its vivid colors, all its dizzying temperatures. Not a neat category of mental power, this Wulpy, but a fleshy, hectic soul, tossed in his last days and nights, indeed an old "King of the Jews," needing female warmth as much as his clarity and courage.

Wulpy is in the mainstream of great Bellow creations, from Tommy to Augie, Herzog to Henderson to Sammler. These are not protagonists of useless make-believe, of movie melodrama, of fancy theory or primitive cultism or cute wordplay, but intelligent, sentient men who think, and act, and feel with adult passion and grown-up confusion. Together they constitute the foremost cast of actors on the stage of contemporary literature since World War II.

Alongside Wulpy, that most serious figure, we have the comic Katrina. Bullied and mocked for her fanciful affair by her tough-cookie sister Dotey, pressured over her children and money by her ex-husband whom she has deserted for Wulpy, haunted by her inability to be creative and unlock her "blocked" elephant story, Katrina charms us—Victor's warning about charm notwithstanding. She is a kind of Judy Holiday of literature, a middle-aged ingenue of beautiful dumb innocence who enchants Victor and the reader as that marvelous comedienne of the fifties charmed her tough guy boyfriends and movie audiences. Raised to be a "nitwit" by her politician, tax-fixing father, Katrina studied foreign languages and became a sorority girl at the University of Illinois and married Alfred Goliger, a crude, wealthy businessman-turned-fancy-art-collector. Now, because of Victor, her life as an Evanston matron has changed sharply; and she is tossed into the confusing realm of heavy intellectual life, meeting the likes of Cage, deKooning, Fuller and trying her best to hold her ground. What she does perfectly is to hold Victor erotically, in the same way she cradles his daughter's fiddle all through their ironic, comical, serious plane journey. This erotic pull is described, very early on, with some of Bellow's best Romanesque detailing:

> Circumstances had made Katrina look commonplace. She did what forceful characters do with such imposed circumstances; she used them as camouflage. Thus she approached Wulpy like a nearsighted person, one who has to draw close to study you. She drew so near that you could feel her breath. And then her lowering, almost stubborn look rested on you for just that extra beat that carried a sexual message. It was the incompetency with which she presented herself, the nearsighted puzzled frown, that made the final difference. Her first handshake informed him of a disposition, an inclination. He saw that all her preparations had been set. With a kind of engraved silence about the mouth under the wide bar of his mustache, Wulpy registered all this information. All he had to do was give the countersign. He intended to do just that. (67)

By means of her sensual power, she secures the great man's confidence and aspires to keep up with his galloping ideas, everything from the poetry of Baudelaire to a novel by Céline, from an obscure joke (which she never gets) to an abstruse interpretation of Valéry. This journey is as humorous as it is arduous. ("'Well,' said Katrina, trying hard, 'let's go back to this statement. It says, "Minds that come from the void into this strange carnival and bring lucidity from outside. . . ."'" Then Dotey cried, '*Which* void!'" [85, ellipses in original]).

Yet there is more to Katrina than a mere secondary role. She is very much a second protagonist, a game, gutsy, aspiring woman, well aware of her role with Victor and her own limited life. In an important way, she inherits the sensitive-helpless gene of Tommy Wilhelm from *Seize the Day*. Like Tommy with his father, she is suckered by her sister (when Dotey mocks her on the phone, Victor advises her: "Bottle up your feelings!" [114]). And also like Tommy, she acknowledges the pressures upon her:

"Everybody has power over me. Alfred, punishing me, the judge, the lawyers, the psychiatrist, Dotey—even the kids. They all apply standards nobody has any use for, except to stick you with" (144). In sum, Katrina is part Holiday and part Wilhelm, a portrait drawn with sympathetic irony and tender criticism, along with pure comedy. By the end, she achieves a touch of something higher, perhaps approaching the heroic. She faces death in the airplane with poise and afterward understands the terms of her life and the men of her life with unsentimental reasoning. It is a measure of Bellow's ability that he makes Katrina more than the merely comical, more than second-fiddle, while staying within her narrow character confines.

Together, Katrina and Victor form a duo that is a dramatic mix of the high and the low, the serious and the comic. It is a relationship at once incongruous, ironic (as they both recognize), and poignant. Victor supplies the high-voltage ideas and intellectual stimulation and Katrina, the touch that resurrects the dead Victor—erotic excitement and, at times, emotional excitement. Each is well aware of the other's needs, wants, deficits, vulnerabilities— they are friends, in other words —and the true odd pull of their union.

This peculiar stew of the two main characters—and especially the serious-comic tone that describes and envelops them—is characteristic of Bellow. It runs through Henderson and Herzog, for example, much as it leavens "What Kind of Day Did You Have?" Again and again Bellow balances on the thin high wire of the comic-tragic, shifting his weight here and there, in sentences, moments, and scenes, without ever falling. With subtle measurement, he judges the weight and value of each character's act or reflection and adjusts his tone, his voice, accordingly.

The result is an unusual performance and, for the reader, a test in reading, as he or she must stay unusually alert, ready to shift responses swiftly and accurately. "What Kind of Day Did You Have?" may be called, for example, a comedy of romance and manners in intellectual America today, or it may be cited as a study of the peculiar fate of the intellectual. Either description without the other, however, minimizes the full flavor and multiple resonances of the tale. The farce of Katrina enhances the tragic note of Victor; the showbiz wizardry and half-baked notions of Hollywood Wrangel are set off against the serious ideas of Wulpy. Even the comic Katrina takes on a graver note alongside the eccentric ways of Krieggstein, the Keystone Kop, and Yulsa, the trickster maid. Through the pair of unlikely loves, Bellow's special dual frequency is sounded, and the unusual charms and seductive powers of American incongruity are felt. To my mind, few writers, if any, since Joyce—with the occasional exception of Nabokov—have so keenly felt and beautifully played the ironic music of modern experience as Bellow has.

In typical fashion, Bellow also makes use of a featured minor character to bring home the full lunatic comedy of native reality. Larry Wrangel, once a student of Victor's in New York and now a successful Hollywood director, follows Wulpy from airport to airport to conduct dialogues with his old mentor. In a Woolworth bandanna and a white fur coat that might have been designed by F. A. O. Schwartz, Wrangel too has a direct descendent in Tamkin of *Seize the Day*—that Dr. Sivana comic-evil shaman who counseled Tommy Wilhelm in life-wisdom and stocks, finally ruining him and disappearing. Wrangel doesn't cause such consequences here, except to infuriate Victor, who finally makes a wildly grotesque face at him and storms off. A *People* magazine celebrity who started out writing for the comic books and graduated to become a "big-time illusionist" (101) in Hollywood with his latest film, *The Kronos Factor*, he has grossed 400 million. Wrangel is a character who " longed to be taken seriously" and was "bearable for about ten minutes" (99). Here, he uses his unique talents to figure out instantly how to rescue Katrina's stuck elephant from the department store, causing her to exclaim: "You are a wizard plotter!" (131). Foxy, feisty Wrangel is an example—a more fulfilled one even than Tamkin—of how Southern California and the big buck turn and twist an able brain and keen energy, revving him up to make movies that infect "the mental life of the country" (127).

Bellow is too honest a writer not to allow the lively and vigorous side of Wrangel's personality to emerge—and too honest not to be sacrificed at the altar of the satire. Wrangel impresses Katrina with his acute observations about American culture and Victor and appeals to the reader as a little dynamo of some real force. Still, he remains an indefatigable operator and con man whiz kid—in other words, a true homespun talent, as shrewd and dangerous as he is ingenious and talented. So immersed is he in his whirring mix of gimmickry, cunning, and celebrityhood that he can no longer tell the true from the illusory and comes to Socratic Wulpy to learn. Wacky Larry Wrangel is a pure Bellow specialty of the house, a sort of Bellow Big Mac, half-tasty, half-sleazy, quick fake food for the duped masses.

Armed with his singular gifts and operating without the crutches of political bias or the mallets of fashionable ideology, Bellow recognizes and evokes the marvelous and dangerous comedy called American reality. The test for Wulpy, as it has been for Bellow, is to get at that reality, to fight through the ingenious maze of distractions and camouflage constructed by the culture. And the best vehicle for this struggle is art, an enterprise inimical to America. As Wrangel explains,

Here art isn't serious. Not in the way a vaccine for herpes is serious. And even for professionals, critics, curators, editors, art is just blah! And it should be like the air you breathe, the water you drink, basic, like nutrition or truth. Victor knows what the real questions are, and if you ask him what's the matter here he would tell you that without art we can't judge what life is, we can't sort anything out at all. Then the "practical sphere" itself, where "planners," generals, opinion-makers, and Presidents operate, is no more real than the lint under your bed. (134)

Let it be said that no one in our literary culture today has undertaken that big-game hunt—seeking the truth undisguised and bringing it back, as it were—with more sustained gusto or intelligence, literary imagination or style, than Saul Bellow. "Concerning the real needs and interests of modern human beings" has meant, for Bellow, searching for a soul amidst the debris of modern life, literary life included. Steadily, for more than four decades—and we must remember here, that, along with Henry James, this is the longest record of accomplishment in American letters—he has produced an art that is at once playful and serious, grand and meaningful, precisely at a time when literature has been corrupted and debased by commercialism, fashion, ideology, and its own practitioners. Just as Eliot's hollow men and Fitzgerald's easy livers dominated the twenties and Hemingway's tight-lipped simplistic creatures the thirties and early forties, so Bellow's reality-hunters, with their special serious-comic voices, have stood out from the fifties onward. Characters such as Augie and Herzog, Henderson and Dr. Braun, Sammler and Wulpy have stood their ground in the ring of the real, taking their blows and hitting back, composite fighters at once American in their street idiom and habits, European in their learning and wisdom, Jewish in their memory and soul.

When the small Cessna bounces around in the stormy skies and it looks as though this might be his last ride, Victor Wulpy rides out the crisis with steadfast courage and poise, taking full responsibility for bringing Katrina along. Death, or its prospect, doesn't daunt him or restrain his intelligence from peering at it. If style is also moral vision, as Proust observed, then Victor at the end remains a man of style, facing the end of life without flinching or lamenting, just as he has faced the powerful and painful absurdities of the American way without flinching, lamenting, euphemizing, distorting, or escaping. His attention remains on the real, the true, as he even discovers his own mistakes of action during the story.

What kind of day did Victor have? Why, not too bad, he might answer, not too bad. And besides, it wasn't over yet. Not by a long shot.

Nor, to our great pleasure and good luck, is Saul Bellow finished giving us more days, more nights, more Wulpies.

Finally, let it be said that for writers, maybe especially for American writers like myself, having a great writer in our time, in our midst, lends a special fragrance to the air of literature and gives an importance, even a legitimacy, to that most civilized task of reading and writing that is so frequently overlooked, and overwhelmed, in the commercial and distracting wilderness of America. For the long-distance runner called the novelist, such a presence also makes us all feel, strangely enough perhaps, a little less lonely on the perennial journey. Like late Matisse, Bellow flourishes, creating fresh and imaginative ways of looking at the world, of perceiving and reconstructing reality, stunning us and expanding our vision with his configurations, his words, his truths, his voice, his most original art.

Works Cited

Bellow, Saul. "What Kind of Day Did You Have?" In *Him with His Foot in His Mouth and Other Stories*, 63–163. New York: Harper, 1984.

RECENT NOVELLAS AND STORIES

♦

Love's Labors Lost: Saul Bellow's *A Theft*

BEN SIEGEL

S aul Bellow has always written short fiction. His first novel, *Dangling Man*, was little more than a long short story, as was the later *Seize the Day*. He has also published two collections of short stories and a cluster of short plays. Still, several reviewers expressed surprise that he published, in 1989, two short paperback novels, *A Theft* and *The Bellarosa Connection*. They had little reason to be surprised. For the past decade Bellow has clearly been a writer in a hurry. He has seemed eager to clear his desk of all unfinished business. Now seventy-eight, he appears determined not to leave unused, in the time left to him, any leftover or salvageable plot line or story fragment. In fact, he seems to be reworking many of his familiar characters and ideas for alternate or additional possibilities. What these reviewers should have also noted is that the plot and character elements in these two short novels differ little from those in such recent longer works as *The Dean's December* or *More Die of Heartbreak*. The only significant shift from his longer novels is that instead of the societal chaos of an *Augie March*, *Herzog*, or *Mr. Sammler's Planet*, Bellow has focused almost exclusively, at least in *A Theft* on the messy lives of several neurotic egocentrics. In short, Bellow presents once again worldly intellectuals more successful in their public rather than private lives. Neither Clara Velde nor Teddy Regler, the two central figures in *A Theft*, experiences any more emotional or marital bliss than did Kenneth Trachtenberg or Benn Crader in *More Die of Heartbreak* or, for that matter, Katrina Goliger in his novella "What Kind of Day Did You Have?". Indeed, *A Theft* seems essentially a reworking of certain aspects of earlier stories such as "The Old System," "A Silver Dish," and "What Kind of Day Did You Have?"

Reprinted from *Saul Bellow Journal* 11, no. 2 & 12, no. 1 (Double Issue 1993): 3-12

I. High-Strung Women and High-Powered Men

Bluntly put, this novella is a narrative fragment Bellow easily could have melded with "What Kind of Day Did You Have?". Each is a tale of a high-strung woman obsessed with a high-powered male whose intellect and worldly wisdom are sought out by political and cultural leaders. If Victor Wulpy was a takeoff of Harold Rosenberg, then Teddy Regler is another view by Bellow of himself. He basically sees Rosenberg and himself as societal pundits or cultural sages who could have done society much good, had society but taken the time to listen to them. Typically, Bellow infuses this self-portrait with a modicum of wry humor. "Ithiel had never been smart about money," he notes with self-deprecating irony. "He was a bad investor—unlikely, careless" (40). Lest the reader still miss his autobiographical slant, Bellow quickly reinforces it. "He was committed to high civility, structure, order; nevertheless he took chances with women, he was a gambler, something of an anarchist" (42). Otherwise, except for several one-liners, his narrative is surprisingly devoid of laughter. The only other possible comic exceptions are his essentially satiric physical and emotional profiles of his heroine. For the central perspective, as in the earlier "What Kind of a Day Did You Have?," is again that of a woman.

Bellow, very likely smarting from the countless misogynist charges leveled at him through the years, has tried to convince interviewers of his high regard for his heroine. "Clara Velde is a composite of all the women I've known," he informed one reporter. "I had a love affair with her in the writing. I was all charged up about her. I took great satisfaction in getting close to a uniquely female intelligence. I've often experienced this intelligence, but for some reason, I've never thought of writing about it. Then I reminded myself that, after all, I did know a great deal about ladies" (Chambers, 66). This particular lady is blond, attractive, "big-boned," and, most tellingly, has an "unusually big" head. But Bellow is quick to add, most likely with tongue in cheek, that whereas in "an inert character, a head of such size might have seemed a deformity," this was not true here. To the contrary, Clara exuded "so much personal force" that her large head "came across as ruggedly handsome. She needed that head; a mind like hers demanded space." For that matter, everything about Clara is enlarged, exaggerated, and "conspicuous, not only the size and shape of her head." She is "a rawboned American woman" from the rural Midwest raised on the Bible and "old-time religion" (1). These factors have shaped but not confined her. As a girl, for example, she had feared "hellfire," and she still quotes the Bible and derides New York as "Gogmagogsville." But she has insisted always on doing "exactly as she pleased" (2). Ever passionate, Clara also has twice attempted suicide because of failed love affairs.

The reader must take on faith much of what Bellow claims for his heroine. Clara may be affectionate, generous, impulsive, and romantic but, strictly speaking, she exhibits few qualities of character or personality a woman from this very Protestant background might be expected to possess. Still, she supposedly has lived her life by a strict American work ethic. After a highly successful journalistic career, Clara, by age forty, had established her own "journalistic agency specializing in high fashion for women." She later sold her company to an international publishing group, where she has remained a top executive and is considered "a czarina of fashion writing" (2). She now resides in a large Park Avenue co-op with her fourth husband, Wilder Velde, and their three young daughters. Clara is fortunate to be so good at her job, as her husband is an unreliable breadwinner. Large, handsome, lazy, and "defiantly incompetent," Wilder Velde spends his time "reading paperbacks—thrillers, science fiction and pop biographies" (3–4) by writers such as P.D. James and John LeCarré. (Apparently he does not read *serious* paperbound novels, such as *A Theft*.) Wilder is not a total fool. He realizes he is "provoking," but he feels he compensates by his "stud power." Her previous "brilliant men" had failed Clara emotionally, but he has provided, he is convinced, the needed "masculine bulk" (3). So self-confident is Wilder that he even videotapes those of her former lovers, especially Teddy Regler, who rate "being interviewed on CBS or the MacNeil/Lehrer programs" (7). (Here Bellow is preening slightly by again making known Teddy Regler's true identity, for he himself appeared with MacNeil/Lehrer.) Clara finds Wilder generally compliant, at times even "sweet," but mostly boring. "To him inertia," she confides to her friend Laura Wong, "is the same as stability" (4).

Wilder Velde never speaks to the reader; Clara speaks for him. Still, he does have some flesh on his bones. Laura Wong does not. She is a phantom. Clara confides in Laura her intimate feelings about her husband and everyone else. The latter is a Chinese-American dress designer who has no function in the story other than to listen to Clara and ask the right questions. She does not even have to react, being the stereotypical inscrutable Oriental. Wilder is fleetingly reminiscent of Wharton Horricker, Angela Gruner's handsome California stud. Clara is reminiscent of several earlier figures; one is that other Midwestern Protestant "voice," Dean Albert Corde, another journalist-turned-administrator. But Clara, to put it bluntly, does not have the good Dean's intelligence or "smarts." Certainly she says or does little to justify Bellow's insistence on her "intelligence." Indeed, Clara differs little from her less-bright Bellovian sisters in failing to comprehend fully her lover's philosophical observations and explanations. In fact, her actions and reactions repeatedly suggest a rather flawed perception or assessment of others. She is keenly aware of her limitations. "Don't ask me for specifics," she warns. "I can't give them. They're always flitting by me" (89). She does not even appear, as Joyce Carol Oates rightly observes, "intelligent enough for her worldly position, nor even for her author's continued investment in her" (Oates, 3).

To make matters worse, Clara seems to have invested little thought or emotion in her marriages or her profession. Her energies in youth were devoted primarily to acquiring "love and happiness" (16) and now to high-style clothes and the latest cosmetics. Other than that, she reveals little interest in her career, never bothering, for example, to describe her professional activities. She does lay claim, however, to being a devoted mother and offers a quick rundown of her daily home routine, especially those chores involving the children. Clara's basic knowledge and intelligence then are meant to be internal, instinctive, maternal. But the children never materialize, so even Clara's mothering skills are never more than hearsay. Much more in evidence is her obsession with Teddy Regler. Clara is painfully aware of the emotional price she has paid for this preoccupation. Their relationship was essentially "a fever using love as its carrier" (21), she thinks. Yet "a real person understands how to cut losses, not let her whole life be wound around to the end by a single desire, because under it all is the uglitude of this one hang-up" (71). At the same time, she refuses to undervalue herself or the love she has expended on Teddy. She is convinced her true value to him has been to provide him with the emotional support he needs to continue functioning as an important public treasure.

Bellow, who emphasizes always the importance of true love to individual self-worth, clearly agrees. Seemingly concerned that this point not be overlooked, he chose to read to an interviewer the passage in which Clara reasons that her love has given truer meaning to Teddy's life than have his significant public achievements. Thinking of the two of them, Clara tells herself:

> You couldn't separate love from being. You could Be, even though you were alone. But in that case, you loved only yourself. If so, everybody else was a phantom, and then world politics was a shadow play. Therefore she, Clara, was the only key to politics that Ithiel was likely to find. Otherwise he might as well stop bothering his head about his

> grotesque game theories, ideology, treaties, and the rest of it. Why
> bother to line up so many phantoms?. (31; see also Miles, 8)

Bellow repeatedly makes it clear that he sees himself as one of the few
writers today grappling with such personal phantoms and public shadow
plays. In effect, he is saying that Saul Bellow, too, needs such ongoing
emotional support from women. This may be why he has Clara describe
Teddy as being "more plainspoken about his own faults than anybody who
felt it necessary to show him up" (13).

II. Women Executives and Their Secret Fears

Bellow has not hesitated on earlier occasions to make known his feelings
about women executives such as Clara Velde. In *More Die of Heartbreak* and
in the related interviews, he put himself clearly on record. Women have
special problems in the business world, he confided to television newsman
Robert MacNeil. They are somewhat uncertain because "a kind of
feminine power has lost its model for the time being." Hence educated
women ambitious to be chief executive officers of companies have to
adopt a masculine model (see MacNeil interview). He expressed himself
similarly in a *Newsweek* interview. Here, too, he stated his concern that
career women, in their determination to achieve equality and freedom,
have rejected the notion (in interviewer Walter Clemons's paraphrase) of
"a gender difference" or a "specifically feminine nature." Indeed, these
business women have adopted the conventional masculine image of
success. "I don't think anyone has seen a distinctively feminine CEO,"
stated Bellow (Clemons, 79).

   In both interviews, therefore, Bellow repeats thoughts expressed by
Kenneth Trachtenberg, whose observations are of Matilda Layamon. But
Kenneth's conclusions apply even more aptly to Clara Velde. "What you
face, then, is modern women who are proud of their education and their
developed minds." Yet these are women "who secretly fear that they
haven't got what it takes to hold the interest of a man who is powerfully
energized by an important task." Kenneth himself believes these women
have relatively little cause for concern. Very few people, after all, are
engaged in important activities. He refers to activities "directed towards a
higher life." Still, these gifted women "*do* worry. And what they're afraid of
is that such a man will be bored by them." They fear he will "find them
out. So they dress, they talk, and they put their moves on you. They act
light but they feel heavy." They are "mortally depressed and gloomy." They
cannot forget that "so much was predicted for them by their parents,

especially by their mothers. These girls were so gorgeous, graceful, gifted, trained to expect high results. But where are they? In outer darkness, where their poor hearts are breaking. And this feminine disappointment and sorrow is [*sic*] very hard on men. They often feel called upon to restore the self-esteem that's been lost" (*More Die of Heartbreak*, 93). Even as he developed Clara Velde's relationship with Ithiel (Teddy) Regler, Bellow may have been thinking of these earlier words from *More Die of Heartbreak*. (They also are an accurate description of the hapless Katrina Goliger and her sense of being inferior to her lover, Victor Wulpy.)

Clara is more independent and assertive than Katrina, but she is as single-minded as was the latter about the important man in her life. Teddy Regler has been Clara's one ongoing passion, with most of the passion on her side. Any Bellow reader should recognize Teddy. He is another of the novelist's all-knowing cultural pundits or political seers. Not surprisingly, he has—like most of Bellow's keen observers—extraordinary eyes. Teddy's large, dark orbs give him not only "a classic level look" (17), thinks Clara, but also appear derived "from Greek mythology" (30). They reflect his inner vision, for he also has a "singular inborn eye" that contributes to "a genius for observing politics" (90) and putting together the "big, *big* picture" (109). Clara may be describing Teddy, but she sounds like Bellow offering his personal evaluation of his own contribution to his time. It is not a modest appraisal. What Teddy has explained to her, Clara recalls, "is that no trained historian will ever do it"—that is, achieve a political portrait of this entire century. So panoramic a work will be achieved, according to Teddy, only by a singular genius such as he has described. Of course Clara's money is on Teddy. He is for her nothing less than "a dark horse in the history of the American mind" (103). Indeed, he may well be the one to "take hold one day," she tells herself, "and do a wrap-up of the century, the wrap-up of wrap-ups" (90). He will do nothing less than "write the book of books about it" (79). In fact, should he choose, Teddy "could be," Clara is convinced, "the Gibbon or the Tacitus of the American Empire" (35). Such thinking by Clara (and Teddy) should not surprise the reader. Teddy Regler is said to be right up there in strategic-policy importance and demand with Henry Kissinger, on whom he is also an expert. Teddy constantly jets off to advise heads of government and of multinational corporations on the latest geopolitical strategies. "A bit of a hyped article, this Teddy," notes David Denby. "He comes off as half talk-show guest, half Richard Goodwin's fantasy of himself" (Denby, 37). Whatever Teddy Regler may be, Saul Bellow is having fun at Teddy's and his own expense.

Teddy and Clara had shared a torrid affair and a Chelsea apartment in the 1960s. Clara bears a strong resemblance to Demmie Vonghel (Charlie Citrine's true love in *Humboldt's Gift*). Indeed the parallels between the two women are numerous enough to suggest they are variations of the same character: Clara, too, had bustled about the apartment in the nude. Clara "had studied Greek" and been a teacher, and Demmie, after studying classics at Bryn Mawr, had "taught Latin at the Washington Irving School." Both women have rather checkered sexual pasts, and Demmie, again like Clara, was "brought up on hellfire and damnation." Their physical resemblance is also striking: Demmie, too, had a "long elegant head" that "grew golden hair" and crowned "a very white sort of face." The ladies even share an enticing flaw. "But I fell first for her legs," recalls Charlie. "And these beautiful legs had an exciting defect—her knees touched and her feet were turned outward so that when she walked fast the taut silk of her stockings made a slight sound of friction" (*Humboldt's Gift*, 19). Clara boasts a like defect in her own legs, one that excited Teddy. Seemingly, however, it had not excited him enough. For she had felt the need to pressure Teddy to marry her, she recalls, with her "revivalist emotions . . . of tears, anguish and emotion" (24). Not only had he refused, but he also had cheated with other women. They had then married other people. Clara now ponders with regret the life they might have had together. "What a waste!" she thinks. "Why should there have been seven marriages, five children!" (50–51).

Clara's previous marriages, sadly enough, are barely mentioned. Each appears to have been more exciting than her present one. Bellow is given to invoking the names of real gangsters to give a gritty, teasing edge to his stories. Here Clara's third husband, "Mad Mike" Spontini, the oil tycoon, was, it seems, an intimate of a radical Italian billionaire publisher referred to only as "Giangiacomo F." Reviewers have quickly identified the latter as the leftist revolutionist Giangiacomo Feltrinelli, who in the 1970s accidentally blew himself to pieces with one of his own bombs. Not surprisingly, Teddy appears much less colorful than Signor Feltrinelli and hardly more of a marital bargain than Mike Spontini. In fact, Teddy's latest wife has just left him, taking with her all the house furnishings. "You wouldn't marry a woman who did value you," a saddened Clara tells him. "[You're] like Groucho Marx saying he wouldn't join a club that accepted him for membership" (54). Bellow appears to be reworking Kenneth Trachtenberg's relationship with the tirelessly devoted Dita Schwartz. Here he puts a harder edge on romance. For Kenneth had hinted that he might be grateful enough for Dita's loyalty and solicitude to reward her ultimately with marriage. Clara cannot expect the same fate. In fact, Ithiel's attitude toward women is curiously like that of Hugh Hefner's *Playboy* magazine: beautiful women are to be displayed, enjoyed, then folded neatly and filed away for future reference or use. Clara's only tangible memento of their youthful affair is a green emerald engagement ring that she had pressured Teddy to buy her for $1200 that he then could ill afford. When later she lost the ring, she grieved deeply for this talisman of the passion she had felt for him. "In it Ithiel's pledge was frozen"(43). Still, she collected $15,000 from the insurance company, and then found the ring wedged in a bed post. Having spent the money, she could not notify the insurance company of the ring's reappearance. Nor could she reinsure it. Now it has disappeared again. Clara is greatly distressed by the loss. Teddy is not. But Clara guesses immediately who has taken it: Frederic Vigneron, the Haitian boyfriend of Gina Wegman, her half-Austrian, half-Italian au pair girl. Gina has come from Vienna to be a student at Columbia University, and seemingly to have a sexual fling, before returning home to marry a man in her father's bank.

The relationship of the two women is only partially developed but still proves suggestive. Clara treats her young charge with patronizing kindness. She worries about Gina's seeming innocence and vulnerability amid New York's "explosive dangers." Clara feels obliged to soften her criticism of Gina because she too had "been a young woman in New York" (63) and had in those years engaged in "reckless experiments" and "chancy relationships." She had done so merely "for the honor of running risks" (11). Indeed, Clara thinks little "of mature women who have evaded" learning about life. "But sometimes the schooling we have to undergo," she concedes, "is too rough" (65–66). She may even have had her own black lover: Clifford, "a convict in Attica" (61), still sends her Christmas cards. Clara also remembers her charged feelings during her romance with Teddy. She informs Laura Wong that "it's conceivable that the world-spirit gets into mere girls and makes them its demon interpreters" (21). Her own erratic escapades cause Clara to wonder about Gina's seeming innocence. She is "such a pretty child," thinks Clara, "and the Italian charm of her looks, so innocent—although innocence is a tricky thing to prove. You can't expect her to forget about being a girl just because the surroundings are so dangerous" (46). Clara is tempted to make "a younger friend" of Gina, but she decides against it. She does not wish to arouse feelings of rivalry in her children. However, she does resolve to use her own experience to protect the young visitor.

III. Innocents, Victims, and Analysts

Here Bellow has tapped into what has proved an increasingly prevalent plotline in recent fiction: the reversal of the familiar Henry James scenario of an experienced, often cynical European confronted by an innocent, uncertain, somewhat gauche American.[1] Asked by interviewer Jack Miles of the *Los Angeles Times* if he intended his novella to be "a kind of inversion of Henry James's *Daisy Miller*," Bellow opted for his own form of innocence. "Bellow laughed," states Miles, but "he was intrigued, mildly." At first claiming he "hadn't thought of that," Bellow then explained that "Luigi Barzini, whose work he admires, calls America the indispensable school for Europe." At that point, reports Miles, Bellow "recalled what young Gina's reasons were for coming to America: to perfect her English and to study music. Yes, perhaps a partial inversion of *Daisy Miller*" (Miles, 8).

Miles does not ask whether Giovanelli, Daisy's Italian suitor, might not have served as model for Frederic Vigneron, Gina's Haitian lover. Nor does either Bellow or Miles suggest that for a time Clara sounds suspiciously like the dowagers Mrs. Costello and Mrs. Walker, who disapproved of Daisy's unconventional behavior. Only at the end does Clara grasp her young charge's true moral character and begin to echo, in a sense, James's belatedly appreciative Winterbourne. Hence Bellow, too, resembles Winterbourne: he seems also to have discovered belatedly interesting possibilities in Gina Wegman. Of course, Bellow might well caution against pushing the Jamesian parallels too far. Certainly Henry James would not have been favorably impressed by the central relationship here between a Protestant woman and the novel's only identifiably Jewish male. But for Bellow the special friendship of Clara and Teddy Regler is emblematic of the times. "At this point, why not?" he explains. "The Protestant dominance in America ended in the 1960s." This means that "in 1989 America, individual Protestants and Jews relate perforce as individuals" (Miles, 8).[2]

Here Bellow challenges again the self-appointed role of "victim." In his early novel of that title, he had pointed up the uncertainties involved in determining whether Asa Leventhal or Kirby Allbee was the true victim. Now Teddy adamantly disdains those who embrace too readily the role of victim, whether for psychological or ethnic reasons. In doing so, he takes swipes at several familiar Bellow targets, especially psychiatry. Clara flies to Washington to console Teddy after his third wife has left him. "I've been despondent," he admits, but he rejects any thought of therapy. "What I've learned, though," he tells her, "is that when people get to talking about their private troubles, they go into a winding spiral about relationships, and they absolutely stupefy everybody with boredom. I'm sure that I can turn myself around" (53). He scoffs at those self-designated victims who wallow in self-pity, including many who claim to have suffered "child-abuse." His father beat him savagely, Teddy admits, but he holds no grudges. "That's my argument with psychiatry: it encourages you to build on abuses and keeps you infantile" (15). He also dislikes the psychiatric profession's habit of offering "cures" where none is needed. "Those guys," he complains. "If a millipede came into the office, he'd leave with an infinitesimal crutch for each leg" (42).

Teddy has passed on to Clara his disdain for psychiatrists. Gazing at her therapist, Dr. Gladstone, she recognizes that "hope brought her here, every effort must be made." Still, when Clara took a good look, when she "looked with all her might at Dr. Gladstone, she could not justify the trust she was asked to place in that samurai beard, the bared teeth it framed, the big fashionable specs, his often baseless confidence in his science." What is she to do? "It would take the better part of a year," she realizes, "to acquaint a new doctor with the fundamentals of her case. She was stuck with this one." But then Gladstone smugly suggests that his going on vacation may be the true cause of her upset at the loss of her ring. After all, he tells her, "my name is Gladstone." The astonished Clara—sounding much like the wisecracking Harry Shawmut of "Him with His Foot in His Mouth"—responds: "You may be a stone, but you're not a gem" (75–76). In fact, she realizes she feels "more than a drop of hatred" for this smug analyst. "Plumbers was what Ithiel called these Gladstone types," she reminds herself. "He had quit analysis because nobody was able to tell him what it took to be Ithiel Regler." Clara feels this "applied to her as well" (98). It could hardly be otherwise: what Teddy thinks, Clara generally thinks also. Yet neither appears aware that despite their shared dislike of professional analysts, they both analyze themselves, each other, and everyone they know.

When not attacking psychiatrists, Teddy takes aim at the Soviet Union. Here, too, he clearly speaks for Bellow, who often has voiced his outrage at Soviet officialdom for its abuse of literary dissidents like Ossip Mandelstam and Andrei Sinyavsky (Abram Tertz). Despite *glasnost* and *perestroika*, both clearly in evidence by 1989, Bellow indicates he is not yet ready to forgive, much less forget. "The Russians," scoffs Teddy—quoting what he describes as "some of the smartest emigres"—delayed announcing "liberalization until they had crushed the dissidents. Then they co-opted the dissidents' ideas. After you've gotten rid of your enemies, you're ready to abolish capital punishment. . . . They strangled the opposition, and now they're pretending to be it" (57). Bellow's skepticism is hardly a surprise. His sense of irony is deeply rooted, as is his conviction that things are never as they appear. His reactions to highly touted "experts" and social prophets have been mixed at best. His grudging admiration for people like economist Milton Friedman, culture critic Harold Rosenberg, sociologist Edward Shils, and all the other intellectual "tough guys" he uses as reference points is generally leavened with an underlying suspicion and frequent disdain. So he may have meant Teddy (like Victor Wulpy) to come off as something of a wise fool. Yet subsequent events in Eastern Europe make Teddy, with his harsh dismissal of *glasnost*, appear a more unalloyed fool than Bellow may have intended. But then Bellow's overall intention here is not clear—as the other male characters hardly speak at all. Wilder Velde and Frederic Vigneron are never heard from directly. Dr. Gladstone and Clara's private detective, Gottschalk, prove men of very few words. Teddy Regler is then the sole male "talker," and he, ironically, should have spoken less.

IV. Thieves, Deceptions, and Tears

Several critics, Joyce Carol Oates among them, have expressed unease at the novel's thief being its one person of "color" (Oates, 3). Laura Wong is Chinese, but seemingly she does not count. Bellow is offering merely a variation, they feel, of Artur Sammler's black pickpocket. Admittedly, Frederic Vigneron is somewhat reminiscent of the pickpocket, who also preyed on unwary New Yorkers and was not above using sex—or at least his bared genitals—as a weapon. But his critics should have recalled that Bellow is much given to theft as a plot device, with the thefts as likely to be committed by women as by men. Bellow launched his investigation of female duplicity early with "Looking for Mr. Green." Then, drawing upon painful personal experience, he described how the wives of Tommy Wilhelm, Moses Herzog, and Charlie Citrine utilized divorce or the divorce courts to part their husbands from their money. Yet his men are hardly without sin. His heroes are as likely to be cheated by their friends, partners, and lawyers, not to mention their uncles, cousins, and brothers, and even an occasional father (as in "A Silver Dish"), as they are by their wives or sweethearts.

But then Bellow can be as ambiguous about a story's true "thief" as he is about its true victim. In *Mr. Sammler's Planet*, for example, the pickpocket is hardly alone in his thievery. Sammler's daughter Shula, his nephew Elya Gruner, and Elya's children Angela and Wallace, as well as the conniving Lionel Feffer, all engage in various forms of theft or deception. In fact, the carping critics should have remembered that Sammler found more to admire in the princely pickpocket than in his victims, whose skulls, he complained, had to be filled "with some kind of stupid mold" (*Mr. Sammler's Planet*, 13). Now, middle-class New Yorkers again are too easily victimized. Thinking of the arrogant French-speaking Frederic and his fellow Haitians, Clara observes that "These people came up from the tropical slums to outsmart New York, and with all the rules crumbling here as elsewhere, so that nobody could any longer be clear in his mind about anything, they could do it" (73). She is tempted, therefore, to dismiss what she terms Gina's "Caribbean romance, or sex experiment," as merely one more "case of being at sea amongst collapsing cultures." But she quickly rejects so glib a pronouncement. "I sound like Ithiel now, and I don't actually take much stock in the collapsing-culture bit." Here at least she appears of one mind with Bellow. For the true cause of the human predicament, individual and in general, as is usual with his people, ultimately lies within. "I'm beginning to see it instead," states Clara, "as the conduct of life without input from your soul." For the real problem is that "essential parts of people [are] getting mislaid or crowded out" (88–89).

Other internal factors, such as restlessness or dissatisfaction, anger or envy, or sheer emotional confusion, also prove troublesome. Clara even considers the possibility that Laura Wong may want Teddy for herself because of the praise Clara has been heaping on him. She decides not to drop her friend immediately but "to spin her off very slowly." After all, Laura knows so many of her secrets that she can hurt Clara with her husband and the insurance company. Also, Laura is "so gifted professionally. We still need her layouts" (90–92). Yet, almost immediately, Clara decides on "an exceptional, a generous action." She will bring Teddy and Gina together so that they can fall in love. Teddy rejects the idea and points up the quirkiness of Clara's thinking. "So you and I will increase our number. She'll enlist with us. And she and I will cherish each other, and you will have the comfort of seeing me in safe hands, and this will be your blessing poured over the two of us" (94–95).

Disconcerted that Teddy so easily discerns her motives, Clara rationalizes her foolish behavior by offering herself a summary of what she considers must be his "underlying view" of human behavior. "The assumptions we make as to one another's motives are so circumscribed, our understanding of the universe and its forces is so false," she writes on a piece of paper, "that the more we analyze, the more injury we do" (93). Her own underlying problem, she decides, is that she (like almost everyone else in Bellow's fiction) wishes to be interesting, singular. "I never feel so bad," she tells Laura Wong, "as when the life I lead stops being characteristic—when it could be anybody's else's life" (83). She had hoped Teddy would provide the "point of rest" in her life. He has failed her, but she also has failed herself. "I have an anti-rest character," she concedes. "I think there's too much basic discord in me." Recognizing now that she is never to experience the blissful serenity for which she has yearned, Clara wishes only to come to terms with her own restless character and to achieve "a quiet life" (90–91). (She could be speaking also for Saul Bellow.)

But in Bellow's fiction as in life, external as well as internal factors are always at work. Money, for instance, often causes disputes between husbands and wives or among family members and friends. Land or property or even a ring also may stir dissension. In "The Old System," for instance, both a land deal and a ring send Tina Braun Fenster on a rampage. Tina is angry with her brother at being excluded from a shopping-center development she had herself rejected. To get even, she "steals" their dead mother's ring, only to return it to her brother when they reunite on her own deathbed. Here Frederic Vigneron *may* be the apparent thief of the title, but this Haitian hustler returns the ring he has taken. Clara Velde, however, has never returned the insurance money she received when she earlier lost (and then found) the same ring. Yet a more serious theft in the story may be Clara's misreading of Gina's true character and thereby robbing the young visitor of her dignity and pride. But then perhaps the major thief is Teddy Regler. He has robbed, or at least deprived, both Clara and himself of a life of shared love and happiness.

His "punishment" consists of being pushed into the background near novel's end. Clara and Gina meet for the last time in a hotel cocktail lounge. Their conversation scene hardly rivals that of Artur Sammler and Govinda Lal or Albert Corde and Dewey Spangler or Benn Crader and Kenneth Trachtenberg, or even Tommy Wilhelm and Dr. Tamkin, but it, too, is meant to illuminate theme and character. No longer the deferential au pair, Gina is confident, self-possessed. At first Clara feels somewhat hostile toward Gina but then quickly dismisses all resentful thoughts. She owes Gina for getting her ring back and for what she has done for her troubled daughter Lucy. "It's false to do the carnal woman number on her," Clara decides. "Let's not get so Old Testament." There is also her own past. "My regular Christmas card from Attica is still arriving." Also, before Gina married that fellow from her daddy's bank she "owed herself some excitement." After all, thinks Clara, "Nobody, but nobody, can withstand modern temptations" (102). So contrite is she that she again toys with the possibility of bringing Gina and Teddy together. But she realizes immediately this is too much of a gesture for her to make. She is astounded when Gina informs her that she had asked Lucy to return the ring and not to mention a word about it. Clara is overwhelmed that her high-strung, disgruntled ten-year-old has proved so reliable.

The two women part with affection and tears. "I believe you pretty well know who you are" (108), says Gina as she leaves. (Readers may feel, however, that Clara's erratic behavior throughout hardly merits so positive an evaluation.) Only then does Clara feel that she clearly understands the girl's true character and "what Gina had done, how the ring had been returned" (109). Clara, like several earlier Bellow characters, cannot restrain her tears. These tears merit consideration. Tommy Wilhelm's uncontrolled sobbing concludes a day of trauma as well as *Seize the Day* itself. (Bellow may have been inspired there by Theodore Dreiser, whom he much admires. For so moved is Dreiser's Jennie Gerhardt by the beauty of the Catholic service for Lester Kane, her deceased lover, that "she cried and cried" [*Jennie Gerhardt*, 365].) Moses Herzog, experiencing his own day of tribulation, stands "in the corridor outside Magistrate's Court" and recalls his mother's death and how his brother "Willie cried in the chapel! It was his brother Willie, after all, who had the tender heart" (*Herzog*, 233). If they have a quasi-baptismal function in Bellow's fiction, tears wash away not so much past sin as the past itself.

Here Bellow's intention, seemingly, is to reveal Clara's "tender heart" under her tough executive exterior. Readers should find familiar both language and imagery. "But now, when Clara came out of the revolving door, and as soon as she had the pavement under her feet, she started to cry passionately. She hurried, crying down Madison Avenue, not like a person who belonged there but like one of the homeless, doing grotesque things in public, one of those street people turned loose from an institution." At that point, "the main source of tears came open. She found a handkerchief and held it to her face in her ringed hand, striding in an awkward hurry. She might have been treading water in New York harbor— it felt that way, more a sea than a pavement, and for all the effort and the motions that she made, she wasn't getting anywhere, she was still in the same place" (109). Like Tommy Wilhelm and Willie Herzog, Clara Velde sobs essentially for herself for her deep sense of loss, frustration, and displacement.

But Bellow cannot resist a concluding reference to himself, in the person of the all-knowing Teddy Regler. "When he described me to myself in Washington," thinks Clara, in the novel's final passage, "I should have taken Ithiel's word for it. . . . He knows what the big picture is—the big, *big* picture; he doesn't flatter, he's realistic and he's truthful. I do seem to have an idea who it is that's at the middle of me. There may not be more than one in a zillion, more's the pity, that do have. And my own child possibly one of those" (109). These closing words, despite their self-congratulatory tone and questionable grammar, link at least three of the characters who merit here more detailed development. They suggest that Bellow wants it known that he is aware he has left unsaid much that readers may feel still needs to be said. Gina Wegman also makes this point. "Which people are the lost people?" she asks, underscoring what is meant here to be a crucial question. "This is the hardest thing of all to decide, even about oneself" (108). Instead of an "answer," she offers only an evasive compliment to Clara: she credits her former employer with being one of modern society's rare "complete" individuals. Clara knows better. Hard knocks and bitter disappointments have taught her just how uncertain and open-ended life can be. In fact, she had only moments earlier posed her own questions. Does life offer "no point of rest?" she had wondered. "Won't the dynamic ever let you go?" (90). In short, when does one achieve stability, certainty, true self-knowledge?

Clara would do well to turn again to Teddy, at least to recall the most sage of his often obtuse observations. "Well, people have to be done with disorder, finally," he has stated, "and by the time they're done they're also finished. When they back off to take a new leap, they realize they've torn too many ligaments. It's all over" (38). These few words may well sum up Teddy's true grasp of the "big picture" and also serve as the narrative key. Bellow has rejected always neat social theories or formulas, whether those of a Marx or Freud or Hegel or Sartre, or of any other school or movement. Certainly he offers here neither pat solutions nor easy nihilism—only ongoing uncertainty and confusion. "You can always get a remedy," thinks Teddy sardonically; "you can tap into solace when you need it, you can locate a mental fix. America is generous in this regard. The air is full of helpful hints." He himself rejects any easy solution or "handy fix" (33). As Clara points out, however, "Cynicism also is unacceptable" (103). It appears then that Bellow expects his readers to imagine for them-selves how Clara Velde, Teddy Regler, and the others will deal with their still unfinished and unfulfilled lives. He allows only one truth to remain evident: Like everyone else, each character will have to cope with that most insidious "thief" of all—his or her own human frailties.

Notes

1. English critic John Bayley recently discussed this point in terms of David Lodge's academic novels *Changing Places* (1975) and *Small World* (1984). In Lodge's two novels, "the two worlds" of Henry James, noted Bayley, "really have changed places: and it is the American man [Morris Zapp] who is knowledgeable and sophisticated, with the confidence of assured wealth and early experience. His English opposite number [Philip Swallow] is uncertain, anxious, timid, and insecure, and comes from a humble though sheltered background" (Bayley, 13).

2. This is a paraphrase by Miles of Bellow's response.

Works Cited

Bayley, John. "Innocents at Home." Review of *A Theft*, by Saul Bellow. *New York Review of Books*, 19 April 1992, 13.

Bellow, Saul. *Herzog*. New York: Viking Press, 1964.

———. *Him with His Foot in His Mouth and Other Stories*. New York: Harper & Row, 1984.

———. *Humboldt's Gift*. New York: Viking Press, 1975.

———. *Mosby's Memoirs and Other Stories*. New York: Viking Press, 1968.

———. *Mr. Sammler's Planet*. New York: Viking Press, 1970.

———. *A Theft*. New York: William Morrow, Penguin Books, 1989.

———. *The Victim*. New York: Vanguard Press, 1947.

Chambers, Andrea. "At 73, Nobel Laureate Saul Bellow Decides He Wants to Be a Paperback Writer." *People Magazine*, 27 March 1989, 65–66, 69.

Clemons, Walter. "The Quest Never Stops." *Newsweek*, 8 June 1987, 79.

Denby, David. "Memory in America." *New Republic*, 1 January 1990, 37–40.

Dreiser, Theodore. *Jennie Gerhardt*. New York: Oxford University Press, 1991.

MacNeil, Robert. Interview with Saul Bellow. "MacNeil/Lehrer NewsHour," June 1987.

Miles, Jack. "Saul Bellow's Life Is an Open Book." *Los Angeles Times*, 30 March 1989, V8–9.

Oates, Joyce Carol. "Clara's Gift." Review of *A Theft*, by Saul Bellow. *New York Times Book Review*, 5 March 1989, 3.

Degrees of Comic Irony in
A Theft and *The Bellarosa Connection*

ELAINE B. SAFER

Of Saul Bellow's fiction, Robert Boyers writes, "Incongruous juxtapositions are as frequent in Bellow as in the routines of seasoned stand-up comics. The difference is that the nonsense in Bellow genuinely comes across as human, all too human, and the big ideas seem very much worth the attention of a decent and thoughtful person" ("Losing Grip," 299). In an interview in 1966, Bellow criticized his first novels, *Dangling Man* and *The Victim,* for their solemnity and their strong sense of complaint and insisted that since then he has been writing comedies. Bellow clearly states, "Obliged to choose between complaint and comedy, I choose comedy, as more energetic, wiser and manlier." He explains that *"Herzog* makes comic use of complaint." "A source of comedy" in the novel is Herzog's desire "to have effective virtues," to arrive "at a synthesis that can satisfy modern demands." All this is treated as a "comic impossibility" (qtd. in Harper, 62, 67, 68). So, too, according to Bellow, the underlying somberness of *Humbolt's Gift* is part of the novel's comedy: "That is to say it's a broad comedy and the theme is death" (qtd. in Dommergues, 17).

In his recent novellas, *The Bellarosa Connection* and *A Theft,* Bellow ironically juxtaposes high-sounding romantic ideas and relativistic or pragmatic behavior. Nevertheless, criticism of these latest novellas has not focused on their irony and humor. Reviewers have commented on their wit and comedy but have placed far more attention on such questions as whether the portraiture in the novellas is strong enough (Oates, 3) and whether the philosophical ideas are integral to the stories (Packer, 675),[1]

Reprinted from *Saul Bellow Journal* 9, no. 2 (1990): 1-19.

without appreciating how the characters' search for answers is treated comically in the novellas, as in Bellow's other works.

Reviewing recent American fiction some thirty years ago, Bellow described a central subject of modern comedy as "the disintegrating outline of the worthy and humane Self." The novelist explains: "The private and inner life which was the subject of serious books until very recently now begins to have an antique and funny look" ("Some Notes," 28). According to Bellow, the sad questions that romantic writers dwelled on are "treated ironically and humorously" by contemporary writers. Such questions are "turned inside-out by the modern comedian." Such things as *"my* moral seriousness, *my* progress, *my* sensitivity, *my* fidelity, *my* guilt—the modern reader is easily made to laugh at all of these" ("Literature," 164).

Sarah Blacher Cohen has pointed out that "throughout most of his novels Bellow has either directly occupied the sphere of comedy or gravitated toward it" (20). Malcolm Bradbury has argued that "Bellow is surely one of the great modern metaphysical comedians" (104). Joyce Carol Oates explains that Bellow is "a writer whose deepest energies incline him, for all his public lamenting of our 'fallen species,' toward the sunlit spaces of comedy and away from the more subtle counterminings of tragedy" (3). Ben Siegel stresses that "Bellow, in recent years, has been focusing increasingly on the comic, the humorous, the light." And Brigitte Scheer-Schaezler, in her comprehensive review of the literature, shows that "now . . . scholars and critics of Bellow are fully aware of the comic in his work" (56).

Bellow has been characterized as a creator of "encyclopedic comedies of knowledge" that have their roots in the "expansive prose" of such writers as Rabelais, Sterne, and Joyce (Shulman, 109). His humorous style also harkens back to that of Jewish writers like Sholom Aleichem, who fuses the sacred and the secular, the mythological and the mundane to "point up the humorous discrepancies existing between [Bellow's] all too fallible characters and . . . grand figures" (Cohen, 18–19). The quick wit, spontaneity, and exuberance of Bellovian prose arise from such stylistic devices as one-liners (Clara Velde's response to her therapist Dr. Gladstone: "'You may be a stone, but you're not a gem'" [*A Theft*, 76]); vivid comparisons ("Mildred had a powdered look, like her own strudel" [*The Bellarosa Connection*, 9]); lively and witty metaphors (Kenneth Trachtenberg's comments on his mother: "As though she would let her own son come flying in over the heads of so many pundits, academicians, the authors of books on *Existenz* and geopolitics. Your mother is the one *goalkeeper* you never can score with" [*More Die of Heartbreak*, 119; second italics added])[2]; and what Cynthia Ozick terms "the private clamor in the writing . . . this sound of a thrashing soul—comic because metaphysical, metaphysical because aware of itself as a farcical combatant on a busy planet—. . . . 'The clever, lucky old Berlin Jew, whose head was like a round sour-dough loaf, all uneven and dusted with flour, had asked the right questions'" (44). It is through comedy that Bellow is able to present the leading issues of our times, enabling us to laugh at his characters' flawed attempts to achieve their goals, and thus enabling us to better accept our own unrealized aspirations.[3]

The Narrative Voice and Comic Irony

Though less direct, another literary approach Bellow often uses for comic purposes is narrative voice. He has frequently highlighted comic irony through the use of a first-person narrator whose obtuseness causes him either to interpret erroneously or to ignore his own motives and those of the other characters in the story. Such narrators exemplify Henri Bergson's point that "a comic character is generally comic in proportion to his ignorance of himself. . . . He becomes invisible to himself while remaining visible to all the world" (71). The reader then alters, reverses, or amplifies the interpretation or description, or supplies his or her own response to fill the narrative void. Bellow has used this method with Augie March's statements on seeking and hoping; Henderson's description of his inner voice that cries "I want, I want"; and Mosby's intellectual generalizations in his memoirs.

Bellow has also used third-person narration to point—with irony and good humor—to his characters' shortcomings, for example: Tommy Wilhelm's upsets and his self-destructive behavior; Herzog's anxieties and his jealousy; wildly liberated Angela Gruner's scatterbrained behavior in *Mr. Sammler's Planet*; and Katrina Goliger's romantic devotion to Victor Wulpy in the novella "What Kind of Day Did You Have?" In *Seize the Day*, *Herzog*, and "What Kind of Day Did You Have?" the third-person narrator sometimes reveals and at other times ignores ironic juxtapositions, for Bellow—as a contemporary writer—obviously does not create a third-person narrator who is all knowing in the traditional sense.

In *A Theft*, the third-person narrator is more than ordinarily obtuse. Evaluations of characters and the related "big ideas" are put forth by a narrator who is no more privileged than any other voice. The narrator ignores or lacks the understanding necessary to appreciate the irony of incongruous juxtapositions. An example is his lack of comment on Ithiel (Teddy) Regler's earnest expressions of devoted love followed that same day by his fleet-footed exit (his departure from the hospital that houses

Clara, who desperately needs him). Although readers may look to the third-person narrator for answers, the narrator continues to be totally obtuse, and, therefore, irony develops.

Mosby and the Narrator in *The Bellarosa Connection*: The Comic Irony of Self Deception

Bellow's method of developing comic irony in *The Bellarosa Connection* (1989) is similar to that in "Mosby's Memoirs" (1968), in which the first-person narrator (referring to himself in the third person) continually makes judgments about characters (including himself) or expresses philosophical views without being aware of contradictions in his perceptions. In fact, the unnamed narrator in *The Bellarosa Connection* can be considered a Jewish Mosby. In "Mosby's Memoirs," Mosby, "the thinker" (161), the successful intellectual, winner of a Rhodes Scholarship and a Guggenheim Foundation grant, has so enraged the academic community by his lacerating method of discourse that Princeton offers him "a lump sum to retire seven years early" (176). Mosby reveals through narration and dialogue he has no emotional concern for others, certainly none for Hymen Lustgarten, the Jew whom he coldly describes in less than human terms: "Strangely meek, stout, swarthy, kindly, grinning with mulberry lips, a froggy, curving mouth which produced wrinkles like gills between the ears and the grin" (164).[4] The narrator, Mosby, is untroubled by the suffering of mediocre humanity and is satisfied with his well-ordered existence. He is an arrogant person, "a fanatic about *ideas*" (160), who treats all with the aesthetic distance of one who can coolly relate that in the scheme of things "Lustgarten didn't have to happen" (183).[5] Notes on Lustgarten serve as a comic digression in his memoirs (175–77). Only at the end of the novella does Mosby realize that his separation from humanity is deadening; it has made his existence as stifling as that in the Mexican tomb which Mosby visits, a tomb whose "mathematical calculations . . . [are] perfect." The tomb, he realizes, is a concrete manifestation of his own death-like existence. This epiphany causes Mosby to look for a way to "get out" (183–84).

Having Mosby as an ignorant interpreter of characters and ideas develops comic irony. He, as narrator-protagonist, is similar in his ignorance, intellectual snobbery, and pretentiousness to Bellow's most recent narrator-protagonist, the unnamed founder in *The Bellarosa Connection* of the Mnemosyne Institute designed to help people remember. This narrator is a modern American, interested in glamour and success. His mansion in Philadelphia is decorated in an eighteenth-century style (by his now-deceased wife, Deirdre), a house furnished from antique shops! In a detached manner, he mentions his own personal history: he is from a family of Russian Jews (2) and Harry Fonstein's aunt was his stepmother (euphemistically called Aunt Mildred), whom he "never loved . . . nor even esteemed" (69). "But, you understand," he explains, "she had a place in my memory, and [he confidently insists] there must have been a good reason for that" (69).

Humor in *The Bellarosa Connection* ranges from the farcical tip of the continuum (as the head of the Memory Institute recalls the tune of a song but cannot retrieve its main phrase—"Swanee River" [70]—to the grim humor that arises as the obtuse narrator unwittingly reveals that by focusing on the theory of memory, he has substituted theory for life, contemplation for emotional involvement. The narrator is a Jewish Mosby, in the sense that he divorces himself from all that is personal—emotional involvement with others and a meaningful connection with his own family and his Jewish roots.

The narrator of *The Bellarosa Connection,* Harry Fonstein—a European Jew, saved from the Nazis by Billy Rose—is a somewhat comic character. The narrator's attitude is similar to Mosby's attitude toward Lustgarten. The narrator savors the irony that the rescue operation for Fonstein was commandeered by Billy Rose, a multimillionaire New York celebrity, a successful songwriter in show biz, owner of The Diamond Horseshoe. For the narrator it all signifies a rerun of *The Scarlet Pimpernel,* "the Hollywood of Leslie Howard, who acted the Pimpernel" (89). The narrator also is intrigued by Billy Rose's continued refusal to meet with Fonstein, the man whose life he saved, a refusal that prevents Fonstein from thanking his benefactor. The narrator explains to Fonstein's wife, Sorella: "I break my head trying to understand why it's so important for Fonstein. He's been turned down? So he's been turned down" (22). He speaks to Sorella with great understatement: "Does it upset him? It could make him unhappy to be snatched from death by a kibitzer" (26).

The narrator's focus throughout is on the connection between Billy Rose, a glitzy Hollywood type, and Harry Fonstein, as well as on the efforts of Sorella Fonstein to make that connection meaningful for her husband. The narrator is unaware of having any emotional involvement with the Fonsteins or with the Holocaust. He engages in superficial comments and light banter rather than showing concern. When Sorella's comments touch on the "black humor, the slapstick side of certain [Nazi] camp operations," he detaches himself. She explains how "some camps were run in a burlesque style" that forced the prisoners to connect grotesquely with their past, practical lives. "Prisoners were sent naked into a swamp and had to croak and hop like frogs. Children were hanged while starved, freezing slave laborers lined up on parade in front of the gallows and a prison band played Viennese light opera waltzes" (28). The narrator records in his memoirs: "I didn't want to hear this, and I said *impatiently*, 'All right, Billy Rose wasn't the only one in show biz. So the Germans did it too'" (28; italics added). The narrator ignorantly thinks of himself as someone other than he is. When reporting a conversation he has with a rabbi from Jerusalem, the narrator speaks of it as a "Jewish conversation" (67). When the rabbi tells him that it would be a "mitzvah" if a homeless relative of Fonstein in Jerusalem could locate and meet with Harry Fonstein, the narrator thinks, "Christ, spare me these mitzvahs" (69).

It takes the narrator a long time to gain insight into the emptiness of his own existence, his "lifelong mistake" (87). While tracking down the Fonsteins (whom he has not seen for thirty years), the narrator goes through his old address books, calling "all over the place" (75) and—in the process—gets more in touch with his own past. As he speaks to people about the Fonsteins, he dwells on subjects that had not concerned him previously: the justice involved in the "Fonstein-Billy thing" and the position of European Jewry as a whole (83–84).

The narrator, tired out, presently begins to dream: "I found myself in a hole. Night, a dark plain, a pit, and from the start I was already trying to climb out. . . . I could see over the edge, but I couldn't crawl out. . . . I was clawing at the dirt for something I could grip" (86). For him, the dream results in an epiphany. The narrator interprets: "It isn't so much a dream as a communication. I was being shown . . . that I had made a mistake, a lifelong mistake" (87). He eventually realizes that the Billy Rose Connection (the Bellarosa Connection) actually is not between the show-biz millionaire and Fonstein but is between Billy and the narrator himself. Harry Fonstein was an Old World European Jew; he lacked the show-biz glitter of a Billy Rose. Billy and the narrator connect because they are assimilated Jews of the New World, a world in which to keep abreast of the glitter of the Hollywood of Leslie Howard, one has to restrict emotional investment. The narrator thinks of the consequent irony: "You pay a price for being a child of the New World" (89).

The narrator gradually realizes he has endured a superficial existence. His concern about memory had related to a method rather than to people. "Memory chains are constructed thematically," he earlier explains. "Where themes are lacking there can be little or no recall. So, for instance, Billy, our friend Bellarosa, could not easily place Fonstein because of an unfortunate thinness of purely human themes—as contrasted with business, publicity, or sexual themes" (76). The narrator's growth can be measured in terms of this early statement he makes in relation to Billy but not in relation to himself, and his gradual realization that he, like Billy, has engaged in shallow relationships. It is only after working hard that he realizes the humane side of life. Once he does, he wishes to talk about the importance of the "roots of memory in feeling" and "what retention of the past really means" (102).

Just as Mosby's memoirs end with his epiphany in the Mexican tomb, his need to move out of a deadening existence, so do the memoirs of the narrator in *The Bellarosa Connection* conclude with an epiphany as he realizes his need to affirm his life force. With awakened feelings and a sense of the true importance of memory, he connects to his personal and his Jewish past. He turns to prayer, a prayer for the dead: "So that the Jews ask even God to remember, '*Yiskor Elohim*.'" (102). These last passages, as in *Mosby*, turn the ironic presentation of the ignorant protagonist-narrator in a positive direction. And the previous irony actually works to strengthen this contrasting humanistic sentiment.

Degrees of Comic Irony in the Third-Person Narrations of "What Kind of a Day Did You Have?" and *A Theft*

In *A Theft* (1989), the third-person narrator, like an obtuse first-person narrator, does not penetrate any of the ironies of situation that are revealed in the novel, particularly the ironies involving the main character, Clara Velde. The narrator records no ironic reaction to Clara's involvement in four loveless marriages to "gesture-husbands" (3), all of whom make odd mates for a sophisticated executive. This situational irony is compounded by the fact that neither the narrator nor Clara's confidante Laura Wong nor any of the other characters see Clara as less than sophisticated, capable, and mature. Saul Bellow, when questioned about Clara and her four marriages ("like her several-times-wed author"), responded casually to the *Publishers' Weekly* interviewer: "Given that 40% of marriages these days go on the rocks, you can't blame a lady for trying again and again" (Steinberg, 60). A similar dismissal of ironic contradictions in Clara's life is evident in the novella as a whole.[6]

In *A Theft*, characters have romantic ideals and speak in terms of them, but their actions directly contradict such "big ideas." Comic irony is developed by the contrast between their romantic fictions and their behavior. The characters speak of categorical imperatives, but they act in terms of relativism. And the narrator is no more privileged with a moral perspective than any of the characters. Situations are structured so that there is a juxtaposition between traditional conceptions (like the romantic notion of a soul mate) and opportunistic action (a sense of relativism, of taking advantage of any opportunity). In *A Theft*, such matters as morality, sensitivity, fidelity, and guilt—subjects dwelled on by romantic writers— are once again "turned inside-out" by the master craftsman of comic irony.

A Theft, like *Herzog*, turns serious complaint to comic purposes. In it two intelligent people—a highly successful businesswoman, Clara Velde, and her lover of twenty years, a Washington man of ideas, Ithiel Regler— become the subject of Bellow's comedy. Despite their intellectual powers, they have grave difficulties in handling crises in love and marriage. Describing her first marriage, Clara says: "This marriage was like a Thanksgiving turkey. After a month the bird is drying out and you're still eating breast of turkey. It needs more and more Russian dressing, and pretty soon the sharpest knife in the city won't slice it. . . . Pretty soon you're trying to eat threads of bird meat" (36). Of her fourth husband Clara comments: "To him inertia is the same as stability" (4). Clara and Ithiel exhibit a struggle similar to Herzog's, what Bellow terms the "portrayal (naturally comic) of the American intellectual trying to come to grips with life" (Gray, 25). The result is a novel blending the comic and the serious.

A Theft is particularly interesting for what it leaves out: the narrator's critical comments that exist in "What Kind of Day Did You Have?," an earlier novella (1974) with which it often has been connected. Clara's romantic dependency is similar to that of Katrina Goliger, heroine of this earlier novella (in *HWFIM*, 1974). Both women are middle-aged; one is married (that is, Clara is for most of her twenty-year love affair with Ithiel), the other in the process of divorcing; and both are involved in extramarital love affairs with great thinkers. Ithiel Regler is in international relations, is successful, has often been on TV; Victor Wulpy (of "What Kind of Day") is "a major figure, a world-class intellectual, big in the art world" (74). He gives lectures for audiences that range from academicians to businessmen. Both married men refuse to invest themselves fully in relationships with the women, and both de-emphasize the kind of full personal life that the heroines desire.

Clara, in *A Theft*, is more sophisticated and successful than Katrina of the earlier novella. In addition to having three daughters, she is an influential executive in a publishing company "specializing in high fashion" (2), and she moves with ease in the business world. Katrina of the 1974 novella is, on the other hand, a distressed housewife ruminating over "what a difference an independent success would make to her" (154). Katrina feels inadequate about her intellect, even though she passed an aptitude test for law with high marks (100) and even though she has learned Latin and French. Katrina feels that she is "just a humdrum housewife," a woman who had been "raised [by her father] to consider herself a nitwit" (77).

The novella "What Kind of Day Did You Have?" treats Katrina, an Emma Bovary type, with dark humor. Her limited interests and her depressive orientation are sardonically reported by the narrator: "Katrina had always tried to widen her horizons. . . . Once . . . she had taken up foreign sports cars, driving round and round the north suburbs with no destination" (100-1). For her, Victor is a life force. For her, "when the current stopped, the dullness and depression were worse than ever" (136).[7] The narrator mocks her obsession for Victor, who excites and frightens her: "She was scared by her own temerity, but even more afraid of being dumb" (121). So, too, her sister Dorothea—in the role of confidante—sarcastically comments on Katrina's romantic desires and offers her own "realistic" assertions, for example, her argument that Katrina's happiness with Victor and his circle of friends will be short lived: "Widows are forgotten pretty fast. So what happens to girl friends?" (77).

The novella sets up ironic oppositions between Katrina and Victor. In contrast to her own meager abilities, Katrina views the wondrous achievements of Victor—"the Thinker Prince" (176), "A New York-style King"—as "first-rate" (75). The narrator comments: "Katrina was enrolled as his [Victor's] only pupil. She paid her tuition with joy" (110). Victor reads widely in the classics; Katrina, because of Victor's instruction, reads Nietzsche and Céline, but it is plain that her most frequent sources of information are plebeian sources like *People Magazine* (116). Victor's writing ranges from such subjects as e.e. cummings to Paul Valery to Marxism in modern French thought (99). Katrina's writing—as well as most of her intellectual effort—centers on a children's story about a frightened elephant. Katrina sees herself as one who "could never generate any brilliancy" or anything inventive. "She could, however, be inventive in deceit" (136). She views herself as "a North Shore mother of two, in a bad, a deteriorating marriage [and] had begun to be available sexually to visitors. . . . But then, a godsend, Victor turned up" (87).

Katrina lacks Victor's sophistication: she not only misses most of Victor's erudite allusions but also finds allusions that do not exist. For example, when she agrees to fly from Chicago to Buffalo to meet him, he responds: "I ask you to meet me and it sounds like an Oriental proposition, as if the Sultan were telling his concubine to come out beyond the city walls with the elephants and the musicians." "How nice that you should mention elephants," says Katrina, whom the narrator describes as "alert at once." The narrator further explains her thoughts, showing how Katrina's romantic view of Victor influences her judgment:

"That he should refer by a single word to her elephant puzzle, her poor attempt to do something on an elephant theme, was an unusual concession. . . . Now he had dropped a hint that ordering her to fly to Buffalo was just as tedious, just as bad art, as her floundering attempt to be creative with an elephant" (89). We laugh at Katrina's "alertness" for it reflects merely wishful thinking. It seems unlikely, given Victor's self-absorption, that he would go out of his way to drop an obscure reference to Katrina's elephant story, which he finds a bore. The incongruency creates comic irony.

Katrina, the narrator wryly reports, "jumped at any chance to rush off and be with Victor" (135), whom she loves. On the other hand, Victor, the narrator points out, muses over such questions as "That she turns me on, does that mean that I love her, or does it simply mean that she belongs to the class of women that turn me on?" (139–40). Victor, because of his habitual "arrogance and detachment" (Knight, 26), rejects deep feeling for Katrina and places her and the relationship, as a whole, in a comic, trivial light: "Katrina was his manifest Eros, this worried, comical lady for whom he had such complex emotions, for the sake of which he put up with so many idiocies, struggled with so many irritations" (123).[8]

Victor's response to Katrina on the flight home, at the end of the day, accentuates her ironic position as lover. Katrina, yearning for a meaningful response, pleads: "If we don't love each other, what are we doing? How did we get here?" He asserts: "We got here because you're a woman and I'm a man" (185).[9] When Katrina finally meets with her two daughters and asks "What kind of day did you have?" (189), the narrator reports that the children answer "nothing at all. . . . Their small faces . . . communicated nothing" (189–91). Their coldness reinforces her earlier brooding concern, which—as usual—is presented with grim humor: "As a mother I seem to be an artificial product. Would that be because I can't put any sex into being a mother?" (122).

Although she has less excuse for such dependence, Clara, the successful, worldly, self-made businesswoman of *A Theft*, finds her extramarital lover of twenty years, Ithiel, as awesome as Katrina finds Victor; yet her extreme romanticism is never pointed out by the narrator. She, unlike Katrina, is never compared to Emma Bovary. Clara is proud of the man "with eyes from Greek mythology" (30), the man who has the aura of being "from antiquity," the person who "could be the Gibbon or the Tacitus of the American Empire" (55). Clara, like Katrina, celebrates her lover's intelligence, sees him as superior to her, although she suspects that he suffers from "the insignificance of the personal factor" (30).[10]

The narrator fails to see the irony that Clara and Ithiel, lovers of twenty years, have never committed to each other in marriage but instead have "'seven marriages between'" them (42); nor any irony that Clara, whom the narrator describes as an authentic self, relies on the emerald engagement ring Ithiel gave her years ago as the sustenance of her life and each time it is lost almost falls to pieces. There also is irony in that Ithiel originally bought the ring because of Clara's insistence, and its loss years later means little to him.

Clara is described by the narrator as attractive, successful, and intelligent with "short blond hair, fashionably cut, growing upon a head unusually big. . . . She needed that head; a mind like hers demanded space" (1). Little evidence, however, is presented in the novella to give credence to the narrator's high rating of Clara's mind—except for her success in the business world. The narrator also reflects on Clara's authentic self: "She must have decided long ago that for the likes of her there could be no cover-up; she couldn't divert energy into disguises. So there she was, a raw-boned American woman" (1). The narrator never acknowledges Clara's gross limitations: excessive romanticism with regard to Ithiel—romanticism that is the equal of Katrina's in the earlier novella; impaired social judgment in four times choosing "gesture-husbands" as mates; and emotional instability as evidenced in two suicide attempts. The contrast between the multiple situational ironies in Clara's life and the praise of her by the narrative voice creates irony that is similar to that achieved by the obtuse first-person narrator in *The Bellarosa Connection*. This irony is compounded by other voices in the novella who accentuate the view of Clara as an honest, authentic self. She is described this way not only by the narrator but also by her confidante Laura Wong, her au pair Gina Wegman, and her lover Ithiel. No voice comments on the irony of Clara's situation.[11]

The narrator describes Ithiel as having deep feeling for Clara, feelings connected to the depths of nature: "His continually increasing respect for her came over the horizon like a moon taking decades to rise." "Seven marriages between us, and we still love each other" she says (42). The emerald ring, which for Clara symbolizes the beauty of their relationship, also evokes the connection between the permanence of nature and the depth of her feelings for Ithiel. The connection moves toward a spiritual level of meaning: "She held the ring to her face, felt actually as if she were inhaling the green essence. . . . Still, this emerald also was an ice. In it Ithiel's pledge was frozen. Or else it represented the permanent form of the passion she had had for this man. . . . It was as real as the *green of the ocean, as the mountains in whose innards such gems are mined*" (43; italics added).

The imagery conveys a sense of timelessness. The richness of nature brings forth a sense of hope, and also the healing quality of nature is felt here.

When Clara was still single and hopeful of marrying Ithiel, she told him: "I love you with my sou'" (33), but her devotion did not deter him from having other "lady friends" (31). When he chastises her for interfering with his life, her plea "Don't go now, I'm in a bad way" (33) does not prevent him from swinging the door shut after him. Then, when he finds out about her suicide attempt, he rushes to the hospital, where he ruminates: "In all the world, now, there wasn't a civilized place left where a woman would say, 'I love you with my soul.' Only this backcountry girl was that way still." But after a very brief stay at the hospital, he abruptly departs. The narrator, with no statement on the self-deceiving hypocrisy of Ithiel, simply reports: "Straight-nosed Ithiel, heading for Washington and the Capitol dome . . . set a greater value on Clara than on anything in *this* place, or any place" (35). Again, without any acknowledgment of an ironic thrust, the narrator introduces the next section of the novella: "It was after this that Clara's marriages began—first the church wedding . . . *Tiffany engravings* . . ." (36; italics added).

Despite such ironic juxtapositions, this novella's conclusion focuses not on the helpless romanticism of Clara but on her authentic self and her ability to draw strength from this self (by herself and with the help of others). At the conclusion she is able to face life anew. The tone throughout is coolly detached—not obviously sarcastic, critical, or ironic with regard to Clara's marriages or her longstanding extramarital love affair with Ithiel. Although such inconsistencies are as easily shrugged off in the novel as they are in Bellow's comment, "You can't blame a lady for trying again and again" (Steinberg, 60), they, as well as other details of the conclusion, call into question the nature of an authentic self.

The last scene in the novella depicts Clara moved to tears by a realization that her au pair risked great danger to recover her ring and also worked with Lucy, Clara's oldest daughter, to place the ring back where it belonged. At the close of the novella, Clara is touched by the affirmation of her au pair Gina: "You were firm, according to *your* lights. I decided that you were a complete person, and the orders you gave you gave for that reason." Even though Clara protests, "I don't see any complete persons. . . . You look around for something to take hold of, and where is it?'" Gina responds, "I see it in you" (107–8). Gina continues, "But when you started to talk about the man in Washington just now, there was no nobody-anybody problem. And when the ring was stolen, it wasn't the lost property that upset you. Lost people lose 'valuables.' You only lost this particular ring." Gina concludes: "I believe you pretty well know who you are" (108).

The reader may ask questions such as "Who is Clara? What is her authentic self?" The reader may also find it ironic that Clara misjudges the Austrian au pair and Clara's oldest daughter, Lucy. Gina not only returns the stolen ring but in addition she is assisted by Lucy, the daughter whose emotional maturity had caused Clara concern. What Clara discovers when she meets Gina at this time is how incorrect her assumptions about Gina had been. Throughout the novella, Clara tries to oversee and protect Gina from the hazards of living in New York City. She stipulates rules and believes that she understands Gina's position. Clara's expectations of disaster for Gina are reversed when Gina—at the novel's end—is not ruined, but is instead self-assured, confident, and appears to be an equal (105–8).

The narrator, however, never comments on Clara's ironic misconceptions. The narrative voice focuses on the communication between Clara and Gina and also between Clara and Lucy. This communication touches Clara with a sense of shared humanity, much as the experience that Tommy Wilhelm, in *Seize the Day*, has when he observes a funeral and weeps. Although everything is different for Wilhelm after his epiphany (that is, he is ready to move toward life rather than death), Clara's breakthrough with regard to Gina and Lucy does not seem to have put her in greater touch with reality as such experiences usually do. Acceptance of the nature of her true self does not seem to have changed her need to look to Ithiel for what is right. Clara still is thinking in the same terms. Her last thoughts are on Ithiel's description of her during her earlier visit to him in Washington, when she comes to his aid after his third wife deserts him: "If anybody were to ask me, Clara, I'd say that you were a strange case—a woman who hasn't been corrupted, who developed her own moral logic" (58). As Clara recalls this conversation, she thinks: "I should have taken Ithiel's word for it. . . . He knows what the big picture is—the big, *big* picture; he doesn't flatter, he's realistic and he's truthful. I do seem to have an idea who it is that's at the middle of me" (109). That her view of Ithiel has not changed undercuts the significance of her revelation about her true self. Her continued need for his approval, his sanction of her, is disappointing and somewhat comic.

The narrator's emphasis on Clara's authentic self because she loves and follows this love ignores multiple ironies in her situation: the voice ignores the contradiction between Clara's dependence on Ithiel to define her nature and her own statement, "who it is that's at the middle of me";

310 ◆ Elaine B. Safer

the narrator ignores the contradiction between "big ideas"—like the authentic self or realness of character—and rather frantic, directionless behavior. In this novella, the reader responds to such ironies and begins to question why the third-person narrator does not. That these ironies are not picked up by any characters in the novel, including Clara's confidante Laura Wong, her au pair Gina Wegman, her lover Ithiel Regler and, of course, by Clara herself, adds to the irony. The reader thus responds to situational ironies that remain unrecognized by the obtuse third-person narrator, who behaves like a first-person narrator—similar, one could say, to the unnamed protagonist in *The Bellarosa Connection.*[12]

Thus in Bellow's most recent novellas we have representations of his comic vision of mankind. In *The Bellarosa Connection,* the first-person obtuse narrator is unnamed, possibly because he represents every man and woman—that is, all of us. In *A Theft,* the third-person narrator—in contrast to reader expectation—is (as in other contemporary novels) a voice that is no more privileged than any other voice. Both novels represent the comic vision that arises from the juxtaposition of characters' high-sounding or romantic assertions and the characters' relativistic behavior. Both novels show Bellow's ability to laugh at characters' foibles and at the human condition. When asked "what function does comedy play" in his novels and how does comedy relate to his major concerns, Bellow has responded: "Sometimes you think, what else can you do but laugh at these things. Perhaps that's the only thing—there's mercy and forgiveness in laughter" (Boyers, "Literature and Culture," 15).

Notes

A shorter version of this essay was presented at the American Literature Association Conference, 31 May–2 June 1990, Bahia Resort Hotel, San Diego, California.

1. See also Boyers, who comments on "the mixture of sweetness and sassiness, tenderness and irony, lightness and weight" in *A Theft* but says: "The ideas are present mainly to confer intellectual tone on the story. That story is hard to take seriously" ("Losing Grip," 299); Josipovici, who speaks of Bellow's "wit and painful humour" in *The Bellarosa Connection* (1181); Scheer-Schaezler, who briefly comments on the depiction of Clara's "clarity of consciousness and improved self-knowledge" at the close as exhibiting "one of Bellow's best tragi-comical scenes" ("Saul Bellow and the Values" 12–13); Pifer, who discusses the close as Clara's "celebrating that original self, or soul, existing prior to its alteration by the conditioning forces of history and culture" (183).

2. See Scheer-Schaezler's discussion of one-liners and metaphors in "Address by Gooley MacDowell to the Hasbeens Club of Chicago" ("Saul Bellow's Humor" 50–52).

3. "If you venture to think in America, you also feel an obligation to provide a historical sketch to go with it, to authenticate or legitimize your thoughts. So it's one moment of flashing insight and then a quarter of an hour of pedantry. . . . One has to feel sorry for people in such an explanatory bind. Or else (a better alternative) one can develop an eye for the comical side of this" (*More Die of Heartbreak* 247).

4. The narrator feels no compassion for the "incompetence" of Lustgarten and his repeated losses: his betrayal by his dental partner, the German dentist, when the black-market dental-supply business in which they are engaged begins to show a profit (164–66); the demolition of the Cadillac that his mother and brother had sent from America, in the hope Lustgarten would make for them a "double profit," but which Lustgarten demolishes in an absurd accident (169).

5. As Daniel Fuchs emphasizes, the "essential relationship [with Lustgarten] remains an afterthought to Mosby" (*Vision and Revision* 300).

6. In this same interview, printed shortly after the publication of *A Theft*, Saul Bellow observes: "I consider it a more straightforward story [than *Henderson the Rain King* or *Herzog*.] I think I've now done all the thinking that I'm going to do. All my life long I have been seriously pondering certain problems and I'll probably continue to do that, but I'm now in a position to use this pondering as a background for the story, and not intrude it so much into the narrative" (Steinberg 60).

7. Marianne M. Friedrich emphasizes that Emma and Katrina "are driven by a romantic longing for a goal that can never be reached. In the story, the disproportionate discrepancy in Katrina between dream and reality is represented comically in the symbol of the elephant [story]" (57).

8. Knight points out that "although she is the great giver in his life and indeed may have kept him in life, he sees her as sex partner and as object for intellectual scrutiny" (34). See also Michael Glenday, who calls Victor "one of Bellow's most biting satirical portraits of the American intellectual" (171).

9. Victor's response serves as a grim parody of Celine's *Journey to the End of Night*, in which the loving woman shoots her man because he refuses to tell her that he loves her. That Victor indeed had suggested that she read the novel compounds the irony. For Daniel Fuchs, Victor's "affection is very muted, the object of it rather dull, and the whole affair more than a bit tacky" ("On 'Him with His Foot in His Mouth'" 5).

10. Ithiel coolly disregards the problem of his third wife's loneliness by stating: "Every morning she [can] decide where to go with her credit cards" (55). This lack of concern does not trouble Clara. She, in fact, is dismayed that his wife could walk out on him: "Precious Francine had no idea what a husband she had. . . . Imagine a lowdown woman who felt that *he* didn't appreciate *her*"(55).

11. The narrator points out: "In a sophisticated boardroom Clara could be as plain as cornmeal mush, and in such a mood, when she opened her mouth, you couldn't guess whether she would speak or blow bubble gum. Yet anybody who had it in mind to get around her was letting himself in for lots of bad news" (40).

12. The emphasis on Clara's authentic self—because she loves and follows this love—contrasts with the focus on the foolishness of Katrina's love in the 1984 novella. This changed emphasis is particularly interesting coming from an author who claimed (in 1987) that "more people die of heartbreak than of radiation" (*More Die of Heartbreak* 107).

Works Cited

Bellow, Saul. *The Bellarosa Connection*. New York: Penguin Books,1989.

———. *Him with His Foot in His Mouth and Other Stories*. 1984. Reprint, New York: Pocket Books, 1985.

———. "Literature." In *The Great Ideas Today*, edited by Mortimer Adler and Robert M. Hutchins, 135–79. Chicago: *Encyclopedia Britannica*, 1963.

———. *More Die of Heartbreak*. New York: Dell, 1987.

———. "Mosby's Memoirs," *Mosby's Memoirs and Other Stories*. 1968. Reprint, New York: Penguin Books, 1988.

———. "Some Notes on Recent American Fiction." *Encounter* (November 1963): 22–29.

———. *A Theft*. New York: Penguin Books, 1989.

Bergson, Henri. "Laughter." In *Comedy*, edited by Wylie Sypher. 1956. Reprint, Baltimore: Johns Hopkins University Press, 1980.

Boyers, Robert, et al. "Literature and Culture: An Interview with Saul Bellow." *Salmagundi* 30 (Summer 1975): 6–23.

———. "Losing Grip on Specifics." Review of *A Theft*, by Saul Bellow. *Times Literary Supplement*, 24-30 March 1989, 299.

Bradbury, Malcolm. *Saul Bellow*. Contemporary Writers Series. London and New York: Methuen, 1982.

Cohen, Sarah Blacher. *Saul Bellow's Enigmatic Laughter*. Urbana: University of Illinois Press, 1974.

Dommergues, Pierre. "An Interview with Saul Bellow." *Delta* [Montpellier, France] 19 (1984): 27.

Friedrich, Marianne M. "Artistic Representation in Bellow's 'What Kind of Day Did You Have?'" *Saul Bellow Journal* 8, no. 1 (Winter 1989): 51–67.

Fuchs, Daniel. "On 'Him with His Foot in His Mouth and Other Stories.'" *Saul Bellow Journal* 5, no. 1 (Winter 1986): 3–15.

———. *Saul Bellow: Vision and Revision*. Durham, N.C.: Duke University Press, 1984.

Glenday, Michael K. "Some Versions of Real: The Novellas of Saul Bellow." In *The Modern American Novella*, edited by A. Robert Lee, 162–77. New York: St. Martin's Press, 1989.

Gray, Rockwell, et al. "Interview with Saul Bellow." *TriQuarterly* 60 (1984): 12–34.

Harper, Gordon Lloyd. "The Art of Fiction: Saul Bellow." *Paris Review* 9, no. 36 (1966): 48–73.

Josipovici, Gabriel. "The Work of Memory." Review of *The Bellarosa Connection*, by Saul Bellow. *Times Literary Supplement*, 27 October–2 November 1989, 1181.

Knight, Karl. F. "Bellow's Victor Wulpy: The Failure of Intellect." *Saul Bellow Journal* 6, no. 2 (Summer 1987): 26–35.

Oates, Joyce Carol. "Clara's Gift." Review of A *Theft*, by Saul Bellow. *New York Times Book Review*, 5 March 1989, 3.

Ozick, Cynthia. "Farcical Combat in a Busy World." Review of *Him with His Foot in His Mouth and Other Stories*, by Saul Bellow. *New York Times Book Review*, 20 May 1984, pp. 1, 44–45.

Packer, George. "Less Brains, Better Legs." Review of A *Theft*, by Saul Bellow. *The Nation*, 15 May 1989.

Pifer, Ellen. *Saul Bellow against the Grain*. Philadelphia: University of Pennsylvania Press, 1990.

Scheer-Schaezler, Brigitte. "Saul Bellow and the Values of the Western World." *Saul Bellow Journal* 8.2 (Summer 1989): 1–13.

———. "Saul Bellow's Humor and Saul Bellow's Critical Reception." *Delta* [Montpellier, France] 19 (1984): 47–65.

Shulman, Robert. "The Style of Bellow's Comedy." *PMLA* 83 (1968): 109–17.

Siegel, Ben. "'Simply Not a Mandarin': Saul Bellow as Jew and Jewish Writer." American Literature Association Conference, 31 May–2 June 1990, Bahia Resort Hotel, San Diego, CA.

Steinberg, Sybil. "A Conversation with Saul Bellow." *Publishers' Weekly*, 3 March 1989, 59–60.

Remembering and Forgetting:
The Holocaust and Jewish-American Culture in Saul Bellow's
The Bellarosa Connection

ALAN BERGER

S aul Bellow's 1989 novella *The Bellarosa Connection* is an extended meditation on the appropriate role of post-Auschwitz memory. In fact, the novella contends that remembering the *Shoah* is the litmus test of Jewish authenticity while seeking to survive as a Jew after Auschwitz. Remarkable in the work of a nonwitnessing author, Bellow's continuing concern with the Holocaust leads him in this novella to juxtapose a variety of antinomies: European Judaism and American Jewish culture—however oxymoronic the latter phrase may be; *Ahavat Yisrael* (genuine love of the Jewish people) and superficial concern; survivors and nonwitnesses; gratitude and indifference; and remembering and forgetting. All of these oppositions revolve around the *Shoah*. Coral Fenster is correct in noting that, "The story's protagonist is the Holocaust."[1] Unlike Steven Spielberg's *Schindler's List*, however, Bellow attempts neither to create a memory where none exists, nor to sensationalize. Rather, this richly crafted tale is a superb character portrait in which the author underscores both the role of memory and the deleterious impact of American culture on this central category of Jewish existence.

Always the metaphysician, albeit in secular garb, Bellow comments on the inadequacy of pre-Holocaust thought to confront the catastrophe of European Jewry. Writing in *To Jerusalem and Back*, the Nobel Laureate observes that::

The Holocaust may even be seen as a deliberate lesson or project in philosophical redefinition: "You religious and enlightened people, you Christians, Jews, and Humanists, believers in freedom, dignity, and enlightenment—you think that you know what a human being is. We will show you what he is, and what you are. Look at our camps and crematoria and see if you can bring your hearts to care about these millions."[2]

How, then, can one remember what defeats humanity itself?

In his longer novels such as *Herzog* and *Mr. Sammler's Planet*, Bellow's protagonists, the nonwitnessing Moses Herzog and the survivor Artur Sammler, attempt to confront the Holocaust; Herzog obliquely and the survivor Sammler directly deriving lessons from the Jewish experience. Yet nowhere is Bellow's insistence on the noncomprehensibility of the *Shoah* more starkly presented than in *The Bellarosa Connection*.[3] The story's nameless narrator, founder of the Mnemosyne Institute in Philadelphia, comes to understand that memory indifferent to the human dimension is useless and, further, that he himself—an assimilated intermarried Jew who had paid a [Jewish] price for "being a child of the New World" (89)—had understood nothing about the Holocaust.

In what follows, I first present the outline of the novella, commenting on the form of the tale in relation to Bellow's artistry. Next, I discuss the post-Holocaust role of memory and witness, while distinguishing three types of response; that embodied by the survivor, by his nonwitnessing wife, and by native-born Americans whose relationship to the *Shoah* is at best tenuous. This is followed by an inquiry into Bellow's understanding of the transrational nature of Jewish identity as it emerges in the relationship between old and new world Judaism. Finally, I conclude with some observations about shaping Holocaust memory in America.

The Bellarosa Connection: Form and Content

Bellow's novellas have thus far been paid little critical attention. As such, they share the fate of much of the author's short fiction. Yet Bellow himself views short narratives as "particularly suitable for the modern life style."[4] As for *The Bellarosa Connection*, I am aware of only three scholarly articles: one on the theme of ironies and insights by Coral Fenster, one on comic irony by Elaine B. Safer, and one on the concept of memory by Regine Rosenthal. In addition, Ruth Miller briefly discusses the novella in her controversial study, *Saul Bellow: A Biography of the Imagination*.[5] These studies, plus a handful of reviews, are hardly fitting for a work as significant as *The Bellarosa Connection* with its ironic, sensitive, and compelling look at the state of American Jewish culture as measured against the vanished world of *Yiddishkeit* with its emphasis on both comedy and the unity of *Klal Yisrael* (the community of Israel). Indeed, Bellow told a 1990 interviewer that, "Somehow I managed to miss the significance of some very great events. I didn't take hold of them as I now see I might have done. Not until *The Bellarosa Connection*."[6]

The novella's anonymous millionaire narrator, Bellow's own voice, after forty years (a biblical generation) in the memory business, longs to "forget about remembering." Like Dr. Braun in Bellow's short story "The Old System," the narrator provides a summing up of the events of his life along with a startling two-fold admission: that he had really understood nothing of importance, i.e., the murder of European Jewry and the necessity of utilizing memory to bear witness rather than recalling mere data. With the institute in the hands of his son, the narrator reflects on his own lifelong preoccupation. He observes that:

> In your twilight years, having hung up your gloves (or sheathed your knife), you don't want to keep doing what you did throughout your life: a change, a change—your kingdom for a change! A lawyer will walk away from his clients, a doctor from his patients, a general will paint china, a diplomatist turn worldly success to the innate gift of memory— a tricky word, "innate," referring to the hidden sources of everything that really matters. (2)

If, as he used to tell clients, "Memory is life," then "there is no retirement except in death" (2).

Bellow's use of the comic is a crucial aspect of *The Bellarosa Connection*. As Elaine Safer's illuminating study shows, Bellow is a writer in the comedic vein. Analogizing him to Sholom Aleichem, she notes that he fuses the "sacred and the secular, the mythological and the mundane."[7] "It is through comedy," she observes, "that Bellow is able to present the leading issues of our times, enabling us to laugh at his characters' flawed attempts to achieve their goals, and thus enabling us to better accept our own unrealized aspirations."[8] Bellow in fact refers to himself as a "comic writer with a weakness for ideas." "If I am granted another twenty years of life," he attests, "I may get it right."[9] One of many examples of Bellow's ironic humor comes in his description of the narrator. Not completely at home in his luxurious surroundings—the Philadelphia mansion with twenty-foot ceilings, the rooms of which contained eighteenth-century furniture chosen by his late wife—the narrator remembers that his origins

were simpler. He'd been the child of Russian Jews from New Jersey and rejected the sham and posturing of those who ignored "the true facts." He
recalls that whenever he was "tempted to fake it, I asked myself, 'And how
are things out in New Jersey?' " This calls to mind Moses Herzog's letter to
his former classmate Shapiro, now a scholar with Anglo-Saxon
affectations. Herzog writes the man: "You are too intelligent for this. You
inherited rich blood. Your father peddled apples." It is the soul, not
material things, which brings truth. In an example of Bellovian humor, the
narrator recalls waking in his "fifty-fifty bed—half Jewish, half Wasp" (88).

Memory and Witness: Three Models

The narrator remembers—of course, memory never fails him—the late
Harry Fonstein and his deceased wife Sorella. These memories are
distinctly different, however, from the type on which he made his fortune.
He confesses at age seventy to being preoccupied "with feelings and
longings, and emotional memory is nothing like rocketry or gross national
product." Again, like Dr. Braun in "The Old System," the narrator of *The
Bellarosa Connection* needs to learn to abandon objectivity in order to get in
touch with his emotions and feelings: characteristics which distinguish
Yiddishkeit from contemporary cultural *naarishkeit* (foolishness, in the form
of denial of identity, self-indulgence, detachment, a desire for possessions,
and a passion only for ostentation—as in the Billy Rose and the show
business culture of America).[10]

Harry Fonstein is a Holocaust survivor. His tale is exemplary for the
narrator's father who hoped that it would be instructive for his son to hear
what the Jews of Europe suffered in the real world while the
thirty-two-year-old American-born Jew was still behaving like a
"twelve-year-old, hanging out in Greenwich Village, immature, drifting, a
layabout, shacking up with Bennington girls, a foolish intellectual
gossip"(5). "I was at the bar of paternal judgement again," notes the
narrator, "charged with American puerility" (5). Bellow here establishes
the initial antinomy between American Jews and the Jews of Europe who
were singled out for extermination.

Fleshing out the typologies, Bellow describes Fonstein as having
"survived the greatest ordeal of Jewish history." One did not "want to play
the fool with Fonstein," whom the narrator sized up as a Central European
Jewish type. As for Fonstein, an *Edel* (well-bred person), Bellow describes
him as viewing the protagonist as an "immature unstable Jewish American,
humanly ignorant and loosely kind: in the history of civilization, *something
new in the way of human types; perhaps not so bad as it looked at first*" (italics

added, 7). Bellow has established both that Jewish-American culture is inchoate and malformed, and that the action of the novel focuses on a battle for the narrator's Jewish soul.

Concerning the pernicious impact of American culture both on Jewish sensitivities and Holocaust remembrance, Bellow pulls no punches. He told an interviewer that at the time of writing *The Adventures of Augie March*:

> Things got away from me. The Holocaust for one. I was really very incompletely informed. I may even have been partly sealed off from it because I had certainly met lots of people in Paris when I lived there who had been through it. I understood what had happened. Somehow I couldn't tear myself away from my American life.[11]

Further, before going to Auschwitz in 1959 when "the Holocaust landed its full weight on me," Bellow observes that he was "still so absorbed in [his] American life that I couldn't turn away from it. I wasn't ready to think about Jewish history. I don't know why. There it is."[12] Now, however, Bellow's position has come full circle. He is defined by Jewish history. In fact, the narrator says that whereas in the beginning he was not inclined to discuss Jewish history with her [Clara], "it put my teeth on edge at first—but she overcame my resistance" (28). He realizes that, "besides, damn it, you couldn't say no to Jewish history after what happened in Nazi Germany" (28).

As noted, Bellow does not sensationalize, but he does provide vivid detail. For example, Fonstein wore a four-inch orthopedic shoe—the narrator refers to him as a "gimpy Galitzianer"—which he never removed because, if it had been stolen, "he would have been caught and killed in his short-legged nakedness. The SS would not have bothered to drive him into a cattle car" (21). Escaping from Poland with his mother, they make their way to Italy where the woman dies. Harry continues to Milan and learns Italian. He serves as an interpreter and even works as a waiter at a party for Hitler. There was no color in the tyrants face, notes Fonstein, because he "wasn't killing anyone that day."

Arriving in America via Cuba, Fonstein enters into an arranged marriage with Sorella. In an adaptation of the Levirite Marriage custom prescribed in the book of Deuteronomy, which prescribes that the surviving brother must marry his deceased sibling's widow, Salkind, Sorella's unmarried uncle, insures the marriage of his brother's daughter. She is obese, educated, and a rememberer. Like her husband, Sorella may be "damaged goods," but both of them join in the common cause of bearing witness. Unlike the obese Tina in "The Old System," size becomes

Sorella. Indeed, "Obesity, for Bellow, is usually an endearing quality."[13] Following the war, Harry and Sorella learn for certain that his life had been saved by the Mafia acting at the behest of Billy Rose. It was under Rose's aegis that the organization arranged to save Harry, and other Jews, from Rome prisons where they awaited execution. Despite Fonstein's repeated attempts to personally thank the entrepreneur for saving his life, Rose refuses to meet with him. Unlike Oskar Schindler, Billy Rose wanted nothing to do with the Jews whom he had rescued.

Bellow's choice of Billy Rose seems improbable. Rose is a multimillionaire showman who associates with hoodlums. Vulgar, small in stature, rumored to be impotent, and sexually immature, Rose is perhaps the least likely person to be involved in rescuing fellow Jews. Yet, Bellow describes "spots of deep feeling in flimsy Billy." The showman "was as splattered as a Jackson Pollock painting, and among the main trickles was his Jewishness" (13). "The God of his fathers," writes Bellow of Rose, "still mattered." Further, Rose "produced" the Madison Square Garden Rally at which the audience could weep publicly and anonymously. Thus, Bellow establishes the fact that Jewishness is not completely expunged by American culture. Traces may remain, no matter how transmuted. Further, in a life defined by a compulsive need for seeing his name in the paper— "he had a bug-like tropism for publicity"—he insisted on keeping secret his European rescue operation.

The character of Sorella is finely drawn and illustrates both Bellow's use of the comic as well as his understanding of the role of bearing witness to the *Shoah*. Initially, the narrator is put off by her obesity and her "preposterous pince-nez." He wonders if such people are "female impersonators, drag queens?" (19). Yet, the narrator quickly realizes that he "was altogether wrong, dead wrong about Sorella" (20). Sorella, whose name can be understood as meaning sorrow, or *tsouris*—she is constantly speaking of Jewish history and the Holocaust—is physically immense. Hence, Bellow's description: "She made you look twice at a doorway. When she came to it, she filled the space like a freighter in a canal lock" (48). Yet, it is this very immensity which enables Sorella to confront the *Shoah*.[14] Bellow observes that: "Maybe Sorella was trying to incorporate in fatty tissue some portion of what [her husband] had lost—members of his family" (48). It is as if Bellow is sketching a physical characteristic necessary to take in the enormity of the loss of European Jewry.

Sorella can also be understood as a secularized version of the *Eshet Hayil*, the woman of valor. Taken from the book of Proverbs and, later, ascribed by kabbalistic thought to the *Shekhinah* (Feminine aspect of God), the *Eshet Hayil* also refers, in the sixteenth-century Kabbalah of Isaac

Luria, to both the Jewish housewife and to the Sabbath itself. Among the characteristics of this woman of valor, whose "price is far above rubies," are the following: "She doeth (her husband) good and not evil, all the days of her life"; "Strength and majesty are her clothing"; "She openeth her mouth with wisdom"; and "Favor is false, and beauty is vain; But a woman that feareth the Lord, she shall be praised." Translated into the example of Sorella Fonstein, it is important to note that she is termed a "Tiger Wife"; her *obsession* is to get Billy Rose to agree to acknowledge Harry's gratitude. Confronting Rose in the King David Hotel, she is described as a "formidable, clever wife. The protection [Fonstein] lacked when he was in flight from Hitler he had found on our side of the Atlantic" (53). She even attempts blackmail to achieve this goal. Moreover, Sorella's indefatigable research into the Holocaust is undertaken "to assist her husband" (28). Further, Sorella is instrumental in Harry's attaining considerable material success. Fonstein patents a thermostat, "and with Sorella's indispensable help he becomes a rich man" (21). Without her, he attests, "there would have been no patent" (21). Fonstein had begun to "go American," which was the narrator's "mental advice." And, indeed, Harry and Sorella did not need such advice. They soon "passed from decent prosperity to real money" (29).

Billy Rose, in contradistinction to both Fonstein and Sorella, has no use for memory. Attempting to jog Billy's memory of Fonstein's many unanswered letters to him, Rose responds, "Remember, forget—what's the difference to me?" (53). Attaching no significance to his rescue of Fonstein, and others like him, he tells Sorella, "Lady, this is one of a trillion incidents in a life like mine. Why should I recollect it?" (53). At this point, the reader recalls Bellow's aphorism that memory is life, and forgetting is death. Yet Rose displays a characteristically American penchant. The narrator observes that the showman may even be emulating, however unconsciously, George Washington's advice against "entangling alliances."

But Bellow shrewdly draws his portrait of Billy Rose. The entrepreneur is far from a one-dimensional character. For example, he remembers one thing with great clarity, telling Sorella that "I did all I could, and for that point of time, that's more than most can say." Bellow, through Rose, then accurately points a historical finger at Roosevelt's "Politics of Rescue," Churchill's complicity, and the ineffectiveness of Jewish leadership, personified by Rabbi Stephen Wise, and the Jewish advisors to Roosevelt such as Sam Rosenman, whom the historian Henry Feingold refers to as "*Sha sha* Jews"; i.e., those to whom their Jewishness was merely an accident of birth. In view of all this, Billy tells Sorella that he abandoned "single-party rescue operations" and began raising money to buy ships in order to get refugees/survivors into British-blockaded Palestine. Billy's defense is both self-serving and sobering. He could, and should, have met with Fonstein. Fonstein himself interprets this refusal as part of the change that comes over immigrants in America. Yet, the showman's statement also underscores the complexity of the rescue issue by pointing up Western bureaucratic complicity in the "Final Solution."

The narrator offers Sorella his own interpretations of Rose's refusal to meet. Perhaps the meeting would have eventuated in a "too Jewish moment"; dragging "him down from his standing as a full-fledged American" (23). Yet the facts of American governmental indifference, not to mention acquiescence in Hitler's extermination of European Jewry, are an integral part of the story of the Holocaust.[15] In a similar fashion, Bellow indirectly engages the ongoing debate over whether American Jewry did all that it could during the *Shoah*.

Sorella's encounter with Billy at the King David Hotel in Jerusalem reveals several points crucial to the novella. For example, both figures are oddities, she physically and he behaviorally. Further, the difference between American culture and Jewish memory concerning the *Shoah* is also emphasized as is the attenuation of Jewish identity in the *Goldeneh Medinah*. Sorella brings a pack of incriminating documents to her meeting with Rose. These documents, containing a mixture of fiscal improprieties and sexual scandal, had been secretly compiled by Ms. Hamet (*khomet*=horse collar), Rose's now-deceased longtime private secretary. Finally unable to appeal to Billy on the human level, Sorella throws the envelope at him. Prior to this, however, there ensues a discussion which reveals the two points referred to above. For example, in response to Sorella's observation that Jews in America, who were not threatened, have a "special duty to come to terms with [the *Shoah*]" (60), Billy pointed out that Fonstein had suffered much less than others; he was not in Auschwitz, had not been tattooed, and was not set to work cremating those who'd been gassed. Rose believes the matter settled. In any event, he is in Jerusalem with the Japanese architect Isamu Noguchi, who is to help him plan the sculpture garden which Billy is donating to the city of Jerusalem.

Sorella interprets the matter as illustrating the enervating effect of American culture on Jewish identity. She tells the narrator the following: "The Jews could survive everything that Europe threw at them. I mean the lucky remnant. But," she tellingly adds, "now comes the next test— America. Can they hold their ground, or will the U.S.A. be too much for them?" (65). The portrait Bellow paints of Billy Rose is, in its own way, a confirmation of this question about the test that America poses for Jews and Judaism. Sorella's interview with Billy is "an American thing." Billy is,

of course, weak, vain, and trivial. Yet, he is—in a childish way—
"big-minded and spacious; . . . dropping fifteen to twenty actual millions
on a rest-and-culture garden in Jerusalem, the core of Jewish history, the
navel of the earth" (75). Bellow is affirming the observation that in
America, Jewish culture is "a mile wide and an inch deep."

The narrator of Bellow's tale is a professional rememberer who only
learns late in life the true meaning and purpose of memory. During the first
part of *The Bellarosa Connection*, he recalls the Fonsteins' attempt to meet Billy.
The second part of the novella, however, is concerned with the narrator's
attempt to find the Fonsteins whom he has not seen in the thirty years since
they had inadvertently discovered each other in Jerusalem. The narrator had
been asked by the Israelis to establish a Mnemosyne institute. Israel,
however, rooted in authentic Jewish memory, requires no such enterprise.

Transrational Nature of Jewish Identity

While clearly different from Sorella, the narrator shares with her a
transrational understanding of Jewish identity. He observes that "There
was also the heart beating in her [in me too] with the persistence of fidelity,
a faith in the necessary continuation of a radical mystery—don't ask me to
spell it out" (40). Thus Jewish existence itself is presented as a mystery, the
meaning of which lies beyond the grasp of the merely rational. Much in
the manner of Elie Wiesel for whom the "essence of Judaism is mystical
and not rational," the narrator views Jewish existence as suprarational. Yet
the narrator, like Fonstein, is also connected to Billy Rose. Unlike the
survivor who owed Billy his life, the narrator's connection is revealed in his
own quest for financial gain, his embrace of the New World, and in his
initial disdain for emotions.

The narrator has not seen the Fonsteins in thirty years.
"Remembering them so well," he muses, "did I need actually to see them?"
But he is also struck by a deep longing for them, especially for Sorella. He
recalls thinking that perhaps he could see them at Passover, but then parses
the word as it is used in the American context, e.g., Passover means to pass
over or ignore family and feelings. The narrator suddenly receives a call
from Jerusalem. A "rabbi x/y" is seeking financial assistance for a
deranged survivor named Fonstein who claims to be related to Harry.
The rabbi wants the narrator's help in locating Harry in order to
substantiate the man's claim.

The call from Jerusalem establishes the ties of *Klal Yisrael* (community
of Israel) which the narrator finds inexplicably irresistible. Further, this call
also signals his transition to a witness bearer. Bellow then sketches a scene

of great comedy. The narrator discovers that he is unable to remember the name Swanee, when he begins singing the song "Swanee River." We recall at this point the aphorism, "Forgetfulness equals death," in this case, death of the comfortable rationalist who unflatteringly but accurately describes himself as being, if "not an assimilationist . . . an avoider of uncomfortable mixtures, and in the end . . . stuck with these 20 rooms"—the Philadelphia mansion (79).

His search for the Fonsteins leads the narrator to make a series of telephone calls, two of which provide further evidence of the extent to which Sorella's query about the Jews being able to hold their own ground in the United States of America must be answered in the negative. The first call is to Hyman Swerdlow, a direct relative of Fonstein. A successful investment counselor, he was very polite and solicitous. Swerlow's character prompts Bellow to accurately observe that "one could assimilate now without converting." Further, Swerdlow, opines the narrator, "had discovered a way to drain the 'Jewish charge' from the ancient Jewish face he'd inherited from his father." Jewish identity has become merely one of the investment counselor's options, rather than his destiny. For example, the narrator's comment to Swerdlow that the *Shoah* shatters the idea of Justice falls on deaf ears. Swerdlow is the perfect bureaucrat, bereft of all emotions and severed from any ties to *Klal Yisrael.*

The narrator then reports a dream in which he, Joseph-like, finds himself in a hole, a dark pit which—struggle though he might—he cannot escape. Moreover, this is no mere hole. Rather, it is a "trap" which has been prepared for him. His struggles to climb out are observed by the shadowy figure who has planned the trap. Realizing the dream as a revelation, the narrator experiences the "complete conviction of error, my miscalculation of strength . . . I had made a mistake, a lifelong mistake: something wrong, false, now fully manifest" (87). This epiphanous moment then yields transforming knowledge. "Revelations in old age" he attests, "can shatter everything you've put in place from the beginning" (87). The new revelation stands in stark contrast to his prior and highly naive assumptions, such as the narrator's earlier belief about the role of Jews in America. Prior to his revelation, the narrator believed that in America, Jews "were equal," strong, "and not [to] be put to death as Jews [in Europe] had been." Realizing the folly of this view, he concludes that while in its grasp, he was incapable of understanding the real facts in the case of Fonstein. "I hadn't understood Fonstein vs Rose, . . . You pay a price for being a child of the New World" (89).

The narrator had spent a lifetime shielding himself from "unbearable . . . recognitions—of murder, of relish in torture, of the ground bass of brutality, without which no human music ever is performed" (90). He recalls his late father's far different response to state-sponsored mass murder. Driving through the vast tracts of empty land in Pennsylvania, the narrator's father tells his son that the Jews in Europe could have been rescued and brought to the state. By this point in his life, the narrator feels like a "socket that remembers its tooth" (79).

The second phone call is to the Fonsteins where the phone is answered by a young man who is house-sitting. At this time, the narrator learns several things. Harry and Sorella are dead, killed in a car crash on the New Jersey Turnpike. "Harry's forty American years of compensation," muses the narrator, "for the destruction of his family in Poland suddenly were up" (97). Second, Gilbert, the Fonstein's son, biographically illustrates the decline of Judaism in American culture. This son of a survivor showed early promise as a math and physics prodigy; Harry had even consulted with the narrator about the boy's education. Now he is in Las Vegas, heavily involved in gambling and sexual licentiousness. Further, Gilbert has written a book on winning at Black Jack. Moreover, while not disowning his Jewish identity, Gilbert is described by the house sitter as "only caring to lead an American life" (97). Sorella's own son is, therefore, proof that America is "too much" for Jews. This prompts the narrator's observation that Gilbert is "more in the Billy Rose vein than the Harry Fonstein vein" (100).

Shaping Holocaust Memory in America

The narrator concludes by embracing a "Jewish" definition of memory. He notes that "the roots of memory are in feeling—about the themes that collect and hold memory." Further, remembering the past involves both man and God. Jews ask even their ancient divine covenantal partner to remember, *Yiskor Elohim*. "If sleep is forgetting, forgetting is also sleep, and sleep is to consciousness what death is to life" (102). Consequently, to remember is both to live and to feel and to be in a relationship with God. But is this possible as Judaism in America hurtles towards the twenty-first Christian century?

Yosef Hayyim Yerushalmi notes that the verb *Zakhor* (remembered) "appears in its various declensions in the Bible no less than 169 times, usually with either Israel or God as the subject, for memory is incumbent upon both" (5).[16] Yet as Yerushalmi observes, memory "flowed [in the Bible], above all, through two channels: ritual and recital."[17] But, and this is Yerushalmi's main point, "In modern times the decline of Jewish collective memory . . . is only a symptom of the unraveling of that common network of belief and praxis through whose mechanism . . . the past was once made present."[18] Surely Bellow, more than most, is keenly aware of this sharp break in the continuity of Jewish living and the ever-growing decay of Jewish group memory. In fact this novella is about little else than the difficulty of remembering the Holocaust in America.

What Bellow offers in place of a collective memorial ritual is a *personal* connection to a world-historical event. The fact that Harry Fonstein is not a blood relative of the narrator marks the difference between European and American responses to the *Shoah*. American Jews are connected to the Event, yet remain at an impenetrable remove. Further, in emphasizing the prominent role played by feeling as opposed to solely rational thought, Bellow brings to mind the Yiddish proverb: "The Heart is Half a Prophet." The narrator comes to realize that memory *theory* is like a body without a soul. Sorella provides a paradigmatic response to memory. She remembers, feels, and acts.[19] Her stance is in opposition to that of Billy Rose and to the narrator's pre-epiphanous life. Moreover, Bellow emphasizes family connections as the lifeforce of memory. In addition, the novella takes evil seriously yet does so while employing the comedic mode. Finally, even though God is the premier rememberer, deity is petitioned to remember those who are dead. Retelling the tales of those caught in the fiery tentacles of the Holocaust insures that the dead live in our memory. To forget means, therefore, that both we and the victims die. They for a second time.

Notes

1. Coral Fenster, "Ironies and Insights in *The Bellarosa Connection*," *Saul Bellow Journal* 9, no. 2 (1990): 21.

2. Saul Bellow, *To Jerusalem and Back* (New York: Viking Press, 1976).

3. Saul Bellow, *The Bellarosa Connection* (New York: Penguin, 1989). Page numbers in the text are from this edition.

4. Cited by Marianne M. Friedrich, *Character and Narration in the Short Fiction of Saul Bellow* (New York: Peter Lang, 1995), 4.

5. Ruth Miller, *Saul Bellow: A Biography of the Imagination* (New York: St. Martin's Press, 1991). Bellow's disagreement with this project is well known.

6. Interview of Saul Bellow in *Bostonia* (November/December 1990): 47.

7. Elaine B. Safer, "Degrees of Comic Irony in *A Theft* and *The Bellarosa Connection*," *Saul Bellow Journal* 9, no. 2 (1990): 2. On the matter of the comic in Bellow, see Sarah Blacher Cohen, *Saul Bellow's Enigmatic Laughter* (Urbana: University of Illinois Press, 1974).

8. Safer, 3.

9.Robert Boyers, "Moving Quickly: An Interview with Saul Bellow," *Salmagundi* 106–7 (Spring–Summer 1995): 41.

10. On the issue of show business in *The Bellarosa Connection*, see Safer.

11. Saul Bellow, *Bostonia* interview.

12. Saul Bellow, *Bostonia* interview.

13. Miller, *Saul Bellow*, 180.

14. Linking Sorella both with sorrow and the comic, David Denby writes, "The comedy of *The Bellarosa Connection* is generated precisely by its improbability, the forced yoking of this extreme of American-Jewish shallowness with a woman so powerfully representing the moral sorrows of the ages." David Denby, "Memory in America," *New Republic*, 1 January 1990, 39. Thus sorrow, rather than Sarah (Surelleh) appears closer to the mark. On Sorella's role as a rememberer as opposed to the indifference of the New World, Denby notes that in Bellow's novella "the Old World Jews & Sorella, generically, is one of them, brought up in grief, can never give up their obsession with dignity and obligation, while the New World Jews are moving too fast to allow themselves to be hindered by any claims at all."

15. The bibliography here is vast. The following are merely representative: Henry Feingold, *The Politics of Rescue: The Roosevelt Administration and the Holocaust* (New Brunswick: Rutgers University Press, 1970); Arthur Morse, *While Six Million Died* (New York: Secker & Warburg, 1968); and David Wyman, *The Abandonment of the Jews: America and the Holocaust 1942–1945* (New York: Pantheon, 1984).

16. Yosef Hayyim Yerushalmi, *Zakhor: Jewish History and Jewish Memory* (Seattle: University of Washington Press, 1982), 5.

17. Yerushalmi, *Zakhor*, 11.

18. Yerushalmi, *Zakhor*, 94.

19. For a discussion of Sorella as a Bellovian heroine see Fenster, 22 and 27.

Works Cited

Bellow, Saul. *The Bellarosa Connection*. New York: Penguin, 1989.

———. *To Jerusalem and Back*. New York: Viking Press, 1976.

———. Interview in *Bostonia* (November/December 1990): 32-47.

Boyers, Robert. "Moving Quickly: An Interview with Saul Bellow." *Salmagundi* 106–7 (Spring–Summer 1995): 35-53.

Cohen, Sarah Blacher. *Saul Bellow's Enigmatic Laughter*. Urbana: University of Illinois Press, 1974.

Denby, David. "Memory in America." *New Republic*, 1 January 1990, 37-40.

Fenster, Coral. "Ironies and Insights in *The Bellarosa Connection*." *Saul Bellow Journal* 9, no. 2 (1990): 20-28.

Friedrich, Marianne M. *Character and Narration in the Short Fiction of Saul Bellow*. New York: Peter Lang, 1995.

Miller, Ruth. *Saul Bellow: A Biography of the Imagination*. New York: St. Martin's Press, 1991.

Safer, Elaine B. "Degrees of Comic Irony in *A Theft* and The Bellarosa Connection." *Saul Bellow Journal* 9, no. 2 (1990): 1-19.

Yerushalmi, Yosef Hayyim. *Zakhor: Jewish History and Jewish Memory.* Seattle: University of Washington Press, 1982.

Something to Remember Me By:
Four Fictions of Memory

S. LILLIAN KREMER

During most of his prolific career, Saul Bellow has written critically acclaimed long and short fiction. In recent years, however, he has forsaken the broad canvas of his novels for Chekhovian brevity, replacing the multiplicity of stories illustrating a theme with a single exemplary tale. He has, as David Denby recognizes, "perfected a method of narrative suspension in which an entire life is encompassed, through expansion and digression, in a day or two of time" (58). In the foreword to *Something to Remember Me By*, Bellow observes that as the millennium ends, the modern reader is "perilously overloaded" and public life is full of distractions: "We have heard it all. We have no time," thereby explaining his recent exclusive adoption of the short fiction mode. Conscious of his own diminishing years, the sage reminds us repeatedly of the dual imperatives of the material and spiritual informing the human condition, increasingly situating his protagonists in incidents that anticipate the re-evaluation of an entire life: the "turntable" on which the character has been spinning becomes a "vortex" into which he is drawn.

A significant portion of Bellow's lyrical short fiction consists of narratives rooted in recollection of the past, often evoking healing nostalgia tempered by an indictment of a century and a contemporary America that have fallen short of their early promise. In the Bellovian universe, rejection of memory is a source of moral decay and enlightened embrace of memory is a source of spiritual and moral growth. Bellow's exploration of the significance of memory is revealed from the middle of the canon through the present in four fictions of old men remembering the past: Willis Mosby in "Mosby's Memoirs," Samuel Braun in "The Old System," the unnamed narrator in *The Bellarosa Connection,* and a dying father, Louie, of "Something to Remember Me By."[1] Each protagonist considers himself or persons of his past, either in obliviousness to memory's relevance or in appreciation of its significance. The first two stories appeared in the same collection as contrapuntal inquiries. The final two tales, one dealing with collective memory and the other with private memory, open and close Bellow's most recent publication. *The Bellarosa Connection* combines, in a single figure, many of the essential attitudes toward remembrance exhibited by Mosby and Braun, and "Something to Remember Me By" begins in the particularity of private memory and concludes with its universal implications. The four stories are united by a common preoccupation with memory and characters who are ready to confront the personal, social, or historic pasts that shaped their lives.

I

Mosby's memoirs focus on his long career and evidence no regrets, no sincere confession of mistakes, no sense of personal failure. A paradoxical figure, Willis Mosby is "erudite, maybe even profound" (151), a man who "thought much, accomplished much, [yet] had made some of the most interesting mistakes a man could make in the twentieth century" (151). A Rhodes Scholar, a professor of political theory at Princeton University until his forced retirement, "a fanatic about ideas" (153), Mosby is guilty of intellectual pride. His hubris is manifested in the conviction that his superior wit and intellect have led to exceptional analysis of the century's major intellectual and political movements and in his denunciation of Princeton for being unable to cope with his "acid elegance, logical tightness, factual punctiliousness, and merciless laceration in debate" (168). Snubbed by Jean Paul Sartre and Claude Levi Straus, disliked by Dean Acheson and Dulles, whom he blames for depriving him of an important postwar position, he feels superior to the men who shaped the world and devotes much of his thought to criticism of their philosophic and practical endeavors.

Mosby intends his memoirs to be an intellectual history of the age, in the manner of Santayana, Malraux, Sartre, or Lord Russell, but he believes that the density of his intellectual and political observations should be lightened by a humorous digression. Determined to avoid what he perceives as the pitfalls of other intellectuals, Mosby settles his satiric gaze on "Jewish Daddy Lustgarten," a bungler he knew in postwar Europe, whose leftist political sympathies he lampoons as he reveals his own admiration of Franco. Aptly described by Elaine Safer as "an ignorant interpreter of characters and ideas" (5), Mosby regards Lustgarten as a chronic loser, a schlemiel, who fails romantically, politically, and economically. Although his analysis embodies a measure of truth, it is nonetheless distorted, and Mosby's detached appraisal of Nazi concentration camps as proof of the rationality of German political ideas is as horrific as it is revealing.

Bellow introduces Lustgarten as a foil to damn Mosby. In contrast to Mosby's unswerving political views, Lustgarten changes his political philosophy from Marxism to Leninism to Trotskyism and then to inept capitalism. Incapable of comprehending Lustgarten's humanity, Mosby understands neither his passion for his family nor his concern for political morality. Lustgarten's love of his children simply inspires Mosby to reflect that Plato considered childbreeding the lowest level of human creativity. Repulsed by Lustgarten's emotional attachments, Mosby unveils his own detachment by exploiting Lustgarten's plight as fodder for his comic digression. "Stone-hearted Mosby, making fun of flesh and blood, of these little humanities with their short inventories of bad and good" (162); "with hate, he pondered their mistakes, their shallowness" (155).

Memory of Lustgarten fails to liberate Mosby. It provides him no human association. Lustgarten is emblematic of ordinary humanity and in betraying him first, through cuckoldry and later, through distorted characterization, Mosby betrays humanity. Mosby also remains unrepentant—unlike Samuel Braun, who learns from his ancestors; the *Bellarosa* narrator, who acknowledges his failure to value the human connections of the past; and Louie, who provides a memoir as spiritual legacy for his son. Albeit writing an intellectual memoir intimates a reflective temperament, Mosby's thought reveals his intolerant spirit. He is certain that he has "disposed of all things human," that he has "completed himself in this cogitating, unlaughing, stone, iron, nonsensical form" (176).

During an unguarded moment of fear in a subterranean tomb, Mosby has a premonition of his own death and realizes the barrenness of a life devoid of meaningful human connection. As Robert Kiernan argues, "Mosby suffers a purgatorial experience of the purest kind: the transcendence of all things human, the absence of God, the sense of living a logical dead end" (135). The purgatorial scene suggests authorial censure. Yet Bellow provides no evidence that Mosby intends to reform. In contrast with the experiences of other Bellow protagonists such as Tommy Wilhelm, Moses Herzog, and Artur Sammler, whose epiphanal experiences promise (or are substantiated in) transformation, Mosby's spiritual insight is fleeting. Unchastened and unconnected to community,

Mosby denies the significance of his brief glimpse of "the grace of life" (176). He is doomed "to live life to the end as Mosby" (174). Incapable of the compassion that Braun, the *Bellarosa* narrator, and Louie summon in their recollections, Mosby reveals himself as a hollow man.

II

Bellow employs conventional flashback in "Mosby's Memoirs" and in *The Bellarosa Connection*. In "The Old System," he introduces more sophisticated and symbolic approaches to counterpoint past and present. Just as eating a bit of cake begins the journey back in time for Marcel Proust's central consciousness, the simple act of washing initiates for Braun a flowing remembrance of times past. Thoughts and feelings about his Jewish past begin to emerge in spontaneous recollection as the biochemist reflects on the difference between his simple act of physical hygiene and the ablutions of his ancestors, for whom every act was religious, "for whom bathing was a solemnity" (48).[2]

Time and juxtaposition of the Hebrew and Gregorian calendars are central to Bellow's complex vision, to his structural schema, and to his thematic concerns in "The Old System." The frame story, set in December of the Gregorian calendar, is controlled by the consciousness of the scientist-narrator, Dr. Samuel Braun, whose malaise leads him to meditate on "the old system." The interior tale, set in the Hebrew New Year season of Rosh-Hashanah and Yom Kippur,[3] unfolds a family saga of love and hate played against the backdrop of religious commitment and disavowal. The vital connection between the frame and interior narratives is found and sustained in the calendar references. Each story is set in a period of reflection as the year draws to a close. Samuel Braun's December meditation is the catalyst for the recollection of his cousin Isaac's high holiday week spiritual renewal. The religious essence of the holy period is *t'shuva*, a return to God through repentance and spiritual renewal. The drama of the inner tale focuses on Isaac Braun's Yom Kippur introspection and spiritual redemption. Its parallel to the frame story lies in the narrator's spiritual stock-taking and reflection on the old system's ethical and ethnic value systems. The frame story occurs on a single day, on the Sabbath, a day in Jewish life devoted to prayer, study, and celebration. A secular Jew, Dr. Braun neglects traditional Sabbath synagogue worship, fails to listen to the week's Torah portion, and ignores the commentaries. Nonetheless, yearning for meaning beyond that which secular success and assimilation afford, he meditates at home on the problems the traditional worshiper ponders: the nature and quality of the human condition, human relationships and passions, and ancestral history. Braun's reflection leads to the discomfiting realization that the old system of Jewish life embraced a dimension of love and human connectedness absent from his assimilated lifestyle.

The narrative, whose title is a direct reference to Orthodox Judaism, explores the spiritual crisis of the twentieth-century American Jew. Bellow parallels both the spiritual angst of a secular Jew who has abandoned Jewish ritual observance but experiences nostalgic longing for traditional Judaism and that of an observant Jew whose fear of perdition is dramatized in religious and economic conflict. Isaac Braun suffers his sister's unsubstantiated allegations that he is harming the family and engaging in religious hypocrisy. A thorough-going materialist, Tina unjustly accuses her brother of denying the rest of the family opportunity to invest in his lucrative real estate business. Isaac strives to restore family harmony by embracing the role of penitent, but Tina repeatedly sunders the unity of their family by spurning her brother's conciliatory efforts, responding with harassment, and seizing every opportunity to reiterate unfounded grievances.

In addition to setting the contemporary conflict in the Yom Kippur period of spiritual self-scrutiny, atonement, and prayer, Bellow elevates the conflict from a materialistic to a moral plane by alluding to the complex biblical schema evoking discord between the Israelites (Isaac) and the Philistines (Tina). Bellow's skillful incorporation of Judaic text and allusive naming direct the reader to interpret the contemporary sibling enmity against the historic discord of biblical Israelites and Philistines. These character analogies reinforce theme and buttress the structural link connecting frame story and inner tale. The second patriarch, Isaac (Israel) settled among the Philistines at Gerar, and devoted himself to husbandry, and his success incurred the envy and wrath of his neighbors. The fictional Isaac settles among American Philistines, worshipers of mammon, and prospers in their midst. Despite a gentle, loving nature, each Isaac witnesses family discord centering on the distribution of wealth. The patriarch's sons, Jacob and Esau, were engaged in a bitter birthright and inheritance quarrel, and Isaac Braun is a central figure in the financial and inheritance disputes of his family. The name *Tina* is emblematic of the character's dramatic function, her early sexual promiscuity, her relentless campaign to denigrate Isaac and turn their brothers against him, her contempt for the praying Jew, and her immoral denial of "the old system," marked by her rejection of Yom Kippur atonement and forgiveness. Completing the triad is the Hebrew name *Samuel*, attributed to the narrative's central consciousness and evoking the judicial function of the biblical Samuel, who lived during the period of the Israelite–Philistine wars. The biblical analogue is essential to interpretation of Samuel Braun's character, for it suggests his reliability as narrator-judge. During several interjections and the concluding frame, Braun meditates on the philosophical and ethical implications of his reverie. Like his namesake, Samuel Braun appraises the private morality of the inner tale and public morality in his judgment that "in America the abuses of the Old World are righted. It was appointed to be the land of historical redress" (67). As did his biblical counterpart and his rabbinic counterpart of the inner tale— an Old World Hasidic rabbi, whose instruction leads to mutual forgiveness and redemption at the heart of the story—Samuel Braun evaluates the motives and behavior of his ancestors and proclaims their guilt and innocence.

Furthermore, comparable to the biblical antecedent, the scientist-moralist enlarges his judgment beyond the confines of the family saga. He asserts that "mankind is in a confusing, uncomfortable, disagreeable stage in the evolution of its consciousness" (48). An exemplary Bellovian critic of contemporary values, Samuel Braun is saddened that "thought, art, belief of great traditions should be— misemployed" (48). Unlike "stone-hearted" Mosby, for whom "unmastered emotion was abhorrent" (165), Braun is moved by "these Jews! Their feelings, their hearts! . . . And these tears!" (83) and revitalized by his memories of Jewish social and religious values. His reminiscence is, according to Alan Berger, "a yizkor (a memorial service) for a Jewish world view which seems increasingly archaic while simultaneously serving as a spiritual yardstick against which one may measure the extent of loss of Jewish identity in the New World" (Berger 136). His Saturday reverie of Jewish times past, dramatizing spiritual redemption, transports Mosby beyond skepticism to knowledge of life and death, to affirmation of "the old system," to comprehension of "a promise that mankind might— might, mind you—eventually through its gift which might—might again!—be a divine gift, comprehend why it lived" (83). Like Bernard Malamud, I. B. Singer, Cynthia Ozick, and other Jewish American authors who write in the redemptive mode of spiritual return, Saul Bellow consistently affirms humankind's spiritual capacity and ethical potential, and nowhere more forcefully than in "The Old System," which he identifies in a *Salmagundi* interview as a favorite among his works.

III

The detachment with which Willis Mosby persists in viewing his past is the initial intellectual posture of the narrator of *The Bellarosa Connection*. The pervasive irony of the novella is that its narrator recognizes at the end of a long career devoted to the mechanics of memory retention that he has been blind to the relevance of personal and collective memory. The lonely septuagenarian, founder of the Mnemosyne Institute, who trained executives, statesmen, and politicians in memory retention and indifference toward the material being processed, prefers to "forget about remembering" (2). He has devoted a lifetime to a misapplied focus on the theory of memory, substituting theory for life and emotional engagement. The man whose professional motto was "Memory is life" has arrived at spiritual death through willful forgetfulness. The story he tells is motivated by a recent revelation that significant memory is necessary for an individual's connection to humanity. An unsummoned memory that begins and dominates the text deals with his cousin and contemporary, Harry Fonstein, a Holocaust survivor. The narrator's reflections on Fonstein's history expose him to Nazi destruction of Jewish life and to Jewish self-denial signified by assimilation in America—issues worthy of meaningful memory.

Bellow resolves the problematics of memory in this novella through juxtaposition of binary points of view of the major characters and several supportive choral voices on the subjects of the Holocaust and the Americanization of the Jew. Harry and his American wife, Sorella, argue for the significance of human connection through historic memory. Billy Rose, Fonstein's rescuer, urges forgetfulness and disengagement, and the narrator wavers between the two positions until his epiphanal recognition of Sorella's position. As Regine Rosenthal observes, "It had been the power of emotional memory that first attracted [the narrator] to Harry Fonstein. . . . It attested to Harry's emotional involvement in and preoccupation with his past, to his rootedness in personal and world history" (88).

In the juxtaposition of Sorella with Billy Rose and the narrator, Bellow explores two faces of contemporary Jewish American response to Jewish identification and historic memory. Opposed to the manner in which the survivor and his wife honor memory, the narrator and Billy Rose are guilty of the historic amnesia Bellow intimates characterizes many American Jews. The narrator will traverse the chasm between one who cannot, according to P. Shiv Kumar, "recognize the human factors that really make memory meaningful" (35) and one who finally understands Fonstein's sense of memory attendant upon human themes.

Reminiscent of Melville's "Bartleby, the Scrivener," a tale as much concerned with its narrator's perceptions as it is with his subject, Bellow's novella focuses, even more so, on the impact of the subject upon the narrator. Despite his desire, in retirement, to resist willed memory, spontaneous recollection of beginning life as the child of Russian Jewish immigrants leads, even before his epiphanal affirmation, to preoccupation with the "feelings and longings, and emotional memory" of Harry and Sorella Fonstein (3). Beginning with his father's interest in Fonstein, the narrator then shifts to memory fragments, creating a minimal outline of Fonstein's wartime struggles. We learn that most of his family perished in Poland while he and his mother escaped to Italy, where his mother soon died and he survived by learning Italian and securing odd jobs. More directly related to the remainder of the tale is his escape from the Nazis, as arranged by operatives of American show business impresario, Billy Rose.

Desire to bury the past is manifest in the rescuer's reluctance to remain responsible for the lives he saved. Following several unsuccessful legitimate approaches, Sorella tries to blackmail Rose into meeting with Harry, whose sole wish has been to express his gratitude to his benefactor. Rose rebuffs her, "I don't need entanglements—what I did, I did. I have to keep down the number of relationships and contacts" (56). The narrator's speculation on Billy's motives in suppressing memory illuminates his own pre-epiphanal character: "Afraid of the emotions? Too Jewish a moment for him? Drags him down from his standing as a full-fledged American?" (23).

Shiv Kumar concludes that "the narrator's use of memory does not strain beyond impersonal and unimaginative registration of facts" (33). This observation is accurate for much of the narrator's life, but unreflective of his post-epiphanal phase. Illustrative of the pre-epiphanal insensitivity is his advice to abandon the effort to contact Billy Rose, to abandon Holocaust memory. His unuttered advice to Fonstein is: "Forget it. Go American" (29). His pre-epiphanal superficiality is evident in the ironic claim that he "never lost sight of Fonstein's history, or of what it meant to be the survivor of such a destruction" (48). The reversal accompanying insight into the connection is achieved after decades of obtuseness. Only in old age does the narrator understand the sterility of his professional concept and use of memory. After three decades of neglect, the narrator realizes that he and the Fonsteins "were meant to be company for one another" (79), that he, like Billy Rose, has evaded meaningful relationships, that his life has been shallow.

The narrator's education is directed by Sorella, a former teacher, "a spirited woman, at home with ideas" (27). As the wife of a survivor, Sorella had sought to understand the Holocaust, "the technics of annihilation, the large-scale industry aspect of it" (28). Sorella's ambivalent student vacillates between reluctance to engage the Holocaust and a morbid fascination with it. "First those people murdered you, then they forced you to brood on their crimes. It suffocated me to do this" (29). Representing the oppositional Jewish American consciousness that feels a strong tie to European Jewish history, Sorella, the novella's moral register, grasps the relevance of historic memory and argues that even though Americans "weren't threatened, we have a special duty to come to terms with [the Holocaust]" (60). Her encyclopedic knowledge of the war against the Jews oppresses the unnamed narrator, who prefers to evade such painful detail. For him, "Hunting for causes was a horrible imposition added to the original 'selection,' gassing, cremation" (29). But listen he does and he cannot dismiss the thoughts once Sorella has informed him. Although he now knows some detail of the genocide, he will not probe the history, rationalizing that "such things are utterly beyond me, a pointless exercise" (29). His hesitance is not based on the Holocaust scholar's recognition that the Holocaust universe will always be beyond the ken of nonwitnesses. On the contrary, it is primarily an exercise of evasion, an effort to spare himself the discomfort of Holocaust encounter. Until the narrator develops an appreciation for Sorella's point of view, he is unable to overcome his failure to understand even the postwar implications of Harry's history. Unlike Harry, Sorella is not easily dismissed. She lectures the narrator on Jewish history, despite his disinclination to listen. But attend he does, and he is moved to recant his hitherto obdurate refusal to think "of the history and psychology of these abominations, death chambers and furnaces" (28–29), to recognition that "you couldn't say no to Jewish history after what had happened in Nazi Germany. You had to listen" (28). Yet the chasm between listening and comprehensive understanding remains.

Newly troubled by his neglect of Fonstein and his professed disinterest in the Holocaust, the narrator experiences a nightmare of symbolic Holocaust import. He finds himself in "a dug hole" (86), a pit from which he is unable to extricate himself because his feet are entangled in ropes or roots, a hole suggestive of the forest graves used for mass killings before implementation of the extensive crematoria system.

Similarly, his identification with the vulnerable refugee is manifest in the image of encumbered feet, recalling Fonstein's orthopedic boot, which would have meant an immediate death sentence had he been sent to Auschwitz. The dream victim's struggles are watched by a booted person, a metonymic completion of the dream's Holocaust context. The dream points to what the narrator now understands was "a lifelong mistake" (87), the American Jew's disengagement from the European Jew's predicament based on his perception of personal security, the essential enigma of the Holocaust for those who were not its direct victims:

> a New World version of reality . . . your strength doesn't give out. . . . European parents . . . were trained in submission, but you were free and bred in liberty. You were equal, you were strong, and here you could not be put to death, as Jews there had been. (88)

The revelation is far more difficult to accept than the dream. His trepidation is founded on recognition that he isn't who he thought he was, he really "didn't understand merciless brutality" (88). The falsity of his Hollywood vision of resistance to Nazism had led him to think, "You couldn't have locked a man like [Douglas Fairbanks] in a cattle car; he would have broken out" (89). The narrator understands that, unlike Fonstein who was "Mitteleuropa," he "was a Jew of an entirely different breed. . . . There was no way, therefore, in which [he] could grasp the real facts in the case of Fonstein. . . . You pay a price for being a child of the New World" (89). Ironically, American privilege is associated here with ignorance and innocence fostered by willful neglect of contemporary history. Exposure to these "illuminated particles of Jewish history" (89) and revelation that he had long avoided "unbearable imaginations . . . recognitions—of murder" (90) lead to self-rebuke, the first step toward spiritual repair, and an effort, after thirty years of neglect, to reestablish relations with the Fonsteins.

Reflective of the narrator's moral transformation is his changed response to the Holocaust. The pre-epiphanal tone is brusk, detached, even flippant and, on occasion, macabre, demonstrating his failure to fathom the enormity of the Holocaust. Representative of the early cavalier attitude is the narrator's reference to the method by which he became familiar with Fonstein's stories, "in episodes, like a Hollywood serial—the Saturday thriller, featuring Harry Fonstein and Billy Rose, or ?? Bellarosa." He asked Fonstein for details of his adventures (his torments) (11–12), interested in them apparently for their connection to the celebrity Billy Rose, show biz producer, business partner of gangsters, protégé of

Bernard Baruch. His recollection of the rescue mission is presented in a tone more appropriate to an adventure saga than a Holocaust chronicle: "it was Billy acting alone on a spurt of feeling for his fellow Jews and squaring himself to outwit Hitler and Himmler and cheat them of their victims" (13). Furthermore, he diminishes the gravity and urgency of the rescue by insinuating the fickleness of its agent, incongruously comparing his dedication to Holocaust rescue with his normally mundane interests. The only saving grace in this assessment is the narrator's modification of the banal in his recognition that "there were, however, spots of deep feeling in flimsy Billy. The God of his fathers still mattered. Billy was as spattered as a Jackson Pollack painting, and among the main trickles was his Jewishness" (13). Although he occasionally reports on Fonstein in the same nonchalant mode he employs for Billy Rose, the narrator shifts to realistic and dour language appropriate for Holocaust tragedy as he assesses Fonstein's probable fate in Auschwitz and concludes soberly with images that directly confront the radical evil of Nazism:

> In Auschwitz he would have been gassed immediately, because of the orthopedic boot. Some Dr. Mengele would have pointed his swagger stick to the left, and Fonstein's boot might now have been on view in the camp's exhibition hall—they have a hill of cripple boots there, a hill of crutches and of back braces and one of human hair and one of eyeglasses. Objects that might have been useful in German hospitals or homes. (4)

Another sign of the narrator's transformation is his newfound sensitivity to Jewish history. In contrast to his earlier sympathetic acceptance of the aloofness of Billy Rose, he now condemns a choral character who espouses emotional disengagement. He presents the character satirically, a bland assimilationist who "settled for good manners . . . wore Brooks Brothers grays and tans" (81). The narrator compares him unfavorably to his immigrant father, whose "ancient Jewish face" he inherited but then found a way "to drain the Jewish charge from it" (81), and distances himself from this adversary for whom justice is forgotten. His frustration with his antagonist's disinterest in contemplating "Justice, or Honor or the Platonic Ideas or the expectations of the Jews" (84) is clearly based on his newfound recognition that historic memory demands thoughtful attention. Sufficiently educated by Sorella at this stage, the narrator perceives the Fonstein–Rose relationship in the national context, arguing that when he considers the particular example he is "liable to see European Jewry also" (83).

The metamorphosis from historic amnesiac to advocate for perpetuation of historic memory is achieved through recognition of distinctions between European and American Jewish experience. A price American Jews paid for the greater freedom and security than European Jews enjoyed was disengagement from Jewish identification and solidarity. That posture contributed to American Jewry's failure to mobilize American government and public support for European Jewry. Here, the narrator comes closest to his moral mentor's concern. Sorella articulates her pessimism about the survival of American Jews as Jews, given the implications of full assimilation. She recognizes that unlike the physical threat Nazism posed for Jewry, assimilation poses a threat to American Jewry's religious/cultural survival. She asks, "Can they hold their ground, or will the U.S.A. be too much for them?" (65).

The narrator, too, comprehends that the Jew who identifies as a Jew religiously, culturally, or politically is spiritually and emotionally enriched. His new historic perspective and understanding of the importance of meaningful memory are manifest in his active search for the Fonsteins, his moderated tone, and his decision to write an account of the Fonstein–Rose story. By the novella's conclusion, the son of Jewish immigrant parents confronts Harry Fonstein's story and, by extension, his own connection to collective Jewish history and memory. His consciousness is awakened to the true importance of memory, and he writes an account of the Fonstein–Rose connection as an act of contrition and a service to the younger generation, represented fictionally by Fonstein's son and his friend, who match their historic illiteracy with willfully distanced demeanors. The narrator has evolved into the true son of his father,who appreciated the educational and humanizing purposes of historic memory, a father who "hoped it would straighten me out to hear what people had suffered in Europe, in the real world" (5).

IV

"Something to Remember Me By" is a superb memory piece. Less diffuse than Bellow's previous works of the type, it is a retrospective glance at the coming of age of an awkward, intellectual adolescent boy, book-learned, but not yet streetwise, capturing the particularity of his life while revealing its universal implications. The tale is shaped as the memoir of a dying old man written for his son for whom he wishes to leave something beyond the material. This remembrance details a shameful incident in the old man's youth, an epiphanic instance of the protagonist's diminished self-image arising from a misadventure with a rapacious prostitute as his mother lay dying of breast cancer. In contrast to Mosby, who admits no mistakes, this memoirist designs his story as a confession, a penance for self-perceived moral failure and a moral inheritance for his son.

Whereas Mosby is emotionally detached from humanity and intellectually distanced from his subject, Louie writes, in a reflective, expansive and good-humored mode, of his Chicago youth (shades of Augie March) teaming with human connection. Set in the Depression era, "Something to Remember Me By" introduces a working-class family and a series of urban types whom Louie encounters in the course of a single day: his loving, but violent father; his physically and emotionally generous mother, so diminished by cancer that she is no longer able to sit up, no longer possessed of breath to speak, patiently waiting for death's release; his older brother, reminiscent of Augie's brother Simon, a shrewd lawyer working for local racketeers and contemptuous of Louie's innocence; and his married sister, whose sole function appears to be promotion of her husband. The human comedy is fleshed out by engrossing urban characters reminiscent of Bellow's Chicago, the corrupt and the heartbroken: a voyeur pseudo-scientist, a prostitute, a world-weary bartender, a speakeasy doorkeeper, a drunkard and his dependent young children, a mother grieving for the death of a daughter. A recurrent juxtaposition in Bellow's fiction, the brute appetites of the city's rough-and-tumble characters in play with ineffective intellectuals, again finds voice through the encounters of a bookish youth with the seamy side of life.

This tale of a youngster's initiation to sexuality and death is set on a cold, bleak, February day in 1933, when he was a seventeen-year-old high school senior. His sexual rite of passage is a mortifying, humiliating experience. During the course of a visit to his brother-in-law's dental office, he inadvertently observes a naked woman, strapped to a table in an adjacent office. A volunteer for a voyeuristic sexology experiment, she evidences no sign of embarrassment at Louie's presence. Rather, she asks for his assistance in releasing her from wires monitoring her responses and dresses slowly and seductively for the aroused adolescent. Feigning a pulled ligament, she asks Louie to escort her home and upon arrival invites him to disrobe. As the naked boy awaits embrace, she tosses his clothes out a window to an accomplice and flees. Through a series of encounters that read like a modern version of the exploits of Hawthorne's country innocent of "My Kinsman, Major Molineux," who sought social initiation and his kinsman, Louie's exposure to contemporary social ills mount when he flees the site of his humiliation clothed in a woman's dress and hat, in search of assistance. Comparable to Robin suffering ridicule and witnessing gluttony and alcohol-induced debauchery in a local tavern where he seeks word of his kinsman, the modern pilgrim searches for his brother-in-law in a speakeasy where he, in turn, is interrogated and mocked by the bartender and patrons for his bizarre appearance and fleecing. Given a dirty shirt, he is told he will have to earn his carfare by escorting a drunkard home and preparing dinner for his children. Hawthorne prolongs Robin's adventure to expose him to multiple encounters with the fallen. Similarly, Bellow protracts Louie's trials among the downtrodden rather than expediting his return home. These obstacles which detain Louie from joining the family deathwatch exacerbate his anxiety and shame.

Throughout the day, Louie has been guilty of indecorous behavior and witness to a virtual vanity fair of sin. Sins of the flesh and assorted misdemeanors appear in his own lust, the prostitute's exploitation of that lust in theft, and a drunkard's failure to care for his children. Censure of these excesses and destructive behaviors is conveyed symbolically in Bellow's allusion to the Judaic dietary laws, one of whose functions is to instill restraint in the religiously observant. Louie's revulsion at handling porkchops for the children's dinner corresponds to his contempt for the drunkard's failed parental responsibility and includes a measure of self-condemnation for his own failed filial duty. As the drunk has forfeited self-control in pursuit of his obsession, so has the lascivious boy succumbed to his lust and delayed filial obligation.

His shame is expressed in language coalescing sexual and death themes: "Instead of a desirable woman, I had a drunkard in my arms. This disgrace, you see, while my mother was surrendering to death . . . a deathwatch. I should have been there" (217). Throughout the day, Louie is plagued by consciousness of his shortcomings, which evolve as a central focus not only of the adolescent protagonist but of the dying memoirist.

As Bellow approaches his final years, he writes frequently of death, of characters anticipating their own or their loved ones' demise. In "A Silver Dish," a mature son considers the death of an aged father:

What do you do about death—in this case, the death of an old father? If you're a modern person, sixty years of age, and a man who's been around, like Woody Selbst, what do you do? Take this matter of mourning, and take it against a contemporary background. How, against a contemporary background, do you mourn an octogenarian father, nearly blind, his heart enlarged, his lungs filling with fluid, who creeps, stumbles, gives off the odors, the moldiness or gassiness of old men. I mean! As Woody put it, be realistic. Think what times these are. The papers daily give it to you—the Lufthansa pilot in Aden is described by the hostages on his knees, begging the Palestinian terrorists not to execute him, but they shoot him through the head. Later they themselves are killed. And still others shoot others, or shoot themselves. That's what you read in the press, see on the tube, mention at dinner. (223)

Whereas Woody Selbst's situation calls for mourning and his withdrawal from the contemporary into memory of his father, the memoirist of "Something to Remember Me By," close to death himself, reflects on his own evasion of his mother's imminent death and his concurrent adolescent indiscretion in a meditation for his son who, in turn, will need to cope with his father's death. A son's aversion to facing his mother's cancer is a recurrent theme in fiction by Bellow, who lost his mother [to cancer] when he was a teenager. Like Herzog, who avoided facing his mother as she succumbed to cancer, Louie is pleased to have reason to leave the house. Yet he feels guilty for being evasive, for indulging in denial, admitting, "I knew she was dying and didn't allow myself to think about it" (187). His after-school job delivering flowers brings him into the home of mourners and to a scene of a dead girl in a coffin. Yet here too he denies a connection with death, "I didn't figure here, . . . this was no death of mine" (193). Even his sexual diversion presses the imminence of death upon his consciousness. The sight of the full breasted body of the naked woman on the doctor's table recalls his "mother's chest mutilated by cancer surgery . . . Its gnarled scar tissue. . . . anything to spoil the attraction of this naked young woman" (196–97). Fifty years after the event, the son still berates himself for failing his mother.

Balancing Louie's self-image as a young fool is Bellow's delineation of the boy as an aesthetically and ethically sensitive budding intellectual. Like the young Zetland of the earlier collection of short fiction, *Him with His Foot in His Mouth,* who had a rough and disapproving father but found sustenance in his adolescent devotion to Kant, Nietzsche, surrealism, and Dada, Louie is at home in the classics and in the great works of modernity. He reads "Prufrock, Mauberly," *Manhattan Transfer, An Enormous Room, A Portrait of the Artist.* Even his decision regarding his mother's cache of money, hidden in her High Holiday Prayer Book and intended for a trip to Europe to see her family, is one that testifies to his moral responsibility and his intellectual promise. He will give the money to his father, except for five dollars that were stolen from him and belong to his employer and five dollars to buy Von Hugel's *Eternal Life* and the *World as Will and Idea.* While his lost clothes caused him immediate embarrassment, he views the loss of a fragment of an untitled book by an unknown author as more serious. It is from this text that he recalls a passage informing the memoir and suggesting the spiritual legacy he wishes to leave his son: "*The visible world sustains us until life leaves, and then it must utterly destroy us. Where then is the world from which the human form comes?*" (193). This is the line he ponders following his witness of a family mourning the death of a young girl. It is the line he will continue to ponder as he returns to his own family deathwatch.

The father in this tale (unlike Bellow's who was a storyteller) teaches his son through the use of his fists, and so the boy seeks guidance in books. It is with gratitude, however, that he accepts his father's blow upon his return home, for that hostile gesture signifies that his mother still lives. Had she died during his absence, his father would greet him with a hug. Unlike "A Silver Dish," in which a hard and truculent father is united, at the end of his life, with a gentle, philosophical, and forgiving son, we do not learn anything about the ensuing relationship of Louie and his father. The education Louie seeks is represented in his return to the alley to retrieve pages that the thief might have discarded. He justifies this act, which he acknowledges his own son may find obsessive, with a statement of the importance of printed matter:

> But remember, there were no redeemers in the streets, no guides, no confessors, comforters, enlighteners, communicants to turn to. You had to take teaching wherever you could find it. Under the library dome downtown, in mosaic letters, there was a message from Milton . . . A GOOD BOOK, it said, IS THE PRECIOUS LIFE'S BLOOD OF A MASTER SPIRIT. (220)

Andrew Gordon astutely assesses this remembrance as the narrator's way of

> open[ing] himself up and giv[ing] of himself to his son. The narrative is an act of love which proves that, despite the odds, Louie has turned into a "mensch" and is trying to be a better father than his own father was, relating to his son through kind words rather than through angry blows. He hopes his son will be a good man and a good Jewish son. (Gordon, 62)

The memory he leaves for his son's edification is not one in which he behaves nobly or heroically, but one that transformed him, one that changed a boy into a man. "This was when the measured, reassuring, sleep-inducing turntable of days became a whirlpool, a vortex darkening toward the bottom" (221). And he had only the wisdom of the pages he lost, but whose wisdom he retained, "to interpret it. . . . They told . . . that the truth of the universe was inscribed into our very bones. That the human skeleton was itself a hieroglyph. That everything we had ever known on earth was shown to us in the first days after death" (221).

This most recent exploration of memory in Bellow's fiction extends his treatment of old men reviewing their lives, seeking to explain themselves, their circumstances and, at least for some, especially those who have learned from their own memories, to leave a moral legacy. Unlike Mosby, who remains blind and deaf to the meaning of human suffering and the value of remorse, Louie, the narrator of *The Bellarosa Connection*, and Samuel Braun appreciate the regenerative value of memory. The reverential Jewish tone and context that close *The Bellarosa Connection* address the importance of relating to one's particular historic/cultural memory and place memory, as did "The Old System," in the sphere of religious obligation: "The Jews ask even God to remember, *'Yiskor Elohim.'* God doesn't forget, but your prayer requests him particularly to remember your dead" (102). In remembering the Jewish dead, and more significantly their history and values, most of Bellow's protagonists achieve communal connection and ethical sensitivity. Like Samuel Braun, whose meditation on the past—family love and strife, religious commitment and apostasy, scenes of sexual initiation and scenes of death, scenes of human intransigence and suffering—left him in tears and ennobled, Louie, too, judges his memories to be worthy of transmittal to the next generation for the revery speaks to human connection and responsibility.

"Something to Remember Me By" poses the transcendental question, "Which world do we really belong to, this world of matter or another world, from which matter takes its orders?" (201) and, as Peter Kemp observes, "points toward the hazy edges of Bellow's fictional terrain where his metropolitan panoramas blur upwards into mysticism" (11). It is the "continuum of spirit" that the dying father strives to bequeath to his son and thereby to help him accept his death. And, perhaps, it is the same for the octogenarian author who, throughout his long, prolific career, has been a master spirit for our age, who dedicates "Something to Remember Me By" not to a single individual, not to a colleague, but to posterity—"To my children and grandchildren."

Notes

1. My analysis of three of the titles have appeared in slightly different form in "Memoir and History: Saul Bellow's Old Men Remembering in 'Mosby's Memoirs,' 'The Old System,' and *The Bellarosa Connection,*" *Saul Bellow Journal* 12,

no. 2 (Fall 1994): 44–58. Also, the position on "The Old System" is drawn from a more comprehensive analysis in "The Old System: Text and Context," in *Saul Bellow and the Struggle at the Center*, Georgia State Literary Series, ed. Eugene Hollohan (New York: AMS Press, 1996).

2. Observant Jews partake in various ritual cleansings to symbolize acts of spiritual purification. The religious discipline of Judaism requires washing the hands on such occasions as arising from sleep, before offering prayers, before eating, and after the elimination of bodily wastes. At other occasions complete immersion in the *mikveh*, the ritual bath, is prescribed.

3. Repentance and reconciliation with fellow humans and God mark the holiday spirit. Rosh Hashanah is designated by two biblical and two liturgical names. Biblically it is identified as a day of Sabbath observance and shofar (ram's horn) blasts. Liturgically, Rosh Hashanah is called *Yom ha-Din* (Day of Judgment) and *Yom ha-Zikkaron* (Day of Remembrance), when humankind is believed to be judged by the Divine. Rosh Hashanah and Yom Kippur are known collectively as *Yamim Nora'im* (Days of Awe).

Works Cited

Bellow, Saul. *The Bellarosa Connection*. New York: Penguin Books, 1989.

——. "Literature and Culture: An Interview with Saul Bellow," *Salmagundi* 30 (1975): 21.

——. "Mosby's Memoirs." In *Mosby's Memoirs and Other Stories*. Greenwich: Fawcett Publications, 1969.

——. "The Old System." In *Mosby's Memoirs and Other Stories*. Greenwich: Fawcett Publications, 1969.

——. "A Silver Dish." In *Him with His Foot in His Mouth and Other Stories*. New York: Pocket Books, 1985.

——. "Zetland: By a Character Witness." In *Him with His Foot in His Foot in His Mouth and Other Stories*. New York: Pocket Books, 1985.

Berger, Alan. "The Logic of the Heart: Biblical Identity and American Culture in Saul Bellow's 'The Old System.'" *Saul Bellow Journal* 11, no. 2 & 12, no. 1 (Winter 1993): 133–45.

Denby, David. "Memory in America." *New Republic*, 1 January 1990, 37–40. Reprinted in *Short Story Criticism*. Vol. 14, edited by David Segal, 55–59. Detroit: Gale Research, 1994.

Gordon, Andrew. "Shame and Saul Bellow's 'Something to Remember Me By.'" *Saul Bellow Journal* 13, no. 1 (Winter 1995): 53–63.

Kemp, Peter. "Expansive Tastes." Review of *Something to Remember Me By*, by Saul Bellow. *Sunday Times*, 2 November 1992, sec. 6, p. 11.

Kiernan, Robert F. *Saul Bellow*. New York: Continuum, 1989.

Kremer, S. Lillian. "Memoir and History: Saul Bellow's Old Men Remembering in 'Mosby's Memoirs,' 'The Old System,' and *The Bellarosa Connection*." *Saul Bellow Journal* 12, no. 2 (Fall 1994): 44–58.

——. "The Old System: Text and Context." In *Saul Bellow and the Struggle at the Center*, Georgia State Literary Series, edited by Eugene Hollohan. New York: AMS Press, 1996.

Kumar, P. Shiv. "Memory Sans Understanding: A Perspective on *The Bellarosa Connection.*" *Saul Bellow Journal* 10, no. 1 (Fall 1991): 32–6.

Rosenthal, Regine. "Memory and the Holocaust: *Mr. Sammler's Planet* and *The Bellarosa Connection.*" In *Saul Bellow at Seventy-Five: A Collection of Critical Essays*, edited by Gerhard Bach. Tübingen: Gunter Narr Verlag, 1991.

Safer, Elaine B. "Degrees of Comic Irony in *A Theft* and *The Bellarosa Connection.*" *Saul Bellow Journal* 9, no. 2 (1990): 1–19.

The Actual

MARK SHECHNER

In a literary firmament that dazzles with sudden comets and flaming supernovae, Saul Bellow has been one of the few fixed stars, since the publication of *Dangling Man* in 1944, more than fifty-three years ago. Born in 1915, Bellow is in his eighties, at an age at which a writer may exercise the privilege of going soft or sour or flat. Bellow has gone none of those things on us; rather, for all the tartness for which he is famed, he has turned remarkably sweet. Surrendering none of his wit, his urbanity, his grace-under-pressure, Bellow has simply sweetened up, sloughed off his former agitations and aggravations like old skins to reveal beneath them a wise passiveness that we could scarcely have imagined in the days of the cranky, pyrotechnic, blockbuster novels—*Henderson the Rain King, Herzog, Mr. Sammler's Planet, Humboldt's Gift*. Conceived in heartache and hell-bent for heart attack, or so they seemed, such novels issued a challenge to the reader: stand and admire or stand aside. Compendia of knowledge and encyclopedias of upheaval and neurosis, they made no concession to the weak of mind or faint of heart, and invariably there was much to admire.

These days we find Bellow more restrained and less noisy, turning out modest novellas such as *More Die of Heartbreak* (1987), *The Bellarosa Connection* (1989), *A Theft* (1989), *Something to Remember Me By* (1991), and now *The Actual* (1997). These read like scale-model novels—assembled with micro-tools and lacquered to a high gloss—that make no demands on the reader except those of art itself, calling to mind the late comedies of Shakespeare: *Pericles, The Tempest, Cymbeline*, similar masterpieces of an abundant talent that settled for flowing serenely within its banks after raging over them for so long. This is a kinder, gentler Bellow than the one who used to pummel readers with his characters' existential trials, marital woes, sexual needs, mystical illuminations, financial upheavals, and truculent humanism.

When Harry Trellman, the protagonist of *The Actual*, is summoned to the home of Chicago trillionaire, Sigmund Adletsky, he is reunited there by chance with his childhood sweetheart, Amy Wustrin. Between Harry and Amy for forty years have stood their respective marriages and long absences, though Harry has carried a torch for the woman who even as a child was his erotic ground zero, his "actual." "Half a century of feeling is invested in her, of fantasy, speculation, and absorption, of imaginary conversation. After forty years of concentrated imagining, I feel able to picture her at any moment of any given day" (18). Such hang-dog devotion was known to Amy's second husband, Jay Wustrin, who once invited Harry to join him and his wife in the shower and then left them alone together. Now with Jay dead and buried next to Amy's mother—he bought the grave site at a discount from Amy's father—Amy is employed by the Adletskys to decorate a new apartment, while Harry, on account of his acute powers of social observation—he is a "first class noticer" (15)—and memory for odd facts, has been hired by Sigmund Adletsky as a personal minister-without-portfolio in charge of random advice.

As the story unfolds, Amy is having her husband exhumed and reburied; her father, who initially sold the plot to raise cash, will soon be needing it for his own burial. At the same time, the Adletskys are negotiating the purchase of an apartment from Bodo and Madge Heisinger, high-income grotesques of a sort that roam freely about in Bellow's fiction. Bodo Heisinger, an elderly toy manufacturer, made his fortune on "muscular, horrendous, laser-armed space aliens for small boys and girls" (45-46), while Madge is one of Bellow's patented Bathshebas, a "real turn-on" who once put out a contract on her husband and did three years in prison for the failed assassination. In homage to such gargantuan passions, her husband has remarried her and lately is "tremendously proud of her."

This is classic mondo Bellow: high-rise passion and folly among business-class Jews, umpteen stories high above Lake Michigan, where everyone has a racket or an angle, a bag man or a hit man, and beneath every skin there lurks a dog: top dog, lap dog, hound dog, mad dog. If the merchandise mart is their synagogue, the board of directors is their minyan. Harry Trellman has had his racket and also his lap dog deficiencies. An importer of distressed antiquities from China, which he restores in Guatemala and sells as the real thing in the States, he made a modest bundle. He might have retired and moved to the Sunbelt, or offshore, but:

in Chicago I had unfinished emotional business. In Boston or in Baltimore I would still have thought, daily and regularly, of the same woman—of what I might have said to her, of what she might have answered. 'Love objects,' as psychiatry has named them, are not frequently come by or easily put aside. 'Distance' is really a formality. The mind takes no real notice of it". (14)

When there had been opportunities, he had hung back emotionally, been in exile from himself, and failed to make his pitch. Thus he had lost Amy twice, the second time to Jay Wustrin, his high school chum who read Eliot and Pound with him but was principally interested in women. But then Jay knew how to be attractive, having been "open, theatrical. I was secretive, uncharitable, prepared to do my neighbor in the eye" (72). Even that morning in the shower, left alone with Amy by Jay, Harry had fallen short, despite having soaped her breasts and her parted thighs, and Amy reminds him years later, "If you cared for me you could have sent a clearer signal" (69). Trellman, like every other Bellow hero, has lived in the shadow of others and been a disappointment, to himself and to those who have expected better things of him. Metaphorically, he is another of Bellow's weak-kneed younger brothers. Like all of Bellow's books, *The Actual* is a sentimental education, in which the hero gets acquainted with life through his failures. "Reality comes in blows," said Moses Herzog, hero of an earlier novel, and it is through the blows to his ego, delivered by men like Jay, that Harry learns to speak up for his desires: to be a man. He is helped along by the most unlikely of Cupids, the nonagenarian Adletsky, who in gratitude to Harry for services sends him around by limousine to the cemetery to aid and comfort Amy during the nasty work of digging up and reburying Jay. Naturally, Harry uses the opportunity to plead his love for Amy in its swivel seats while Jay's coffin is being hoisted from one grave to another. As Jay's coffin slides into a fresh grave, Harry turns from random chit-chat to the business at hand, and proposes marriage. Was ever a woman this way wooed? Was ever a woman this way won?

The romantic-erotic folderol that had earlier Bellow heroes on their knees is handled here with a sly tongue-in-cheek. The spirit of the story is Shakespearean: we are all fools for love, but if we are lucky and live long enough we may have a second chance, or a third or a fourth. This is decidedly a premodern sentiment that identifies Bellow as a humanist, a believer in moral improvement, though the lessons may be bitter and the goal, after all, only a juicier love life. But then, Bellow is a romantic who has always taken love as a philosophical issue of the utmost urgency.

In telling a story of old flames rekindled after many years, Bellow is recycling earlier stories, dusting off, for example, Charlie Citrine's torch for his adolescent sweetheart, Naomi Lutz, in *Humboldt's Gift*. "When I loved Naomi Lutz," recalls a moony Citrine, in a phrase that could be equally at home in *The Actual*, "I was safely *within life*" (76). "There was nothing alien in Naomi. My feeling for her went into her cells, into the very molecules that, being hers, all had her properties" (214). This is virtually the same language of bedrock love with which Harry Trellman extols his Amy in *The Actual*, a love Harry calls "straight and simple, an involuntary music" (71). Naomi too, like Amy Wustrin, had been confused by her suitor's intellectual talk and married a businessman instead.

Even before *Humboldt's Gift*, though, Bellow had introduced the dream of childhood passion reawakened in midlife in a one-act play titled *A Wen*, which was published in *Esquire* magazine in 1964. There he has a world-class atomic scientist named Solomon Ithimar seek out a childhood playmate, Marcella Menelik, in order to reenact a primal moment in their mutual childhoods, the game of show-me-yours-and-I'll-show-you-mine. During their games he had seen a wen, a birthmark, on her vagina, and the vision had been burned into his imagination. Many years later, he has interrupted a trip to a scientific conference to seek her out and beg to see the birthmark one more time.

> My spirit has attached itself to it and gravitates about it. To the scientist only a drop of pigment, perhaps, a small concentration of melanin, a purplish or rosy or mulberry discoloration; but to me a fixed star, an electromagnetic potency, a phenomenon which makes me ache, adore, throb, long to merge, and in fact seems to contain the secret of life. (74)

Sound familiar? It's the same rapture for the primal, in the familiar high-concept lingo, that lingers on through *The Actual*, and which women might well take for B.S., though it is only a shy intellectual's way of expressing desire:

> There has been time, as I was roller-skating to my laboratory, or talking to the President, when that little mark would suddenly appear to me. Sometimes like a closed bud or tinier. Sometimes the size of an egg. Or as if you held that egg to a powerful light, all transparency. Finally, the same diameter as the sun. The sun itself, where the fusion process goes on, pouring on subatomic particles. Lastly, explosions within me like whole novae, scattering my matter through sidereal space to cool again. Finally, I had to see you. I had to fly. I was driven. I had to know. (74)

Was ever a woman that way wooed? Was ever a woman that way won? Marcella, understanding scarcely a word of this big-bang theory of herself, is bowled over by so much verbal passion anyway, and as a hurricane bears down upon the house, she ducks behind a couch with Ithimar and a flashlight for a final, midlife game of show-me-yours before the house is lashed by the storm.

A Wen was a charming jeu d'esprit, a touch of soft-focus fetishism from a future Nobel Prize winner: nothing raspy or hard-core or violent. And in later replays, that fascination would simmer down into nostalgia for childhood love, as Marcella and her birthmark are sublimated upward into Naomi Lutz and Amy Wustrin, the romantic-erotic soulmates of men struggling to return from exile. There is no mistaking the continuity, however, and no mistaking the power of nostalgia, of Eros, of love, that drives these stories. They may sound different notes, but together that are decidedly a chord.

What are we to make of all this? Matters of artistry aside—and I regard *The Actual* as a delightful miniature—I suppose we should start by taking Bellow's romanticism seriously, not just as "Bellow's romanticism" but as a fully integrated vision, something essential to the way he sees the world and writes his books. He is, finally, as he has been since the novel *Henderson the Rain King* in 1959, a writer of the erotic, and a man for whom sex and love are more than passions: they are personal metaphysics. They grapple with the universe itself. Why not take Bellow seriously about this and, beyond pegging him thematically, actually lend an ear? That is how we best respect our writers, after all: by reading them as though they were, as Lionel Trilling once said, delivering the news. Of course, if this particular news is that first love is best love, we may not want to give our assent too easily, but then who hasn't had those twinges of nostalgia for old, half-forgotten, and deeply buried romances or childhood crushes? Who hasn't suffered regret for words unspoken? That Bellow from time to time brandishes that torch only tells us that at the core he is a romantic and even a Romantic, but then we've always known that.

Such considerations don't much affect our estimation of *The Actual*, which stands or falls on its own production values, like any other book: how skillfully the plot is managed, how well the characters are developed, how rich is the verbal texture, etc. In such scaled-back productions, there is a premium on incidentals, and Bellow's little gifts of perception and phasing are all around. Says Adletsky about a banker: "He's got a condom over his heart" (14). And Harry on adolescent love: "It strikes you at seventeen and, like infantile paralysis, though it works through the heart, not the spinal cord, it, too, can be crippling" (73). Harry Trellman on his own Oriental appearance: "I have Japanese legs, straight from one of Hokusai's bath scenes. The thighs are muscular, and the shins are concave. I'd look even more Japanese if I were to shorten my hair and wear a fringe. I began to revise my image accordingly" (16). Bellow has these touches strung together so tightly that they ring like chimes, and though this book does not change the face of literature, it does soften the profile of its author.

Works Cited

Bellow, Saul. *The Actual.* New York: Viking Penguin, 1997.
——. *Humboldt's Gift.* New York: Viking, 1964.
——. "A Wen." *Esquire* (January 1964): 72-74, 111.

Bellow's Short Fiction:
Selected Bibliography

BLAINE HALL

Alhadeff, Barbara. "The Divided Self: A Lainian Interpretation of *Seize the Day*." *Studies in American Jewish Literature* 3, no. 1 (1977): 16-20.

Alter, Robert. "Kafka's Father, Agnon's Mother, Bellow's Cousins." *Commentary* (February 1986): 46-52.

Avery, Evelyn. "Book Reviews." Review of *The Bellarosa Connection*, by Saul Bellow. *Studies in American Jewish Literature* 10, no. 2 (1991): 225-27.

Bach, Gerhard P. "'Howling like a Wolf from the City Window': The Cinematic Realization of *Seize the Day*." *Saul Bellow Journal* 7, no. 2 (1988): 71-83.

Birindelli, Roberto. "Tamkin's Folly: Myths Old and New in *Seize the Day* by Saul Bellow." *Saul Bellow Journal* 7, no. 2 (1988): 35-48.

Bloom, Steven. "Why Billy Rose? Bellow's Use-Misuse of the Real Billy Rose in The Bellarosa Connection." In *Saul Bellow at Seventy-five: A Collection of Critical Essays*. Vol. 9 of Studies & Texts in English, edited by Gerhard Bach, 189-200. Tübingen: Gunter Narr Verlag, 1991.

Bordewyk, Gordon. "Nathanael West and *Seize the Day*." *English Studies* 64, no. 2 (1983):153-59.

———. "Saul Bellow's Death of a Salesman." *Saul Bellow Newsletter* 1, no. 1 (1981): 18-21.

Bouson, J. Brooks. "The Narcissistic Self-Drama of Wilhelm Adler: A Kohutian Reading of Bellow's *Seize the Day*." In *Saul Bellow Journal* 5, no. 2 (1986): 3-14. Revised version reprinted as "Empathy and Self-Validation in Bellow's *Seize the Day*." In *The Empathic Reader: A Study of the Narcissistic Character and the Drama of Self*, 64-81. Amherst: University of Massachusetts Press, 1989. Reprinted in *The Critical Response to Saul Bellow*. Vol. 20 of Critical Responses in Arts and Letters, edited by Gerhard Bach, 83-99. Westport, Conn: Greenwood, 1995.

Bowen, Robert O. "Bagels, Sour Cream and the Heart of the Current Novel." *Northwest Review* 1, no. 2 (1957): 52-56.

Chavkin, Allan. "Bellow's *A Theft*." Review of *A Theft*, by Saul Bellow. *Saul Bellow Journal* 8, no. 1 (1989): 68-70.

———."'The Hollywood Thread' and the First Draft of Saul Bellow's *Seize the Day*." *Studies in the Novel* 14, no. 1 (1982): 82-94.

———."Suffering and Wilhelm Reich's Theory of Character-Armoring in Saul Bellow's *Seize the Day*." *Essays in Literature* 9, no. 1 (1982): 133-37.

———."Wordsworth's 'Ode' and Bellow's *Seize the Day*." *ANQ* ns 3, no. 3 (1990): 121-24.

Chavkin, Allan, and Nancy Feyl Chavkin. "Shawmut's Hostile Joking and Stereotyping in 'Him with His Foot in His Mouth.'" *Saul Bellow Journal* 11, no. 2 & 12, no. 1 (1993-94): 22-29.

Clark, Michael. "Saul Bellow's *Seize the Day* and *Oedipus Rex*." *Saul Bellow Journal* 6, no. 1 (1987): 28-33.

Clayton, John J. "A Rich Reworking." *Saul Bellow Journal* 6, no. 2 (1987): 19-25.

———. "Saul Bellow's *Seize the Day*: A Study in Mid-Life Transition." *Saul Bellow Journal* 5, no. 1 (1986): 34-47.

Cohen, Sarah Blacher. "Adaptations in and of Saul Bellow's 'The Old System.'" *Saul Bellow Journal* 11, no. 2 & 12, no. 1 (1993-94): 108-23.

———. "Velvel, the Fair-Haired Hippopotamus." In *Saul Bellow's Enigmatic Laughter*, 90-114. Urbana: University of Illinois Press, 1974.

Costello, Patrick. "Tradition in Seize the Day." *Essays in Literature* 1, no. 1 (1987): 117-31.

Cronin, Gloria L. "The Seduction of Tommy Wilhelm: A Post-Modernist Appraisal of *Seize the Day*." *Saul Bellow Journal* 3, no. 1 (1983): 18-27.

Denby, David. "Memory in America." Review of *The Bellarosa Connection* and *A Theft*, by Saul Bellow. *New Republic*, 1 January 1990, 37-40.

Dutton, Robert R. "'Sunk Though He Be.'" *Saul Bellow*. Vol. 181 of Twayne United States Authors Series, 83-97. Boston: Twayne, 1971. Revised edition, 1982, 75-90.

Fenster, Coral. "Ironies and Insights in *The Bellarosa Connection*." *Saul Bellow Journal* 9, no. 2 (1990): 20-28.

Friedrich, Marianne M. "Artistic Representation in Bellow's 'What Kind of Day Did You Have?'" *Saul Bellow Journal* 8, no. 1 (1989): 51-67.

———. "Bellow's Renaissance Courtier: Woody Selbst in 'A Silver Dish.'" *Saul Bellow Journal* 9, no. 1 (1990): 21-35.

———. *Character and Narration in the Short Fiction of Saul Bellow*. Vol. 5 of Twentieth-Century American Jewish Writers. New York: Peter Lang, 1995.

———. "'Cousins': The Problem of Narrative Representation." *Saul Bellow Journal* 11, no. 2 & 12, no. 1 (1993-94): 80-107.

———. "A Theft: Bellow's Clara Between Anarchy and Utopia." In *Saul Bellow at Seventy-five: A Collection of Critical Essays*. Vol. 9 of Studies & Texts in English, edited by Gerhard Bach, 177-88. Tübingen: Gunter Narr Verlag, 1991.

——. "Two Women Protagonists from Bellow's Short Stories: Character Conception and Its Artistic Realization." In *Saul Bellow: A Mosaic.* Vol. 3 of Twentieth Century American Jewish Writers, 73-85. New York: Peter Lang, 1992.

Fuchs, Daniel. "Bellow's Short Stories." In *Saul Bellow: Vision and Revision,* 280-304. Durham: Duke University Press, 1984.

——. "On *Him with His Foot in His Mouth and Other Stories.*" *Saul Bellow Journal* 5, no. 1 (1986): 3-15. Reprinted in *The Critical Response to Saul Bellow.* Vol. 20 of Critical Responses in Arts and Letters, edited by Gerhard Bach, 282-92. Westport, Conn.: Greenwood, 1995.

——. "Seize the Day." In *Saul Bellow: Vision and Revision,* 78-97. Durham: Duke University Press, 1984.

Galloway, David D. "Saul Bellow: 'The Gonzaga Manuscripts.'" In *Die Amerikanische Short Story der Gegenwart: Interpretationen,* edited by Peter Freese, 168-74. Berlin: Schmidt, 1976.

Giannone, Richard. "Saul Bellow's Idea of Self: A Reading of *Seize the Day.*" *Renascence* 27, no. 4 (1975): 193-205.

Goldman, L. H. "Seize the Day: Tommy Wilhelm's Tragedy." In *Saul Bellow's Moral Vision: A Critical Study of the Jewish Experience,* New York: Irvington, 1983.

Goodheart, Eugene. "Parable of the Artist." Review of *Him with His Foot in His Mouth and Other Stories,* by Saul Bellow. *Partisan Review* 52, no. 2 (1985): 149-53. Reprinted as "Saul Bellow's *Him with His Foot in His Mouth and Other Stories.*" In *Pieces of Resistance,* edited by Eugene Goodheart,167-70. New York: Cambridge University Press, 1987.

Gordon, Andrew. "The Hero as Sucker in Saul Bellow's Early Fiction." *Saul Bellow Journal* 6, no. 2 (1987): 47-63.

——. "It Doesn't Ring True." Review of *A Theft,* by Saul Bellow. *Saul Bellow Journal* 9, no. 1 (1990): 79-83.

——. "Shakespeare's *The Tempest* and Yeats' 'Sailing to Byzantium' in *Seize the Day.*" *Saul Bellow Journal* 4, no. 1 (1985): 45-51.

Handy, William J. "Bellow's *Seize the Day*." In *Modern Fiction: A Formalist Approach*. Crosscurrents/Modern Critiques. Edited by William J. Handy, 119-30. Carbondale: Southern Illinois University Press, 1971.

————. "Saul Bellow and the Naturalistic Hero." *Texas Studies in Literature and Language* 5, no. 4 (1964): 538-45.

Holinger, Richard. "Him with His World Intact." *Saul Bellow Journal* 8, no. 1 (1989): 24-34.

Howe, Irving. "Introduction to Seize the Day." In *Classics of Modern Fiction*, edited by Irving Howe,457-66. New York: Harcourt Brace and World, 1968. 2nd ed. 1972. 511-20; 3rd ed. 1980. 457-66.

Hyland, Peter. "Novels of the Eighties." In *Saul Bellow*. Modern Novelists, 107-18. New York: St. Martins, 1992.
————. "Novels of the Fifties." In *Saul Bellow*. Modern Novelists, 40-47. New York: St. Martins, 1992.

————. "Short Stories." In *Saul Bellow*. Modern Novelists, 119-27. New York: St. Martins, 1992.

Ikeda, Choko. "Narrative Devices in Saul Bellow's 'A Silver Dish.'" *Kyushu American Literature* 29 (1988): 31-39.

Jefchak, Andrew. "Family Struggles in *Seize the Day*." *Studies in Short Fiction* 11, no. 3 (1974): 297-302.

Johnson, Gregory. "Jewish Assimilation and Codes of Manners in Saul Bellow's 'The Old System.'" *Studies in American Jewish Literature* 9, no. 1 (1990): 48-60.

Kiernan, Robert F. "Him with His Foot in His Mouth." In *Saul Bellow*. Literature and Life: American Writers, 190-216. New York: Frederick Ungar-Continuum, 1989.

————. "Mosby's Memoirs and Other Stories." In *Saul Bellow*. Literature and Life: American Writers, 113-35. New York: Frederick Ungar-Continuum, 1989.

——. "Seize the Day." In *Saul Bellow. Literature and Life: American Writers*,57-75. New York: Frederick Ungar-Continuum, 1989.

Kindilien, Glenn A. "The Meaning of the Name 'Green' in Saul Bellow's 'Looking for Mr. Green.'" *Studies in Short Fiction* 15, no. 1 (1978): 104-07.

Knight, Karl F. "Bellow's Shawmut: Rationalizations and Redemption." *Studies in Short Fiction* 24, no. 4 (1987): 375-80.

——. "Bellow's Victor Wulpy: The Failure of Intellect." *Saul Bellow Journal* 6, no. 2 (1987): 26-35.

——. "The Rhetoric of Bellow's Woody Selbst: Religion and Irony." *Saul Bellow Journal* 8, no. 1 (1989): 35-43.

——. "Sexual Irony in Bellow's 'What Kind of Day Did You Have?'" *Notes on Contemporary Literature* (March 1987): 10-12.

Kremer, S. Lillian. "An Intertextual Reading of *Seize the Day*: Absorption and Revision." *Saul Bellow Journal* 10, no. 1 (1991): 46-56.

——. "Memoir and History: Saul Bellow's Old Men Remembering in 'Mosby's Memoirs,' 'The Old System,' and *The Bellarosa Connection*." *Saul Bellow Journal* 12, no. 2 (1994): 44-58.

——. "*Seize the Day*: Intimations of Anti-Hasidic Satire." *Yiddish* 4, no. 4 (1982): 32-40.

Kulshreshtha, Chirantan. "The Victims: *Seize the Day*." In *Saul Bellow: The Problem of Affirmation*, 77-94. New Delhi: Arnold-Heinemann, 1978.

Kumar, P. Shiv. "Memory Sans Understanding: A Perspective on *The Bellarosa Connection*." *Saul Bellow Journal* 10, no. 1 (1991): 32-36.

Lelchuk, Alan. "Recent Adventures of Saul Bellow: Reflections on 'What Kind of Day Did You Have?'" In *Saul Bellow: A Mosaic*. Vol. 3 of *Twentieth Century American Jewish Writers*, 59-71. New York: Peter Lang, 1992.

Lister, Paul A. "The 'Compleat Fool' in *Seize the Day*." *Saul Bellow Journal* 3, no. 2 (1984): 32-59.

Loe, Thomas. "Modern Allegory and the Form of *Seize the Day.*" *Saul Bellow Journal* 7, no. 1 (1988):57-66.

Machida, Tetsuji. "Seize the Day." In *Saul Bellow, a Transcendentalist: A Study of Saul Bellow's Transcendentalism in His Major Works from the Viewpoint of Transpersonal Psychology*, 53-68. Osaka: Osaka Kyoiku Tosho, 1993.

Malin, Irving. "The First Story." In *Saul Bellow's Fiction.* Crosscurrents/Modern Critiques, edited by Irving Malin, 3-8. Carbondale: Southern Illinois University Press; London: Feffer, 1969.

———. "The Characters." In *Saul Bellow's Fiction.* In *Saul Bellow's Fiction.* Crosscurrents/Modern Critiques, edited by Irving Malin, 56-84. Carbondale: Southern Illinois University Press; London: Feffer, 1969.

Marotti, Maria Ornella. "Concealment and Revelation: The Binary Structure of *Seize the Day.*" *Saul Bellow Journal* 5, no. 2 (1986): 46-51.

Marovitz, Sanford E. "That Certain 'Something': Dora, Dr. Braun, and Others." *Saul Bellow Journal* 12, no. 2 (1994): 3-12.

Mathis, James C. "The Theme of *Seize the Day.*" *Critique* 7, no. 3 (1965): 43-45.

McCadden, Joseph F. "[*Seize the Day*]." In *The Flight from Women in the Fiction of Saul Bellow*, 89-108. Lanham: University Press of America, 1980.

———. "[Short Stories]." In *The Flight from Women in the Fiction of Saul Bellow*, 213-42. Lanham: University Press of America, 1980.

McCormick, John. "The Urbane and the Urban: Iris Murdoch and Saul Bellow." Review of *The Bellarosa Connection*, by Saul Bellow. *Sewanee Review* 98, no. 1 (1990): 159-65.

Morahg, Gilead. "The Art of Dr. Tamkin: Matter and Manner in *Seize the Day.*" *Modern Fiction Studies* 25, no. 1 (1979): 103-16. Reprinted in *Saul Bellow.* Modern Critical Views, edited by Harold Bloom, 147-59. New York: Chelsea, 1986.

Morganroth-Gullette, Margaret. "Saul Bellow: Inward and Upward, Past Distraction." *Saul Bellow Journal* 9, no. 1 (1990): 52-78.

Nakajima, Kenji. "A Study of Saul Bellow's 'A Sermon by Dr. Pep.'" *Kyushu American Literature* 17 (1976): 12-19.

———. "A Study of Saul Bellow's 'Looking for Mr. Green.'" *Kyushu American Literature* 18 (1977): 5-18.

Nelson, Gerald B. "Tommy Wilhelm." In *Ten Versions of America*. Edited by Gerald B. Nelson, 129-45. New York: Knopf, 1972.

Newman, Judie. "Saul Bellow and Social Anthropology." In *Saul Bellow at Seventy-five: A Collection of Critical Essays*. Vol. 9 in Studies & Texts in English, edited by Gerhard Bach, 137-49. Tübingen: Gunter Narr Verlag, 1991.

———. "Saul Bellow and Trotsky: 'The Mexican General.'" *Saul Bellow Newsletter* 1, no. 1 (1981): 26-31.

Opdahl, Keith Michael. "Come Then, Sorrow." In *The Novels of Saul Bellow: An Introduction*, 96-117. University Park: Pennsylvania State University Press, 1967.

Park, Sue. "Chinese Boxes, Rings and Words: Repetition in Saul Bellow's *A Theft*." *Conference of College Teachers of English Studies* 57 (1992): 5-13.

Pauwels de la Ronciere, Marie-Christine. "Bellow's Hero and the 'Reality Instructors': Just a Punch and Judy Show?" *Saul Bellow Journal* 9, no. 2 (1990): 29-37.

Phillips, K. J. "Sacrificing to Baal: Bellow." In *Dying Gods in Twentieth-Century Fiction*, 93-96. Lewisburg: Bucknell University Press, 1990.

Pifer, Ellen. "The Heart and the Head: *Seize the Day* and *Mosby's Memoirs*." In *Saul Bellow Against the Grain*. Penn Studies in Contemporary American Fiction, 79-95. Philadelphia: University of Pennsylvania Press, 1990.

Pinsker, Sanford. "A New Look at 'The Old System.'" *Saul Bellow Journal* 11, no. 2 & 12, no. 1 (1993-94): 54-65.

Porter, M. Gilbert. "The Scene as Image: A Reading of *Seize the Day*." In *Saul Bellow: A Collection of Critical Essays*. Twentieth Century Views, edited by Earl Rovit, 52-71. Englewood Cliffs, NJ: Prentice, 1975. Reprinted in revised form as "*Seize the Day* A Drowning Man." In *Whence the Power? The Artistry and Humanity of Saul Bellow*, 102-26. Columbia: University of Missouri Press, 1974.

Pugh, Scott. "Stylistic Indeterminacy and the Opening of Seize the Day." *Kyushu American Literature* 28 (1987): 29-37.

Raper, Julius Rowan. "The Limits of Change: Saul Bellow's *Seize the Day* and *Henderson the Rain King*." In *Narcissus from Rubble: Competing Models of Character in Contemporary British and American Fiction*, 12-36. Baton Rouge: Louisiana State University Press, 1992.

———. "Running Contrary Ways: Saul Bellow's *Seize the Day*." *Southern Humanities Review* 10, no. 2 (1976): 157-68. Reprinted in *The Critical Response to Saul Bellow*. Vol. 20 of Critical Responses in Arts and Letters, edited by Gerhard Bach, 73-83. Westport, Conn.: Greenwood, 1995.

Richmond, Lee J. "The Maladroit, the Medico, and the Magician: Saul Bellow's *Seize the Day*." *Twentieth Century Literature* 19, no. 1 (1973): 15-25.

Rodrigues, Eusebio L. "Koheleth in Chicago: Quest for the Real in 'Looking for Mr. Green.'" *Studies in Short Fiction* 11, no. 4 (1974): 387-93.

———. "Reichianism in Seize the Day." In *Critical Essays on Saul Bellow*. Critical Essays on American Literature, edited by Stanley Trachtenberg, 89-100. Boston: Hall, 1979.

———. "A Rough-Hewn Heroine of Our Time: Saul Bellow's 'Leaving the Yellow House.'" *Saul Bellow Newsletter* 1, no. 1 (1981): 11-17.

———. "*Seize the Day*." In *Quest for the Human: An Exploration of Saul Bellow's Fiction*, 81-107. Lewisburg: Bucknell University Press, 1981.

Rooke, Constance. "Saul Bellow's 'Leaving the Yellow House': The Trouble with Women." *Studies in Short Fiction* 14, no. 2 (1977): 184-87.

Rosenthal, Regine. "Memory and the Holocaust: *Mr. Sammler's Planet* and *The Bellarosa Connection*." In *Saul Bellow at Seventy-five: A Collection of*

Critical Essays. Vol. 9 of Studies & Texts in English, edited by Gerhard Bach, 81-92. Tübingen: Gunter Narr Verlag, 1991.

Roudané, Matthew C. "Discordant Timbre: Saul Bellow's 'Him with His Foot in His Mouth.'" *Saul Bellow Journal* 4, no. 1 (1985): 52-61.

Salomon, David A. "The Brotherhood of Unfulfilled Early Promise: Tommy Wilhelm in Saul Bellow's *Seize the Day* and 'You' in Jay McInerney's *Bright Lights, Big City.*" *Saul Bellow Journal* 12, no. 2 (1994): 37-43.

Satlof, Marilyn R. "Bellow's Modern Lamed Vovniks." *Saul Bellow Journal* 8, no. 2 (1989): 39-46.

Scheer-Schaezler, Brigitte. "The Dread Is Great. The Soul Is Small." In *Saul Bellow.* Modern Literature Monographs, 59-75. New York: Ungar, 1972.

Scrafford, Barbara L. "Saul Bellow's Maternal Icon." *Saul Bellow Journal* 10, no. 2 (1992): 65-71.

———. "Water and Stone: The Confluence of Textual Imagery in *Seize the Day.*" *Saul Bellow Journal* 6, no. 2 (1987): 64-70.

Sharma, J. N. "Seize the Day : An Existentialist Look." In *Existentialism in American Literature,* edited by Ruby Chatterji, 121-33. Atlantic Highlands: Humanities Press, 1983.

Shear, Walter. "'Leaving the Yellow House': Hattie's Will." *Saul Bellow Journal* 7, no. 1 (1988): 51-56.

———. "Steppenwolf and *Seize the Day.*" *Saul Bellow Newsletter* 1, no. 1 (1981): 32-34.

Shechner, Mark. "The Noble Savage." In *After the Revolution: Studies in the Contemporary Jewish American Imagination,* 131-34. Bloomington: Indiana University Press, 1987.

Shiels, Michael. "Place, Space, and Pace: A Cinematic Reading of *Seize the Day.*" In *Saul Bellow at Seventy-five: A Collection of Critical Essays.* Vol. 9 of Studies & Texts in English, edited by Gerhard Bach, 55-62. Tübingen: Gunter Narr Verlag, 1991.

Sicherman, Carol M. "Bellow's *Seize the Day*: Reverberations and Hollow Sounds." *Studies in the Twentieth Century* 15 (1975): 1-31.

Stevick, Philip. "The Rhetoric of Bellow's Short Fiction." In *Critical Essays on Saul Bellow*. Critical Essays on American Literature, edited by Stanley Trachtenberg, 73-82. Boston: Hall, 1979. Reprinted in *Critical Response to Saul Bellow*. Vol. 20 of Critical Responses in Arts and Letters, edited by Gerhard Bach, 271-81. Westport, Conn.: Greenwood, 1995.

Stout, Janis P. "Suffering as Meaning in Saul Bellow's *Seize the Day*." *Renascence* 39, no. 2 (1987): 365-73.

Sudrann, Jean. "Goings and Comings." Review of *The Bellarosa Connection*, by Saul Bellow. *Yale Review* 79, no. 3 (1990): 414-20.

Tanner, Tony. "The World's Business." In *Saul Bellow*. Writers and Critics. Edinburgh and London: Oliver, 1965; New York: Barnes, 1965; New York: Chips, 1978. 58-70.

Trowbridge, Clinton W. "Water Imagery in *Seize the Day*." *Critique* 9, no. 3 (1967): 62-73.

Tuerk, Richard. "Tommy Wilhelm—Wilhelm Adler: Names in *Seize the Day*." In *Naughty Names*, edited by Fred Tarpley, 27-33. Commerce: Names Institute Press, 1975.

Walsh, Thomas. "Heroism in Bellow's 'The Mexican General.'" *Saul Bellow Journal* 1, no. 2 (1982): 31-33.

Weatherford, Kathleen Jeannette. "*The Bellarosa Connection* and the Hazards of Forgetfulness." *American Studies in Scandinavia* 24, no. 2 (1992): 65-82.

Weinstein, Ann. "Ijah, 'Our Cousins' Keeper': Bellow's Paradigm of Man." *Saul Bellow Journal* 7, no. 2 (1988): 58-70.

———. "A Toast to Life, L'Chayim: Saul Bellow's 'A Father-to-Be.'" *Saul Bellow Journal* 2, no. 1 (1982): 32-35.

Weiss, Daniel. "Caliban on Prospero: A Psychoanalytic Study on the Novel *Seize the Day*, by Saul Bellow." *American Imago* 19, no. 3 (1962): 277-306. Reprinted in *Saul Bellow and the Critics*, edited by Irving Malin, 114-141. New York: New York University Press, 1967; In *Psychoanalysis and American Fiction*. Edited by Irving Malin, 279-307. New York: Dutton, 1965; In *The Critic Agonistes: Psychology, Myth, and the Art of Fiction*. Edited by Eric Solomon and Stephen Arkin, 185-213. Seattle: University of Washington Press, 1985.

Wilson, Jonathan Wilson. "*Seize the Day*." In *On Bellow's Planet: Readings from the Dark Side*. Edited by Jonathan Wilson, 96-111. Rutherford: Fairleigh Dickinson University Press, 1985.

INDEX

♦